"Bachman, confronting conventional wisdom and bias, gives us a fascinating portrait of a man who for so long lived as a 'man without footnotes.' This book supplies plenty of them. Bachman's research is meticulous. His analysis is sound. And though he writes as one who knows that pitfalls abound, it is quite evident that he values and executes an even-handed approach to telling an otherwise awkward story. . . . Bachman has written an important addition to the canon of Minnesota history and one that should stimulate much conversation."

—WILLIAM D. GREEN, *Minnesota History*

"[Bachman's] extensive endnotes encourage further exploration, providing a real treasure map for researchers. *Northern Slave, Black Dakota* creates a fascinating picture of slavery in pre-statehood Minnesota. . . . The book provides a balanced, factually based account of the two series of trials conducted by General Henry Hastings Sibley's military tribunal that does much to discount the simplistic sensationalism that usually describes them. . . . An essential new reference on the tragic conflict that may have been the most important event in Minnesota history."

—STEPHEN E. OSMAN, *Journal of Military History*

"I cannot overstate the important contribution that *Northern Slave, Black Dakota* makes to our understanding of race and class in the formative period of Minnesota history. Through meticulous and wide-ranging research, Walt Bachman has reconstructed the life of Joseph Godfrey, a little-known slave who fought with the Dakotas in the U.S.-Dakota War of 1862. The result is a fascinating biography, but it is also much more than one man's story. . . . The archival research that undergirds this work is of the highest caliber, and indeed, Bachman has tapped sources unexplored by other scholars of Minnesota history that will be of great benefit to future scholars."

—MARY LETHERT WINGERD, author of *North Country: The Making of Minnesota*

"To this reviewer's knowledge, no one has ever studied the original record of the Dakota trials and the circumstances surrounding them with the care that Bachman has, nor has any historian brought to the task his familiarity with courtroom procedures and nineteenth-century legal customs. His conclusions about how the trials were conducted are even-handed enough to displease partisans of both sides, and they yield a vivid picture of human feeling, fear, and frailty."

—RHODA GILMAN, author of *Henry Hastings Sibley: Divided Heart* and *Stand Up! The Story of Minnesota's Protest Tradition*

NORTHERN SLAVE BLACK DAKOTA

The Life and Times of Joseph Godfrey

WALT BACHMAN

UNIVERSITY OF NEBRASKA PRESS | LINCOLN

© 2026 by Walt Bachman
Originally published in 2013 as *Northern Slave, Black Dakota* by Pond Dakota Press.

All rights reserved

The University of Nebraska Press is part of a land-grant institution with campuses and programs on the past, present, and future homelands of the Pawnee, Ponca, Otoe-Missouria, Omaha, Dakota, Lakota, Kaw, Cheyenne, and Arapaho Peoples, as well as those of the relocated Ho-Chunk, Sac and Fox, and Iowa Peoples.

∞

First Nebraska paperback printing: 2026

This publication was made possible in part by the people of Minnesota through a grant funded by an appropriation to the Minnesota Historical Society from the Minnesota Arts and Cultural Heritage Fund. Any views, findings, opinions, conclusions, or recommendations expressed in this publication are those of the author and do not necessarily represent those of the State of Minnesota, the Minnesota Historical Society, the Minnesota Historic Resources Advisory Committee, or the Pond Dakota Heritage Society.

For customers in the EU with safety/GPSR concerns, contact:
gpsr@mare-nostrum.co.uk
Mare Nostrum Group BV
Mauritskade 21D
1091 GC Amsterdam
The Netherlands

Library of Congress Cataloging-in-Publication Data can be found at search.catalog.loc.gov:
ISBN 978-1-4962-4599-1 (paperback)

For Elizabeth,

who gave her unfailing support and encouragement

throughout the years this book was being researched and written,

and whom I love even more than sticky toffee pudding

CONTENTS

List of Illustrations and Maps / viii
Preface / ix
Introduction: A Negro Leading Them / xv

Part I: Northern Slave

Chapter 1: Godfrey's Early Years / 1
Chapter 2: Flight to Freedom / 29
Chapter 3: Fugitive Slave, New Reservation / 58

Part II: Black Dakota

Chapter 4: The War / 81
Chapter 5: Camp Release / 117
Chapter 6: Godfrey's Trial / 138
Chapter 7: Chained Alone / 167
Chapter 8: The Cookhouse Trials / 199
Chapter 9: Waiting for Lincoln / 228
Chapter 10: Atop the Pile of Cases / 251
Chapter 11: The Prison Years / 285
Chapter 12: Life and Death at Santee / 318

Afterword / 341
Appendix: Whiting-Ruggles Report / 352
Acknowledgments / 357
Abbreviations / 361
Works Cited / 363
Index / 376

ILLUSTRATIONS

1. Courtney's voucher / 6
2. Faribault cabin / 40
3. Fort Ridgely voucher, Jenny and Joe / 65
4. Fort Ridgely voucher, William and Jane / 66
5. Whiting-Ruggles report / 257
6. Missionaries' prison list, Godfrey / 268
7. Missionaries' prison list, Caske-ite / 269
8. Missionaries' prison list, Wasicun / 270
9. Missionaries' prison list, Wasicunna / 271
10. Godfrey, by Sweeny / 274
11. Stevens panorama / 328
12. Joseph Godfrey's grave / 334

MAPS

1. Minnesota Territory, 1849 / 45
2. The Dakota War, 1862 / 104
3. Minnesota and the Santee Reservation, 1866 / 319

PREFACE

Researching and writing the remarkable life of Joseph Godfrey has taken me down many roads. On some I found that my travel was smoother due to my study of law and the twenty-two years I spent as a trial lawyer in Minnesota. On others, however, I was keenly aware that my formal education covered very little history of Native Americans, African Americans, military tactics and practices, and American slavery.

During the extensive research phase of this book, I was often struck by the similarities between studying the intricate history of the Dakota War and handling complex lawsuits involving many witnesses and thousands of documents. As a lawyer, I enjoyed the paper chase challenge of such cases, the process of sifting through stacks of relevant records and reams of transcripts of pretrial testimony to locate the best possible evidence required to advocate a client's cause in court. In law as in history, I found, a tedious and careful examination of original records often unlocks basic truths. Even a tiny fragment of overlooked evidence can yield enormous breakthroughs in understanding a complex case or complicated historical stories.

This book relies, whenever possible, on primary sources that are meticulously cited. Anyone who disagrees with my contentions can easily go back to those sources to determine whether I have used them accurately or not. In most instances, I hope and believe, readers who quarrel with my findings will discover, upon examination, that they disagree not with me but with the underlying source or with previous historians' representations of it.

To gather primary sources relating to Godfrey's story, I spent years combing through records at the Minnesota History Center and at the Brown, Stearns, Blue Earth, Hennepin, Scott, and Chippewa County historical societies. I also spent months in Washington, D.C., examining and copying old military and Dakota-related files at the National Archives.

One of my research projects deserves emphasis. After learning that old army paymasters' records at the National Archives contain information from which it is possible to reconstruct a clearer history of slavery in the United States Army (and thus help illuminate Godfrey's early life in slavery), I embarked on what I believe to be the first-ever comprehensive examination of the 1,735 boxes containing those records. This portion of my research alone consumed about three full years. From that massive collection, I culled and digitized all of the records that relate to army-financed slavery in Minnesota, many of which have never been seen or cited by any other historian. The story they tell of army slavery in 1850s Minnesota, and in other Northern states and territories, is presented here for the first time.

I also found that my work as an appellate lawyer (one who argues cases to higher courts during posttrial appeals) proved helpful in understanding the role played by Godfrey during the trials of 410 Dakota War–related cases before military courts during 1862 and 1863. Most nonlawyer historians have struggled to interpret the 392 Dakota trials held in 1862; no other history even mentions two additional sets of Minnesota military trials that are discussed in this book.

As a lawyer, I argued more than thirty cases before the Minnesota Supreme Court. In the American legal system appellate lawyers are required to adhere scrupulously to the content of the written record of the trial under appeal. Any lawyer foolish enough to "misstate the record" during arguments on appeal will pay a high price for his or her error. As I read accounts of the postwar trials and legal proceedings, I realized that I might be able to clarify some of the points scholars trained only as historians have missed or misstated.

Another phase of my legal career proved particularly relevant to this book: the four years I served as chief deputy Hennepin County attorney, during which I presented more than one hundred homicide cases to the grand jury. Each of those cases required me to read the police and medical examiner reports and determine which witnesses and which documents to use to permit the grand jurors to decide whether to indict a defendant for murder or return a "no bill." In that capacity I gained a thorough knowledge of Minnesota's murder and manslaughter laws. And those abbreviated presentations of murder cases to the grand jurors, I found, were not unlike the short postwar military trials of the Dakota defendants.

As a prosecutor I learned that, contrary to what most laypeople believe, murder cases are usually rather simple—provided that there is no dispute about the identity of the suspect and that the evidence necessary to prove the case is not circumstantial. Very few murder cases present anything like the circumstantial evidence puzzle of the O. J. Simpson case. In the majority of homicide cases I handled, the suspect conceded that he had shot the gun, plunged the knife, or shot the arrows (yes, even in 1980s Minnesota a man killed a woman with a hunting bow) that caused the victim's death. Typically the only dispute in the case was over which one of the three degrees of murder best fit the evidence or whether self-defense or legal insanity could be argued as a defense.

The military trials of the thirty-eight men who were hanged at Mankato in 1862 used procedures that differ significantly from those employed in the twentieth century and today. So as not to make anachronistic comparisons, I examined Civil War–era military trials that did not involve Indian defendants and reviewed other contemporaneous laws and practices. Some of the criticisms of the Dakota trials by modern historians, I discovered, focus on criminal-justice practices that were standard for the times. For example, while it seems unthinkable today to regard a murder case as fair unless each defendant is provided with a good defense lawyer, mid-nineteenth-century lawyers (including President Lincoln) would have found nothing unusual about that practice, even in capital punishment cases.

The simultaneous hanging of thirty-eight men following the conclusion of the 1862 trials raises a particularly sensitive topic: the death penalty. I personally have long opposed capital punishment on both moral and practical grounds. When I prosecuted murder cases, I was grateful that Minnesota was among the minority of states that did not (and still does not) impose the death penalty for any crime. Had the state enacted capital punishment during my tenure as a prosecutor, I would have declined thereafter to handle murder cases.

Consistent with my beliefs, I wish that no Dakota man, no matter how heinous his crimes, had been executed at Mankato. Whether I would have felt the same had I been born in 1844 rather than 1944, I'll never know. (In 1862 the death penalty was almost universally accepted throughout America. Even the most pro-Dakota missionaries and clerics did not challenge the morality or legality of hanging men convicted of murder or rape.)

I urge those of you who share my views on the death penalty not to refuse to examine the facts adduced in the trials simply by virtue of your opposition to capital punishment. One of the key questions that needs to be answered about the Dakota War is, How many Dakota warriors committed murder, rape, or other war crimes that justified the imposition of the law's maximum penalty? The answer to that question is crucially important for the sake of history. It is, I believe, a historical cop-out to argue that the guilt of individual Dakota defendants is subsumed by the death penalty issue.

As for the other parts of Godfrey's story, I often found myself wishing that I had a decade or two to immerse myself in four areas of study: American slavery, African American history, the Dakota language, and Native American history. I claim no professional expertise in any of these fields, but I have done my best to read and understand enough about each of them to place Godfrey's life in its proper perspective.

Because I have only the most rudimentary knowledge of the Dakota language, and because of the importance for this book of linking each Dakota trial defendant with the correct case, I have used the phonetic spellings of Dakota names as they are found in the 1862 trial transcripts. Dakota-language scholars inform me that, especially by today's conventions, numerous errors were made in 1862 in recording those names. But I believe I would only compound the problem and confuse readers by substituting different spellings for those found in the trial records.

The writing of this book required me to confront and discuss some of the ugliest chapters in American history. Some have argued that there was a "Minnesota nice" version of slavery, but I do not share that view. In the following pages I present evidence of beatings, abuse, and even murder of Minnesota slaves, not because I relish those brutal details but because I believe they need to be discussed to understand our history. The same is true of antiblack racist statements, whether uttered by whites or by Dakotas. Though some scholars have told me they would never use the "N word" in any book, I feel that the deletion of that epithet from quoted sources would sugarcoat a chapter of history that needs emphasis, not euphemisms.

Writing about the Dakota War raises a host of other issues and sensitivities. In general, older histories of the war tend to wallow in inflated tales of "barbaric savages" while underplaying the real suffering endured by Dakota people both before and after the war. But most histories written since 1970 have, by one means or another, sanitized evidence that reveals the unique features of the war. The Dakota War remains so fascinating—and so divisive—precisely because it involved the most extensive intentional killing of American noncombatants in any war fought between 1776 and September 11, 2001. It was a war in which the majority of the hundreds of white victims slain were defenseless civilians murdered away from battle sites, while every Dakota who was killed during the hostilities was an armed, adult male warrior.

We now know that the entire Dakota nation has paid a grievous and extreme price for the wanton killings committed during the war by no more than about two hundred of its warriors. But life is not lived with the benefit of foresight. If we blur together the later, horrific acts of white vengeance with the grim realities of the 1862 Dakota killings, we run the risk of missing the real lessons of history. If we downplay the violent deeds of Dakota warriors, we are left to conclude that blind white racism alone can explain the paroxysm of anger and vengeance that swept through Minnesota after the war.

We regard ourselves today as largely free of such extreme racist views, and thus we take comfort in our distance from the events of the 1860s. But consider what would happen today if a militant group, be they foreign terrorists or domestic zealots of any stripe, were to fan out into a region of rural America and kill hundreds of ordinary citizens in their homes or while they were attempting to flee to safety. Would we wring our hands over the legitimate grievances that may have prompted the group to commit such an attack? Would we argue that, above all else, the perpetrators of such deeds should be treated as fairly as possible under the law? Would we decline to demonize and punish the larger group from which the murderers emanated? Or might we, in our collective fury, call for the mighty hammer of American retribution to descend with full and merciless force on the people who perpetrated such deeds?

Ask yourself those questions, and then read this book. There are good reasons why Joseph Godfrey's story is still relevant today, but only if we look at our history clearly and grasp its lessons.

INTRODUCTION

A Negro Leading Them

Fifteen Minnesota men—all German Americans from New Ulm—rolled slowly along in five horse-drawn wagons on a fine Monday morning in August 1862. It was a festive group, armed with nothing more than brass musical instruments and a thirty-four-star flag. Their mission was to fill Brown County's quota for Civil War enlistees—to recruit the young men working on nearby farms to join the Union army. One of the leaders of the group, a cabinetmaker by trade, was my great-great-grandfather, Ernst Dietrich.[1]

The recruiters' noontime destination was the hamlet of Milford, located on the Fort Road seven miles west of New Ulm. There they planned to stop at Anton Henle's house, which doubled as a wayside inn called the Travelers' Home. Henle himself, having gone into town to hear Sunday's patriotic speeches, was seated in one of the rear wagons. Ambling past reddening sumac and the ripening crops of the local white farmers, the recruiters likely planned to drink Henle's whiskey and beer once they reached the inn. Assuming that the fires they saw in the distance rose from burning crop stubble, they unsuspectingly advanced into the bloodiest uprising of Indians ever to occur in the American West.

As the recruiters neared the houses strung along the road at Milford, the men in the first wagon laughed when they heard a slurred Germanic call from someone lying beside the road's edge. They suspected that one of the local yeomen had begun the day's festivities early and was already feeling the effects of too much strong drink. The lead wagons halted as men in the rear jumped out to investigate. The prostrate man was identified as Joseph Messmer, Henle's neighbor and brother-in-law. He was writhing in pain with mortal injuries: an arm and an ear had been cut off, and there was a deep gash on his head. Those near him yelled, "This man is wounded! He has been partly scalped! Men, that looks like the work of Indians."[2]

At that moment, Dietrich and the other men in the front looked down the road and saw a sight that added to their confusion. Four Indians, dressed only in breechcloths, their bodies smeared with war paint, were running along the road. But one of the four stood out from the rest. He was a black man.

Thinking that they had come upon the scene of a crime and that the culprits were fleeing, the men in the first two recruiting wagons reacted swiftly. Whether motivated simply to scare off the offenders or to capture them, they resolved to make a show of bravado. Sounding a charge with their brass instruments, the men whipped the horses forward toward a small bridge over a ravine. Horns blaring and flag waving, they realized their mistake only as they reached the bridge, where a larger body of well-armed Dakota Indians fired from ambush positions in the brushy lowlands. Dietrich, John Schneider, and Julius Fenske were shot and died on the spot. A fourth man, Adolph Steimle, took a bullet through the throat. He survived only a few days.[3]

After the ambush Steimle and some of the other men in the first two wagons jumped out and ran to the rear. The three trailing wagons turned around and were not pursued by the Indians. A few men raced ahead to New Ulm to sound the alarm, while the retreating wagons followed more slowly.

Brown County Sheriff Charles Roos, after listening to the first reports of the killings, rounded up a posse of thirty men and rode to Milford to investigate. He left instructions for New Ulm to be barricaded against further attacks. About halfway along the road, Roos met up with the wagon carrying Steimle, who was unable to speak due to his injury. Steimle, though in pain, wrote out the names of the three recruiters who had been killed. He also drew Roos a map indicating the location of the attack, showing where the assailants had concealed themselves.[4]

When the sheriff arrived at Milford, the Indians were gone. The posse found the bodies of Dietrich and Schneider beyond the bridge, though their wagon and another had been taken by the Dakotas. Fenske's body lay not far to the east. The Travelers' Home was a scene of devastation: Henle's wife, having run away and hidden in the brush, was still alive, but eight-year-old Anton Henle and four-year-old Mary had been tomahawked to death. Despite three gashes on his head, Henle's eighteen-month-old baby survived. Martin Henle, twelve years old, had tried to run away from a sword-wielding Indian on horseback. Repeatedly slashed on his head and upper body, Martin sustained many deep and painful wounds, which had caused him to collapse. Roos and his men found similar scenes at other Milford homes.[5]

Returning to New Ulm, Roos put together such accounts as he could gather by the end of the day. He then wrote an emergency dispatch to send to Minnesota's governor, Alexander Ramsey. The sheriff described the killings at Milford and the ambush of the recruiting party, ending his plea with this sentence: "It was, as I am informed, Wabashaw's band, a *negro leading* them, who committed the murders."[6]

This book was spawned in the electric moment when, in 1996, I first read Sheriff Roos's emergency message in the files of the Brown County Historical Society. I was in New Ulm seeking information about my ancestor's death, hoping to add details to sketchy family stories that I had heard as a boy growing up in Minneapolis.

But no one in my family had ever mentioned that a black man was at the scene of Dietrich's death, let alone that he was reported to have led the Dakota attackers. Almost immediately, questions swirled through my head about this mystery man, some of which I am still struggling to answer. Who was this "Negro"? Why had he joined the Indian attackers? Was he really their leader? How could a black man have assumed such a role in such times? Could he have been an agent provocateur, sent by the Confederacy to instigate a new rebellion in America's West? Was he the harbinger of some new alliance between oppressed blacks and Indians?

I soon confirmed that the black man's name was Joseph Godfrey.

He makes brief to moderately long appearances in almost all histories of what is now called the U.S.-Dakota War of 1862. He was the only non-Indian to fight on the Dakota side during that war, though he is much better known for the role he played in postwar trials, during which he was initially charged with murder but then gave state's evidence testimony against many Dakota men. Over time, Godfrey has been both glorified and reviled, but today's writers tend to accord him more revulsion than glory.

As soon as I found answers to my initial questions, others popped up in their stead. How had a black man come to live in early Minnesota at a time when virtually all residents were Native or white? How, and why, did he make the transition from living within the white community to waging war with the Dakotas? How did he, a man whose background and race set him apart from the Indians-versus-whites framework of the 1862 war, relate to the Dakotas and to the whites? And how did they view him?

My fascination with the black man in war paint became an obsession. I ultimately spent several years on a quest for more information about his obscure life, making lengthy visits to archival and library collections from Minnesota to Washington, D.C. My goal was to gather buried historical nuggets about Godfrey, to put as much flesh on the bare bones of his life story as I could. Along the way, hidden facets of history emerged.

Because I was searching for references to a lowly and easily overlooked man, I made a point of examining original documents at the National Archives and elsewhere. Over time, I saw that the struggle to document Godfrey's life also unveiled fresh evidence about such subjects as the incidence of slavery in the region, the presence and plight of African Americans during the 1862 war, racism on the frontier, differing white and Indian perspectives of warfare, and the manner in which postwar justice was meted out to the Dakotas.

History is often a matter of perspective, and Godfrey, throughout his life, saw his world from a unique viewpoint. No matter where or with which community he lived, he spent his life as an outsider. Godfrey was always odd man out, never fitting into prevailing racial or cultural patterns. He also was buffeted by a series of life-threatening challenges that most of us are never required to face. No matter what your preconceptions or opinions regarding early Minnesota history or the 1862 war and its aftermath, seeing those events through Godfrey's eyes may be jarring or provoke discomfort. I make no apologies for that possibility. It is the inevitable byproduct of delving into the life of a man who seldom knew true comfort.

NOTES ON INTRODUCTION

1. Sources for the ravine ambush at Milford and the Roos posse include *New Ulm Review*, August 7, 14, 1912, September 12, 1946 (account of Sheriff Charles Roos; account of Charles Pfau); Fritsche, *History of Brown County* (account of Theresa Henle, 198–201; account of Christopher Spelbrink, 182–94); *St. Paul Pioneer and Democrat*, August 26, 1862 (statement of "Antoine Henry"/Anton Henle); Roddis, *Indian Wars of Minnesota* (account of John W. Young, 92–94). See also Sioux Uprising, New Ulm, Roos Letters and Accounts, Brown County Historical Society; Berghold, *Indians' Revenge*, 90–91; Nix, *Sioux Uprising*, 87–88; and Bachman, *"Death of Ernst Dietrich."*
2. *New Ulm Review*, September 12, 1946; Berghold, *Indians' Revenge*, 91.
3. A lonely stone monument with a brass plaque located on the north side of Brown County Road 29 commemorates the place where the four recruiters were slain. Some of the brass letters have been chipped by modern bullets. The ravine is now a gentle swale in farmed fields; the dirt road has long since been paved.
4. Sioux Uprising, New Ulm, Roos Letters and Accounts, Brown County Historical Society.
5. See also *St. Paul Pioneer and Democrat*, August 26, 1862 ("statement of Antoine Henry"), referring to the injured baby, and *St. Paul Pioneer and Democrat*, September 3, 1862 (death of "Martin Hawley," described as "horribly mutilated" by the Indian "fiends").
6. *St. Paul Pioneer and Democrat*, August 22, 1862 (emphasis in original).

NORTHERN SLAVE, BLACK DAKOTA

PART I

NORTHERN SLAVE

CHAPTER 1

Godfrey's Early Years

Joseph Godfrey is mysteriously absent from official and historical records created before the 1862 Dakota War. His name cannot be found on any census taken in preterritorial, territorial, or poststatehood Minnesota. There is no pre-1862 documentation of Godfrey's birth, baptism, schooling, or marriage. His name appears in no known family Bible. None of the many fur trade account ledgers lists him as a buyer or seller of goods. He is mentioned in no newspaper articles or books.

Yet we know from Godfrey's own account, related late in 1862 to soldier-historian Isaac Heard, that up to that point he had lived virtually his entire life in what would become Minnesota. He described his background before he joined the Dakotas in one succinct paragraph: "I am twenty-seven years old. I was born at Mendota. My father was a Canadian Frenchman, and my mother a colored woman, who hired in the family of the late Alex. Bailley. I was raised in Mr. Bailley's family. My father is, I think, living in Wisconsin; his name is Joe Godfrey. My mother is also living at Prairie du Chien. I last saw my father and mother at Prairie du Chien seven years ago. I lived with Mr. Bailley at Wabashaw, and also at Hastings and Faribault."[1]

Godfrey said that he was born in Mendota, Minnesota, while his "hired" mother was working in the household of the prominent fur trader Alexis Bailly. All four of the towns in which Godfrey said he had lived with "Mr. Bailley's family" are located in Minnesota. Mendota, originally called

St. Peter or St. Peter's, was eclipsed first by St. Paul, then by Minneapolis.² Today it is a small enclave surrounded by the much larger Twin Cities suburb of Mendota Heights. But in the 1830s the sorry-looking collection of log huts scattered along the southern bank of the Minnesota (or St. Peter's) River was the economic, cultural, and residential hub of non-Indian settlement in Minnesota, occupied by Indian traders, tradesmen, and voyageurs.³ At that time, Mendota and Camp Coldwater (situated nearby, across the river) were the only civilian communities of whites in the southern two-thirds of Minnesota. Located near the confluence of the Mississippi and Minnesota Rivers, Mendota was well positioned to serve as the headquarters for the river-oriented fur trade. The peltries of beaver, muskrat, otter, and other fur bearers trapped throughout the region funneled through the hamlet on their way to their next downstream destination, Wisconsin's Prairie du Chien, and thence onward to eastern and European markets.

Almost everyone in 1830s Minnesota was either Native American or employed in some capacity related to the Indians. Fort Snelling, located across the Minnesota River from Godfrey's birthplace, housed the largest aggregation of whites: four companies of the First Regiment, U.S. Infantry, whose mission was to keep the peace in what was then the northwest corner of the American frontier. Operating from two stone buildings just outside the fort, Maj. Lawrence Taliaferro—the local agent for the federal Office of Indian Affairs—dealt with the Dakotas (or Sioux) in the southern half of the region and Ojibwes (or Chippewas) in the northern half.⁴

Alexis Bailly and his father-in-law, Jean Baptiste Faribault, were among the leading fur traders in early Mendota. They and their families lived in two of the village's larger log huts. Bailly and Faribault were, to use Godfrey's phrase, "Canadian Frenchmen," both well-educated immigrants from the British possessions to the north. Faribault, sixty years old in 1835, was the respected dean of the area's fur-trading business, and his sons, Alexander, David, and Oliver, were following him into the trade. Alexis Bailly, described by one biographer as having "great vices and also great virtues," married into the Faribault family when he wed Lucy, daughter of Jean Baptiste, in 1826.⁵ Until 1834 Bailly held the highest rank in the Minnesota fur trade as the principal district representative of John Jacob Astor's powerful American Fur Company.

To describe Mendota as a white community is somewhat misleading, since many of its inhabitants—including all of the Baillys and all of the Faribaults except Jean Baptiste—were of mixed white and Indian heritage. To use the Canadian term, they were métis. Jean Baptiste Faribault had married Pelagie Ainse, a mixed-blood Dakota woman. Alexis Bailly, like many Canadian-born fur traders, had Indian blood, being one-quarter Ottawa.[6] All of the Faribaults and Baillys thus had Dakota relatives. Mendota also had a few black residents, one of whom was Godfrey's mother.

If Godfrey and his mother lived in the house of one of the most prominent citizens of the day, and if Godfrey continued to reside with that family for years, why is there no mention of his existence in any contemporaneous records or accounts? The answer lies in the same peculiarity that shaped his life from birth to manhood and beyond: Godfrey was a slave who was born and raised in Minnesota in bondage. The void in documentation arose, at least in part, from Godfrey's nearly anonymous condition as human chattel, no more deserving of notice than a horse.

Like most slaves, Godfrey's mother was never accorded the dignity of a surname by her masters. She was known during her bondage only as Courtney, which she retained as her first name once she secured her freedom. Courtney was born into slavery in about 1812 in the home of James Garland, a prominent Virginian who later served in the U.S. Congress. Garland had a small plantation and practiced law in Livingston, Virginia, a town located about twenty-five miles due north of Appomattox, where Robert E. Lee surrendered to Ulysses S. Grant near the end of the Civil War. In 1820 Capt. John Garland returned to his home state to visit his older brother, James. The Third Infantry army captain had recently married and was interested in procuring a household servant, so he bought eight-year-old Courtney during his visit.[7]

The price Captain Garland paid for Courtney is unknown, but slaves were cheap in Virginia during the 1820s due to a considerable surplus. It's unlikely that he paid more than $150—perhaps much less because the seller was his brother. In the marketplace for human beings, the price of slave children was far lower than that of adults; they were less productive and the buyer took on the costs of raising them as well as the risks (considerable in the nineteenth century) of death by disease or accident.

Captain Garland had an incentive for acquiring a slave. As an army officer, he was eligible for a perk given to no other group of federal employees: extra pay for keeping a "private servant." This bonus pay was not automatic; it could be drawn only if an officer actually kept a servant, either free or enslaved. The army also required each officer to furnish a written description of his servant on a pay voucher every time he claimed the extra pay.[8] Captain Garland first named "Courtney, Negro" as his servant on a pay claim that covered the months of October and November 1820. He was entitled to draw $116.60 in base pay for those two months, but extra servant pay of $28.04 boosted his income by almost 25 percent. When drawing his pay in Detroit, Michigan, in 1821, Garland noted nine-year-old Courtney's age on his pay claim.[9]

Servant pay was paid to the officer, not the servant. Captain Garland and other officers received the same amount under the statutory formula, no matter what it cost them to keep a servant. If an officer wanted to "hire" (rent from his or her owner or hire a free individual) a well-trained adult who cost him more than the allotted amount, the officer had to absorb the extra cost. At the other extreme, if an officer wished to buy or hire a cheap child slave, he could pocket any difference between his costs and the servant pay allowance. The army pay system thus encouraged the use of children, especially slaves, as servants.

Courtney, as far as we know, never again saw any members of her Virginia family after Captain Garland bought her. She was among a vast number of Virginia slaves, particularly children, who, between 1820 and 1860, were separated for life from their parents and other family members as "surplus" people were sold in America's largest internal slave diaspora. Most of those slaves were "sold South" to cotton, rice, and sugar plantations to help fill an insatiable demand for their labor.[10] But Courtney, as an army slave, was not taken to Alabama, Mississippi, or Louisiana. When her new master's regiment was posted along the Great Lakes, she was taken north. And, as Captain Garland was transferred from one northern post to another, Courtney remained enslaved in supposedly "free" territories for the next ten years. Her name appears repeatedly on pay claims Garland submitted in Detroit, at Minnesota's Fort Snelling, and at Wisconsin's Fort Crawford. Courtney later said that her master also took her to Wisconsin's Fort Howard, near Green Bay.[11]

From 1821 to 1826 Courtney labored mostly in Detroit, a relatively small town with a population of less than two thousand. The years Captain Garland and Courtney spent in this small frontier community suggest the possibility of intriguing intersections. As one of the area's higher-ranking officers in the federal army, Garland would almost certainly have had both official and social contacts with Detroit's principal federal politician, Solomon Sibley, a distinguished lawyer who was then serving as Michigan Territory's representative in Congress. Thus Garland quite likely also would have met the congressman's son, Henry Hastings Sibley, who was about Courtney's age. Though an illiterate female slave child and a young white prodigy who was tutored in Greek and Latin came from opposite ends of the social spectrum, it is also possible that young Henry would have met Courtney in Detroit and remembered her when their paths crossed later in Minnesota.

In 1826 Captain Garland was transferred to Fort Snelling. Col. Josiah Snelling had been acting both as commandant and quartermaster of the Minnesota fort that bore his name, even as he supervised the deployment of the Fifth Infantry Regiment in the region. But the quartermaster's office in Washington was not happy with Snelling's handling of the fort's business, so it directed Garland to take over as quartermaster for the regiment.[12] Soon after his arrival at Fort Snelling, Captain Garland tendered his first pay claim, covering the months of July and August 1826. There he specifically described Courtney as a slave.

It is curious that Garland had never indicated Courtney's status as a slave on any of the pay claims he had filed in Michigan but that he did so immediately at Fort Snelling. Slavery was unlawful in both areas under the terms of the Northwest Ordinance of 1787 (east of the Mississippi River, including the western Great Lakes area) and the Missouri Compromise of 1820 (west of the Mississippi, including the site of Fort Snelling). It appears that Garland viewed Fort Snelling as a more hospitable place to

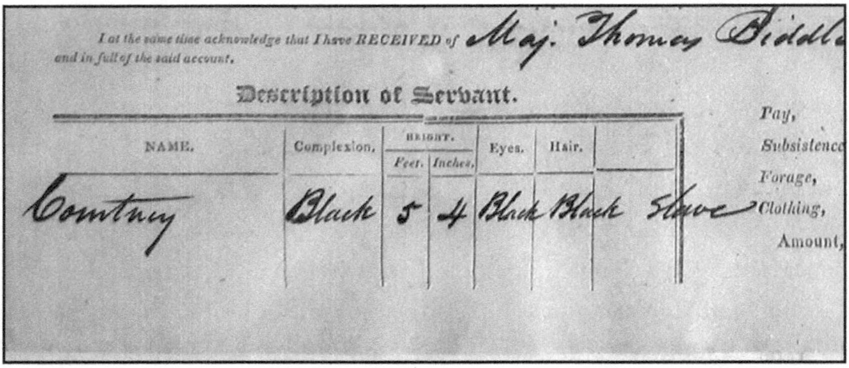

I at the same time acknowledge that I have RECEIVED of Maj. Thomas Biddle
and in full of the said account.

Description of Servant.

NAME.	Complexion.	HEIGHT.		Eyes.	Hair.	
		Feet.	*Inches.*			
Courtney	Black	5	4	Black	Black	Slave

Pay,
Subsistence
Forage,
Clothing,
Amount,

Fig. 1 Pay voucher filed September 1826 by Capt. John Garland, adjutant and quartermaster at Fort Snelling, declaring that his servant, Courtney, was a slave. Courtney, Godfrey's mother, first appeared on Garland's pay vouchers in 1820, when he was posted in Detroit. Garland's Detroit pay voucher for July 1821 indicated that Courtney was then nine years old and four feet tall. Pay Vouchers, National Archives. Record Group 217, Entry 516, Settled Accounts, Army Paymaster.

declare that Courtney was—as she had been from birth—enslaved.[13]

Slaveholding by army officers had been quite limited at Fort Snelling before Courtney's arrival there. From the time the Fifth Regiment was sent to begin the construction of Fort Snelling in 1819 until Garland's arrival there in 1826, fewer than 10 percent of the officers of that regiment used enslaved servants, either at Fort Snelling or at Fort Crawford (its downriver companion post at Prairie du Chien, Wisconsin). The local Indian agent who held sway from his headquarters just outside Fort Snelling, Virginian Lawrence Taliaferro, had brought at least two of his slaves to the area, and he had occasionally loaned or hired them out to officers at the fort before 1826. Colonel Snelling was among the officers who used Taliaferro's slave William as a servant for short periods. Perhaps it was Taliaferro's presence with slaves that made Garland feel comfortable in disclosing Courtney's legal status on a pay form. In any event, Garland was among the first officers at that post to do so.[14]

Courtney, about fourteen years old, was not the only female slave in the vicinity of Fort Snelling in 1826. Eliza, who was about the same age, had been brought to Minnesota from Virginia by Taliaferro. The Indian agent had been allowing a young married officer, Capt. Joseph Plympton, to use the young girl's services for more than a year.¹⁵ When Plympton learned that he would be transferred back to the East Coast, he asked Taliaferro if he could purchase Eliza. The Indian agent recorded his response in his journal: "Capt. Plympton wishes to purchase my Servant Girl Eliza. I informed him that it was my intention to give her her freedom at a limited time but that Mrs. P could keep her for two years or perhaps three."¹⁶ The Plymptons took Eliza with them to New York and later to St. Louis, Missouri, where she served them for more than two years before she was returned to her owner, Taliaferro.¹⁷

After arriving at Fort Snelling in 1826, Courtney would also have become acquainted with Maria Fasnacht, an African American woman in her twenties who worked as a servant for at least two officers at the post. Fasnacht was an indentured servant, her status created by the terms of an 1816 Illinois indenture that cast her into servitude until 1833. Her master took her to Prairie du Chien and there, in 1824, she met and married Jacob Fasnacht, a former army private who had served at Fort Crawford. Maria probably told Courtney of her hopes that she or her husband could raise the money to buy out the remainder of her term of indenture. Maria's unique story—the only known black indentured servant ever to work at Fort Snelling and the only black woman in servitude in the region who legally married a white man—may have opened Courtney's eyes to the possibility of a future life in freedom.¹⁸

Two other officers at Fort Snelling were using enslaved servants at the time of Courtney's arrival. Second Lt. Nathaniel Harris, who the year before had graduated from the U.S. Military Academy at West Point, New York, used Taliaferro's slave William. And Dr. Benjamin F. Harney, brother of the brutal Indian fighter William S. Harney, was spending a one-year interlude at Fort Snelling that punctuated his long career as an army surgeon in Baton Rouge, Louisiana. Dr. Harney's importation of his Louisiana slave, Peter, was a harbinger of future developments at Fort Snelling. Shortly after Courtney's arrival the doctor took Peter back south, where he remained an army slave for at least eighteen more years.¹⁹

Slaveholding officers were still an anomaly at Fort Snelling in 1826, but the use of slaves had been on the upswing for about a year. There is no evidence that even a single African American up to that time had lived in freedom anywhere in the southern half of Minnesota. By law, the region was supposed to be slavery-free, but the reality for blacks was not in accord with legality. Up to this point the limited slavery at Fort Snelling had followed an expected pattern: Southerners like Captain Garland, Dr. Harney, and Indian agent Taliaferro brought their slaves north and sometimes shared them with or hired them out to other officers, including Northerners. But that mold was broken in dramatic fashion during the second year of Courtney's tenure at the fort, when Commandant Snelling himself purchased two slaves.

Massachusetts-born Josiah Snelling was proud of his Boston roots. Since his assignment to the Fifth Regiment in 1819, he had spent most of his career at northern posts. Yet he entered the ranks of slave owners in 1827 when he bought a woman named Mary and her daughter, Louisa (age unknown), in St. Louis. He promptly brought them north to Minnesota and declared them both as slaves on his pay claims. Snelling thus became the first slave-owning commandant at the post. More important, the fact that the Northern-born commander of all regional troops posted on the Upper Mississippi River now owned slaves sent a powerful message within the rank-conscious military. If Snelling was willing to ignore the antislavery law enacted by Congress, and if the army freely permitted him to do so and knowingly subsidized his slaveholding with federal funds via servant pay, there was no impediment to other officers following his lead.[20]

Lt. Martin Scott, the army's keenest marksman and one of the most colorful members of the Fifth Infantry's officer corps, did not wait for Colonel Snelling. Scott bought a young slave, a boy named Jack, while posted at Fort Crawford, Wisconsin, in 1826. Scott, from Vermont (a state that still proudly proclaims that it was the first to abolish slavery), had kept a succession of white servants before he purchased Jack, whom he described on an October 1826 pay claim as "a negro boy and a slave." The next year Courtney would have met Jack when Scott brought him up to Fort Snelling. Over a period of almost twenty years, Scott used Jack as his servant at a succession of Northern posts in Minnesota, Wisconsin, and Michigan.[21]

Courtney, Jack, Mary, and Louisa had one crucial feature in common: all were sold *north* into slavery. Their masters were army officers who knew at the time of purchase that their human chattel would be kept in slavery in Northern "free" territories. Southern slaves may have looked upon the North Star as the shining light of freedom, but Courtney and other African Americans in Minnesota knew from bitter experience that America's northwestern frontier was de facto slave country—and that Southerners were not their only oppressors.

By 1828 the Fifth Infantry had been posted at Fort Snelling for nine years. Of the fifty officers who rotated through the post between 1819 and 1828, Courtney's master was one of only eight who declared slaves on their pay claims. The vast majority of Fifth Regiment officers had never kept a black servant. But that pattern was about to be broken in dramatic fashion. Colonel Snelling's slaveholding was a watershed development in the history of Minnesota slavery, but it was soon subsumed by a deluge that occurred when the army decided to send Zachary Taylor's First Infantry Regiment to Fort Snelling in 1828.[22]

Josiah Snelling and Zachary Taylor personified their respective regiments. Snelling, the Bostonian who sought Brahmin status through a military career, became a slave owner only during his last two years of army service. Taylor, raised in Louisville in a family whose father who was one of Kentucky's major slaveholders, had been served from birth by people held in bondage. During tours of duty in the Deep South, Taylor had adopted the First Infantry headquarters post, Baton Rouge, as his residence. He purchased plantations in both Louisiana and Mississippi, acquiring more slaves with each transaction. Taylor was already well on his way to owning more than one hundred slaves by the time he replaced Snelling on the northern frontier. He later became the last U.S. president to keep slaves in the White House.[23]

In both their sectional composition and their slaveholding practices, the First and Fifth Infantry Regiments mirrored the polar opposites of their commanders' backgrounds. When the First was transferred to the northern forts in 1828, twenty-three of the thirty-three men who formed its officer corps (almost 70 percent) were Southerners, compared to an overall average throughout the army of just 40 percent Southern officers.

Seven of the First's ten top-ranking officers hailed from the South. At the time it was sent north in 1828, the First Infantry was the most regionally imbalanced regiment in the entire army.[24] In sharp distinction, only ten of the thirty-four officers assigned to the Fifth Infantry in 1828 (about 30 percent) were Southerners. Only two of that regiment's top ten officers came from the South. Thus, overall, there was a 40 percent differential in the North-versus-South breakdown of the two regimental officer corps.[25]

On May 23, 1828, Lieutenant Colonel Taylor disembarked at the Fort Snelling steamboat landing with his two slaves, Jane and Glascon. When Taylor settled into the commandant's quarters at the post, the heyday of Minnesota slavery commenced. For the ensuing nine years, until the First Infantry departed in 1837, the practice of slavery in Minnesota flourished to an extent unrivaled in any other epoch.[26]

As other First Regiment officers made their way north to join Taylor at Fort Snelling, most of them brought along their slaves. Never before had a majority of the officers at Fort Snelling kept slaves, but after 1828 it was an exception when one did not. This new slaveholding regime lasted the full length of the First Infantry's nine-year tour of duty (1828 to 1837). Of the thirty-eight officers stationed at Fort Snelling during those years, thirty-three (more than 85 percent) used an enslaved servant at some point. For the first time in the fort's history, slaveholding was the norm. The total number of slaves skyrocketed from only seven under the Fifth Infantry to thirty under the First.[27]

Courtney was the only officer's slave not affected by the change in regiments. Because Captain Garland was assigned to the Third Regiment and posted in Minnesota on quartermaster duty, he remained at Fort Snelling during the 1828 transition.[28] Colonel Snelling, as was typical, took his slave Mary to his new posting in Washington, D.C.[29] With the sole exception of Courtney, therefore, all of the slaves kept by officers of the First Regiment at Fort Snelling between 1828 and 1837 were new to the region.

The army's own records show that military authorities in Washington would not have been surprised at this wholesale importation of slavery into the free Missouri Compromise territory. The First Infantry's officers had long engaged in legal slaveholding in slave states, and—absent any directive to the contrary—the generals in Washington could have easily foreseen that the order uprooting the First Regiment from its Baton Rouge base would result in many officers bringing their enslaved property with them to their new posts. Yet there is no indication that anyone in the army gave a moment's thought to the effect this redeployment of troops would have on the incidence of slavery in Minnesota or elsewhere in the Northern territories.

Not all First Infantry officers who brought slaves to Fort Snelling were Southerners. First Lt. William Day was a New Yorker. Today, like Dred Scott's master, Dr. John Emerson, Day is better known for the slave he kept, James Thompson, than for his undistinguished military career. Thompson occupies a unique role in regional African American history, for he was the only known former Fort Snelling slave to settle in the area that became Minnesota.

James Thompson, like Joseph Godfrey, had a white father and an enslaved black mother. Like Courtney (Godfrey's mother), Thompson was born into slavery in Virginia. He and his siblings and other relatives had been owned by George Monroe, nephew of U.S. president James Monroe. George Monroe's gambling debts compelled him to sell off Thompson and five of his kin, a transaction that apparently separated Thompson forever from others in his enslaved family. Brought to St. Louis, Thompson was resold to John Culbertson, a sutler licensed to sell merchandise to the First Infantry. About the time Culbertson and Lieutenant Day went to Fort Snelling with the First Infantry in 1828, Day purchased Thompson. Day repeatedly identified "James, Slave" (whose surname he never used) as his servant on pay vouchers.[30]

Army officers always played the most dominant role in Minnesota slavery, but the impact of the First Infantry's embrace of slaveholding from 1828 to 1837 radiated beyond the military. This is the only period during which local private citizens are known to have participated in buying and selling slaves. Indian agent Taliaferro, who had previously loaned out his slaves for short periods to Fort Snelling officers, now seized the opportunity to import more of his Virginia slaves for purposes of hiring them out or selling them—Southern-style commercial slave dealings transacted within Minnesota that lacked only an auction block. Always the biggest local slaveholder, Taliaferro became Minnesota's principal slavery profiteer after the arrival of the First Infantry.[31]

When the army decided to rebuild Fort Crawford, in 1829, Colonel Taylor moved his regimental headquarters from Fort Snelling to the Wisconsin post. Captain Garland, who was tapped to supervise the reconstruction project, brought seventeen-year-old Courtney along as his servant.[32] While serving the Garland family in Prairie du Chien, Courtney would have renewed her contact with Maria Fasnacht. She almost certainly would have learned the exciting news that Maria (or her husband) had raised the sum of $210, enabling her to buy off the last four years of her indenture. In August 1829 Maria received the equivalent of a slave's coveted "free papers" when her master signed and filed a document with Wisconsin authorities formally releasing her from servitude. Courtney's exposure to the black woman in her twenties who had procured her freedom and settled in Prairie du Chien with her white husband must have left an indelible impression, for it was uncannily similar to the path Courtney herself would follow seven or eight years later.[33]

In the summer of 1830 Captain Garland hired Courtney out to 2nd Lt. Thomas Stockton, a young, married West Pointer who had been posted at Fort Snelling. We can only speculate about the reasons her master no longer wished to keep Courtney as the Garland family's servant after she had served in that capacity for a decade. Courtney, at eighteen, may have been pregnant or already have borne her first child, and some officers preferred not to be encumbered with a slave child in their household. Or Garland may simply have seen the chance to capitalize on his investment in Courtney, for her value would have increased greatly since he had acquired her as a child. In any event, Courtney was sent back to Fort Snelling and, as far as we know, never again worked for Captain Garland. Courtney's name appeared for the last time in the army's files on Stockton's pay claim for November 1830, which described her as a black slave with curly hair.

Ten years earlier Captain Garland had listed her height as less than five feet; now she had grown to her adult stature of five feet six inches.[34]

Courtney had lived from childhood to maturity as an army slave, but now her master, Garland, had decided to sell her. The Stocktons were logical purchasers, for they were interested in acquiring a female slave. But they too may have wished to avoid adding a slave child to their family. Instead of buying Courtney, Lieutenant Stockton sent Elias T. Langham, Taliaferro's subagent at the Indian agency, to St. Louis in late 1830 for the express purpose of buying a single female slave. Langham secured a young woman named Rachel on the Stocktons' behalf and brought her back to Fort Snelling.[35] Rachel thus became yet another slave who was sold to a Northern officer posted in Minnesota (Stockton was a New Yorker). Since both of them served as slaves within the Stockton family, it is a virtual certainty that Courtney and Rachel would have become acquainted during Rachel's year at Fort Snelling. After that, Stockton took Rachel to his next posting, in Washington, D.C., and then, in 1832, to Fort Crawford.[36]

Captain Garland's 1831 sale of Courtney to Alexis Bailly is referenced in many works of Minnesota history, though her name is not mentioned. Taliaferro, writing during the middle of the Civil War, claimed, "The only colored woman purchased [in Minnesota] was by Alexis Bailly of Major Garland." Bailly's purchase was said to have been "by bill of sale," and an entry in one of Bailly's ledgers for 1831—"To Cash Paid Major John Garland: $450"—appears to confirm both the timing of the transaction and the amount paid by Bailly. Bailly "used her as a house servant and as a maid for his mixed blood Indian wife."[37] With this transaction, Courtney moved from the peripatetic life of an army slave to ownership by a private citizen.

There can be little doubt that Captain Garland's purchase of Courtney had been a profitable endeavor. Over the years, through servant pay, the army had subsidized his slaveholding by an amount exceeding $600, and Bailly now paid him an additional $450 for her.[38] The relatively high amount of Courtney's 1831 sale price (Snelling had paid only $400 for a woman and her daughter four years earlier), coupled with a later report of a black child in the Bailly household, both underscore the likelihood that Courtney was either pregnant or had already given birth to Godfrey at the time of Bailly's purchase. The value of an enslaved woman could increase sharply once it was known that she could deliver healthy children, for her owner automatically acquired another slave with each birth. In 1862 Joseph Godfrey said he was twenty-seven years old, but the weight of evidence suggests that he was Courtney's first child and that he was born earlier than 1835. Slaves were often unaware of their true age, and the many conflicting birth years given for Godfrey (ranging from 1826 to later than 1835) serve as an example of this phenomenon.[39]

Godfrey's father, also named Joseph Godfrey (sometimes spelled Godfroi or Godfroy), whom he described as a Canadian Frenchman, worked as a low-ranking trader for Bailly. There is no indication that Joseph Godfrey Sr. and Courtney were married, either legally or informally, nor is anything known about the nature of their relationship. Under the basic principles of American slavery, neither the race nor the legal standing of Godfrey's father mattered, for his mother's status meant that he was born into slavery. The applicable legal doctrine was *partus sequitur ventrem* (offspring follows the condition of the mother).

Either by purchase or by birth, Godfrey became the property of Alexis Bailly. Godfrey thus is one of the few African Americans to have been born into slavery in Minnesota and the only one known to have grown from birth to adulthood there.[40] Bailly has been identified as the "first Minnesota slave holder, except for some of the members of the military at Fort Snelling" and as the "only resident" of Minnesota who owned a slave.[41] But a 1925 article in the *Minneapolis Tribune* offers rare proof of a citizen-to-citizen slave sale and adds Bailly's father-in-law as another resident slave owner. The box at the top of the next page reprints an entry in an 1833 credit book recording the transaction between Bailly and Jean Baptiste Faribault.

Bailly thus sold "1 Negro wench" to Faribault for $350 in 1833. Was Godfrey's mother this female slave? Probably, but we can't rule out the possibility that Bailly owned another woman in addition to Courtney. In this intra-family transaction, nominal ownership of Courtney might have

J.B. Faribault, Dr. [Debtor]
To 15 barrels of flour at $7.50......................$115.
1 lot of cattle...147.
1 Negro wench..350.
Balance of account last year........................<u>124.51</u>
$736.[42]

been transferred to Faribault merely as an account-balancing procedure; Courtney remained, apparently, in the Bailly home as long as she lived in Mendota (as Godfrey's comments in 1862 indicate). Note, too, that the sale price was $100 less than Bailly had paid for Courtney two years earlier. That could have been because the 1833 sale did not include young Joseph or because, as a relative, Faribault paid Bailly an artificially low price. Or perhaps the "Negro wench" was not Courtney at all. Whatever one's interpretation, however, the 1833 document shows conclusively that both the Bailly and Faribault families owned slaves.

One glimpse into the Bailly household helps us to visualize Godfrey's treatment there as a young slave. Philander Prescott had worked for Bailly before Henry Sibley's arrival in Mendota. Since 1823 Prescott had been married to a full-blood Dakota woman named Nehanamenah (Spirit of the Moon), who took the English name Mary. During the winter of 1833–34, Lucy Bailly asked Mary to permit her young daughter (also named Lucy) to live in the Bailly home. Though Lucy Prescott was then only five or six years old, Mrs. Bailly wished her help in caring for the Bailly children.[43]

Mary Prescott consented to this live-in arrangement but was horrified when little Lucy "had not been there long before she got a whipping" and promptly removed the girl from the home. Lucy Bailly was "offended" and saw to it that the Prescotts were denied nearby housing in retaliation. Not surprisingly, given the whipping of his child, Philander Prescott viewed Lucy Bailly as a "miserable, revengeful" person. According to Prescott, Mrs. Bailly's mistreatment of his daughter was not an isolated occurrence. She was, he unsparingly recalled, "remarkably fond of whipping other people's children." Prescott then gives us an insider's look at Lucy Bailly's dark side: "And whilst I am speaking about the whipping business—Mrs. Bailly had a little black child raised in the family and a young Sioux girl. Those two children, I actually believe, would get from 25 to 50 lashes a day and sometimes more, every day almost. I frequently would leave the house to get away from the miserable crying of those children when she was cowhiding them."[44] Godfrey himself was likely a victim of these repeated whippings, for he is the only "little black child" who can be placed in the Bailly household at the time of Prescott's observation (1833–35). If Lucy Bailly's treatment was sufficiently brutal to raise an anguished outcry from a local fur trader, imagine the horrors that Courtney experienced as she was forced to listen to the cries that accompanied the "cowhiding" of her own child.

In the Bailly household Courtney would have been exposed to a strikingly different life than she had experienced either in her upbringing in Virginia or during her years of service at army forts. Her new master and mistress had kinship ties to the Dakotas with whom Bailly traded, and Dakota and French were most likely the dominant languages spoken within the home. Young Joseph would have learned to talk in this environment. To his mother, both the words and the customs may have seemed alien, but Joseph Godfrey was raised and learned to cope as a slave in this setting. Courtney would have been acquainted with the slave James Thompson from her time at Fort Snelling, but both she and her young son almost certainly had further contacts with him while they lived in Mendota. Thompson is known to have associated closely with the Dakotas who frequented the Bailly and Faribault trading posts. In 1833, while still enslaved at Fort Snelling, Thompson married a daughter of Chief Cloudman, the leader of the Dakota band whose village was near Lake Calhoun, in what is now Minneapolis. Thus Thompson, through his marriage, and Godfrey, by growing up with the Baillys, became the only two local slaves who are known to have learned the Dakota language; they also both received significant exposure to Dakota culture.[45] By contrast, most Minnesota slaves, like their white masters, had limited contact with the Indians and, also like their white masters, may have viewed them with fear and apprehension.

While Godfrey and his mother were in Mendota, Rachel, the young woman who had replaced Courtney as the slave of Lieutenant Stockton's family at Fort Snelling in 1831, courageously launched a freedom lawsuit in St. Louis. Stockton had taken Rachel and James Henry, the son born to her at Fort Crawford in 1834, to St. Louis, where he sold them to an infamous slave dealer. Rachel's lawyer contended that *Winny v. Whitesides*, an 1824 Missouri Supreme Court decision, entitled her to emancipation because she had resided with her master in two different free territories where slavery was prohibited by law: the Missouri Compromise region (Fort Snelling) and the Northwest Ordinance territory (Fort Crawford). Rachel thus became the first slave of an army officer to seek freedom through the courts.[46]

Stockton risked loss of the proceeds from his sale of Rachel if she won her freedom, so it was he, not the slave dealer, who presented the only defense in the Missouri litigation. The lawyer defending against Rachel's suit, relying on Stockton's statement, argued that army officers, because they were sent to their posts under federal orders, were exempt from all territorial antislavery laws. Late in 1834 a St. Louis trial judge agreed with him, ruling that Rachel and her child must remain in bondage. News of this decision must have traveled swiftly upriver and would have been greeted favorably at Fort Snelling, where most of the officers, including Commandant Maj. John Bliss, were keeping slaves.[47] Rachel's lawyers immediately filed notice of their intention to appeal her case.

As Rachel's case was making its way to the Missouri Supreme Court, the fur trade in Minnesota was undergoing its most significant transformation. Alexis Bailly had represented the interests of the American Fur Company in the territory off and on since 1823. But by 1834 he had outworn the goodwill of his absentee partners and had alienated Indian agent Taliaferro. The owners of the fur company wanted to ease Bailly out of power without pushing him into competition; Taliaferro was determined to strip him of his fur-trading license for his persistent clandestine liquor trafficking to the Dakotas. The company decided it needed a new, more diplomatic trader who could charm Bailly into accepting a subservient interest and mend fences with Taliaferro so as to preserve control of the local fur trade.[48]

Henry Hastings Sibley was just twenty-three years old when, in the summer of 1834, the new American Fur Company, presided over by Ramsay Crooks, purchased John Jacob Astor's fur-trading interests. To manage the new firm's business in Minnesota, Crooks recruited Sibley to serve as the on-the-scene partner of what was called the Western Outfit. Sibley would be headquartered in Mendota.[49]

Sibley may have been young in years, but his family was long on pedigree, tracing its American roots to John Sibley, who had emigrated from England in 1629.[50] Befitting his family's station, Sibley's formal education at the Academy of Detroit was supplemented by private tutoring. He also studied law for two years, actively encouraged by his father to follow him into the legal profession. But Sibley yearned for a "more active and stirring life," and so, at the age of eighteen, he procured a clerkship in Astor's fur company in Mackinac, Michigan. For the next five years, he learned the fur trade, earning Crooks's respect in the process.[51]

When Sibley traveled from Mackinac to Mendota in 1834 to assume his new position, he met up with Bailly at Prairie du Chien.[52] In late October and early November Sibley and Bailly trudged two hundred miles overland to Mendota, stopping for a night at the cabin of Augustin Rocque near the location of the present river town of Wabasha, Minnesota. Sibley later described the structure as "the only habitation of a white man" along the entire route. But Rocque, like Bailly, was a métis whose mother had been a sister of the first Dakota chief, Wabasha. Sibley may have regarded Rocque as white due to his residence in a cabin and his relative acculturation, but Rocque described himself, in the parlance of the times, as a "half-breed."[53]

Such ethnic distinctions, which were considered important and real in the nineteenth century, help to highlight a major and symbolic transition: the passing of the fur-trading torch from Bailly, a Canadian-born métis, to Sibley, a patrician American WASP. While French Canadians had intermarried openly with the Indians, Sibley and most of the other Anglo-Americans who came to Minnesota after 1834 refused to solemnize their sexual liaisons with Native women. Within the course of a single generation following Sibley's arrival, a massive wave of white settlers would largely supplant both métis and Indians in Minnesota.

Like his father, Sibley would ultimately serve as a territorial representative to Congress. After Minnesota achieved statehood, he became its first governor. He has been described as "the most prominent figure in Minnesota" from 1834 to 1891, the state's George Washington.[54] And, from November 1834 until May 1835, during a frigid Minnesota winter that he described as "remarkable for its length and severity," Henry Sibley lived in Mendota in the Bailly's small log hut.[55] During those six months Courtney worked as the household slave and Godfrey was routinely whipped by mistress Lucy.

Sibley's unfinished autobiography, written in the 1880s and published posthumously in 1932, speaks with great warmth about his "uniformly pleasant" stay with Lucy and Alexis Bailly during his first winter in Mendota. Lucy, in his memory, was "a handsome, well formed lady" who had "received some advantages of education." She "warmly welcomed" the young man destined to take over the fur-trading business from her husband. Despite his mission to nudge Bailly aside, Sibley came to look upon the older man as a lifelong friend and mentor.[56] Sibley failed to mention either Godfrey or his mother in his autobiography, but that was hardly unusual. At the time, domestic servants—whether slaves or not—were relatively invisible members of a host's household. Similarly, Sibley mentions no Bailly children in the house, referring only to his host's "family."

Given the silence that later shrouded the subject, it is difficult to say with certainty how many contemporaries of Godfrey (aside from the Bailly and Faribault families) knew that he was a slave. But Sibley surely knew. After Godfrey's death, a respected historian wrote that Godfrey had "acted as an errand boy" for Sibley.[57] Since the Baillys moved from Mendota in 1835, the young slave's errands probably were run in 1834 or 1835. And, since he kept in contact with Bailly for more than two decades, both personally and through the fur-trading business, Sibley would have known that Joseph Godfrey remained a slave of the Bailly or Faribault families in years to come.

After spending the 1834–35 winter with the Baillys, Sibley established his own bachelor residence in Mendota. He soon built a large and gracious stone house that today is open to the public as a state historic site. In his memoirs Sibley reported that his cook and servant was "a mulatto man named Joe Robinson."[58] In her Sibley biography, historian Rhoda Gilman discusses Robinson's likely status: "The presence of a black servant, when slavery was practiced frequently though illegally at Fort Snelling, has raised the question of whether Sibley was at this time a slave owner. A note in [one of Sibley's 1837] memorandum books . . . suggests that Robinson may indeed have been a slave, but that if so, he belonged to [Hercules] Dousman and had been loaned to Sibley."[59] Given evidence of the region's proslavery milieu, Gilman's suggestion that Sibley may have used slave labor in his own home is even easier to credit. Any black person working in the vicinity of Fort Snelling in the 1830s was likely to have been enslaved.[60]

Sibley himself provides other indirect evidence of Robinson's enslavement. Though Robinson "could cook plain food moderately well," Sibley wrote, he was also "wasteful" and "not entirely cleanly in his methods." Had an employee shown such shortcomings, he would probably have been fired or docked in pay. Instead, Sibley tells how he dealt with the "faults" of Robinson: "I was compelled to reprimand him frequently, and severely." Whether Sibley administered twenty-five lashes of cowhide, as did Lucy Bailly, we cannot know. But it would be naïve not to conclude that Sibley used some form of corporal punishment. In so doing, he would have been applying the standard form of discipline for errant or recalcitrant slaves.[61] Gilman's supposition that Robinson was loaned to Sibley by Hercules Dousman, his senior partner, may offer a clue as to how private citizens such as Sibley might have deflected questions about owning slaves in a supposedly free territory. If asked, Sibley could truthfully have said that he did not own Robinson. If pressed, he could have added that he had "hired" Robinson—which may well have been true, in the sense that Sibley most likely gave something to Dousman in return for the use of his human property.

But, at least in Sibley's first few years in Minnesota, such a subterfuge would hardly have been necessary. In the vicinity of Fort Snelling and throughout southern Minnesota, slavery was the prevailing status for blacks at the time, and many of the region's leading citizens were slaveholders. The major fur traders, the sutler and most of the officers at Fort Snelling, and the local Indian agent and his assistant were all slave masters during this period. Indeed, if one were to compile an abbreviated "Who's Who in Mid-1830s Minnesota," a majority of the prominent white residents listed would be slaveholders. In this respect and others, there are striking parallels between the patterns of slavery in frontier Minnesota and that in the original colonies in America's Northeast. Edgar McManus's classic book *Black Bondage in the North* notes that slaveholding in colonial New England "reflected social as well as economic standing" and that slaves were seen as "visible symbols of rank and distinction." It was the "leading families" who kept slaves in the very states later known for their abolitionist sentiment.[62]

While the evidence documenting Godfrey's birth into slavery at Mendota is convincing today, it is important to note that this key aspect of his life was never mentioned when he was catapulted to notoriety after the Dakota War of 1862. The first written references to his enslavement did not appear until early in the twentieth century. As might be expected from such delayed accounts, many of their details are contradictory or now known to be false. In a two-page biography of Godfrey prepared for the Minnesota Historical Society in 1907, historian Clarence Paine claimed that Godfrey's mother was a slave named Polly who was brought from St. Louis to Minnesota and that his father was a "Frenchman named Godefroi."[63] In 1909 a Nebraska newspaper reported that "Godfrey and his mother were said to have been slaves in St. Louis, and were brought to St. Paul as the property of a steamer."[64] Finally, Mary Schwandt Schmidt, a captive during the 1862 war, offered a 1913 account: "I afterwards learned that his [Godfrey's] mother was a slave brought north by an officer at Fort Snelling and later became a servant in the Faribault family."[65] This statement, the only one made by someone who had actually met Godfrey in the 1800s, proved, as we shall see, to be the most accurate.

The long-delayed disclosure of Godfrey's birth into slavery raises obvious questions about who, in 1862, knew and kept quiet about his status. Godfrey had his own reasons for not mentioning his enslavement. But we should also consider the knowledge Godfrey would have had about slaveholding in Minnesota, including, quite possibly, by Sibley himself. Godfrey likely would have known the legal status of Robinson, Sibley's black servant. He also knew that Sibley's closest associates in the fur trade, as well as many of his friends in the officer corps at Fort Snelling, had been Minnesota slave masters. And Sibley obviously knew about the enslavement of both Godfrey and Courtney within the Bailly family. Both men thus apparently knew facts that, while common knowledge among the few non-Native residents of Minnesota in the 1830s, would have been highly charged secrets during the years from 1861 to 1865, when slavery divided the nation and drove it to war. When in 1862 the paths of Sibley and Godfrey crossed again, while the Civil War was raging, each had memories the other would not have wished to be revealed.

NOTES ON CHAPTER 1

1. Heard, *History of the Sioux War,* 191.
2. An 1849 Minnesota census listed many distinguished Mendota residents, including two men who would become governor of the state (Henry Sibley and Alexander Ramsey), future U.S. senator Henry Rice, and the Faribault family. Though Ramsey and Rice were apparently temporary residents, this census illustrates the unique role played by the village of Mendota well into the 1840s. See Minnesota Territorial Census Schedules, 1849–55, MHS, roll 1, frame 76.
3. H. Sibley, *Unfinished Autobiography,* 29–36.
4. Ibid., 29–30.
5. Belliveau, "Life of Alexis Bailly," 1. On Bailly's marriage, see Woolworth biography in "Jean B. and Pelagie (Ainse) Faribault and their Descendants," Woolworth Papers, MHS; Alexis Bailly affidavit, #49, Scrip Rolls. Though Woolworth identifies Lucy Bailly as the daughter of Jean Baptiste and Pelagie Faribault, there is reason to doubt her parentage. See 1855–56 affidavits: Alexis Bailly, #49; Augustin Rock (Rocque), #50; Alexis Bailly Jr., #219; and Alexander Faribault, #222, all in Records Relating to Mixed-Blood Claimants under the Treaty of Prairie du Chien, 1855–56, NA, RG 75, Miscellaneous Reserve Papers (hereafter, Scrip Rolls). These affidavits all claim that Lucy Bailly's mother was a "full-blood Sioux." Since all of the other children of Jean B. and Pelagie Faribault are identified in the scrip affidavits as being quarter-bloods (indicating that their mother was a half-blood), it appears that Lucy Bailly may have had a different mother. She thus may have been the half sister of the other Faribault children (Alexander, David, and Oliver Faribault and Emily Fowler). Alternatively, Alexis Bailly may have falsely overstated his wife's Dakota blood so as to assure his family's qualification for scrip benefits.
6. Upham and Dunlap, *Collections of the Minnesota Historical Society,* 14:28; Belliveau, "Life of Alexis Bailly," 1.
7. *Courtney v. Rayburn,* 1836, Circuit Court Case Files, Office of the Circuit Court–St. Louis, Missouri State Archives, Office of the Secretary of State (hereafter, St. Louis Freedom Suits). Available online at http://stlouiscourtrecords.wustl.edu, accessed March 20, 2012. I gratefully acknowledge assistance from two scholars: Barbara Luecke, coauthor of *Snelling: Minnesota's First First Family,* verified Garland's marriage and other facts relating to his family; Professor Lea VanderVelde, author of *Mrs. Dred Scott,* alerted me to the existence and online availability of records relating to Courtney's freedom suit.
8. Army officers' pay claims from 1816 to early 1861 are found in a massive collection of 1,735 boxes of army payroll documents at the National Archives, NA, RG 217, E516, Settled Accounts, Army Paymaster, cited hereafter as Pay Vouchers.
9. For early pay claims that mention Courtney, see Pay Vouchers, boxes 121, 125 and 139. For a short period the paymaster in Detroit used a pay form that required officers to give the age of their servant(s); it was on such a form that Garland indicated, in 1821, that Courtney was nine years old.
10. For an excellent basic discussion of the internal slave trade from 1810 to 1860, see Kolchin, *American Slavery,* 95–97. Kolchin cites scholarly estimates that the odds of an "Upper South" child slave being "sold South" were about 30 percent.

11. See *Courtney v. Rayburn,* 1836, St. Louis Freedom Suits. At least twenty-three of Garland's pay claims, covering a period of forty-two months, name Courtney as his servant. Although Garland declared a white woman as his servant on the pay claims he submitted at Fort Howard, they do not contradict Courtney's statement that she too served the Garlands at that post. Garland's rank entitled him to draw pay for only one servant, but it was not uncommon for officers who had the financial means to use extra servants. It appears that Garland sometimes elected to list his free servant, rather than his slave, on his pay claims. See Pay Vouchers, boxes 121–307.
12. See Luecke and Luecke, *Snelling,* 164 et seq. for an excellent discussion of Garland's replacement of Snelling as quartermaster and the ensuing testy relationship between the two officers.
13. The image of the servant description comes from the only pay claim on which Garland described Courtney as a slave. See Pay Vouchers, box 222. As discussed later in the chapter, Lieutenant Stockton also described her as a slave on his pay claim. Some officers regularly recited the legal status of their servants, while others never did so or included it only occasionally. The army's form did not require an officer to declare whether a servant was free or enslaved, so that fact was added at an individual officer's discretion.
14. Colonel Snelling listed "William Thompson, a black man and slave" for January and February 1826. Curiously, Taliaferro noted an arrangement to permit Snelling to use William's services from April until October 1826 in exchange for furnishing "his Victuals and Clothes," but Snelling did not seek reimbursement for William on his pay claims during those months. See *Taliaferro journal,* March 31, 1826, Taliaferro Papers, MHS; and Snelling's pay vouchers. Other officers who apparently used Taliaferro's slave William include Nathaniel Harris and Alexander Johnston. See Pay Vouchers, boxes 150, 214, and 222.
15. That Eliza was a favored slave is shown by the fact that she was the only one (out of twenty or more) who remained in the Taliaferro home in Pennsylvania in later years. Eliza Johnson, black, age thirty-eight, was listed in the 1850 census as living in the Taliaferro household. Eliza's "mulatto" daughter, Susan, age sixteen, also appeared in the same census. Several facts suggest that Taliaferro may have been Susan's father, but we may never know her true paternity. That the Plymptons used Eliza's services at Fort Snelling is shown by a unique retroactive pay voucher Captain Plympton submitted from New York late in 1826. There he indicated that E. Johnson, black, 4' 8" had served him for his last fourteen months at Fort Snelling (April 1825 through May 1826), for which he drew a substantial amount in additional back pay. See Pay Vouchers, box 220.
16. *Taliaferro journal,* May 29, 1826, Taliaferro Papers, MHS.
17. Plympton drew servant pay for "E. Johnson" or "E. Johnston" in New York in 1826 and 1828 and in St. Louis in 1827. Pay Vouchers, boxes 220, 222, 228, and 264. He never referred to her as a slave, but Taliaferro's journal leaves no doubt about her legal status; Eliza remained in slavery until at least 1839, and perhaps much longer. Her daughter, Susan, was born into slavery in Minnesota in about 1834.

18. The spelling of Fasnacht's surname (also spelled Forsnot, Fatchnaught, Faschnot, and Fashnaght) and her husband's rank as a private are from the December 1822 post return for Fort Crawford, NA, RG 94, Returns from U.S. Military Posts, 1800–1916, M617. The terms of Maria's 1816 indenture were generously provided to me by James Hansen of the Wisconsin Historical Society, by e-mail, October 28, 2008. Capt. Robert McCabe and 2nd Lt. Henry Clarke listed Maria "Fashnaght" as their servant at Fort Snelling from May 1826 to May 1827. Pay Vouchers, boxes 222 and 228. Slaves often married other slaves informally, but such unions were not accorded legal status; in contrast, Maria wed Jacob before a justice of the peace and their union was entered into official records. See "Crawford County, Wisconsin, Marriages," 46.
19. For Harris's use of "William, Slave," see Pay Vouchers, boxes 214 and 222. Dr. Harney did not identify Peter as a slave on his pay claims while he was posted at Fort Snelling, but he repeatedly did so in Baton Rouge both before and after his Minnesota service. Peter, still enslaved, last appeared on Dr. Harney's pay claims in 1842.
20. For Snelling's pay claims regarding Mary and Louisa, see Pay Vouchers, boxes 231 and 245. Luecke and Luecke, *Snelling*, 261, citing Snelling's journal, refers to the purchase of Mary and Louisa in 1826.
21. For relevant Scott pay claims, see Pay Vouchers, boxes 150, 202, 204, 222, 280, and many others.
22. The statistical statements and summaries in this paragraph and throughout the first three chapters of this book are derived from my collection and analysis of relevant officers' pay vouchers in the National Archives, which I intend to publish in upcoming works about army slavery.
23. For general discussions of Taylor's slaveholding, see two Taylor biographies: Bauer, *Zachary Taylor*, 105–8; and Hamilton, *Zachary Taylor*, 32–40.
24. Using data from 1830, Skelton noted that 60 percent of the First Infantry's officer corps were Southerners, making it the most Southern regiment in the army. See Skelton, *American Profession of Arms*, 155–57. I developed the statistics in the text using 1828 data from the *Army Register*, which show an even more extreme North-South imbalance.
25. This analysis is based on the 1828 regimental rosters published in *American State Papers: Military Affairs*, 3:666–67. Officers' regional roots are as stated in Heitman, *Historical Register*. Throughout this book, and consistent with the practice of many other scholars of slavery, "South" and "Southern" include states (whether or not they joined the Confederacy) in which slavery was still legal at the commencement of the Civil War. I am aware that these statistics present more extreme regional differences than those described by military scholars (see Skelton, *American Profession of Arms*; and Watson, "Professionalism, Social Attitudes, and Civil-Military Accountability"), either because those scholars dealt with a later time period or because they defined "South" more stringently.
26. Taylor, on his first pay claim filed at Fort Snelling in 1828, described his two servants as "Jane, dark, slave" and "Glascon, dark, slave." See Pay Vouchers, box 269.
27. Statistics based on my analysis of the Pay Vouchers. These figures understate the full scope of slavery at Fort Snelling, for they do not include slaves whose names were not recorded in the Pay Vouchers, such as very young children.
28. The only other officer who was not transferred away from Fort Snelling in 1828 was the post surgeon, Dr. Robert C. Wood. Surgeons were assigned to posts by the U.S. surgeon general and did not automatically move when regiments were changed. Before the arrival of the First Infantry, Dr. Wood had not used an enslaved servant at Fort Snelling. Captain Garland was thus the only slaveholding officer at the fort who remained there following the 1828 transition.

29. Snelling listed Mary as one of his servants on all pay claims he submitted from the time he purchased her until his death in Washington, D.C., in August 1828. But Mary's daughter, Louisa, was not listed after Snelling's arrival in Washington early in 1828. Her fate is unknown. See Pay Vouchers, boxes 232, 245, 253, and 255.
30. For biographical information about James Thompson, see Newson, *Pen Pictures of St. Paul*, 9–12; Nancy Fitzgerald, "Ex-Slave Helped Found Historic St. Paul Church," *St. Paul Pioneer Press*, August 28, 1949; Spangler, *Negro in Minnesota*, 19–20; and Turner, "Analysis of Negro Slavery," 12. Though James Thompson is often said to have been purchased by Lieutenant Day at Fort Snelling, an earlier voucher showing James as his servant at Jefferson Barracks ("James, Slave," March and April 1828, Pay Vouchers, box 260) suggests that the purchase may have occurred even before Day's arrival at Fort Snelling.
31. One isolated page of Taliaferro's private accounts for part of 1832, which he (apparently inadvertently) included when he donated his papers to the Minnesota Historical Society, documents some of his slave-related transactions in Minnesota. Taliaferro recorded $112 income from hiring out two slaves, Horace (to army officers) and Frederick (to the assistant Indian agent), plus $500 for his sale of Horace to A. S. Miree, the fort sutler. For the same period, Taliaferro also entered his income for a half-year's service as Indian agent ($650). Thus, for the limited period for which such financial data is available, Taliaferro's own records show that he made almost as much from his Minnesota slave dealings as he did from his federal salary. See Taliaferro Papers, MHS, roll 4, frame 49. Taliaferro's own documentation of his sale of Horace also undercuts his later claim that he freed all of his slaves.
32. Courtney appears on Captain Garland's pay claims at Fort Crawford for January through June 1829 and August through September 1830. From July 1829 until July 1830 Garland named a white servant, Martin Gregorich. See Pay Vouchers, boxes 259, 288, 316, and 317. Garland, whose rank permitted him to draw extra pay for only one servant, may have chosen to list Gregorich even though Courtney was still serving his family, but it is also possible that he had hired out her services to a local citizen.
33. Documentation of the formal release of "Maria Fatchnaught" from the terms of her indentured servitude was provided by James Hansen, Wisconsin Historical Society, in e-mail dated October 28, 2008. According to Hansen, the release was filed in Crawford County's deed records on August 8, 1829, upon payment of $210.
34. Courtney's name appears on two pay claims submitted by Stockton, covering July through November 1830. Pay Vouchers, box 317.
35. *Rachael, A Woman of Color v. Walker*, 4 Mo. 350, 1836.
36. "Rachel, black" appears as Stockton's servant on his pay claims submitted between January 1831 and October 1832. Though Stockton never referred to her as a slave when drawing his pay, Rachel's freedom suit leaves no doubt as to her legal status.
37. Ledger, 1831, Alexis Bailly Papers, MHS. The best evidence of Bailly's ownership of Courtney for five years comes from her affidavit in *Courtney v. Rayburn*, 1836, St. Louis Freedom Suits, discussed more fully in chapter 2. Taliaferro wrote that the slave Garland sold to Bailly was a woman. Taliaferro, "Auto-Biography," 235. See also Holcombe and Bingham, *Compendium of History*, 46 ("used her as a house servant"); and *Minneapolis Tribune*, July 26, 1925 ("Negro slave woman"). Other sources, apparently incorrectly, claim that Garland sold Bailly a male slave. Baker, "Address at Fort Snelling," 297 ("negro man"); Neill, "Occurrences in and around Fort Snelling," 115; and Hubbard et al., *Minnesota in Three Centuries*, 2:67 ("negro man" bought "in about 1840"). Also see Appell, "Slavery in Minnesota," 41. Godfrey's story verifies that at least one slave held by Bailly was a woman.

38. Pay vouchers that name Courtney as a servant show a total in excess of $600.
39. Several facts place Godfrey's year of birth earlier than 1835. That year Courtney gave birth to another son, William, who was sold with her in St. Louis later in 1835. See *Courtney v. Rayburn*. Barring the extremely unlikely possibility that Courtney gave birth to twins and that Bailly kept one baby while disposing of the other, the only way Godfrey could have been born in Mendota (as he said in 1862) was if he had been born earlier than 1835. Also, Prescott's account of a "young black child" who was old enough to be lashed with a whip (see discussion later in the chapter) must refer to a slave child who was born well before 1835. Godfrey's tombstone indicates that he was born in 1827, though that date is probably too early.
40. In 1834 a "mulatto" woman, Susan Johnston, was also apparently born into slavery in Minnesota. Taliaferro's journal refers to other slaves born there as well. VanderVelde noted that the 1850 census for Bedford County, Pennsylvania, lists both Eliza and Susan (sixteen years old, born in Minnesota) as living in Taliaferro's household. The identification of Susan (but not her mother) as a "mulatto" raises obvious questions about the identity of her father, and Taliaferro is a prime paternity candidate. See VanderVelde and Subramanian, "Mrs. Dred Scott," 1058n103. Godfrey's younger brother was also born into slavery in Minnesota but soon gained his freedom (see chapter 2).
41. *Minneapolis Tribune*, July 26, 1925; Hubbard et al., *Minnesota in Three Centuries*, 2:67.
42. *Minneapolis Tribune*, July 26, 1925, 1. I have not been able to locate the underlying original record, though I have no reason to doubt the authenticity of this copy.
43. Affidavit of Philander Prescott, #55, Scrip Rolls (Lucy, married name Pettijohn, was twenty-seven years old in 1855–56); Parker, *Recollections of Philander Prescott*, 116, 152.
44. Parker, *Recollections of Philander Prescott*, 152. The 1850 Wabashaw County, Minnesota, census lists the members of the Alexis Bailly household, including Angelique Skaya, age twenty, born in the Indian village of "Capozia." If this is the "young Sioux girl" to whom Prescott referred, she would have been just three or four years old at the time she was whipped by Lucy Prescott—about the same age as Godfrey.
45. Thompson's half-breed scrip affidavit, #68 (signed with an "X"), Scrip Rolls, gives 1833 as the year of his marriage to Mary, a full-blood Dakota woman. See also Thompson biography, Woolworth Papers, MHS.
46. Detailed records of Rachel's freedom suit are available online in *Rachel v. Walker*, 1834, St. Louis Freedom Suits.
47. On his pay claims at Fort Snelling, Commandant Bliss referred to two black servants, Hannibal and Jane. See Pay Vouchers, boxes 380–81, 391–92 ("Hannibal, black" and "Jane, black") and boxes 394, 406, 423, 427, 435, and 438 ("Hannibal, black" and "Fanny," a blue-eyed "light" woman). Though Major Bliss never described Hannibal or Jane as slaves on his pay claims, his son later wrote that both were enslaved and that his father had purchased them in St. Louis while he was en route to Fort Snelling. See Bliss, "Reminiscences of Fort Snelling," 336.
48. Gilman, *Henry Hastings Sibley*, 36–46. Gilman describes in superb detail the steps by which Bailly was dislodged from his position of control and Sibley took charge of the American Fur Company's interests.
49. Ibid., 37–38.
50. J. Sibley, *Sibley Family in America*.
51. H. Sibley, *Unfinished Autobiography*, 10–27.
52. Ibid. Sibley, understandably but rather disingenuously, omits all of the business schemes of his partners to wrest control of the territory from Bailly.

53. Ibid., 29; and Augustin Rock (Rocque) affidavit, #31, Scrip Rolls, where Rocque describes himself as "a Half Breed of the Medawahkanton band."
54. Folwell, *History of Minnesota*, 1:162; H. Sibley, *Unfinished Autobiography*, 3.
55. H. Sibley, *Unfinished Autobiography*, 31.
56. Ibid., 30–34.
57. Two-page biography of Godfrey by Clarence Paine, October 4, 1907, MHS, M582, roll 1. Paine was born in Minnesota and was a director of the Nebraska State Historical Society, a position he held at the time he wrote the Godfrey biography. In his cover letter to the Minnesota Historical Society Paine said that his account of Godfrey's life "is very largely his version of the part he took in the Indian troubles in Minnesota," a statement that suggests that Paine either interviewed Godfrey or had sources that quoted him.
58. H. Sibley, *Unfinished Autobiography*, 35.
59. Gilman, *Henry Hastings Sibley*, 242n5.
60. The only free black person known to have lived near Fort Snelling anytime before 1840 was James Thompson, who had been enslaved at the fort for many years but was emancipated when a missionary purchased his freedom (at Fort Crawford, not in Minnesota) in 1837.
61. H. Sibley, *Unfinished Autobiography*, 35. The word *severe* was often used as code for corporal punishment. See McManus, *Black Bondage:* advertisement for disobedient slave who "needs a severe master," 28; slaves were "severely punished" under the auspices of black magistrates, 97; flogging was a standard punishment for slaves, while white indentured servants could either be flogged or have their terms of service extended, 56–57; "master could legally use whatever force was needed to enforce his commands," 90.
62. See McManus, *Black Bondage*, 1, 39–42.
63. Clarence Paine, Godfrey biography, October 4, 1907, MHS, M582, roll 1. I attempted to locate Paine's sources at the Nebraska State Historical Society and elsewhere, but without success. See Paine to Warren Upham, October 4, 1907, files of the Organization of American Historians, Indiana University, Purdue University, Indianapolis. One incorrect version of Godfrey's origins came from Rev. Stephen R. Riggs, who wrote to his wife on October 20, 1862, "I think Maj. Cullen brought him [Godfrey] up into the country when he first came as superintendent [of Indian Affairs]." See Riggs letters, CCHS.
64. *Niobrara (NE) Tribune,* July 8, 1909.
65. "Reminiscences of Mary Schwandt Schmidt as told to Mrs. Edna Sandford Ward," 1913, 23, Schwandt Schmidt Papers, MHS, M581. A fourth account, provided by a former Minnesotan asked to give his recollections about Godfrey, does not specifically say that he was a slave but suggests it. According to S. B. Egbert, a man named Brown brought the "niger boy" and his "wench" mother from New Orleans to Minnesota, adding that Godfrey later "ran away." S. B. Egbert to Theodore Carter, February 3, 1910, Carter Papers, MHS, box 2.

CHAPTER 2

Flight to Freedom

Courtney gave birth to another son in Mendota in April 1835, when Godfrey was about five years old. Henry Sibley was still living with the Bailly family when the new slave baby, William, was born. Alexis Bailly was about to hand over the reins of the fur trade to Sibley. Because the company wanted to distance the controversial trader from Indian agent Taliaferro's wrath, Bailly agreed to move away from Mendota. He initially went to Prairie du Chien but soon moved back to far southern Minnesota, to the new Mississippi River town of Wabasha—the second location where Godfrey, in his 1862 statement, said he had lived with the Bailly family. The Baillys apparently never again lived in Mendota.

Godfrey may have been taken to Prairie du Chien with the Baillys in 1835, or he may have remained temporarily in Mendota with the Faribault family. In any event, within a few months Bailly decided to keep Godfrey as a family slave but to sell Courtney and baby William, thus permanently separating young Godfrey from his mother.[1] Within a few months of leaving Mendota, Bailly took Courtney and William to St. Louis and sold them to a prominent slaveholding businessman, Samuel S. Rayburn. Almost immediately after that transaction, Courtney made her way to Charles D. Drake, a respected Missouri lawyer who was willing to accept enslaved clients in freedom suits. (More than ten years later Drake appeared briefly as the first attorney for Dred Scott in the country's most famous freedom litigation.)[2]

We don't know how Courtney became aware that the courts of Missouri offered her a chance to escape slavery, but it's likely that she received advice and encouragement from either Maria Fasnacht (whom she would have seen again in Prairie du Chien) or Rachel (who was in St. Louis, awaiting the final outcome from the appeal of her own freedom suit). However Courtney came to the decision, it required great courage, for the loss of a freedom suit could bring fearful retribution from a slave master.

On November 2, 1835, Courtney scratched her "X" on an affidavit Drake had prepared. It was the only sworn statement she ever signed, the only written recital of her life in slavery. It begins, "Your petitioner, Courtney, a woman of color, about twenty three years of age, respectfully represents, that she was born in the State of Virginia and belonged to a man named Garland; that when quite young she was sold by him to his brother Major John Garland of the United States Army, who took her to Detroit in Michigan." Whether Drake or Courtney provided the estimate of her age is not known, but it coincided perfectly with Captain Garland's notation on his 1821 pay voucher. Both documents indicate a birth year of 1812.

Recounting that she "did not remember" how long she had been held by Captain Garland at Detroit, Green Bay, and Prairie du Chien, Courtney then briefly summarized her time as a Minnesota slave and the sale to Rayburn:

> She lived with Mr. Bay [Bailly] about five years at St. Peters [Mendota] on the Mississippi River, that somewhere about four months hence Mr. Bay removed to Prairie du Chien and brought her with him, and that she has been there with him since a short time ago, when she was brought by him to the City of St. Louis, and there sold by him to Mr. Samuel S. Rayburn as a slave, and . . . Rayburn now holds her in custody as a slave. . . . Alexi Bay at the time of selling her sold also to . . . Samuel S. Rayburn, an infant child of hers, a boy, about seven months old, named William, who was born at St. Peters, while she was there in the service of Mr. Bay.

Courtney's estimate that she had lived with "Alexi Bay" in Mendota for five years would suggest that she began to serve the Baillys in 1830. Since it is quite possible that Bailly "hired" her from Garland before buying her in 1831, her estimate may be correct.

Courtney's petition also sought freedom for seven-month-old William, making him the only slave born in Minnesota to become a plaintiff in an emancipation lawsuit. But why did Courtney's claim omit her older son, Joseph Godfrey, who was also born in Minnesota and had lived there longer than his brother, William? The answer is straightforward. Godfrey was not and never had been present in the state of Missouri, and thus the court in St. Louis had no jurisdiction over him. Courtney probably told Drake about her older son, but the lawyer would have informed her that he was powerless to take any action on Godfrey's behalf. Also, any mention of Godfrey's name might have undermined Courtney's case by highlighting one of the cruelest ironies of regional slavery laws: for slaves who labored in "free" Minnesota, the best chance of securing freedom was via the courts of the slave state of Missouri.

That Missouri gave more protection to freedom-seeking slaves than its neighbors (including the adjacent free state of Illinois) was, not surprisingly, a controversial political topic in the state. Any reference to Godfrey in Courtney's petition would have reminded Missourians that their state was enforcing slave rights that other states and territories, supposedly "free," were ignoring and thwarting. For both jurisdictional and political reasons, therefore, it made sense for Drake to exclude Godfrey from his mother's plea for freedom.

Courtney's suit did not immediately go to trial. Perhaps either her lawyer or the judge thought it prudent to await the decision of the Missouri Supreme Court in Rachel's case. Depending on the appeal court's reasoning in deciding Rachel's fate, Courtney's case would be either weakened or strengthened.

Courtney waited about eight months, until the Missouri Supreme Court issued its decision in Rachel's case in June 1836. The appellate judges gave short shrift to the trial judge's conclusion that army officers were exempt from antislavery laws. Declaring that keeping a slave at Fort Snelling was "contrary to law" under the terms of the Missouri Compromise and that slavery was also "forbidden" at Fort Crawford by the Northwest Ordinance of 1787, the judges reasoned that a wholesale exemption of army officers from these laws would effectively repeal all antislavery laws. Rhetorically, they asked, "Shall it be said, that because an officer of the army owns slaves in Virginia, that when as officer and soldier, he is required to take command of a post in the non-slave holding States or territories, he thereby has a right to take with him as many slaves, as will suit his interests or convenience?" That, the court unanimously ruled, "surely cannot be the law." The judges thus ordered that Rachel and her infant son should be set free.[3]

After Rachel's victory, both Rayburn and Bailly would have seen the folly of continuing with the case. Courtney had been kept by an officer in free territories for ten years and by a private citizen for another five years in Mendota. Her case for freedom was thus far stronger than Rachel's. Rayburn, as her new owner, and Bailly, as the person who stood to lose for having sold a slave of whom he did not have proper ownership, would have wasted their money by incurring additional legal fees in opposing a case that was now indefensible. Though the official court record is silent on the timing and nature of the final disposition of Courtney's case, there can be little doubt that the defense soon agreed to grant both Courtney and William their freedom. William was freed for the same reason Rachel's baby was emancipated: once the court had determined that Rachel became free by virtue of her residence in free territory, it automatically followed that any child born during or after that residency would also be free.

Courtney soon brought William back to Prairie du Chien, where both of them made their homes for many years to come. Courtney probably got help from Maria Fasnacht in settling there initially. Then, in less than two years, Courtney followed Maria's lead by marrying a local Canadian-born white man, Benjamin Boudre. The official entry of that wedding ceremony in the records of a Wisconsin justice of the peace on July 4, 1838, removes all doubt that Courtney was living as a free woman.[4]

By the time his mother married, as he told Isaac Heard in 1862, Godfrey was living in Wabasha, in southern Minnesota, where Bailly had established a new trading post along the Mississippi River. At that location Bailly presided over a fur-trading enterprise called the Lake Pepin Outfit, from which he traded with members of the nearby Dakota bands who were led by a succession of chiefs named Wabasha and by Chief Wakute. From his experience with Courtney's lawsuit, Bailly knew that Missouri judges would have ruled that Godfrey too was entitled to court-ordered emancipation. But Bailly also must have been aware that Indian agent Taliaferro and the officers posted at Fort Snelling continued to bring and hold slaves there even after the decision in Rachel's case and that Henry Sibley, Bailly's successor in the fur trade, also used an enslaved servant.

In May 1836, one month before the decision in Rachel's case, the First Infantry's Col. William Davenport replaced Major Bliss as the commandant at Fort Snelling. Davenport brought along his two long-term slaves, Julius and Nancy, and kept them at the post until his regiment was transferred from the North in mid-1837. Lower-ranking First Infantry officers also named slaves on their pay claims after Rachel's case was decided.[5]

More important for the history of American slavery, Dr. John Emerson brought his slave, Dred Scott, to Fort Snelling during the same month that Colonel Davenport assumed command of the post in 1836. As a surgeon, Emerson was assigned to a post rather than a regiment. Thus the doctor and his slave remained at Fort Snelling when, in mid-1837, the Fifth Regiment moved in to replace the First.

The incidence of slavery at Fort Snelling dropped off dramatically in 1837. But that was because the First Regiment was transferred south to serve in Florida's Seminole War, not because the army had decided to adhere to the terms of the Missouri Compromise or to react to the Missouri decision in Rachel's case. The Fifth Infantry returned from its Great Lakes postings to garrison both Forts Crawford and Snelling starting in May 1837. As had been their practice in the 1820s, officers of the Fifth kept few slaves. But Capt. Martin Scott, who commanded Fort Snelling briefly after the Fifth Infantry's takeover, did not hesitate to join Emerson in notifying the army on his pay claims that he was still using the services of his slave, Jack.[6]

On pay claims Emerson submitted in 1836–37 and again in

1839–40, the doctor regularly declared a servant whom he called "Etheldred, Slave" or "Dred, Slave."[7] By keeping Dred Scott at Fort Snelling for almost four years after the decision in Rachel's case, Emerson thumbed his nose both at the federal law prohibiting slavery in the region and at the Missouri high court's enforcement of that law. More important, the army as an institution was fully aware of and complicit in these illegal acts and routinely approved the use of federal funds to subsidize them.

If the army, the Indian agent, and the leading fur traders all were willing to flout the law and court decision prohibiting slavery in Minnesota, it is hardly surprising that Bailly would feel comfortable in keeping Godfrey in Northern bondage in Wabasha. Moreover, Bailly, upon moving to southern Minnesota, had settled in a place that he claimed was beyond the reach of the law. Under the terms of an 1830 treaty (the provisions of which were said to have been orchestrated by Bailly), a large tract of land on the western bank of the Mississippi River had been set aside for Dakota "half-breeds." This ill-defined reserve extended the entire length of Lake Pepin (not a lake but a widening of the river) and southward, encompassing today's city of Wabasha and beyond.[8]

Since the Lake Pepin tract had been ceded by the Dakotas to their mixed-blood kin under terms as yet undefined, it fell outside the jurisdiction of the Indian agent and other authorities; at the same time, it was not open for white settlement. Ensconced in his home and store there, Bailly had found the ideal place from which to conduct not only a legitimate fur business but also a liquor trade that would have been harassed by authorities elsewhere. Bailly held such a preeminent position on the reserve that he was sometimes referred to as "the Emperor." Both its isolation and its unique legal status also made Wabasha a perfect place to keep a slave, despite the fact that Bailly had been identified in the decision in Rachel's case.[9] The Missouri courts were powerless against him, and the local authorities were themselves violating the same laws.

In the Lake Pepin environs, Godfrey would have been surrounded by Mdewakanton Dakotas, with the band of the famed Chief Wabasha to the south and Chief Wakute's Red Wing village to the north.[10] Since Bailly sent his children away to be educated at boarding schools, Godfrey's main peer interactions (to the extent permitted by his masters) would probably have been with Dakota children.[11] After living in Mendota, in a house where English, French, and Dakota were spoken, Godfrey now became more closely linked to the culture and language of the Dakota people. The friendships and associations he made during his Lake Pepin years help explain why, much later, he was living with Dakotas who were members of bands led by Wabasha and Wakute.

It is more difficult to document Godfrey's life at the next location he mentioned to Heard: Hastings. A Mississippi River city located about twenty-five miles southeast of the modern Twin Cities, Hastings was not dubbed with Henry Sibley's middle name until the 1850s; peviously, it was known as Oliver's Grove. Confederates of Alexis Bailly, including members of the Faribault family, had used the spot as their dropping point for liquor smuggled to the Indians. Alexander, Oliver, and David Faribault, sons of Jean Baptiste and Bailly's brothers-in-law, all were involved in this illicit trafficking.[12] While there is no account placing Godfrey at Oliver's Grove, it is likely that he lived there for some time; he may even have worked in the clandestine liquor trade.[13] If so, he again would have been immersed in a culture dominated by Indians, since the smugglers' principal dealings were with the Dakotas.

While Godfrey was laboring at remote river-trading outposts, separated from his mother and brother, he probably had very little, if any, contact with other African Americans. He may not have known that his mother and brother had gained their freedom or that a Missouri court had issued a decision that, in effect, implicated his master in unlawful slaveholding. Nor, if word reached him about the presence of blacks at Fort Snelling, would it have offered him any reason to believe that his bondage was unlawful, for they continued to be enslaved.

While Godfrey was at Wabasha, James Thompson parlayed his knowledge of the Dakota language into a ticket to freedom. When his owner, Captain Day, was reassigned downriver to Fort Crawford in 1836, he took Thompson with him. As was common in the practice of slavery, the bondsman's Dakota wife was left behind.[14] As Captain Day undoubtedly knew, Thompson's eight years of residence at Forts Snelling and Crawford gave him, like Courtney, an even stronger claim to court-ordered freedom than Rachel. Day owned an intelligent, highly skilled male slave in the prime of his life, but a cloud of defective title hovered over his ownership rights. Thus when Day learned that Rev. Alfred Brunson was interested in buying Thompson in order to emancipate and employ him as a Dakota interpreter, Day seized upon the opportunity. Without disclosing his defective-title predicament to Brunson, Day extolled Thompson as a man with an "unspotted character," a pious nature, rare interpretive expertise, and jack-of-all-trades skills. Brunson immediately launched an appeal for money to purchase and emancipate Thompson.[15]

Brunson's fervent letters back to the mission headquarters in Cincinnati, appealing for a fund-raising crusade to free Thompson, reflect both his sincere enthusiasm and his naïveté. The Cincinnati publisher of the *Western Christian Advocate* printed Brunson's letters and embraced his cause with a passion. During the winter of 1836–37, the *Advocate*'s plaintive pleas asked for donations from the faithful: "Thompson must be redeemed. . . . Let all whose minds lead them to spread the gospel, send in their mites, and the work will be done. Can you, reader, spare a dollar! Perhaps you can spare 5, 10, or even 20, or even 50 dollars."[16] As money flowed in from parishioners in Ohio, Illinois, and Iowa, the *Advocate* published plaudits to contributors. Donors' letters show that some were motivated by the desire to enhance the Methodists' efforts to bring Christianity to the Indians, while others welcomed the chance to rescue one good man from slavery.

On April 3, 1837, Brunson sent the exultant message that immediately became an *Advocate* headline: "JAMES THOMPSON IS FREE." By May 16 Thompson was back at Fort Snelling, a free man. Less than a week later he and missionary David King inaugurated the Methodists' new mission in Little Crow's village, located on the Mississippi ten miles south of the fort. Thompson's freedom and new position allowed him to reunite with his Dakota wife (who had taken the English name Mary). The couple soon had a daughter, Sarah, and later a son, George.[17]

Thompson thus apparently became the first free African American person to reside within one hundred miles of Fort Snelling. He also possessed the most treasured document a slave could acquire: free papers, signed by a former white owner, offering sufficient and permanent proof that he had lawfully broken the fetters of bondage. Since Minnesotans would know nothing of Thompson had he not fortuitously been freed and returned there to settle, his story raises a question about how many other slaves might have married Indian women but then were transported elsewhere by their masters without their Native wives. Given the scores of slaves known to have resided at Fort Snelling, such connections would seem highly probable, if difficult to prove.[18]

According to all extant Minnesota histories, Dred Scott was the last slave kept at Fort Snelling by any army officer. Nor, with the exception of Henry Sibley's possible holding of a slave, is there any mention of slaves being kept anywhere in Minnesota from 1840 (when Scott departed) until after 1857, when Southern tourists and settlers, emboldened by the recent Supreme Court decision in the Dred Scott case, brought a few slaves to the area.[19] If it was true that there was a seventeen-year hiatus in Minnesota slaveholding, Godfrey's retention in slavery would have made him the only person kept in bondage during this entire period.

But the army's own records show that officers kept bringing slaves to "free" Northern posts until 1845, when the buildup to the Mexican-American War began siphoning off most of them. Lt. Col. Henry Wilson, a Pennsylvanian who commanded both at Fort Snelling in 1844–45 and then at Fort Crawford, brought along his two long-term slaves, Dan and Abe. Several other officers also brought slaves to Fort Crawford in the mid-1840s, freely describing them as such on their pay claims.

The most significant change in local army slavery, as compared with the 1830s, was that officers no longer purchased slaves for the express purpose of importing them to serve at the Northern forts. And, following Taliaferro's resignation as Indian agent and his departure in 1839, no regular slave purveyor stepped into his shoes to hire slaves to officers. It's likely that Rachel's case had a deterrent effect on officers who might have sent away to purchase a slave in St. Louis, as Stockton had done, or might have purchased slaves there while en route to Fort Snelling, as had Commandants Snelling and Bliss. But the army's files show that Godfrey was not the only slave remaining in Minnesota in the 1840s. Again, if word filtered down to him, Godfrey could only have been discomfited by the news that high-ranking officers continued to defy antislavery laws covering the region.

Godfrey told Isaac Heard that Faribault was the last place he had lived, a reference that brings to mind the current town of Faribault, on the Cannon River about forty-five miles south of Minneapolis. A fur-trading post had been established there as early as the 1820s. By the time Godfrey might have lived there, Alexander Faribault, Alexis Bailly's brother-in-law, supervised the large post. (It was for Alexander, not his father, Jean Baptiste, that the town was named.)

But there is no evidence that either Godfrey or the Bailly family ever lived on the Cannon River. So why did Godfrey tell Heard that he had lived in Faribault? This conundrum is resolved by a single source that provides two crucial facts. First, at some point, probably in the 1840s, Godfrey left the Bailly household and was kept as the slave of Oliver Faribault, Bailly's brother-in-law. This move is not surprising, given the close familial, business, and slave-trading ties between Bailly and the Faribaults. If Godfrey's mother was the "negro wench" sold to Jean Baptiste in 1833, the transfer of Godfrey to the Faribaults may have compensated for the loss of Courtney following her freedom suit. Second, in 1844 Oliver Faribault established his own trading post on the Minnesota River at the current site of Shakopee, and Godfrey lived there as Oliver's slave. Oliver's post was referred to as Faribault Springs, or the Faribault post, so that probably was the place to which Godfrey referred when he said he had lived at Faribault.[20]

By moving from the home where whip-wielding Lucy Bailly presided to the household of Oliver Faribault, Godfrey did not necessarily improve his plight. Oliver's later neighbor, missionary Samuel W. Pond, saw Oliver as the family's black sheep, especially in comparison with his father and better-liked brothers, Alexander and David. Pond, and later his son, Samuel Jr., described Oliver as "somewhat autocratic and self-willed," "not so good a man as his father," a man who was "treasuring up wrath against the day of wrath," possessed with "wickedness."[21]

Though Oliver Faribault's trading post was located just twenty miles upriver from Fort Snelling, it was still remote from white communities in the 1840s. Godfrey's life in Mendota, Wabasha, and Hastings would have been punctuated by the steady passage of steamboats and visitors making their way up and down the Mississippi. But before 1851, the Minnesota River was off-limits to any whites not expressly authorized to enter by the Indian agent. During his first years at Faribault Springs, Godfrey would have had few contacts with non-Indian visitors—and virtually none with other black persons.

Oliver built his tamarack-log cabin and then an adjacent warehouse in order to trade with the large Dakota band headed by Chief Shakpaydan (after whom Shakopee is named).[22] Godfrey probably worked on the construction of the buildings, and then he must have lived in the "crowded log house" with Oliver, his family, and other fur-trading assistants.[23] Miraculously, the cabin where Godfrey was last kept in bondage is still in excellent condition and open to public visitors as part of a Minnesota River Heritage Park called The Landing, located in Shakopee. The cabin's curators, however, know nothing about its role in the state's slavery history.[24] At the trading post countless tasks might have been assigned to a slave: supplies and trade goods that Faribault exchanged for furs would have to be toted and warehoused; when furs arrived they would need to be counted, sorted, bundled, and loaded for transport downriver; and sundry nineteenth-century household chores such as water drawing and fire tending would have kept Godfrey very busy.

Six hundred Dakotas lived not far from Oliver's post in tipis and bark huts at Shakpaydan's village. The Indians called the settlement Teentahotonwa, meaning "the village of the prairie," but whites used the prosaic translation Prairieville. Chief Shakpaydan and his band had the reputation of being "turbulent and warlike," among the Dakotas most resistant to white intrusion. The chief had, before Oliver's arrival, refused to permit any missionaries or mission schools in his village.[25] When Godfrey was first brought there in the 1840s, it is likely that he became the only person in the vicinity with no Indian blood. Of necessity, he would have deepened

Fig. 2. Oliver Faribault's trading post, built around 1844, was the last place where Godfrey was kept in slavery. In the 1970s the well-preserved cabin, constructed of tamarack logs, was moved from its original location at Faribault Springs to a nearby historic park, The Landing, 2187 East Highway 101, Shakopee. The cabin is preserved and managed by the Three Rivers Park District, furnished as it might have been in the 1840s. Photo 2012 by Derek J. Dickinson, courtesy of ThreeRiversParks.org.

his knowledge of the Dakota language and customs.

Three years after Oliver Faribault established his post near Shakpaydan's village, the chief had a change of heart and decided to invite missionaries to build a school nearby. Samuel Pond, who with his brother Gideon was the earliest Protestant missionary to the Dakotas in Minnesota, accepted the chief's call. In 1847 Samuel Pond built the first frame house located away from Fort Snelling on the Minnesota River.[26] Situated on the opposite side of Faribault Springs from Oliver's post, Pond, his wife, and their three small children struggled to teach Dakota children under conditions that were, notwithstanding the chief's invitation, often adverse or even hostile. To ward off potential attacks and thwart the incessant pilfering of their livestock and garden, Pond erected a sharp-stick stockade around his home. The sturdy house was built so as to be bulletproof. School lessons were sometimes interrupted and classes cancelled when Dakotas opposed to the white presence forcibly removed pupils from Pond's small school and forbade the children to return.[27]

The Pond family's presence in Prairieville increased the likelihood that other missionaries who were working farther up the Minnesota River would stop by the Faribault post while traveling to and from Fort Snelling. The Riggs, Williamson, Hopkins, and Huggins families all were engaged at Presbyterian mission stations among Dakotas located upstream. Such layovers would have brought them into contact with Godfrey. One such encounter, which took place in the late 1840s, led to the most dramatic transformation of Godfrey's life. Alexander Huggins, an Ohioan who was one of the most militant abolitionists among the Minnesota missionaries, paid a routine visit to the Faribault-Pond compound and had a talk with young Joseph.

Whether Godfrey knew it or not, Huggins was the ideal Minnesotan from whom a slave could have sought counsel. Huggins and Sibley had been two of the four "Ruling Elders" who helped to establish Minnesota's first Presbyterian church at Fort Snelling in 1835, but they differed in their perspectives on slavery.[28] Huggins became so stridently abolitionist that in the early 1850s he left the Dakota Mission because its parent organization, the American Board of Commissioners for Foreign Missions, refused to expel slaveholders from its governing board.[29] Huggins saw slavery in an apocalyptic light. Long before the Civil War, he "predicted terrible disasters as a judgment on our national sins [slavery]." His son, Eli Huggins, later recalling his father's "fiery" views, said he "would have made a choice member of John Brown's band."[30]

At the time he met with Godfrey at Faribault's post, Alexander Huggins may already have been wracked with personal guilt over profiting from slavery, a dark personal obsession that later led to his eight-month commitment to a hospital for the insane. Earlier, Huggins's father had moved to Ohio from North Carolina, where he had owned a family of slaves. Though he wanted to bring his slaves to Ohio and free them there, North Carolina required payment of a substantial bond and the slaves were reluctant to go to a cold northern climate where almost no blacks lived. So Alexander's father sold the slaves to a relative, and his son knew that he was in line to inherit some of the morally tainted proceeds from that transaction.[31]

When he met Godfrey in the late 1840s, Alexander Huggins was living in Traverse des Sioux, located about forty miles upstream from Oliver Faribault's post. Later, Eli Huggins offered his thoughts as to what his father might have said to Godfrey during the fateful encounter: "Father usually made a trip once a year to Kaposia [the Dakota camp in present-day South St. Paul] and relating visit to Pond. While there he saw the mulatto Godfrey . . . who at that time was living at the Faribault trading post. I have no doubt father gave him good advice and some religious instruction. At all events, he gained Godfrey's confidence."[32] Huggins's kindness and expressions of concern apparently prompted Godfrey to see him as a man who might help him break the bonds of slavery, for he almost immediately resolved to run away from his master and to seek Huggins's help.[33]

How runaway slave Godfrey, at the age of about seventeen, made his way from Prairieville forty miles southwest to the Alexander Huggins home at Traverse des Sioux is not known. Most likely he traveled on foot following Indian trails. At some point he would have had to cross the river. Perhaps he did so near Huggins's home, for Traverse was named for and located at a shallow spot in the Minnesota River that had long been used as a fording place by the Dakotas.

When Godfrey appeared on Huggins's doorstep, he told the missionary that "he had been beaten and abused and could stand it no longer."[34] Other than those few words and the inferences that can be drawn from Prescott's recollections of Lucy Bailly's whippings, we know no details of the torments Godfrey suffered as a slave. But his travails must have been severe, for his flight to freedom in the late 1840s was a risky and courageous act. The law then offered few protections to fugitive slaves. Had Godfrey been recaptured by his master, he would have faced the prospect of even worse physical abuse—plus the dreaded possibility of being sold down the river to a Southern plantation. At the Huggins's home, Godfrey left a "powerful" and lasting impression on six-year-old schoolboy Eli Huggins, who never forgot seeing his "first Negro slave." Years later, Huggins recalled the youth's appearance: "Rather darker than the average Sioux, and with wooly hair, but not strongly marked African features."[35]

When Godfrey became an infamous figure in 1862, Alexander Huggins was no longer living, so Eli asked his mother to recount Godfrey's contacts with the Huggins family. In a 1918 letter to historian William W. Folwell, Eli repeated her story. He alerted Folwell to the existence of a letter that Alexander Huggins had written to Oliver Faribault immediately after Huggins welcomed Godfrey into his mission home.[36] That letter, unfortunately, has never been located. But Eli summarized his father's message to Faribault: "He [Alexander Huggins] wrote that he was harboring Godfrey, he did not believe slavery was right, and would not lend himself to any effort to take Godfrey with the view of remanding him to servitude, whether he could legally be regarded as a slave or not, but he thought proper to write and explain the circumstances."[37]

With these words Alexander Huggins threw down the abolitionist's gauntlet. He bravely vowed that he would defy the law, if necessary, and would never return Godfrey to a life of "servitude." Huggins did not accuse Faribault of violating the law by keeping a slave. Instead, the zealous missionary staked out a moral, even heroic, position, declaring that he was willing to harbor Godfrey no matter what his legal status.

While Huggins was waiting for a response from Faribault, he put Godfrey to work digging potatoes. But the frightened slave fled before Faribault's reply arrived. "He [Godfrey] was with us three days and left in the night without saying goodbye," Eli stated. "Father heard soon afterward where he was living with the Indians. Mother thought his flight was because he feared Faribault meant to seize him and sell him."[38] Faribault's reply to Huggins probably arrived after Godfrey had left: "F[aribault] replied saying that if anyone had a legal claim on G[odfrey] it was some army officer. He, F[aribault] had no use for him, it was a good riddance, or to that effect."[39]

If Huggins had received this letter before Godfrey slipped away, he might have tried to reassure him about his status. But even if Godfrey had known about the letter, it hardly afforded him any clear protection. Faribault did not deny that Godfrey was a slave or that he had been treated as one; he merely said that any legal claim of title to him was held by an unidentified army officer.

Faribault's response may have been truthful. It is possible that Garland had retained title to Godfrey when Courtney was sold to Bailly or that he might have been sold later to another officer and then rented or loaned back to Bailly or the Faribaults. But it seems more likely that the army officer story was a ruse to cover up Faribault's illegal involvement in slavery—or to lull Huggins into complacency so that Faribault could retake his property. Either way, Godfrey was in a position of continuing risk. If an army officer had reappeared to assert his title, it is entirely possible that he would have succeeded, with or without the blessing of local authorities. Or if Faribault had recaptured Godfrey and taken him south, he could have sold him either outright or subject to the claims of the supposed absentee owner.[40]

Slaves were uniquely vulnerable in the days before Minnesota achieved territorial status in 1849, for the rudimentary law enforcement system afforded them virtually no protection. If evidence of a serious crime arose, John H. Fonda, a coroner and constable whose offices were in Prairie du Chien, was sometimes summoned to investigate. Thus, when the body of a female slave was discovered near the Pig's Eye Slough not far below Fort Snelling sometime between 1845 and 1849, the constable's services were called upon. Fonda recognized the victim, whose corpse showed that she had been "cruelly cut and bruised," as a woman "belonging to a certain [army] Captain." But when the officer claimed he did not recognize her, the inquest failed to point a finger of blame, and the official file was closed.

In his written reminiscences, Fonda used this story as an example of how "evil-disposed persons . . . perpetrated deeds of violence with perfect impunity" in those early days. After the case had been closed, he wrote, "Soon after it came to light that the woman was whipped to death, and thrown into the river during the night; but no investigation was made and the affair blew over." Constable Fonda failed to explain why he made no effort to reopen this homicide case based on the new evidence.[41]

Fonda's account offers graphic evidence that the risks Godfrey and other local slaves faced were not limited to beatings or to the prospect of being sold South. Had Godfrey, after his flight to freedom, been recaptured and then killed in vengeance by his masters, there is little chance that any legal sanction would have been imposed for the crime.[42]

Godfrey was not freed by the act of running away. Unlike James

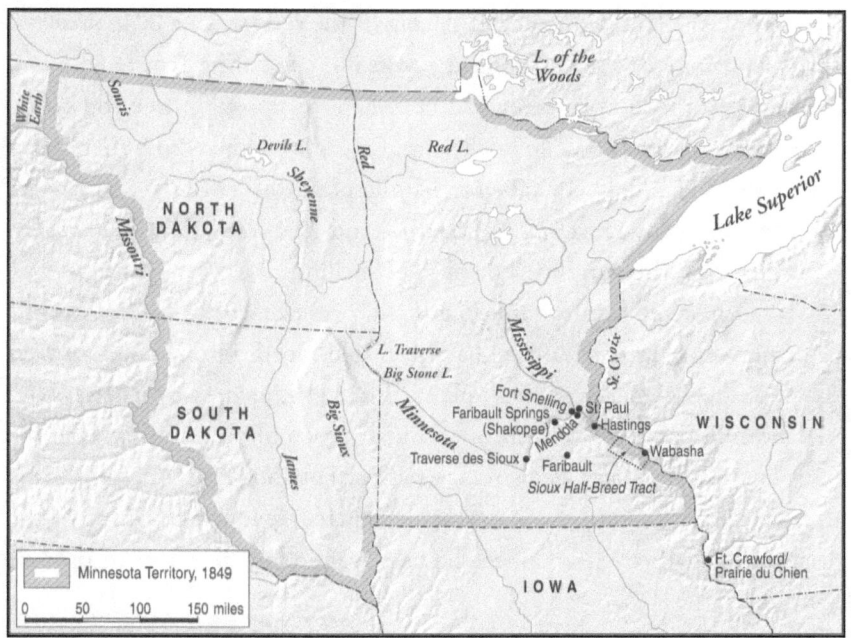

Map 1. Minnesota Territory, 1849. Courtesy of the Pond Dakota Heritage Society.

Thompson, he lacked the all-critical emancipation papers that would have protected him from being taken back into slavery. That he was never again held as a slave does not erase the real jeopardy he faced, especially after the passage of the Fugitive Slave Act in 1850. That law provided an expedited legal procedure by which a slave owner could extradite an escaped slave without a jury trial. Godfrey's unnamed owner (if he existed) could have appeared at any time with proof of his ownership, or the Baillys or Faribaults could have brought a claim either on their own behalf or for an alleged absentee owner, and the legal apparatus set up by the Fugitive Slave Act would have required that Godfrey be surrendered into bondage.

While Godfrey was laboring at Oliver Faribault's trading post, Dred Scott and his wife, Harriet, belatedly commenced the most important freedom suit ever brought by American slaves. Following the same path taken by Rachel and Courtney, they sought the services of a St. Louis lawyer in 1846 and filed their claims in a Missouri court. The Scotts also based their case on the fact that they had been kept in slavery in free regions by an army officer. Harriet, like Rachel and Courtney, recounted in her sworn petition how she had been taken to Minnesota by her owner—in Harriet's case, Indian agent Lawrence Taliaferro—and had been sold there to Dr. John Emerson, the army surgeon at Fort Snelling.[43]

Three key features linked this trio of freedom suits. First, Rachel, Courtney, and Harriet Scott all had been sold North into Minnesota slavery. Second, each enslaved adult plaintiff had been owned by masters who were born in free states or territories. Finally, each of the adult slaves in the three lawsuits had been kept in servitude at Fort Snelling.[44] A full decade after Rachel and Courtney had procured their freedom, the courts of the slave state of Missouri remained the best avenue for the Scotts to procure their liberty.

Dred and Harriet Scott soon would pay the price for delaying their lawsuit, for during the decade that separated the successful cases brought by Rachel and Courtney from the commencement of the Scotts' case, the highest court in Missouri had undergone a profound shift that favored pro-slavery interests in the state. Newly added judges on that court were more than willing to overturn years of freedom litigation precedents, including the decision in Rachel's case. Unsuccessful in their pleas to those Missouri judges, the Scotts' lawyers were forced to file their case in federal court, where the protracted litigation was finally decided by the U.S. Supreme Court in 1857.[45]

Three years after the Scotts began their freedom case, in 1849, Minnesota became a territory. In 1858, the year after the U.S. Supreme Court finally ruled against the Scotts, Minnesota became the thirty-second state to enter the Union. In the intervening years the region was transformed from a place where Indians were preeminent, both numerically and geographically, to an area populated by burgeoning hordes of white settlers who soon vastly outnumbered the Dakotas and Ojibwes.[46]

Godfrey's whereabouts and activities during the years 1848 to 1853 are as hard to reconstruct as his time in slavery. Where did he go after he ran away from Huggins's house? We can only guess from his later associations that he must have fled to the area he knew best—the Mdewakanton Dakota villages along the Mississippi River where Chief Wabasha and Chief Wakute lived with their bands. To avoid capture, Godfrey surely would have shied away from Bailly's trading post in Wabasha and Oliver Faribault's Prairieville post, and he would have stayed clear of Shakpaydan's band. But those limitations left large sectors of southeastern and central Minnesota where Indians outnumbered whites by a wide margin, where a runaway slave could integrate quietly into the Dakota world.

In other regions of America escaped slaves commonly sought sanctuary among their Native American neighbors. In Florida, for example, significant numbers of fugitive slaves lived among and intermarried with the Seminoles. Their presence added a major complication when American troops tried to remove the tribe from its homelands by force, for the slaves feared they would be killed or returned to vengeful former masters. Fugitive bondsmen, understandably, put up fierce resistance to the invading U.S. troops.[47]

But the picture was different in Minnesota. Harsh winters almost eliminated the thought of any fugitive slave living off the land for a lengthy period of time, as was possible farther south. Moreover, most Minnesota slaves were kept by army officers and had little contact with Native people. Dred Scott and his wife, for example, were both said to have disliked Indians, so they and other slaves who shared their views would have been unlikely to seek refuge among the Dakotas.[48]

Nor did the Underground Railroad offer a means of escape for Godfrey, as it apparently did not get on track in the region until after he was living with the Dakotas. William Taylor, a black St. Paul barber in the 1850s, was the informal leader of a small group of citizens who assisted slaves who had managed to make their way to the North or whose masters had brought them into the region.[49] But significantly, Huggins had not plotted to spirit Godfrey away to freedom in Canada via a series of safe houses. Godfrey too may have felt safer living with the Indians than if he had taken his chances on fleeing to another state or to Canada. Many other slaves saw Northern white communities as beacons of freedom, but Godfrey's life story hardly would have led him to share that perspective. As far as we know, Godfrey was the only Minnesota slave to seek refuge among the Dakota people. He was also the only bondsman born in Minnesota to secure his freedom by running away from his masters but remaining in the area.

Godfrey, who was about seventeen when he ran away from slavery, would have been eligible to join the Dakotas' arduous hunting expeditions. Also, since boys of sixteen qualified to join older warriors, he could have accompanied his male friends on war parties against the Ojibwes.[50] After fleeing Oliver Faribault, it seems Godfrey rejoined his childhood friends from Wabasha's or Wakute's bands. His acceptance might have been eased because he appeared at a time when they were undergoing their own coming-of-age transitions and could welcome him into their young warriors' circle. For the next five years, until the Dakotas were moved in 1853 from their eastern Minnesota homelands to a new reservation along the Minnesota River, Godfrey probably spoke the Dakota language almost exclusively, though he may sometimes have been called upon to translate for his Dakota kin.

To appreciate the risk and rarity of Godfrey's flight to freedom and his continuing residence in Minnesota as a former local slave, one need only look carefully at the 1850 census for Minnesota Territory. The year after Minnesota gained territorial status from Congress in 1849, it took part in its first official U.S. decennial census. The 1850 census-takers were asked to indicate the race of residents: "white," "black," or "mulatto." Full-blood Indians were not counted in the tally.[51] Census-takers recorded thirty-nine persons as "B" (black), "M" (mulatto), or "colored" in Minnesota Territory.

At first glance that total appears to represent a sizeable increase over the estimated fifteen to twenty enslaved blacks who lived in Minnesota at the peak of local slavery between 1828 and 1837. But the white population of about five hundred in 1835 had mushroomed to about six thousand by 1850, drastically reducing the ratio of blacks to whites.[52] There were twenty-five to thirty-five whites for each black Minnesotan in the 1830s; by midcentury the ratio had risen to almost two hundred to one.[53]

In 1850 a substantial majority of black Minnesotans (thirty of thirty-nine) lived in the city of St. Paul. But even that number made up barely 1 percent of the population of Ramsey County—a huge drop in the proportion of blacks in the part of Minnesota where the black population was concentrated. Outside of Ramsey County there were five hundred white residents for every black person, confirming that anyone of Godfrey's race would have been a rare sight except in St. Paul.

Because slavery in Minnesota has usually been depicted as temporary and aberrant, and because the practice was not openly discussed once the political climate changed during the Civil War, little thought has been given to the ultimate fates of the people once enslaved in the state.[54] As difficult as it is to document slavery in the area, it is even harder to reconstruct the later lives of Minnesota slaves. Did they, like Godfrey, remain in Minnesota? The 1850 census offers a clear answer to this question: most of the slaves who lived in Minnesota between 1820 and 1845 no longer resided there in 1850. Nor, as far as we can tell, did their offspring.[55] There appears to be almost no overlap between the list of known slaves who had been held at or near Fort Snelling and the black residents, all ostensibly free, named in the 1850 census. By one means or another most slaves had left the region, and a completely different group of blacks had replaced them. James Thompson was the only black resident listed in the 1850 Minnesota census who was definitely brought to Minnesota as a slave.

The most obvious explanation for this turnover in the black population lies in the itinerant nature of military and frontier government service. Most of Minnesota's slaves were brought there as the possessions of army officers and the Indian agent. When these officials left Fort Snelling for other postings, or when they retired from public service, they took their property—including slaves like Rachel and Dred and Harriet Scott—with them.[56] Courtney's case was atypical. When she was sold to Bailly, a private and long-term citizen of Minnesota, she and her son were effectively removed from this cycle.

The 1850 census for Minnesota Territory lists no slaves, but there is reason to question the methodology used in that count. In Southern states census-takers were instructed to make a tabulation of all free people and all slaves, but in Northern regions, where slavery was unlawful or presumed not to exist, all residents were assumed to be free. In circumstances exactly analogous to those in Minnesota, the 1850 census-takers in Oregon Territory were asked to enumerate the people living at the army's Columbia Barracks (later known as Fort Vancouver). In the family of Capt. Llewellyn Jones they listed a forty-nine-year-old black woman named Monimia Travers, reciting that she was born in Virginia. As was standard practice in Northern states and territories, the printed census form used in Oregon (the same one used in Minnesota) indicated at the top of each page that it listed "Free Inhabitants." Thus Travers was recorded in the 1850 census as a free person. But, within army circles, Captain Jones made no secret of the fact that Travers was a slave. He described her as such on pay claims submitted in both Missouri and Oregon. And in 1851 Jones signed a document indicating that he was freeing "Mommia Travers" from slavery.[57] These circumstances clearly suggest that Jones had not concealed his slave's true legal status from the census-taker. Travers was not enumerated as a slave because the 1850 census procedures assumed there were no slaves to count in a part of America where slavery was presumed not to exist.

Given this clear example in Oregon, is it possible that one or more of the thirty-nine "free" blacks listed in the 1850 census for Minnesota Territory were, in fact, slaves? There are at least two names, it appears, that justify asking that question. One person listed as a "free inhabitant" of "Fort Snelling and Vicinity" in Minnesota's 1850 census was a thirty-year-old "colored" man, born in the slave state of Kentucky, whose name was recorded on the census only as Charles. The same summer as that census was taken Maj. Samuel Woods, while posted at Fort Snelling, listed a "Yellow" (mulatto) servant named Charles (no surname) on his pay claim, though with no indication that he was a slave. Later in 1850, however, Woods, when drawing his pay in St. Louis, described Charles as a "Yellow Slave." Thus at least one slave was apparently listed in Minnesota's 1850 census as a free person.[58]

Away from Fort Snelling, in the southern region of Minnesota where Godfrey was then presumably living, a far more intriguing name appears in the 1850 census. At that time a massive entity called Wabashaw County included the southern quarter of modern Minnesota, stretching westward from the Mississippi River far into present-day South Dakota.[59] Of the hundreds of residents living in that county in 1850, the only black person listed (recorded as "mulatto") was "Godfroy Courtney," age twenty-four, laborer, born in Minnesota Territory. And the official census-taker who wrote down that name was none other than Alexis Bailly, Godfrey's former master.

Bailly indicated that "Godfroy Courtney" was living in the household of Samuel Pond, the missionary who lived next door to Bailly's brother-in-law, Oliver Faribault, but Bailly's misnaming of all of Pond's children and his wife suggests that he did not actually visit their house. Bailly, who likely knew that Godfrey had sought refuge with a missionary, may have presumed Godfrey had fled to Samuel Pond's family. Or his entry of "Godfroy Courtney" may have been Bailly's way of making sure that Godfrey got counted someplace, for there is ample evidence that Bailly and other census-takers in Minnesota were so anxious to boost the tally that they double-counted entire families to enhance the territory's standing.[60]

At the time of the 1850 census the Dakota people still retained most of their ancestral homelands in Minnesota Territory and whites were still prohibited from settling in vast areas to which the Indians still held title. But that was about to change.

NOTES ON CHAPTER 2

1. *Courtney v. Rayburn*, 1836, St. Louis Freedom Suits.
2. Ibid.; and *Scott v. Emerson*, 1846, St. Louis Freedom Suits.
3. *Rachael v. Walker*, 4 Mo. 350 (1836). Technically, the appeals court merely decided that Rachel should get a new trial. But no second trial was necessary and none was held, since the Missouri Supreme Court's decision made the outcome a foregone conclusion. Similarly, no trial of Courtney's case was necessary after the decision in Rachel's appeal.
4. "Crawford County, Wisconsin, Marriages," 41.
5. Colonel Davenport did not identify Julius and Nancy as slaves while he was posted at Fort Snelling. But he declared them slaves on pay claims filed both before and after that tour of duty. Lower-ranking First Infantry officers who named slaves at Fort Snelling between June 1836 and May 1837 include Capt. Thomas P. Gwynne ("Lucy, Slave") and 2nd Lt. William H. Price ("Etheldred, Slave" and "Wilson, Slave"). See Pay Vouchers, boxes 391, 431, 436, 443, 472, 494, and 634.
6. Captain Scott served as commandant at Fort Snelling from July 16 to August 20, 1837. He drew servant pay for those weeks by declaring "Jack, Black Slave" as his servant. Pay Vouchers, box 473.
7. For Emerson's pay claims at Fort Snelling naming Dred Scott, see Pay Vouchers, boxes 430, 460, 471, 472, 493, 525, and 539. Dr. Emerson was away from Fort Snelling for part of the 1836–40 period, serving at Fort Jesup, Louisiana. For part of that time, Dred Scott was hired out to other officers at Fort Snelling.
8. Folwell, *History of Minnesota*, 1:159, 270–74, 482–86, quoting William Quinn: "Alexis Bailly was at the bottom of it [the half-breed grant of 1830]" (1:484n40).
9. Goodman and Goodman, *Joseph R. Brown*, 239–41; and H. Sibley, *Unfinished Autobiography*, 34. For Bailly's residence in Prairie du Chien and Wabasha, see Belliveau, "Life of Alexis Bailly," 9–12.
10. Goodman and Goodman, *Joseph R. Brown*, 98n33.
11. Bailly's children attended boarding schools in Kentucky and Illinois. Belliveau, "Life of Alexis Bailly," 9.
12. For an excellent discussion of one confrontation between the Indian agent and Bailly's liquor-smuggling cohorts, see Goodman and Goodman, *Joseph R. Brown*, 118–19.
13. There is evidence that neither Bailly nor the Faribaults gave up their liquor trafficking in the 1830s. Bailly was implicated in the liquor trade in the mid-1840s, and David Faribault was said to be smuggling liquor to the Dakotas as late as the early 1850s. It is unlikely that the full extent of such dealings, which would have been kept quiet, will ever be known. See Goodman and Goodman, *Joseph R. Brown*, 239–42; and Samuel W. Pond to Gideon Pond, January 5, 1951, Pond Family Papers, MHS, box 6 (Indians drunk after David Faribault furnished liquor to Shakopee's band in Prairieville).
14. Alfred Brunson to Rev. B. F. Hoyt, March 28, 1859, NMM, MHS, box 19 (Thompson's wife was left behind "[a]s was usual in such cases.").
15. The letters of Alfred Brunson and related articles about James Thompson are in the *Western Christian Advocate*, December 2, 1836 ("unspotted character"), and February 17, March 3, 10, April 21, 28, July 27, 28, and September 15, 1837.
16. Editor's note, *Western Christian Advocate*, February 17, 1837.

17. Thompson scrip affidavit, #68, Scrip Rolls. George was born in about 1842. See also 1850 census, Scott County, MN.
18. One indication of the possible existence of a child resulting from a slave-Dakota liaison comes from the 1862 Dakota Trial Records. The defendant in trial 260 was called Washechoonsapa, which is the Dakota term for *Negro*. A later prisoner list, compiled in 1866, gives the same man's age as thirty-six. He thus would have been born in about 1830, when James Thompson and other male slaves resided at Fort Snelling.
19. See Lehman, *Slavery in the Upper Mississippi Valley*, 114–41.
20. Eli Huggins to William Folwell, August 9, November 12, 1918, Folwell Papers, MHS, Box 47. I gratefully acknowledge Carrie Zeman for drawing this source to my attention.
21. Pond, *Two Volunteer Missionaries*, 187; interview of Samuel Pond Jr., June 23, 1915, Folwell Papers, MHS, box 114, vol. 88; S. W. Pond to Gideon Pond, October 16, 1850, Pond Family Papers, MHS, box 3.
22. There was more than one hereditary Dakota chief named Shakopee. The chief in power in the mid-1840s was Shakopee II, also called Standing Cloud. Diedrich, *Famous Dakota Chiefs*, 118.
23. For descriptions of Oliver Faribault's post, see Pond, *Two Volunteer Missionaries*, 180–90. For Godfrey's presence at the post, see Eli Huggins to William Folwell, August 9, November 12, 1918, Folwell Papers, MHS, box 47.
24. The fur-trading cabin was moved a short distance, from its original site next to Faribault Springs to The Landing. When I visited the cabin in 2011 no one connected with the historic park was aware that Oliver Faribault had once kept a slave there or that Godfrey had commenced his run to freedom from that cabin.
25. Pond, *Two Volunteer Missionaries*, 180–90.
26. Ibid., 185.
27. Ibid., 180–93.
28. Minutes, June 11, 1835, First Presbyterian Church (St. Peter's) records, MHS. Sibley left the church sometime in the late 1830s, and when Sibley joined the Episcopal Church in the 1840s, Williamson wrote to welcome the "returning wanderer," suggesting that he now had left behind "worldly amusements" and "temptations" to return to Christianity. Williamson to Sibley, January 18, 1845, Sibley Papers, MHS, M164, roll 3. The reasons for Sibley's parting with the Presbyterian Church are not clear, but the letters from Williamson suggest that Sibley may have bristled at the lectures he received on his conduct as an Indian trader, for example, for doing business on the Sabbath. See letters from Williamson to Sibley, 1835–57, Sibley Papers, MHS, M164, roll 1. Though no letters survive that discuss the points, the Presbyterians probably strongly disapproved of Sibley's fathering one or more children with Dakota women out of wedlock, the baptism of his Dakota daughter, Helen, into the Catholic Church, and possibly his employment of a slave as a household servant.
29. Willand, *Lac Qui Parle*, 221–22.
30. Eli Huggins to Folwell, November 12, 1918, Folwell Papers, MHS, box 47.
31. Ibid. The Huggins family secret concerning Alexander's "mental aberration" and treatment in an Ohio insane asylum was revealed in a letter by his son, Eli, to historian William Watts Folwell. Eli was concerned that Folwell might pick up the story from others and wanted Folwell to know the true story, though he emphasized that this sensitive information was "for your eye only."
32. Eli Huggins to Folwell, August 9, 1918, Folwell Papers, MHS, box 47.

33. Another source confirming that Godfrey "ran away" to join the Dakotas is found in two letters: S. B. Egbert to Theodore Carter, February 3, 1910, and Carter to Egbert, January 28, 1910, Carter Papers, MHS, box 2. Though Egbert does not say that Godfrey was a slave, his claim that Godfrey and a "wench" had been brought to Minnesota from New Orleans (though wrong) leaves little doubt that he had heard that Godfrey was a slave. Oliver Faribault's death is sometimes reported as having occurred in 1850 and sometimes in 1851, but it is authoritatively fixed in October 1850 by the detailed letter of S. W. Pond to Gideon Pond, October 16, 1850, Pond Family Papers, MHS, box 3.
34. Eli Huggins to Folwell, November 12, 1918, Folwell Papers, MHS, box 47.
35. Eli Huggins to Folwell, August 9, 1918, Folwell Papers, MHS, box 47.
36. Another of Eli Huggins's letters to Folwell makes it clear that it was Oliver Faribault to whom he was referring, though the August 9, 1918, letter refers only to "Faribault" at Shakopee. See Eli Huggins to Folwell, December 9, 1918, Folwell Papers, MHS, box 47.
37. Eli Huggins to Folwell, August 9, 1918, Folwell Papers, MHS, box 47.
38. Ibid.
39. Ibid.
40. I considered but rejected three alternate claims as to how Godfrey came to live with the Dakotas, all of which omit the key fact of his enslavement. (1) A sensationalist in *True West* magazine asserted that Godfrey was raised by Lucy Bailly (misidentified as "Mrs. Alexander Bailey") because he was "unwanted by his parents." Because he was "in trouble as a boy, Godfrey soon became an outcast . . . [and] renounced all whites as well as Negroes and went to live with the Indians. . . . [He] turned his back on the two races that made up his ancestry to go and live with still another race." This version of Godfrey's story, like much in the article, was apparently invented by the author. Shannon, "Black Judas," 22–23, 36. (2) Godfrey's father-in-law by his third wife claimed, in the early 1900s, "Joseph Godfrey [was] a full-blooded nigger, who grew up with this tribe. . . . This nigger's family all died and he was given to the chief of the Santee Tribe, and he grew up with the tribe." Deposition of William Goodteacher, George Blackowl Estate, NA, RG 75, BIA, LR, CCF 1907–39, E121, file 34941-1915 (350) (hereafter, George Blackowl Estate.). (3) Another Dakota source, who later earned his living as a snake oil salesman, billing himself "Dr. George Quinn," claimed that he had been acquainted with Godfrey since he was "a little boy" and that his sister had "raised and educated him." But Quinn acquired a reputation for his unreliable versions of history, so no weight can be placed on his story. McIntyre to Carter, February 14, 1910, citing the statements of Quinn, copy in Woolworth Papers, MHS. (The original appears to be missing from the Carter Papers at MHS).
41. Fonda, "Reminiscences of Wisconsin," 277. Because Fonda included the fact that the unnamed captain responsible for this murder was posted at Fort Crawford at the time of his investigation, it is often presumed that this killing took place in Wisconsin. But his reference to the Pig's Eye Slough, not far downriver from Fort Snelling, suggests that the brutal whipping took place near there and that the culprit dumped his slave's body into the river. Officers often shuttled back and forth between Forts Snelling and Crawford, for both posts were garrisoned by the same regiments.
42. Another record suggests a similar unpunished crime in Iowa Territory. When a black man named Nat (probably a slave) was whipped to death in 1840, a Galena, Illinois, newspaper reported matter-of-factly, "Died in Dubuque [Iowa], Nat, a negro, whipped to death on September 6th." "Vital Statistics from Galena Newspapers," 1828–1850, September 11, 1840, http://jodaviess.ilgenweb.net/vitals/VS1a.htm, accessed March 22, 2012.

43. VanderVelde, relying on the Civil War–era assertions of slavemaster Taliaferro, contends that Harriet Scott was set free rather than sold to Dr. Emerson. VanderVelde, *Mrs. Dred Scott*, 115–18, 274. VanderVelde's argument, however, is contrary to the sworn claims of Harriet herself and to those of Adeline Russell, another witness in the Scotts' case. The text reflects my conclusion that Harriet was sold to Dr. Emerson in Minnesota.
44. Rachel's owner, 1st Lt. Thomas B. W. Stockton, was born in and commissioned to the army from New York. Courtney was owned by Alexis Bailly, who was born in Canada and was a long-term resident of preterritorial Minnesota. Harriet Scott was owned, for most of the period she was kept in free territory, by Dr. John Emerson, who was born in and commissioned to the army from Pennsylvania. See Heitman, *Historical Register*, 405, 927.
45. The lengthy process by which the Dred Scott case wove its way through the Missouri and federal courts from 1846 to 1857 is chronicled in detail in Fehrenbacher, *Dred Scott Case*, 250–304.
46. The convulsions experienced by Minnesota's Native peoples during this period are covered with thoroughness, sensitivity, and clarity in Wingerd and Delegard, *North Country*.
47. To induce Seminoles to surrender, U.S. army officers sometimes offered the fugitive slaves in their midst protection from their former masters. See Bauer, *Zachary Taylor*, 86.
48. See VanderVelde and Subramanian, "Mrs. Dred Scott," 1078–83; and Holcombe and Bingham, *Compendium of History*, 45–46 ("Dred Scott and his wife . . . did not like the Indians").
49. For an account of Taylor's role in the local Underground Railroad, see Swanson, "Joseph Farr Remembers."
50. Laviolette, *Dakota Sioux in Canada*, 47, 59.
51. Though Indians were generally not included in the 1850 census, one notable exception was the wife of James Thompson, who was listed in Ramsey County under her English name, Mary Thompson. She was full-blood Mdewakanton Dakota. James Thompson affidavit, #68, Scrip Rolls. Other Native women who were married to or living with white men were also sometimes counted in the census. See the Washington County census, which designated Indian wives with the initial *S* (apparently denoting either *Sioux* or *squaw*). For county-by-county tabulations from the 1850 census for Minnesota, see De Bow, *Statistical View*, 332.
52. The census forms gave no guidance for the treatment of persons of mixed Indian and white blood, and individual marshals treated Indian "half-breeds" very differently in the 1850 census. Some counties, such as Itasca and Washington, made a careful record of residents who were nonwhite mixed-bloods, usually with the designation "1/2 B" for "half-breed." On the other hand, Dakota County, which had a significant number of mixed-blood residents, counted them all as "white." In practice, marshals designated race only for those who were not white.
53. One difficulty in making comparisons between the 1830 and the 1850 census arises from the variable treatment of persons with mixed white and Native backgrounds. The 1830s lists invariably include large numbers of "half-breeds," who were viewed as white if they maintained a "civilized" lifestyle.
54. One noteworthy exception to this depiction of slavery in Minnesota is VanderVelde, *Mrs. Dred Scott*.

55. Only four of the thirty-nine black residents listed in the 1850 census were born in Minnesota, three of whom can be identified with ease. Two were the children of James Thompson (who were never enslaved because their mother was a Dakota woman and they were born after their father was emancipated), and the third was George Bonga, the free Ojibwe-black son of a well-known black man, Pierre Bonga, who lived in northern Minnesota. The fourth person, "Godfroy Courtney," is more mysterious.
56. In several instances the army's pay records indicate the paths taken by former Minnesota slaves as their officer-owners were transferred to new posts. For example, Zachary Taylor's pay vouchers show that Jane (one of the slaves who spent a year at Fort Snelling while Courtney was there, followed by several more years at Fort Crawford) was taken to Florida when her master was dispatched to fight the Seminoles in the late 1830s. Later, while Taylor was ascending to national hero status as a U.S. commander in the Mexican-American War, Jane attended him south of the border. She remained in bondage to Taylor as he was running for president in 1848, and she was almost certainly one of the slaves Taylor took with him to the White House when he was sworn into office in 1849. While Jane's personal travelogue followed an extraordinary path, the fact that she was involuntarily rotated from post to post as the army transferred her owner was typical of the fate of most former Fort Snelling slaves. Taylor often described Jane as a slave on his pay vouchers. He named her as one of his servants in Kentucky (1826), Louisiana (1827–28), Fort Snelling (1828–29), Fort Crawford (1829–32), Florida (1838–40), Arkansas (1842), Mexico (1846), and Louisiana (1848–49). See Pay Vouchers, boxes 223, 250, 259, 269, 288, 315, 316, 478, 494, 504, 534, 763, 922, and 1064.
57. Llewellyn Jones, from 1849 to 1851, identified "Mommia," "Memmia," or "Monimina" as a slave in both Missouri and Oregon. See Pay Vouchers, boxes 1138 and 1201. For her emancipation, see Shine, "Slave Freed at Fort Vancouver." Travers is not an isolated example; I have documented other examples of slaves being listed in the 1850 census as free persons in Northern free states by contrasting the information on army pay claims with census data. These findings call into question the regular practice of relying on census data as proof of the supposed nonexistence of slavery in free regions. As the Oregon case of Monimia Travers shows, the listing of "Godfroy Courtney" in the 1850 census does not indicate that Bailly believed that Godfrey was a "free inhabitant" of Minnesota Territory.
58. In the census Charles is listed in the household of a clerk, Benjamin H. Randal. The absence of a surname for an adult black man is one possible indicator that he was enslaved. Also, knowing that Major Woods was using a black servant named Charles at that time, it is significant that there is no entry under Woods's name in the census for Charles or for any other servant. This omission, when coupled with Woods's subsequent pay claim in St. Louis naming Charles as his slave, may indicate that the census-taker recorded Charles under the name of an army clerk rather than as the servant of his master, Major Woods. For Woods's pay claims, see Pay Vouchers, boxes 1167 and 1170.
59. Minnesota Territory in 1850 was significantly larger than the present boundaries of the state of Minnesota. Wabashaw County's western boundary was the Missouri River, including a large portion of what today is South Dakota. The eastern border of Wabashaw County was the Mississippi River, and the northern border began about twenty miles south of the present city of Minneapolis. The county extended southward from there to Iowa.

60. The families of Oliver Faribault and Samuel Pond were both double-counted in the 1850 census, once in Dakotah County by census-taker Henry Tilden and a second time in Wabashaw County by Alexis Bailly. Tilden accurately recorded the full names and ages of Pond, his wife, and the couple's three children, but he made no mention of any black person in the household. Bailly, in contrast, inserted apparently invented first names for Mrs. Pond and the children; he also got the ages of everyone in the Pond family wrong. Bailly also erroneously noted that Samuel Pond had been born in Ohio (Tilden correctly recorded Connecticut). Significantly, the name "Godfroy Courtney" was inserted at the end of the long list of erroneous identifications recorded by Bailly. This suggests that Bailly did not visit the Pond household at the time of the census and simply approximated information. If "Godfroy Courtney" had in fact been living with the Ponds in 1850, it seems that the name would appear on Tilden's report.

CHAPTER 3

Fugitive Slave, New Reservation

A few years after Godfrey joined the Indians, the Dakotas entered into the treaties of 1851 by which they ceded thirty-five million acres of land to the U.S. government. These pacts were the product of a classic combination of carrot, stick, and trickery. Sibley, the entire Faribault family (though not Oliver, who had died the year before), and Alexis Bailly all were involved on the white side of the treaty negotiations.[1]

As was customary, territorial governor Alexander Ramsey headed the commission that negotiated the treaties. Bailly was his "commissary," in charge of the massive outpouring of gifts, food, liquor, and other forms of inducements and hospitality that would put the Dakota chiefs in the best possible mood to give up their lands.[2] Sibley, the Faribaults, and Bailly all had large sums of money at stake in the outcome of the negotiations, provided they could evade the federal law against direct payment of trading debts with treaty funds. In the end, Sibley and the other traders managed to receive substantial payment for alleged Dakota debts by getting the chiefs to sign side deals—so-called traders' papers. Some Dakotas later asserted that they did not understand the effect of these separately signed documents.[3]

The 1851 treaties required the Dakotas to move to a reservation that extended for ten miles on either side of the upper Minnesota River, starting about seven miles west of the current town of New Ulm and extending westward to a point about twenty miles beyond Minnesota's western boundary. This beautiful area had long been part of the Dakota people's territory, but it was only a remnant of their sweeping ancestral homelands and did not include their traditional hunting grounds.

If local slavery had died out before Minnesota became a territory in 1849, as most existing histories suggest, Godfrey's status as a fugitive slave might be only an asterisked exception to the received story in which the days of Dred Scott had long passed. Assuming that all other African Americans in the territory were free and that Minnesota was steadily advancing toward entering the Union as a free state, any notion that Godfrey might actually be in a position of risk as a fugitive slave would seem farfetched. But the army was called on to beef up its presence in Minnesota for the 1851 Dakota treaty negotiations; a stronger peacekeeping force was required. Experienced officers from the Sixth Infantry Regiment were sent to fill that new need, and they brought their slaves along.

The lull in openly declared slave-keeping at Fort Snelling that had prevailed (no officer described his servant as a slave there from 1845 through 1850) was not due to any change in army policy or to any social, demographic, or political changes occurring within Minnesota. Rather, it was a reflection of the fact that the army's resources had been moved, first to Mexico, and then to Texas, California, Washington, Oregon, and the new southwestern territories acquired after the Mexican-American War.

The army brass in Washington must have known they would be reestablishing a slavery foothold in Minnesota when they dispatched Lt. Col. Francis Lee and Capt. Thomas L. Alexander to Fort Snelling in 1851, for both officers had been reporting for many years that their servants were held in bondage. Lee was a Pennsylvanian, but as a young lieutenant he had married a Louisiana woman, the sister of Henry Hopkins Sibley (a distant cousin of Minnesota's Henry Hastings Sibley who went to West Point and became a general for the Confederacy during the Civil War). After the death of his father-in-law, Lee, in 1826, purchased the Sibley family slave, Jenny, to save her from being auctioned off to strangers.[4] For the next twenty years, as he rose in rank, Lee repeatedly declared "Jenny, Slave" on his pay claims. When his rank permitted him to draw extra pay for two servants, he added "Joe, Slave." Starting in June 1851 Lee named Jenny and Joe as his enslaved servants as he commanded at Fort Snelling, and he continued to do so for the full three-and-a-half years he was posted in Minnesota. Once again, the highest-ranking federal officer in Minnesota was a slaveholder.[5]

Capt. Thomas Alexander, a West Pointer who had been born in Virginia and commissioned to the army from Kentucky, kept a man named Wesley as his long-term servant. Alexander, like Lee, had no compunctions about describing his servant as a slave; he had done so frequently since 1838, and he continued to list "Wesley, Slave" on his pay claims until 1861. While the captain was stationed in Minnesota Territory between 1851 and 1853, he referred to his slave on ten pay vouchers.[6]

Godfrey would have relocated with the Dakotas when, in about 1853, the Mississippi River bands settled on the eastern edge of the new Lower Reservation—about twelve miles west of what was soon to become the pioneer German settlement of New Ulm. Chiefs Wabasha and Wakute pitched their tipis on the southern side of the Minnesota River, about ten miles from Minnesota's newest military base, Fort Ridgely.

After the signing of the treaties of 1851, Sibley, then serving as Minnesota Territory's representative in Congress, had urged the establishment of an army post in the vicinity of the new reservations. The small contingent of officers who traveled through snow in November 1852 to select its prairie site was led by Lieutenant Colonel Lee, the slaveholding commandant at Fort Snelling. Construction of the post's sprawling buildings commenced in 1853. As one early state history bluntly put it, the fort was located inside a military reserve on the new reservation because it was deemed "necessary to preserve order among the savages."[7]

When Fort Ridgely's officer quarters were ready for occupancy, Commandant Lee himself, still attended by Jenny and Joe, moved from his Fort Snelling headquarters to take command at the post in June 1854. Later that year he named two other slaves, Hetty and Lucy, on pay claims he submitted at Fort Ridgely. By the end of 1854, when Lee concluded his tour of duty as the highest-ranking army official in Minnesota, he had signed thirteen separate pay claims identifying his servants as slaves. Another slaveholding officer, 1st Lt. Lewis Armistead, reported for duty a few months after Fort Ridgely was occupied, promptly identifying his servant as "Sarah Ann, Slave."[8]

At this point slavery had been unlawful in western Minnesota under the terms of the Missouri Compromise for thirty-four years. Yet during these decades officers of the U.S. Army frequently and flagrantly violated the antislavery law. There is no direct evidence that Godfrey knew about the army slaves so close to his new reservation home. But it seems likely that he, as perhaps the only other black person living in proximity to Fort Ridgely, would have become aware of them. Given Godfrey's unresolved legal status, the news that federal officers were openly keeping slaves nearby would have been unsettling. His own enslaved mother had been brought to Minnesota by an army officer, and Godfrey probably viewed Fort Ridgely as an unsafe place for a black man who lacked free papers.

About two years after moving to the reservation, Godfrey took a long journey. Isaac Heard quoted him as saying, in 1862, that, "I last saw my father and mother at Prairie du Chien seven years ago." Godfrey traveled from the reservation to this river town in Wisconsin in about 1855—a trip of more than three hundred miles that would have involved passage down the Minnesota and Mississippi Rivers. It seems likely he financed his passage by working, perhaps as a roustabout on a boat.[9] We don't know if Godfrey had received any reports from or about his mother since Bailly had cruelly separated them in 1836, though this 1855 trip suggests that their reunion was not coincidental. The fact that Godfrey journeyed to Wisconsin suggests that by the mid-1850s he felt reasonably comfortable that he would not be shanghaied back into slavery—as long as he stayed away from slave states. Perhaps his concerns were allayed by the fact that his last master, Oliver Faribault, had then been dead for five years and no one had sought to claim him in the interim.

On arriving in Prairie du Chien, Godfrey must have marveled at the story of his mother's path to freedom and at the relatively prosperous life she had established in a predominantly white community. Courtney, who took the surname Boudre during her first marriage, had given birth to three children during that union, Godfrey's half siblings: Margaret (born 1840), Benjamin (1843), and Catherine (1845). Godfrey's brother, William, whom Bailly had sold with Courtney in St. Louis in 1835, had also taken his stepfather's surname. The Boudres ran a bakery in Prairie du Chien. In 1846 Boudre enlisted in a company of the Wisconsin militia that manned Fort Crawford while the soldiers from the regular army were off invading Mexico. In October of that year Courtney was widowed when Boudre, just forty-two years old, died.[10]

Courtney probably continued operating the family bakery after her husband's death, but her life as a former slave with four children could not have been easy. She apparently got some help from her old friend Maria Fasnacht, who by that time had married a second white husband, a farmer named Era Putnam who lived nearby. The Putnams agreed to take in William Boudre as a farmhand; the fifteen-year-old appears in their household in the 1850 census with the notation that he was engaged in farming.[11]

In about 1852 Courtney married another local baker, German immigrant Charles Weidimer. Two years before Godfrey's 1855 visit she gave birth to another son, Jonas. The remarkable parallels between the lives of Courtney Weidimer (as she was known for the rest of her life) and Maria Putnam were now complete. The two women who had met while they were in servitude to officers at Fort Snelling had each procured freedom, settled in the same small Wisconsin town, and married two successive white husbands.

After almost twenty years of separation, Godfrey's mother must have been fascinated and moved on hearing the saga of his enslavement by the Baillys and at Oliver Faribault's fur-trading outpost, his escape to freedom, and the new life he had made for himself as a fugitive living among the Dakotas. Godfrey, too, must have been impressed by the fact that all of his siblings had been raised in freedom. We can only speculate about the details of this mother-son reunion, but one fact hints at its poignant impact: Courtney Weidimer's last child, born during the year of Godfrey's visit, was named Joseph, the same name as her firstborn, long-lost son.[12] In retrospect, we might wonder why Godfrey did not remain in Prairie du Chien, where his mother and Maria Putnam had integrated into the dominant culture despite their history as slaves. Wisconsin had been admitted to the Union as a free state in 1848, while a return to territorial Minnesota would expose him to a greater range of legal risks as a former slave without free papers.

But perhaps romance lured Godfrey back to Minnesota, for not long after his return, he married a Dakota woman named Takanheca, which is roughly translated as "Sinewy."[13] She was the daughter of Wahpaduta, a member of Wakute's band (also known as the Red Wing band).[14] We do not know if Godfrey followed the Dakota custom of paying a bride price to Takanheca's family or if he eloped with her. The couple married by Indian custom rather than in a church.[15] That Godfrey married Takanheca does not necessarily mean he had joined Wakute's band at the time of his flight to freedom; Dakota men usually married women from outside their village, and Godfrey may have followed this custom.[16] When he was single he might have identified with the nearby Wabasha's band (Sheriff Roos, in his August 1862 emergency dispatch, linked him to Wabasha). But after his marriage Godfrey lived with his wife's family in Wakute's village, a few miles east of the Lower Sioux Agency. Godfrey and Takanheca soon became parents. Their son, born in 1857 and later known as Joseph Godfrey Jr., would have been called Chaska, the traditional Dakota childhood name for a firstborn male.[17]

While Godfrey had become thoroughly integrated into the tribe, neither *Joseph* nor *Godfrey* was easy for Dakotas to pronounce, so it appears they shortened his name. He was called "Gusse," pronounced, and sometimes spelled, "Gussay" (sometimes spelled Gusse, Gusa, Kasa, Kosi, and Kusa). Whites, upon hearing this name, sometimes referred to him as Gus or Augustus, anglicizing the Dakota pronunciation.[18]

Recorded sightings of Godfrey living among the Dakotas before 1862 come from the late-in-life reminiscences of a white settler, S. B. Egbert. In 1910, conceding that it was "a long time for one to remember things correctly," Egbert wrote about seeing Godfrey in the 1850s.[19] At that time Egbert was enrolled in school in Glencoe, a small town situated about sixty miles due west of St. Paul and about forty miles northeast of Godfrey's home on the reservation.

Egbert saw Godfrey during some of the last traditional Dakota winter hunts held in Minnesota. No mere sportsmen's outings, these were major, multi-week expeditions in which almost every Dakota man, woman, and child took part. Tipis were pitched in hunting grounds located many miles from summer homes, and the entire encampment moved as fortunes dictated. Deer were the primary quarry, but any edible animals were fair game; raccoons were particular favorites.[20] From time immemorial, winter hunts had been a cornerstone of the Dakotas' annual hunter-gatherer cycle. A successful hunt brought celebration and feasting; a poor hunt led to hardship and even starvation. As Egbert's letter confirms, the Dakotas kept up their winter hunting traditions in the 1850s, ranging far from the boundaries of their new reservation. But it must have been a wrenching experience for them to witness the influx of white settlers, who, every year, occupied more and more of their customary territory and destroyed hunting habitats with permanent settlements and agriculture.

Though Godfrey and his Dakota band primarily camped about nine miles northeast of Glencoe, Egbert wrote, they also stayed less than a mile southwest of the town, along Buffalo Creek, for about a week while en route back to the reservation. Indians were often seen in this area, but the rare sight of a black man "prompted us scholars to investigate after school was dismissed." Egbert and his classmates saw Godfrey "several times [and] . . . we learned to know 'Joe'—he would talk Sioux." Egbert was uncertain about dates, but one of his statements—"I saw him a winter later and learned that he had a squaw wife then"—may place Egbert's contacts with Godfrey in the mid-1850s.[21]

Just as Godfrey's birth into and life in slavery, until very recently, has been overlooked by historians, the myth that the institution of slavery was absent from Minnesota during the lead-up to statehood has been a fixture of the North Star State's history. But the crack that Godfrey's story opens in these foundational presumptions widens to a veritable chasm with the realization that slavery persisted in Minnesota throughout the 1850s.

Godfrey was probably oblivious to the passage of the Kansas-Nebraska Act of 1854, which repealed the Missouri Compromise's prohibition of slavery that had applied to Fort Snelling since 1820 and to Fort Ridgely from its inception. That enactment helped awaken antislavery sentiments in Minnesota and helped trigger the creation of the Republican Party in the territory. But Godfrey would have noticed no change in his reservation neighborhood: officers kept slaves at Fort Ridgely before the 1854 law became effective and continued to do so afterward.²²

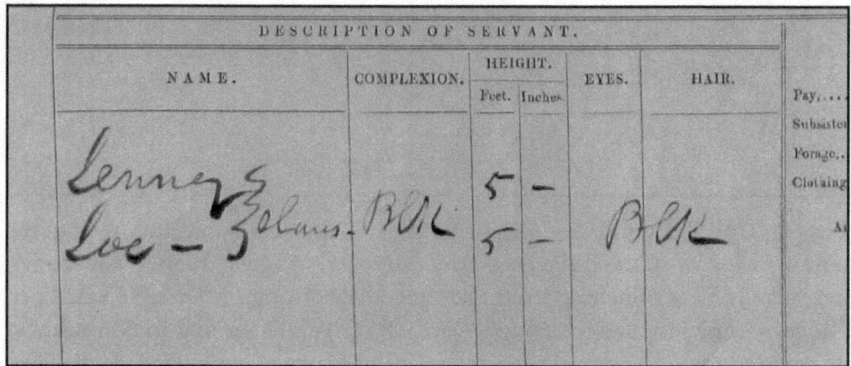

Fig. 3. Pay claim for Col. Francis Lee, June-July 1854, indicating that his servants, Jenny and Joe, were slaves. Lee commanded Fort Snelling from June 1851 through June 1854, where he repeatedly identified Jenny and Joe as slaves on his pay vouchers. Lee took Jenny and Joe with him when he assumed command of Fort Ridgely in July, 1854. In December 1854 Lee's pay voucher named two different slaves, Hetty and Lucy, as his servants at Fort Ridgely. Pay Vouchers, National Archives Record Group 217, Entry 516, Settled Accounts, Army Paymaster.

Commandant Lee and his regiment were transferred away from Minnesota in early 1855, but their departure (with their slaves) did not signal the end of local army slavery. That year Secretary of War Jefferson Davis supervised the creation of the new Tenth Infantry Regiment, which, after a brief training period, was sent to garrison the forts in Minnesota and Wisconsin. Lt. Col. Edmund B. Alexander, a Virginian and long-term slave master, was appointed to lead the Tenth Infantry. The new regiment's arrival at Fort Snelling in 1855 ushered in a stunning revival of army-sanctioned slavery in Minnesota. From 1855 until 1858 five officers reported to the army that they were keeping no fewer than nine slaves there. Not since Godfrey's mother and James Thompson had procured their freedom in the 1830s had so many army slave masters kept their human chattel in Minnesota.²³

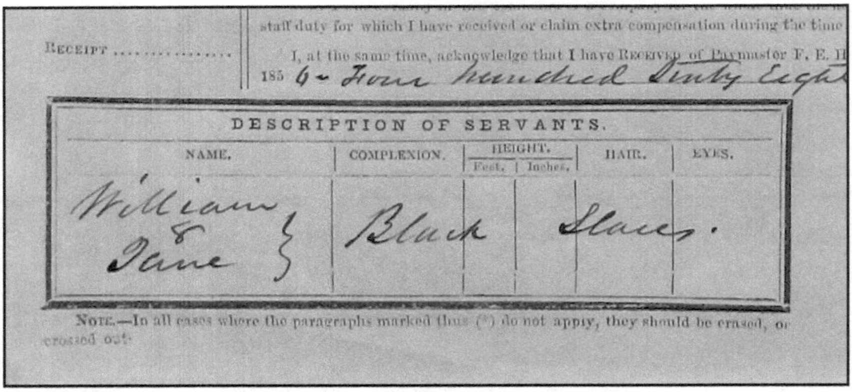

staff duty for which I have received or claim extra compensation during the time

Receipt ....

I, at the same time, acknowledge that I have Received of Paymaster F. E. H

185 6 – Four hundred Sixty Eight

DESCRIPTION OF SERVANTS.

NAME.	COMPLEXION.	HEIGHT. Feet.	HEIGHT. Inches.	HAIR.	EYES.
William & Jane	Black		Slaves.		

Note.—In all cases where the paragraphs marked thus (*) do not apply, they should be erased, or crossed out.

Fig. 4. Col. Edmund B. Alexander's pay voucher, submitted while he commanded at Fort Ridgely during July and August 1856. Alexander commanded Fort Snelling from October 1855 through June 1856 and Fort Ridgely from July 1856 through April 1857. While serving in Minnesota, Alexander named enslaved servants on all of his pay vouchers. At both Fort Ridgely and Fort Snelling, Besides William and Jane, Alexander also named a third slave, Margaret. The Fort Ridgley Military Reserve was part of the Lower Reservation until 1858. In total, four different officers kept at least nine people in bondage on the Lower Reservation during the years Godfrey lived there as a fugitive slave. Pay Vouchers, National Archives Record Group 217, Entry 516, Settled Accounts, Army Paymaster.

This dramatic upsurge in Minnesota slavery was not reported by the local press and is not mentioned in any state history, but it is a virtual certainty that James Thompson and other prominent black residents would have known about it. Army officers were powerful figures in frontier America, and the knowledge that such august representatives of the federal government had brought numerous slaves to Fort Snelling must have sent shudders through the growing black community in St. Paul.

One way or another, the African American grapevine probably communicated this alarming slavery revival news to Godfrey. Because James Thompson's wife was eligible to receive Dakota annuity payments, he probably traveled to the reservation each summer for that purpose. Either Thompson or another black resident could have brought Godfrey the news of the renewed presence of slaveholders at Fort Snelling.

Even if word of the developments at Fort Snelling did not reach Godfrey, however, he almost surely was informed—and worried—when Lieutenant Colonel Alexander, accompanied by three of his slaves, assumed command of Fort Ridgely in June 1856. For the next twelve months, both Alexander and one of his key officers, Capt. Barnard Bee, regularly notified the army that they were keeping servants in bondage at the army post nearest to Godfrey.[24] While whites saw Fort Ridgely as a protective outpost, Godfrey and other black Minnesotans would have shared a much more wary attitude toward federal officers who were importing slavery back into their midst.

The same year Godfrey's first child was born, in 1857, the U.S. Supreme Court's decision in the Dred Scott case threw all racial and slavery issues into turmoil, especially in the North. The court declared that Scott, because he was black, was a noncitizen who lacked the right to bring a claim in federal court. In words that are inscribed in the annals of Supreme Court infamy, Chief Justice Roger B. Taney opined that, throughout the "civilized and enlightened portions of the world" at the time of the drafting of the Constitution, blacks were "so far inferior, that they had no rights which the white man was bound to respect." The decision also struck down, as unconstitutional, the Missouri Compromise law that had, prior to passage of the Kansas-Nebraska Act, guaranteed that slavery in the Northern territories would be "forever prohibited."[25]

The proslavery judges on the court in the Dred Scott case reached out to strike down a law that already had been nullified by Congress, apparently because the judges wished to bring an end to the country's political controversies about slavery in the territories. But the effect was precisely the opposite, as the decision exacerbated rather than calmed the rifts between pro- and antislavery advocates. The *St. Paul Daily Times*, in common with many other Northern newspapers, decried the decision as one expounded by five slaveholding judges (joined by two Democratic colleagues). While the holding of the case was limited to territories, the sweeping language used in the decision, the *Daily Times* noted, threatened the right of Northern states to outlaw slavery within their borders.[26]

During the year the Dred Scott case was decided, Minnesotans were anticipating their admission to the Union as a free state the following year. Although some participants in the 1857 state constitutional convention, including its president, Henry Sibley, had winked at the wholesale disregard of antislavery laws in the 1830s, they enshrined the territory's longstanding (if often previously violated) prohibition of slavery in Minnesota's new constitution: "There shall be neither slavery nor involuntary servitude in the State."[27] The constitution did, however, limit voting rights to "white citizens." An effort to strike the word "white" was defeated by a two-thirds majority of the delegates.[28] By the late 1850s Godfrey's fears of recapture may have eased, but he could not cast a ballot in the place of his birth.

Like many politicians who set their sails to the changed winds of public opinion, Sibley went beyond mere silence in discussing the history of slavery in Minnesota. Sometime, probably in the 1850s, he wrote a detailed history of the varying legal entities that had evolved to form the state. Wrapping himself in the cloak of Northern antislavery sentiment, Sibley exulted in the fact that slavery had always been prohibited in the area. That longstanding law was, he effused, "an exhibition of magnanimity and devotion to the public weal, without parallel in our history."[29] Sibley probably sincerely believed, in the years before the Civil War, that Minnesota was fortunate to have inherited a legal framework that outlawed slavery. But such words—coming from a man who probably employed a slave himself, whose close associates in the fur trade were slave owners, and who knew about slave-keeping by army officers and other prominent early residents—smack more of hypocrisy than a change of political heart.[30] To the many African Americans who had been held in bondage in Minnesota, including Godfrey, legal pledges such as those Sibley extolled had been utterly empty promises.

The last army slaveholder departed just as Minnesota became a state, though it would be a mistake to attribute that fact to the army's respect for local antislavery laws. The Tenth Infantry left the region because it was needed in Utah, where, it was feared, a war would be fought with restive Mormons. Had there been a similar military crisis in Minnesota the slaveholding officers would have remained in place, even after the state's constitution had outlawed slavery.

But, as evidenced by the groundbreaking scholarship of Christopher P. Lehman, and as the *Daily Times* predicted, some Southerners were emboldened by the Dred Scott decision to bring their enslaved servants to the new state of Minnesota. In St. Cloud a few settlers, including Democratic activist Sylvanus Lowry, kept slaves to work as household servants. No legal action was taken against him or a handful of other resident slaveholders, just as no legal proceedings of any nature had been brought in Minnesota against the army officers who practiced slavery at Forts Snelling and Ridgely.[31]

The continuous presence of slaveholders within Minnesota throughout the 1850s would have reminded all black residents that they faced unique and dire risks. Throughout the decade stories abounded of false claims of servitude leading to the deportation of free blacks, and the presence of slave catchers in Northern states sent waves of apprehension through every black community. As late as 1860 Governor Ramsey offered a $250 reward for the apprehension of a man who kidnapped an "alleged fugitive slave" in Minnesota "without any legal forms or any warrant."[32]

As Godfrey looked over his shoulder for possible slave-nappers, the army career of the man responsible for bringing Godfrey's enslaved mother to Minnesota was thriving. John Garland had risen to the rank of brigadier general in 1847. By the 1850s he was commanding the vast Department of New Mexico, which included the American southwestern frontier that stretched from Texas to the California border. After he sold Courtney to Alexis Bailly, General Garland had named a long list of other slaves on his pay claims, a pattern suggesting that he may have transported other people in bondage from his home state of Virginia to places where he was posted and sold them, too, at a profit. Being identified in Courtney's Missouri lawsuit as an illegal slaveholder and as the officer who had sold her unlawfully to a private citizen in Minnesota had not tarnished Garland's reputation in the army's eyes, nor had those facts discouraged the army from using federal funds to subsidize his profitable slaveholding.[33]

As evidenced by the voting laws, the antislavery posture taken in Minnesota's Constitution did not equate with full acceptance of African Americans. Fearing they would be inundated with freed slaves, many Northern states that had abolished slavery passed laws restricting or prohibiting black immigration.[34] In Minnesota a "Black Law" that would have required a $300 to $500 bond from any black person who wished to move to the territory was defeated in the House by a ten to six vote.[35] Outside of St. Paul the antiblack attitude was more extreme. The *Mankato Weekly Record* exulted in 1859 that there was not a black person in town and probably not one in the whole of Blue Earth County, a fact that prompted the editor to remark that the region was "peculiarly blessed in this respect."[36] Similarly racist remarks appeared with regularity in the Minnesota press.

As the Dakota people were pressured to become more like whites, they too began to learn the rudiments of racial discrimination. When they first encountered blacks in Minnesota, Dakotas had reacted with curiosity, amusement, and apparently, acceptance. After all, a chief's daughter had married James Thompson while he was enslaved.[37] But over the span of Godfrey's life in Minnesota, Dakota toleration eroded as they absorbed the racist ideas of the whites with whom they had increasing contact. The Dakotas coined a neutral word for *Negro* (Wasicunsapa) and a pejorative equivalent of *nigger* (Hasapa).[38] By the time the Civil War erupted the Sioux Indian agent opined that the Dakotas had "an instinctive hatred of a negro"—a claim that surely reflected attitudes picked up from white bigots.[39] Racism by the 1860s was not nearly as virulent among the Dakotas as it was in the white community, but it did exist and probably affected Godfrey on a regular basis.

The percentage of black residents in Minnesota continued to decline during the 1850s as the overall population ballooned from about 6,000 in 1850 to 172,000 in 1860, almost a thirtyfold increase. Blacks increased in absolute terms in the same decade, from 39 to 259 (less than a sevenfold increase), while their proportion of the total population shrank to an all-time low. By 1860 white residents outnumbered blacks in the state by more than six hundred to one.

By the late 1850s Godfrey's family was living with, or close to, his father-in-law, Wahpaduta. In 1858 some Dakota chiefs signed another treaty, ceding all of their reservation lands north of the Minnesota River. At the same time Indian agent Joseph R. Brown, following policies of the Office of Indian Affairs, greatly accelerated longstanding efforts to coerce Dakotas to give up their seminomadic lives as hunter-gatherers.

Dakota men were not asked merely to take up farming as an occupation. To receive the many rewards the agent offered those willing to settle down and raise crops, they were also required to renounce some of their most deeply established customs. One superintendent of Indian affairs described what he demanded: "Those who are desirous of becoming agriculturists [should] make *public avowal* of their abandonment of their Indian habits of life. . . . [They must dress in] useful garments civilized man has adopted, . . . yielding up their trappings, plumes, and decorations. . . . [They must] yield all their alliances with the superstitions of their nation, submit themselves to be shorn of their long cherished 'scalp-lock' . . . and to be stripped of the blanket, the garment emblematic of their indolent life." Dakotas who acceded to this humiliating and culture-destroying routine were asked to do so in a formal ceremony conducted not in a government office but "in the presence of the tribe."[40]

Wahpaduta and Chief Wakute must have submitted to these "civilizing" measures, since by 1859 both were listed as members of the farmers' bands. Wahpaduta was one of the earliest to accept an agricultural life, for his name appears as one of only thirteen (out of ninety-two) households in Wakute's band on the farmers' lists.[41] The Indian agency leaders had no illusions about the hostile reaction the new farmers would provoke within the greater Dakota community: "Those . . . who are willing to become pioneers . . . must bear the scoffs and taunts of their former companions."[42] To sweeten this bitter pot, the agency offered the Dakotas numerous inducements to make a public renunciation of cultural traditions. Houses were constructed for the farmer Indians: frame houses for chiefs and principal leaders and log houses for others. Wahpaduta probably received a log house. Government-paid farmers then broke ground on two to five acres of land near the houses, enabling the farming novices to plant crops readily. Even cash annuities were boosted, with double payments going in 1859 only to those heads of households who, like Wahpaduta, accepted farming life.[43]

The lists of distributions to the farmers' bands show the other valuable items Wahpaduta received in 1859: one pair of oxen and an ox bow; clothing (one coat, one pair of pants, two pairs of stockings, and two shirts); and basic foodstuffs (one barrel of flour, one-fifth barrel of pork, and thirteen pounds of sugar). Since one of the government's goals was to downgrade the influence of hereditary chiefs, Wakute got only a little more: one-eighth barrel of salt, twenty pounds of soap, and a chest of tea.[44]

The reverse side of this system of reward was punishment. When Dakota war parties traveled north to attack their traditional enemies, the Ojibwes, they subsisted largely off the land. By the late 1850s small farms dotted the route, offering opportunities for the warriors to pilfer pigs or cattle. The Indian agents received many claims and complaints relating to such "depredations," and Agent Brown sometimes raised the money to pay settlers back for their losses by withholding annuity payments from every warrior who went with the group, whether they took part in the stealing or not. Thus, during the June 1860 annuity distribution, Brown noted the names of more than 130 men whose regular twenty-dollar payment was withheld because they had gone on a war party that committed depredations. Many of these men appear to have been prominent warriors in the 1862 war.[45]

During this same period the soldiers' lodge, the Dakota quasi-military society that traditionally decided when to go to war and set the ironclad rules that governed any conflict, began to serve as the forum for the most militant warriors to discuss their grievances against whites. Stripping such men of their much-needed annuities fanned the flames of discontent and alienated the very group most likely to precipitate a war against whites.[46]

Godfrey, as a non-Dakota, did not receive annuities or other benefits. But his wife and son were both eligible for payments, which were most likely disbursed via Godfrey's father-in-law. Wahpaduta received 1859 annuities for one adult man (himself), two adult women (his wife and, likely, Takanheca), and one child (probably Takanheca and Godfrey's son).[47] Just three years earlier, before Godfrey had married Takanheca and before the birth of their child, Wahpaduta had drawn annuities only for one man (again, himself), one woman (presumably his wife), and one child (presumably Takanheca).⁴⁸ At some point Godfrey and Takanheca had a second child, a daughter. She was given the customary Dakota birth name Hapan (second child, if female). She was most likely born in 1862; it is possible that Takanheca was pregnant at the time of the 1862 hostilities.⁴⁹

One last pre–Dakota War sighting of Godfrey was documented by Eli Huggins in 1861, more than a decade after the runaway slave sought refuge with the Huggins family in Traverse des Sioux. In 1861 Huggins was a volunteer soldier stationed at Fort Ridgely, not far from the Lower Sioux Agency. At the agency he saw a "mulatto whom I took to be Godfrey." Huggins's only comment was that Godfrey "was not wearing a blanket." As might be expected from his father-in-law's adoption of agriculture, Godfrey had apparently accepted white patterns of dress, similar to those of the Dakota farmers who lived in the vicinity of the agency.⁵⁰

A state legal case heard not long before the start of the Civil War offers the only known example of an attempt to use Minnesota courts to protect the rights of slaves. When a wealthy Mississippi planter named Colonel Christmas vacationed in Minnesota in the summer of 1860, he brought along his household slave, Eliza Winston. The colonel stayed at a cottage on the shores of Lake Harriet. A small group of local abolitionists secured a writ of habeas corpus and brought the question of Eliza's status before an antislavery judge. Relying on the Minnesota Constitution's prohibition of slavery, Judge Charles E. Vanderburgh issued an order freeing Eliza. Before any appeal could be brought, however, abolitionists spirited her, via the Underground Railroad, out of Minnesota to Canada. This extralegal action strongly suggests that local abolitionists still lacked confidence that slaves brought to Minnesota could be freed by the state's judiciary.⁵¹

While by the late 1850s most Minnesotans probably would have opposed any attempt to return Godfrey to slavery, the most distinguished lawyers of the era might have debated his legal status at the time of the Winston case and even beyond. Theoretically, if Godfrey's long-absent putative owner had reappeared with proof of title, he could have clamped

Godfrey into irons and sent him downriver at any time until the Civil War (or, if he was from a Northern slaveholding state, even later). An abolitionist judge like Vanderburgh would have made short shrift of any such claim. But a Democratic judge with copperhead sentiments could have reached the opposite conclusion. In some respects Godfrey was even more vulnerable than Eliza, who had been brought to Minnesota in violation of the new state's constitution. By contrast, Godfrey's enslavement in Minnesota had occurred under the territorial laws that the Supreme Court had retroactively nullified in the Dred Scott case. An owner could argue, therefore, that Godfrey's bondage had been lawful and that he was a fugitive who could be removed by court order to a slave state.[52]

As the fateful month of August 1862 arrived, Godfrey and Takanheca were living peacefully with their five-year-old son not far from Godfrey's father-in-law. The family had sown a crop of hay, and Godfrey was busy harvesting in mid-August.

On August 18 Godfrey would spring onto history's stage.[53]

NOTES ON CHAPTER 3

1. For an extensive discussion of the plans and negotiations that led to the signing of the 1851 treaties and the notorious traders' papers, see Folwell, *History of Minnesota*, 1:266–304, and his appendix dealing with the subsequent investigation of Ramsey, 1:462–70.
2. Folwell, *History of Minnesota*, 1:279.
3. See Kane, "Sioux Treaties and the Traders."
4. For a detailed account of Lee's purchase of Jenny, see Thompson, *Confederate General of the West*, 14–15.
5. For numerous pay claims naming Jenny as Lee's servant (often describing her as a slave), see Pay Vouchers, boxes 288–1356.
6. Starting in 1838 and continuing through the rest of his career, Alexander declared enslaved servants on his pay claims more frequently than almost any other officer in the army. He first listed Wesley as his slave while serving as the commandant at Iowa's Fort Atkinson in 1848–49 (Iowa had entered the Union as a free state in 1846) and repeatedly named him thereafter. See Pay Vouchers, boxes 473–1720 (Alexander vouchers) and 923, 941, and 1033 (vouchers at Fort Atkinson).
7. Hubbard et al., *Minnesota in Three Centuries*, 2:327.
8. See Pay Vouchers, boxes 1222, 1238, 1277, 1295, 1308, 1310, 1315, 1330, 1337, 1356, and 1394.
9. Another possible explanation for Godfrey's appearance in Prairie du Chien in about 1855, is the movement of a large contingent of officers and soldiers from Fort Snelling sent to Fort Crawford from Fort Snelling in 1855. Godfrey might have worked as a teamster or laborer on that expedition. See Mahan, *Old Fort Crawford*, 267–68.
10. James Hansen, Wisconsin Historical Society, e-mail message to author, October 13, 2008; Wisconsin vital statistics in *Minnesota Genealogical Journal* 1 (May 1984); 1850 and 1860 census for Prairie du Chien.
11. The 1850 census shows, in the household of Era and Mariah Putnam, "William Boudrie," mulatto, age fifteen, occupation "farming," born in Minnesota.
12. Since it is unclear when Godfrey began using the first name Joseph, it is also theoretically possible that Godfrey took the first name of his mother's last child following his visit to Prairie du Chien.
13. I am grateful to Louis Garcia for this translation.
14. The pre-1851 treaty annuity rolls recorded Chief "Wahcoota" as the leader at "Red Wing's Village." Wahpaduta can be placed in Wakute's band by reference to the Office of Indian Affairs annuity rolls for the St. Peter's Agency, though his name was spelled in varying ways: Wahpaduta (1851); Wahpadoota (1852–53), Wapaheduta (1856), and Worpeduta (1859 annuity roll and 1859 farmers' roll). See annuity rolls, MHS, M405, roll 1. Because Wahpaduta's name does not appear on some of the annuity rolls, it is possible that he, like many Dakotas, used alternate names.

15. Godfrey's son later speculated that the marriage was by Indian custom, and all other available sources support that conclusion. Takanheca was later called Louise Godfrey, but apparently not until she lived at the Santee Reservation. Deposition of Joseph Godfrey Jr., October 21, 1912, RG 75, CCF, entry 121, file 110773-1913(312) (hereafter, Godfrey heirship file. For a discussion of Dakota marriage customs, including the so-called bride price, see Pond, *Dakota or Sioux in Minnesota*, 137–40.
16. Marriage within a village was "rare." Meyer, "Red Wing Indian Village," 30.
17. Joseph Godfrey Jr.'s age is recorded in many Santee Reservation census lists; he also gave it under oath in a 1912 deposition in the Godfrey heirship file.
18. For various iterations of Godfrey's name, see Carter to Egbert, February 8, 1910, Carter Papers, MHS (Gusse, pronounced Gussay, and not commonly referred to as Joe or Joseph); *Morton Enterprise, July 23, 1909* ("Gusa Godfrey"); Sweeny letter, March 27, 1886, *St. Paul Dispatch*, March 28, 1886 (Gusse); Henry Two Bear Papers, Collection R-E2784, Saskatchewan Archives Board, Regina, Saskatchewan, Canada (Kosi); and many other variants.
19. S. B. Egbert to Carter, February 3, 1910, Carter Papers, MHS, box 2.
20. For a discussion of traditional winter hunts, see Pond, *Dakota or Sioux in Minnesota*, 43–53.
21. S. B. Egbert to Theodore Carter, February 3, 1910, Carter Papers, MHS, box 2. Egbert estimated Godfrey's age at seventeen or eighteen, seven or eight years younger than his actual age (about twenty-five in 1855).
22. For a helpful and succinct discussion of the effect of the Kansas-Nebraska Act in Minnesota, see Wingerd and Delegard, *North Country*, 231, 242, 245. Even Minnesota's antislavery press discussed the potential effects of the new law in theoretical terms; it is unknown whether the editors of those papers were ignorant of, or simply chose not to report, the presence of slaves at local army forts. See *St. Paul Daily Times*, November 16 and 22, 1854. Lieutenant Armistead declared that he was keeping a slave at Fort Ridgely during the very month the Kansas-Nebraska Act was passed; Commandant Lee brought his slaves to that post starting in June 1854. See Pay Vouchers, box 1356.
23. Officers who kept slaves in Minnesota from 1855 to 1858 include Lt. Col. Edmund B. Alexander (Anderson, William, Margaret, and Jane, 1856–57), Dr. Ebenezer Swift (Fanny, 1856–57), Paymaster Franklin E. Hunt (Margaret, 1855–57, identified as a slave at Fort Leavenworth, his next post); Quartermaster Alexander W. Reynolds (1858, Tom and James); and Capt. Barnard Bee (William, 1855–57). See Pay Vouchers, boxes 1421–1604. This count does not include several other officers who also brought black servants to Minnesota during this period, some of whom were almost certainly enslaved.
24. Pay Vouchers, boxes 1420, 1469, 1497, 1517, and 1586.
25. *Scott v. Sandford*, 60 U.S. 393, 407 (1857). Because every one of the nine justices wrote opinions in the Dred Scott case, it is no easy task to distill their hydra-headed reasoning into collective principles. The basic approach taken in the text is consistent with the thoughtful analysis of the case in Ehrlich, *They Have No Rights*, 169–78.
26. *St. Paul Daily Times*, March 25, 1857.
27. 1858 Minnesota Constitution, Article 1, Section 2. For Henry Sibley's participation in the 1857 Constitutional Convention, see Green, "Minnesota's Long Road to Black Suffrage," 74.

28. Spangler, *Negro in Minnesota,* 38. In 1849 Benjamin Brunson, the son of the man who bought James Thompson's freedom, introduced a bill in the territorial legislature that passed in the House, giving only white males the right to vote in the territory. See Green, "Minnesota's Long Road to Black Suffrage," 69.
29. Sibley's four-page history in his own handwriting is in the Sibley Papers, MHS, M164, roll 1, frames 11–12.
30. An almost exact parallel is found in Sibley's writings about the possibility of marrying or having a sexual relationship with a Dakota woman. In the draft of an unpublished autobiography written late in his life, Sibley described a scene in which a Dakota father tried, almost literally, to put his daughter into Sibley's Mendota bed. Sibley did not content himself with saying that he simply rejected the offer, adding that he had "no intention" of taking an Indian for a wife and that his "categorical" refusal of the proposal was necessary because such an alliance would make the other Indians with whom Sibley needed to trade "jealous." See H. Sibley, *Unfinished Autobiography,* 38–39. Read against the now-known backdrop of Sibley's having taken at least one Dakota woman as his wife, Sibley's embellishments show strong parallels with his changed stance on slavery. See Gilman, *Henry Hastings Sibley,* 75–76, for a discussion of Sibley's mixed-blood daughter, Helen.
31. Lehman, *Slavery in the Upper Mississippi Valley.* Lehman recounts that Lowry, whose political supporters denied his slaveholding, was exposed as a Minnesota slave master by Jane Swisshelm. Samuel Hays, a federal civil appointee, also brought two slaves to St. Cloud in 1857–58. Lehman identifies other possible slaves in Stillwater and elsewhere, though in some instances proof of continuing enslavement is uncertain.
32. Spangler, *Negro in Minnesota,* 28, citing the *New York Tribune,* August 3, 1860. Long before passage of the Fugitive Slave Act, free Northern blacks had been kidnapped for sale in the South. McManus, *Black Bondage,* 182–83.
33. Between 1832 and 1858 Garland named at least seventeen additional slaves on his pay claims, an unusually high number for such a high-ranking officer who was known to have owned slaves. The appearance of so many different slaves on his pay claims suggests that he may have bought them on furlough visits to his Virginia home and sold them at a profit, as he had Courtney, while stationed at distant army posts. See Pay Vouchers, boxes 352–1560. See also Kellogg, "Lincoln's New Mexico Patronage"; and *New-York Tribune,* December 31, 1860.
34. See Litwack, *North of Slavery,* 64–71; and Green, "Minnesota's Long Road to Black Suffrage," 74.
35. Spangler, *Negro in Minnesota,* 27.
36. Ibid., citing *Mankato Weekly Record,* November 15, 1859.
37. Taliaferro, "Auto-Biography," 235.
38. Williamson, *English-Dakota Dictionary.* The fact that both words were in usage by 1862 is shown in the trial translations of the testimony of a Dakota-speaking witness. See use of both *nigger* and *Negro* in the testimony of Wahpaduta (Godfrey's father-in-law), trial 11, Dakota Trials Records (1862 Dakota trials records, three microfilm rolls. Original records in NA, Center for Legislative Archives, U.S. Senate Records (for further details, see chapter 4, note 2). See also Hans, *Great Sioux Nation,* 340 ("Negro" spelled Wa-xi-cun-sa-pa; "nigger" as Ha-sa-pa).
39. Deposition testimony by Thomas J. Galbraith, October 10, 1863, in U.S. Department of the Interior and U.S. Sioux Commissioners, *Claims for Depredations,* 8.
40. W. J. Cullen to A. B. Greenwood, September 15, 1859, in *Report of Commissioner of Indian Affairs for 1859,* 51–52; italics in original.

41. Mdewakanton and Wahpekute annuity rolls, St. Peter's Agency (listing names of those in the "farmers' bands"), MHS, M405, roll 1. The Chief Wakute who enrolled as a member of the farmers' band was not the same Wakute who led his band earlier. The elder chief died in about 1858. See Meyer, "Red Wing Indian Village," 35–36.
42. W. J. Cullen to A. B. Greenwood, September 15, 1859, in *Report of Commissioner of Indian Affairs for 1859*, 51–52.
43. See Brown to Cullen, September 30, 1858, in *Report of Commissioner of Indian Affairs for 1858*, 51 (houses and acres plowed); and Cullen to Greenwood, September 15, 1859, in *Report of Commissioner of Indian Affairs for 1859*, 59.
44. The purpose of these extra distributions is made clear by Agent Brown's comment that they were made "to induce them to assume the dress of the whites, and to promote their agricultural improvement and civilization." Certification of Joseph R. Brown, 1859 "farmers' bands" distribution lists, MHS, M405, roll 1.
45. For the names of the 130 men denied payment, see MHS, M402, roll 1.
46. For a discussion of the soldiers' lodge and further details about the denial of annuities for depredations, see Anderson, *Little Crow*, chapters 5–7 (annuities, 111).
47. 1859 annuity rolls, MHS, M405, roll 1. In the summer distribution eighteen dollars per person was distributed. So Godfrey's wife and son would have received, between them, thirty-six dollars.
48. 1856 annuity rolls, MHS, M405, roll 1.
49. Depositions of Henry Trudell and Joseph Godfrey Jr., October 21, 1912, Godfrey heirship file. Godfrey Jr. said that his siblings were "quite small" when they died, and Trudell gave Hapan's name and placed her death at Fort Snelling, which indicates that she must have died in the fort's internment camp sometime during the winter of 1862–63. Though her precise age is not known, the reference to her as "quite small" suggests a possible birth year of either 1861 or 1862. Godfrey's trial testimony is conflicting on the subject of his children; he referred once to his "wife and children" but also said, "I have one child." It is possible that Takanheca was pregnant in 1862 and that the child was born late that year, or the trial reference to "one child" may be mistaken. The heirship file refers to a third child, George, who also died in infancy, year of birth unknown. Joseph Godfrey Jr. testified that his father's second marriage took place "about the first time the Santees moved [to Nebraska]" in 1866, suggesting that his father remarried not long after his release from prison. So George, the third child of Godfrey and Takanheca, may have been born and died in Minnesota between the births of Joseph Godfrey Jr. and Hapan.
50. Eli Huggins to Folwell, August 9, 1918, Folwell Papers, MHS, box 47. Huggins said that Alfred Riggs confirmed that the "mulatto" man he saw was Godfrey.
51. See Spangler, *Negro in Minnesota*, 29–32; *Minneapolis Sunday Tribune*, March 14, 1926; and Green, "Eliza Winston."
52. The Eliza Winston case was highly controversial in Minnesota. The *Stillwater Democrat* on May 19, 1860, railed at any "odious creature" who would "invade the family circle [i.e., slaves in the family]." Cited in Spangler, *Negro in Minnesota*, 29.
53. Heard, *History of the Sioux War*, 191.

PART II

BLACK DAKOTA

CHAPTER 4

The War

G odfrey was mowing hay in bright sunshine near his Lower Reservation home on August 18, 1862, when he heard the startling news that war had broken out. He was helping a neighbor, Wazeyeta, cut and transport his crop, in exchange for which Godfrey had been promised the loan of oxen to bring in his own hay. The men were making their way by wagon to his neighbor's house when a Dakota man rode up on horseback, "hallooing."[1] Godfrey and Wazeyeta had no inkling of the feverish, nightlong deliberations that had led to a declaration of war by members of the Lower Soldiers' Lodge. The rider announced that the people at the Lower Sioux Agency "were all murdered," two hundred Indians were coming after him, and they were going to "kill all the whites."[2]

    The messenger, who had his gun cocked, looked menacingly at Godfrey. Perhaps he wondered how this black man fit into the declaration to "kill all the whites." To Godfrey, the rider looked "strange." Twice the Dakota asked Godfrey where his loyalties lay, or "which side I would take." As Godfrey later recalled, the man on horseback "held his gun as if he would kill me" and "came near killing me." But the rider held his fire, instructing Godfrey to go to his house and put on warrior's dress—a breechclout.[3]

    When he arrived home, Godfrey and Takanheca at first decided to flee to safety. They grabbed a sack of flour and ran two hundred yards into the woods. Wahpaduta said he would close up the house and come after them, then changed his mind and yelled for them to return. Back at the house, another Dakota man, Takanheca's uncle, scolded them for trying to flee, telling them "we would be killed if we went toward the white folks." He told Godfrey he would be safe only if he joined the warring Indians, urging him to put on the breechclout. So dressed, Godfrey was instructed to follow men who were heading off "to kill all the Dutch [German] farmers."[4] Not far down the road the Dakota soldiers gathered to paint themselves for war. Godfrey was told that he too must be painted, and as he later submitted, "I was afraid to refuse."[5]

The grievances that led the Dakotas to try to regain some or all of their historic homelands had long been building. A great many factors contributed to their decision to commence a war in 1862, but most stemmed from three root causes: complaints about treaties, assaults on Dakota culture, and the effects of the Civil War.[6]

Treaty grievances were foremost. The Dakotas were convinced, with substantial justification, that they had been bullied and tricked into ceding their lands for less than their true value. The scheme concocted by Sibley and Ramsey to divert large sums from the 1851 treaty proceeds into the pockets of the Indian traders was perhaps the single most detested injustice in Dakota eyes. But others were also upset when their chiefs agreed to cede the northern half of their reservation in an 1858 treaty. Again, much of that treaty's proceeds went to white traders, and Congress fixed a purchase price that was well below the value of the lands.[7] The Indians also complained that the government was not adhering fully to its promises, that they were being shortchanged in the performance of treaty terms.

Even if the treaties had been relatively fair and carried out to the letter (they were not), many Dakotas would have remained fiercely angry at the insistence of white authorities that they abandon traditional ways. They may have reluctantly signed papers to sell some of their lands, but the majority of Dakotas did not accept the notion that they had bargained away their customs and culture. While white Indian agency leaders and missionaries saw acculturation as bringing the benefits of education, agriculture, and Christianity to the reservation, many Dakotas perceived it as an all-out attack on their most hallowed values.

The cultural assaults were large and small. Agent Thomas Galbraith had continued his predecessor's system of rewarding Indian men who took up farming, an endeavor that the traditional warrior-hunters derided as women's work. Pressures mounted on the Dakotas to abandon their spiritual practices, cease holding their dances, forego warfare with their long-term Ojibwe enemies, and yield to the advancing tide of white settlers now disturbing their formerly far-reaching hunting grounds.

The Civil War was a sine qua non for the Dakota War, and its impacts were felt in many ways. The Dakotas noted the departure from both civilian and military ranks of many white men of fighting age: if ever the whites were vulnerable to attack, it was during the war. Cash annuities, typically distributed in midsummer, were delayed due to national shortages of gold coin occasioned by the costs of war. Throngs of Sissetons and Wahpetons who lived near the western edge of the reservation and had assembled to collect their money were upset. Some endured near starvation when they were required to camp far from their hunting grounds to await the distribution.

Agent Galbraith, in a surfeit of Union patriotism but a deficit of wisdom, responded to Lincoln's call for five hundred thousand additional recruits by raising a company of white and mixed-blood reservation residents, grandly called the Renville Rangers. Even before the annuity money had arrived, he marched them off the reservation, adding grist to the Dakota rumor mill that the government was in such dire straits that it might not pay the basic treaty entitlements.

Another aspect of the Civil War's effects must have fallen heavily on Godfrey, for Lincoln's political opponents (including most of the Indian traders, who, like Sibley, voted Democratic) sometimes disparaged the war as the president's misguided policy of philanthropy toward black Americans. Such politically loaded rhetoric was common throughout the country, but it fell on credulous ears in the Dakota villages, contributing to the growth of rumors and engendering disquiet. Galbraith, Lincoln's appointee, graphically noted this feature of the buildup to the 1862 war. "Half-breeds and others who could read the news kept telling the Indians all kinds of exaggerated stories about the [civil] war. Sometimes that the *niggers* had taken, or were about to take, Washington; that the Great Father and the agent were friends to these *niggers*; that the Great Father was . . . *cleaned out*; that the Indians would get no more money; that the *niggers* would take it, or that it would be used to pay for the war."[8]

On August 17 Galbraith and his Rangers were feted by the townsfolk in New Ulm. The agent delivered a rousing patriotic speech, urging the German immigrants (who were staunchly antislavery and pro-Lincoln) to do their part by enlisting even more recruits. The people cheered, provided lodgings for the Rangers at Turner Hall, and furnished ample free libations to the recruits. They accepted Galbraith's assurances that all was calm on the Indian reservation. A committee of five, appointed to spearhead Brown County's campaign, made plans to launch a recruiting expedition the next day.[9]

The spark that ignited the war came on the same day as Galbraith's speech, when a small group of Dakota hunters killed five white settlers at Acton, forty miles north of the reservation. Even these murders might not have spilled over into war, for hindsight suggests many "ifs" that could have averted the conflict. If only Agent Galbraith had not left the reservation. If only the Dakotas had known that the annuity money in gold coinage was even then being transported by stage to Fort Ridgely. If only more had been done to provide for the immediate needs of Dakotas awaiting their annuity monies. If only the Acton killings had come a week after the annuity distribution. It is impossible to read accounts of the lead-up to the Dakota War without concluding that even small changes in circumstances might have altered the course of history in major ways. But all of the Dakotas' grievances were still festering when the Acton killers returned to the reservation on their stolen horses on the night of August 17. The shedding of white blood at that precise moment immediately led to a full-scale conflagration.

All-night meetings within the soldiers' lodge in the early morning hours on August 18 culminated when the warriors descended on Little Crow's home to ask him to give his blessing to the war. Initially reluctant, the chief consented when his courage was challenged. Despite his endorsement, Little Crow could shape war objectives and tactics only by using his persuasive powers, for the soldiers' lodge had the last word under Dakota governance traditions. For as long as war lasted, the edicts of the lodge's head soldiers—rather than the opinions of the more-moderate chiefs—would govern the waging of war.[10]

At the break of dawn Dakota warriors raced to the traders' stores at the Lower Agency, and emissaries soon radiated in all directions to proclaim the outbreak of war to their kinsmen. Hated traders such as James Lynd, Andrew Myrick, and George Divoll were among the first to be shot at the agency; no women or children were killed there, though many were taken captive.[11] Still, the rumor was spread by Dakota messengers that "all the whites" had been slain.

The reasons for the Dakotas' comparatively selective killings at the agency are debatable. Little Crow may have asked the warriors to kill only adult male adversaries, the distraction of lucrative booty in the traders' stores (especially weapons, shot, gunpowder, and other war-related items) may have deflected the Indians' attention and permitted escapes, or the mixed-blood families of the traders may have protected their kin and friends from harm. But, despite contrary claims made in some histories that the Dakotas "killed the men and carried the women and children into captivity," the Lower Sioux Agency was the only location where that killing pattern prevailed.[12]

The experience elsewhere was quite different. At the Upper Sioux Agency, the headquarters on the Sisseton and Wahpeton reservation, the vast majority of white residents (alerted and aided by Dakotas) managed to flee across the prairies to safety. In that area few whites were killed or taken into captivity. But on the eastern end of the reservation Mdewakanton and Wahpekute bands killed more women and children than they took into captivity at each site where appreciable numbers of whites were slain.[13]

When the war commenced, the settlement closest to the eastern edge of the reservation was Milford, a hamlet populated entirely by immigrant German families. The houses in Milford straddled the east-west road that led from the Lower Agency to New Ulm. By setting off in an eastward direction the morning of August 18, the Dakotas had selected the very destination toward which Ernst Dietrich and his recruiting-party wagons were then ambling.

About fifteen to twenty Dakotas descended on the farmhouses of Milford, not with wild whoops of war but with cunning and deceit. By one means or another they pretended that they had no hostile intentions. They gained entry to homes by asking for food or water and then killed most if not all of the occupants. If anyone asked why they were dressed in warrior garb, they led their victims astray by telling them they were looking for enemy Ojibwes.[14]

At the first house, occupied by the Massopust family, the Dakotas asked for water to get inside the home. They immediately killed Wilson Massopust and his two daughters, but a son managed to run away.[15] The six members of the Zettel family, who lived just to the east of the Massopusts, were slaughtered—husband, wife, and four children age two to eight. The Indians moved from house to house, systematically killing all the occupants they could. They tried to extinguish the lives of all six members of the Mey family, but three young children left for dead with tomahawk wounds survived.[16] Two other Milford residents survived the day but soon expired from ghastly injuries suffered from swords or tomahawks.[17]

According to Godfrey, the Dakotas told him during the course of the Milford attack, "If you don't kill a white man we will kill you." They thrust a hatchet into his hand and pushed him into a house, where, he said, he struck an old man "on the shoulder with the flat of the hatchet." Though the members of that family tried to flee, all (including the old man) were killed by the Dakotas.[18]

On their deadly sweep through Milford, the Dakotas killed forty-eight people: twenty children, nineteen men, and nine women. They took no captives. There are no reports that they intentionally spared any adult or child, though a handful escaped. No effective resistance was offered by any white settler; not one Dakota warrior was killed. What happened at Milford was a massacre—not the only massacre of the conflict, but the worst in terms of loss of life.

The term *massacre* is a sensitive one, but the historical misuse of the word in connection with the 1862 war has further heightened feelings about the term. For many years whites incorrectly referred to the overall war as a massacre or misapplied the term to describe battle scenes. But the killings at Milford and at other locations during the Dakota War fit dictionary definitions of a massacre: the killing of a number of defenseless people in an indiscriminate and cruel manner. Including Milford, there were eight sites at which the Dakotas massacred thirteen or more helpless civilians away from the scene of any military battle—the majority of whom, at each location, were women and children.[19]

Shortly after the Dakotas had begun to drink Anton Henle's liquor at the Travelers' Home, they looked down the road and saw the approaching wagons of the recruiting party. Most of the Indians concealed themselves in a ravine so as to ambush the wagons, but Godfrey and a few Dakotas stood in the road.[20] After Dietrich and the other men in the foremost recruiting wagon had been shot by the ambushers, the Dakotas seized the two lead wagons and took the brass musical instruments that the recruiters had intended to play to drum up support for their mission. The four men killed in the recruiting-party ambush brought the death totals at Milford to fifty-two, still with no Dakota fatalities.

Recruiter Henry Behnke, who survived the ambush, raced seven miles back to New Ulm to sound the alert. After Sheriff Roos returned from viewing the extent of the massacre at Milford, Behnke was assigned to carry an urgent message asking for reinforcements. Saddling up a fleet horse at midnight, he rode thirty miles through the night until he reached the home of state supreme court justice Charles Flandrau near Traverse des Sioux, an exploit that earned him the title of New Ulm's Paul Revere. Flandrau, immediately exchanging his judicial robes for firearms, recruited a company of St. Peter volunteers and rode to the defense of the German town.[21]

As the Dakotas turned westward after the ambush of the recruiting party, Godfrey was given the task of driving one of the recruiters' wagons, which soon was piled with plunder from the settlers' homes. Stopping at the Massopust house to gather more booty, Godfrey saw the bodies of the two girls, both of whom had been partially disrobed (a Dakota custom of humiliating an enemy, not a sign of sexual attack, as whites mistakenly supposed). One girl had been decapitated, her head nowhere to be seen. An old Dakota man named Wazekootay lectured the retreating warriors against committing such mutilations, and he drew both girls' dresses down to cover their naked bodies.[22]

The inebriated warriors left Milford on horseback and in heavily laden booty wagons; preceded by a crazed herd of stolen cattle, they presented a fearful and motley sight. Some of the Dakotas blared away on the brass instruments taken from the recruiting party. As the Indians crested a hill, a wagon of whites fleeing toward New Ulm saw the horns "glistening in the sun" and at first believed that a group of soldiers was coming to their aid.[23]

This hapless wagon was driven by Francois Patoille. He, two other men, and three young women had already driven many miles when the Milford attackers came upon them. According to survivor Mary Schwandt, Patoille stayed in the wagon as the Indians approached and was immediately shot and knifed, his head beaten "all to pieces."[24] The other five occupants of the wagon jumped out and ran to a nearby slough, but the men were quickly caught and killed. Mary Anderson, a young Swedish woman, was shot in the back and gravely wounded. Mattie Williams, a "highly cultured young lady from the East" who was visiting her uncle in Minnesota, and fourteen-year-old Schwandt were taken captive.[25]

As was the Dakota custom, the brave who seized each woman was entitled either to kill her or to claim her as his captive.[26] It is not clear why the same warriors who had spared no one earlier in the day now decided to take captives. Perhaps they saw the young women as suitable for captivity, or perhaps they simply felt more comfortable taking captives now that they were so close to home and had wagons in which the women could be transported. Similar life-and-death decisions were made by Dakotas throughout the region, and decisions about who was killed and who was allowed to live often appear to have been based on the whims of the actors.

Mattie Williams and the injured Mary Anderson were put in one wagon, while Mary Schwandt was placed in the wagon being driven by Godfrey. Schwandt, who later gave many (sometimes conflicting) statements about her flight and captivity, had deeply mixed reactions about

Godfrey. Her varying accounts described him as a "demon in human form" but also as having the "sweetest voice I ever heard in a man." She reviled him as one of her attackers but conceded that he was unarmed and that she didn't see him "lay his hands on" anyone. The Indians, she said, were drunk, but Godfrey was sober. His belt was garishly festooned with six to eight watches taken from Milford victims.[27]

Godfrey apparently had been instructed by the Dakotas to deliver Schwandt to his chief, for he brought her to Wakute's house and told her that the other two captives were already there. Schwandt's ambivalence toward him is reflected in her reluctance to leave the wagon: "So I begged this black man, in spite of my loathing for him, to take me with him to his house." But the Indians forcibly removed Schwandt from the wagon and delivered her to Wakute.[28]

The fates of the three young women in the Patoille wagon illustrate the widely differing treatment given to the more than one hundred whites taken captive by the Dakotas in 1862. Mary Anderson died an agonizing death from her gunshot wound while still at Wakute's. Mary Schwandt was sold by her captor for the price of a pony to a Dakota woman named Snana, who treated her as her own daughter, with great kindness. And the "highly cultured" Mattie Williams was claimed by her "horribly pockmarked" captor, Tazoo, who took her to his tipi and raped her.[29]

In some respects the killings at Milford followed the practices carried out for eons by the Dakotas against their traditional adversaries, especially the Ojibwes. Enemy women and children were not spared when the Dakotas waged war, though it was considered unmanly to dispatch them with a gun. Missionary Samuel Pond noted that "unless they chose to take them captives, they commonly killed [women and children] with knives, spears, war-clubs, or hatchets."[30]

Another major distinction between intertribal wars and the 1862 conflict lay in the reactions of the Dakotas' enemies. Native adversaries, raised from infancy with tales of preparedness for war, reacted swiftly and furiously and resisted to their last breath when an enemy was sighted. Both sides in Indian wars knew that passivity or attempts to surrender to a hostile force, even by women or children, might bring no quarter from the adversary. Some newcomer immigrant whites learned this reality of Indian warfare too late to defend themselves. Similarly, no Ojibwe over the age of five would have become confused, as did many whites in 1862, upon seeing Dakota braves smeared in war paint. Samuel Pond noted this important difference: "Indians were not slaughtered like sheep without any attempt at resistance, as many of the white settlers on our frontier were in 1862."[31] The Dakotas sometimes used the same sheep simile in recounting how easy it was to kill the whites in the first days of the conflict.[32]

Godfrey had lived long enough within the Dakota warrior society to have absorbed their customs in intertribal warfare, including their elaborate rules for awarding honors to their warriors. Individual battle heroics were valued over casualty statistics, and the highest esteem went not to the soldier who shot a man but to the warrior who first touched him, even if the enemy was mortally wounded by a gunshot or already dead.[33] Touching qualified as a "kill," even if the man who had contact with an enemy casualty did nothing to physically harm him. Bravery in attack, not proximate causation of death, was rewarded. Moreover, up to five Dakota soldiers in a war party were given credit—and a feather—for a slain enemy, even if some were just in close proximity at the time of the killing. Combining the concepts of touching or approaching victims with the custom of multiple awards, it was possible that a Dakota man with many "kills" to his credit had never actually slain anyone.[34] Dakota men returning from battle were expected to recount their killings in detail, partly to gain credit for their deeds and partly to permit the band to determine who was entitled to receive military honors. Warriors openly boasted of their conquests, and everyone in the village feted them with feasts and glory.[35]

Godfrey, acting under life-threatening duress or not, was entitled to premier status under this system of battle honors. He had entered houses in Milford with small groups of men where multiple victims had been slain, and he was thus eligible to boast about his many "kills." Striking the old man with a hatchet, even if it caused no injury, would have been seen by the Dakotas as the highest form of heroism and would have qualified Godfrey to count all of that house's victims as his "kills."

Godfrey did brag about his exploits, though we will never know if he did so as a temporary convert to the Dakota cause or as a means of deflecting the continuing hostility of the Dakotas toward a non-Indian man in their midst. Within earshot of mixed-blood captives, Godfrey boasted that he had "killed" seven men as well as an unspecified number of children. A white woman held captive, writing forty years after the conflict, claimed that he had bragged of "killing seventeen women and children," relating "how they fought for their lives before they were killed."[36] The Dakotas, as they often did in times of war, bestowed Godfrey with a new name. For the duration of the war, they called him Otakle, or Many Kills.[37]

After the Milford attack Godfrey led both the Dakotas and their captives to believe that he was a willing participant in the war. He displayed no reluctance and even made himself a prominent presence in the Dakota camp. One white captive later recalled a scene, apparently from an en masse march to a new camp: "The negro Godfrey is one who always stands out most prominently in my memory. . . . He was everywhere; up and down the line he rode, passing us twenty times an hour and always trying to frighten the captives by his hideous antics."[38] Even making allowances for the fact that a black man dressed as a Dakota warrior would have offered a memorable image, it appears that Godfrey went out of his way to convince everyone that he was a full-fledged partisan of the Dakota cause after he reluctantly joined those who committed the Milford killings.

Especially in light of the stance taken by Godfrey after the war, one must ask whether his wartime boasts and "antics" were, at least in part, an act to keep the Dakotas from killing him, as they had repeatedly threatened to do.[39] Theodore Carter, a thoughtful white soldier who became acquainted with Godfrey after the conflict, believed that his boasts were a form of self-defense: "He had to act and talk in the presence of Indians so as to avoid suspicion, or lose his life."[40] Marion Satterlee, a journalist and amateur historian, trying to be sympathetic but couching his defense of Godfrey in racist terms, wrote off his bragging as "nigger prattle."[41]

A crucial unaddressed question relates to Godfrey's boastful statements and deeds during the war: How did the Indians view and act toward African Americans during the conflict? If the Dakotas treated other black men as they treated white men, the likelihood increases that Godfrey's claims of duress were true and that his boasts were a façade put forth for his own protection.

When the Dakota War broke out three African American men were in the immediate vicinity of the Lower Agency. William Taylor, a well-respected black barber and musician from St. Paul, was visiting during the time of the anticipated annuity distribution in order to make money plying his twin trades. Godfrey, of course, lived on the reservation with his wife and son.[42] And James Thompson, the emancipated slave, lived in a house near the agency with his Dakota wife, Mary, and the couple's eighteen-year-old son, George. The Thompsons' twenty-four-year-old daughter, Sarah Thompson Barnes, was also on the reservation (apparently without her white husband), probably to collect annuities for herself and her three children, ages two, four, and seven.[43]

When the rallying cry rose up among the Dakotas on August 18 to "kill the whites," no one issued decrees about where to draw racial lines. Were white men or women married to Dakotas to be slain? Were those of mixed white and Indian heritage to be killed? Did it make a difference what quantum of Indian blood one had? Were blacks to be treated the same as whites? What about those few people with mixed black and Dakota ancestry?

Since Godfrey and Thompson both were married to Dakota women, they would have been safe if kinship by marriage and adoption of many Dakota customs gave one protection from attack. But the 1862 victim lists indicate that the Dakotas used race more than kinship as the primary determinant of which males they killed and which were spared. There were scores of men of mixed Dakota and white blood who remained on the Dakota side of the conflict. Some of them, like Godfrey, joined the fighting on the Indian side, sometimes with the same claims of duress. Others were considered captives, many of whom believed their lives were in jeopardy from Dakota threats.

But only one man with any quantum of Indian blood is known

to have been killed by the Dakotas.⁴⁴ Even mixed-blood traders who had taken an active role in negotiating the hated treaties of 1851, such as David Faribault Sr., were not harmed. In contrast, white men married to Dakota women, such as Philander Prescott, James Lynd, and Peter Quinn, were killed in or near the eastern half of the reservation.⁴⁵

William Taylor's fate offers the clearest proof that Dakota calls to "kill the whites" did not exclude black men. Taylor, a key figure in Minnesota's Underground Railroad, was killed while fleeing from the Lower Agency on the first day of the conflict. Missionary Emily J. West recalled, "As we were wandering along the prairie without any path . . . we met ten or twelve white people, men women and children. . . . Among them was a colored man from St. Paul who had been at the Agency three or four weeks. . . . [C]hanging our course a little we were soon separated. I afterward learned that not long after they left us they met a party of Indians who killed the black man and took the rest prisoners."⁴⁶

If any man's story could serve as a litmus test for the hazards Godfrey faced by remaining on the Dakota side during the conflict, it is James Thompson's. Thompson, though he was older than Godfrey, was situated almost identically to him. Both had white fathers and black, enslaved mothers, and both were called "mulattoes." Both men were born into slavery. Both had lived in Minnesota in its early years, both had married Dakota wives there, and both had fathered tri-racial black-white-Dakota children. Both spoke the Dakota language fluently.

How did Thompson react to the outbreak of war? He sought the sanctuary offered by Fort Ridgely, leaving his wife, his two children, and his three grandchildren on the Dakota side. His name on the roster of survivors of the siege on the fort was, perhaps, overlooked because it was mistranscribed as "Jones Thompson."⁴⁷ Not long after Thompson fled the reservation, Dakota warriors came to his house to kill him. Finding him gone, they vented their fury by taking all of his possessions and burning them.⁴⁸ Though staying away from his family during such a crisis may appear to be an act of cowardice, subsequent events established that Thompson had correctly judged where the members of his mixed-race family would be safest.

The story of Thompson's son, George, also demonstrates the kind of racial distinctions the Dakotas made. Though they tried to kill his father, the Indians sought to conscript eighteen-year-old George to join their war. His mother's novel ploy to keep him out of the hostilities was set forth in a letter from missionary Jane Williamson, who wrote, "Jim Thompson's wife said she kept her son out of several battles by going herself and driving away part of the cattle after hearing there was to be a battle and sending him after them. When he was call[ed] for she replied he was gone after the cattle. But she could not always succeed though he did what he could to evade the battles."[49] George, like others with Indian blood, was exempt from the Dakotas' killing edicts.

Applying the lessons of Taylor's death and the attempt to kill Thompson to Godfrey's plight, it is easier to understand why Godfrey might have felt the need to flaunt his pro-Dakota stance (or, as he later claimed, to pretend to do so) during the war. The Taylor and Thompson stories demonstrate that black men were not protected, even if they had embraced Dakota culture and had marital kinship. These parallels do not prove that Godfrey was coerced to join the Indians or that his boasts were feigned, but they confirm that his life was in peril during the conflict for reasons that did not apply to almost any other person on the Dakota side.

Since Godfrey's choices were to stay with the Dakotas or to try to flee to Fort Ridgely, one crucial fact distinguishes his circumstances from both Taylor's and Thompson's: he was still a fugitive slave without papers to prove his right to live in freedom. Godfrey's mother was brought to Minnesota by an army officer, he was enslaved within Minnesota longer than any other person, and he lived nearby as officers kept slaves at Fort Ridgely. All of these facts, when coupled with his unsettled legal status, would have led Godfrey to view Fort Ridgely as a risky place to seek sanctuary.

Back in the state capital, St. Paul, Governor Ramsey, upon receiving emergency dispatches about the outbreak of war, immediately appointed a man with no prior military experience to lead state militia forces in fighting the Dakotas: Henry H. Sibley. Ramsey and Sibley, now twinned to lead Minnesota's civil and military response to the war, were the very men who had conceived and carried out the 1851 scheme to divert Dakota treaty money to the fur traders. Colonel Sibley's ill-equipped army of fresh recruits, lacking adequate munitions, supplies, and horses, slowly made its way to the relief of Fort Ridgely, which was besieged by Dakota warriors for ten days. Ferocious battles were fought at three different sites before Sibley arrived and relieved the fort.

On August 18 the only early engagement that could qualify as a military battle was an ambush of fifty soldiers led by Capt. John Marsh, who had marched south from Fort Ridgely toward the Lower Agency when news of the uprising reached the fort. As they had at Milford, the Indians pretended they had no hostile intentions; at a ferry crossing a Dakota man on the opposite shore calmly told the soldiers to cross (the plan being to launch the attack once the men were floating helplessly in the middle of the river). By the time the fort contingent detected the deception, they were surrounded by a much larger Dakota force. Marsh's company was nearly wiped out, suffering twenty-five fatalities against only one Dakota casualty. This overwhelmingly successful attack greatly buoyed the Dakotas' warrior spirits and led them to believe that white soldiers could be killed almost as easily as the sheeplike settlers.[50]

Also on August 18 and again the next day, Dakota bands swept through the small white farming communities north of the river. Defenseless settlers living near the streams that flowed into the river were slain in large numbers at Middle Creek, Beaver Creek, and LaCroix Creek (Birch Coulee). Simultaneously, at the small town of Leavenworth to the south of Milford, the entire population of twenty-three settlers was extinguished.

By sundown on August 19 almost all whites within thirty miles of the Lower Agency had been killed or captured or had managed to reach the relative safety of Fort Ridgely or New Ulm. With the exception of those two enclaves, the Dakotas, using a combination of deceit, terror, and mass killing of civilians, had effectively cleansed the entire region of its white population. Up to that point more than two hundred whites had been killed at the cost of just one Dakota soldier (at the ferry battle), and the vast majority of those victims were slain in Milford-like attacks on defenseless noncombatants.

Attempting to complete their conquest, the Dakotas launched fierce attacks on New Ulm and Fort Ridgely. On August 19 the German town was defended by a disorganized group of citizen-soldiers, some armed only with pitchforks. Only the timely arrival of volunteer reinforcements and a thunderstorm that rendered it difficult for the Indians to keep their gunpowder dry saved the residents from wholesale murder. New Ulm was attacked again on August 23, when the defenders barely held a tiny central compound of buildings while the remainder of the town burned around them.

Godfrey fought with the Dakotas at the second New Ulm battle, later saying that he and the mixed-blood men had been conscripted by Little Crow. Standing on the sidelines ("afraid of both sides," he later said), he fired five shots "into a house" from a distance. He had no idea whether his salvos killed or injured anyone.[51]

Fort Ridgely, crowded with refugees, similarly withstood two pitched assaults, on August 20 and 22. Again, Godfrey was present at the second battle only. As he drove a wagon toward the fort, unarmed, Godfrey was threatened by a Dakota wielding a knife and saying, "When you are over the river you will be dead." Once he was at the fort Godfrey teamed up with David Faribault Jr., the twenty-three-year-old nephew of his last master. While the battle raged the two men ran into the fort stables and stole horses, though the mare Godfrey got was immediately taken away from him by a Dakota man. Neither Godfrey nor Faribault fired any shots at the fort battle.[52]

Also by August 20, Dakota war parties had begun to make forays farther afield. Up to that point most of the white victims had been German settlers, reflecting the ethnic populations that lived closest to the Lower Agency. On the twentieth one Dakota band attacked a group of Swedish settlers about eighty miles north of the Lower Agency, in Kandiyohi County, killing twenty-three.[53] To the southwest about fifty-five miles, an isolated white community near Lake Shetek was attacked on the same day. After killing a few people the Dakotas promised protection to the rest, who had run to hide in tall grasses. Again, Dakota deceit led to the loss of lives, for as they emerged, many of those who surrendered were slain at the place immortalized as Slaughter Slough. A total of seventeen people were killed at Lake Shetek, and the Dakotas sustained their only fatality to occur away from a battle scene.

The twelve hundred refugees and surviving residents of New Ulm, huddled into four barricaded blocks to guard against another attack, decided on August 25 to evacuate the town. Just before leaving, they prepared a malicious gift to leave behind for the Dakotas: a barrel of whiskey laced with "enough strychnine in it to destroy the whole Sioux nation." The poisoned whiskey was apparently never consumed.[54]

Pauline Dietrich, Ernst Dietrich's widow, survived the siege with her four small children, including two-year-old Hedwig (who later married my great-grandfather, Henry Bachman). Like many white survivors of the conflict, Pauline did not stop when the town's evacuees reached Mankato or St. Peter. She traveled on to St. Paul, where she found modest lodgings and, nearly destitute, subsisted on small relief payments from the state's refugee fund. She never again lived in New Ulm.[55]

Sibley's forces reached Fort Ridgely after the majority of the frontier settler killings were over. Still short of horses and supplies, the colonel drilled his troops and sent out scouting parties before proceeding farther west. The Dakotas, meanwhile, moved their camp westward to distance themselves from Sibley's army. Little Crow, by this time, had conceived a bold plan to attack the town of Mankato, located one hundred miles southeast on the Minnesota River. The chief, according to Godfrey, announced that anyone who refused to go on the expedition would be killed. Still associating with David Faribault Jr., Godfrey set off with the assembled war party of two hundred men. Godfrey later explained why such a small contingent might dare to assail a town the size of Mankato, with more than one thousand residents: "They [the Dakotas] thought that the Winnebagoes [whose reservation was south of Mankato] would . . . attack the lower settlements."[56]

At the same time, Sibley sent a contingent of men out from Fort Ridgely to dig graves for dead settlers whose bodies had lain exposed for many days. After interring scores of the Dakotas' victims, the members of this expedition camped overnight on an unprotected plateau near a rivulet called Birch Coulie. There Little Crow's war party chanced upon them.

By dawn on September 2 the Dakotas had surrounded the unsuspecting encampment. At first light they rained lead into the sleeping compound. Since few white soldiers were awake, the initial fusillade was aimed at their tents and horses. Godfrey later admitted, "I shot just the same into the tents." Only by hunkering down behind the bodies of their own horses and dead comrades did the Birch Coulee contingent survive a thirty-six-hour siege that could well have presaged Custer's Battle of the Little Bighorn. When Sibley sent an artillery-equipped relief column out from Fort Ridgely, the Dakotas considered attacking it. But, according to Godfrey, Little Crow "said it was no use to shoot against the cannon."[57] So the Indians retreated to their new center of operations, near the Upper Sioux Agency.

The casualty figures for the Birch Coulee battle were, once again, lopsided in the Dakotas' favor: nineteen whites died and more than fifty were seriously wounded, while only two Indians lost their lives. Nearly as important from a military standpoint, the loss of almost one hundred horses left Sibley's army more foot-bound than ever.[58] The near catastrophe at Birch Coulee made Sibley even more cautious. He remained at Fort Ridgely for almost three weeks, drilling his green troops and awaiting reinforcements and supplies.

Sibley, though inexperienced in warfare, knew firsthand of the deep cultural schisms that had cleaved the Dakota nation prior to August 18: militant warriors in the soldiers' lodge versus their more pacific chiefs; mission congregants and spiritual traditionalists ("pagans," to white missionaries); farmers and hunters; frame-house versus tipi dwellers; pantaloons versus breechcloths. Sibley knew that "half-breeds" were more fully accepted by their Indian relatives than by whites but that many of them were oriented toward their white half nonetheless. He understood that while war was being waged under terms decreed by the soldiers' lodge, any peace would be made with the chiefs—and that both the legal and moral authority of the militants would collapse if the Dakotas were defeated in battle.

One of Sibley's main concerns now was to find a way to wrest more than one hundred white captives (and many more mixed-bloods) from their Dakota captors. Seeking to capitalize on the divisions within the Dakota ranks, the colonel dispatched a series of messages to Little Crow and, secretly, to the Dakotas' more peace-oriented factions. His velvet-gloved words would ultimately ease the Dakotas' surrender more than the mailed fist of his plodding troops.

Little Crow also knew that the white captives were his trump card in any negotiations. The chief's messages to Sibley made vaguely menacing threats about the captives (whom he called prisoners), but the same mixed-blood men who brought Little Crow's missives also confirmed that the Indians were "divided in sentiment and . . . quarreling among themselves."[59] Sibley's response to the chief was chastising and noncommittal. Even with the captives' lives in peril, he would make no peace that would prevent him from hanging Little Crow.[60]

The extent of the divisions in the Indian camp was more dramatically confirmed when one of Little Crow's messengers, Tom Robertson, secretly revealed that he also bore a "private" message from two chiefs, Wabasha and Taopee, who (despite Wabasha's reluctant appearance at battles) styled themselves as dissidents.[61] Writing off Little Crow ("He has now got himself into trouble that we know he can never get himself out of"), the chiefs asked Sibley to designate a place where they could flee with as many white captives as possible, suggesting the mouth of either the Redwood or Cottonwood Rivers, claiming they had refrained from helping the whites more openly under threats of death.

Sibley sent his secret reply back with Robertson on September 12: "I have come up here with a large force to punish the murderers of my people. It is not my purpose to injure any innocent person. If you and the others who have not been concerned in the murders and expeditions will gather yourselves, with all the prisoners, on the prairie in full sight of my troops, . . . [displaying] a white flag . . . you can come forward and place yourself under my protection. My troops will be all mounted in two days' time, and in three days . . . I expect to march."[62] Sibley's claim that his slow-paced foot soldiers were about to be transformed into a fearful mounted army was a patent canard (if a justifiable military deception), since he was simultaneously complaining to headquarters that he could count only twenty-five cavalry and expected to advance at the pace of the infantry.[63]

Seeking to exploit the divisions within the Indian ranks and to add yeast to the brewing foment among the Dakotas, Sibley now crafted his verbal wedge in the form of an open letter, dispatched on September 13:

> To those of the Half-Breeds and Sioux Indians who have not been Concerned in the Murders and Outrages upon the White Settlers: I write a few lines by Simon [Anawangmani] to say to you that I have not come into this upper country to injure any innocent person, but to punish those who have committed the cruel murders upon innocent men, women, and children. If, therefore, you wish to withdraw from these guilty people you must, when you see my troops approaching, take up a separate position and hoist a flag of truce and send a small party to me when I hoist a flag of truce in answer, and I will then take you under my protection.[64]

These "few lines" were vintage Sibley, and this carefully worded script was to be the core of his stance for the next month.

Reaching beyond the goal of wholesale capitulation, Sibley must also have had in mind the reality that the Dakotas were marshaling their forces for one last stand when he wrote these messages. By seeking to isolate the minority of Indians who had murdered settlers, Sibley must also have considered the impact of his words on the fighting spirit of the rest. Reluctant warriors, or those who had had a change of heart, would take solace in the fact that defeat in battle was not—as would have been true in intertribal warfare—synonymous with their destruction. If Sibley could be trusted, anyone who had not yet murdered whites now had hope of being spared. If the gist of Sibley's messages filtered down to Godfrey, he may well have contemplated surrender. Despite his braggadocio and his presence in the thick of the Milford massacre, Godfrey claimed he had killed no one.

While Sibley was sending divide-and-conquer messages to the Dakotas, a new military commander arrived in St. Paul. Because he appeared on the scene not long before the 1862 fighting ended, Gen. John Pope is often depicted as not much more than a figurehead background character in histories of the conflict. In a purely military sense, that is an accurate depiction. But Pope, as we shall see, had a profound impact on the fate of the Dakotas via an imperative series of blustery and conflicting orders.

Pope came to Minnesota in disgrace, having commanded the Union troops that lost the crucial second battle of Bull Run in the Civil War. He was seething with resentment at Lincoln for removing him from his Virginia command. One of his staff aides described him in a private letter in scathing terms: "like a bear with a sore head," "ambitiously crazy," "deceitful," and obsessed with making "war on the President in a mean and babyish manner."[65] While traveling to his new post in St. Paul to command the army's Department of the Northwest, Pope, bristling to redeem his reputation, pledged to take the field himself against the warring Dakotas.[66]

But Pope never got closer to the theater of war than the comfortable headquarters he established for himself and his sizeable entourage at St. Paul's International Hotel. One of his first acts was to order that the telegraph line be extended to the hotel so that Washington could quickly receive his urgent demands.[67] Within two weeks of his September 15 arrival, Pope let it be known that he did not favor halfway measures, that he was bent on exterminating the Dakotas.[68] Even as the season for war was drawing to a close, he demanded that a large contingent of ten thousand troops be sent to bolster Sibley's expedition.[69]

Within the same two weeks Pope sent Secretary of War Edwin Stanton his grandiose scheme for solving problems in white-Indian relations by treating all Native Americans in the region, not just the Dakotas, as "wild beasts" or "maniacs." He envisioned an open-air asylum in some remote western locale where all Indians would be relocated and "cheaply fed and clothed" by the government. Pope had nothing but scorn for Indian traders and agents—such as Sibley and some of the men surrounding him on his expedition—whom he blamed for polluting the Indians' native nobility. Under Pope's plan, all treaties would be unilaterally scrapped by the U.S. government and annuities promised under them immediately stopped.[70]

The most practical and immediate effect of Pope's arrival was to federalize the army that Sibley was commanding in the field. Minnesotans welcomed this transfer of authority, if only because it meant that the national government would henceforth shoulder the costs of waging war.[71]

Sibley, meanwhile, hopeful that his messages had weakened the Dakotas' resolve, had ordered his troops to commence a deliberate march west toward the Indian camp. On September 18 the military expedition crossed the Minnesota and followed the federal wagon road upriver. Little Crow, whose scouts informed him of Sibley's every move, plotted a final surprise attack. Almost every able-bodied man was conscripted to the Dakota cause, including some who harbored private wishes that Little Crow would fail.[72]

The anticlimactic Battle of Wood Lake on September 23 was the only engagement of the war in which Dakota casualties outnumbered white ones: seventeen Dakotas and seven white soldiers were killed.[73] Godfrey, like many of the recalcitrant warriors on the Dakota side, never fired a shot. Sibley viewed it as a "serious" conflict, but Pope, accustomed to the massive casualties of Civil War battles, termed it a "skirmish."[74] Little Crow, after the Battle of Wood Lake, railed at the lack of fighting spirit in his men, ascribing his loss to "traitors in our midst."[75] Who knows how many Dakotas went through the motions of war at the denouement without committing to the fight or how many retreated with undue haste, in reliance on Sibley's promises of peace and protection.

When word of Sibley's success at Wood Lake reached Washington, victory-starved Lincoln was anxious to reward one American commander who could bring him good news. The president, to Pope's apparent chagrin, immediately appointed Sibley to the prestigious rank of brigadier general in the Union army. But it would take weeks for official news of that appointment to reach Sibley in the field. In the meantime, Sibley remained a colonel in the state militia.[76]

As hostilities drew to a close after the Wood Lake battle, the killing of civilians also ended. For many years, exaggerated rumors inflated the white death totals from the conflict to eight hundred to one thousand or more.[77] But even the documented reality shows that Sibley had many potential candidates for his "murderers will be punished" doctrine. The overall body counts, according to the war's first statistician, Marion Satterlee, were enormously lopsided: 447 identified whites killed versus 29 Dakotas—a ratio of fifteen to one.[78] But the real story is obscured by aggregate statistics, for one of the most startling features of the Dakota War is the widespread killing of helpless, noncombatant settlers. A substantial majority of white victims were killed away from scenes of battles, most of them in their homes or while attempting to flee to safety.

No Indian women or children were slain during the hostilities, while at least one hundred settler children and fifty white women were killed.[79] These stark statistics, better than any others, bring home the essence of the war that so infuriated white Minnesotans. As they defined murder—the killing of helpless noncombatants away from a battlefield—about two-thirds (more than three hundred) of the whites killed in 1862 had been murdered. Almost half of those victims were women and children.[80]

After the Dakotas lost the Battle of Wood Lake, the schism between Little Crow's followers and those who wanted to surrender to Sibley widened to an unbridgeable chasm. The Indian peace faction, at considerable risk to themselves, gained control over almost all of the white and mixed-blood captives. By this time many Dakotas from the western Sisseton bands had already returned to their wintering grounds on the prairies, but Little Crow and others who wished either to continue the war or to escape Sibley's retribution now also departed, taking with them a few white captives.

Sibley kept up his drumbeat of messages to the dissident Dakotas. On September 24 he wrote to Tatankanajin, a Sisseton chief. Explicitly seeking to alienate them from their easterly kin, Sibley said he had "not come up to make war upon any bands who have not been concerned in the horrible murders upon the white people. . . .Such of the Indians as have not had anything to do with the murders of the whites will not be injured by my troops; but, on the contrary, they will be protected by me when I arrive, which will be very soon." He counseled the chief not to permit his people to "mix yourselves together" with the guilty bands, "for I do not wish to injure any innocent person." In contrast, "I intend to pursue the wicked murderers with fire and sword until I overtake them."[81]

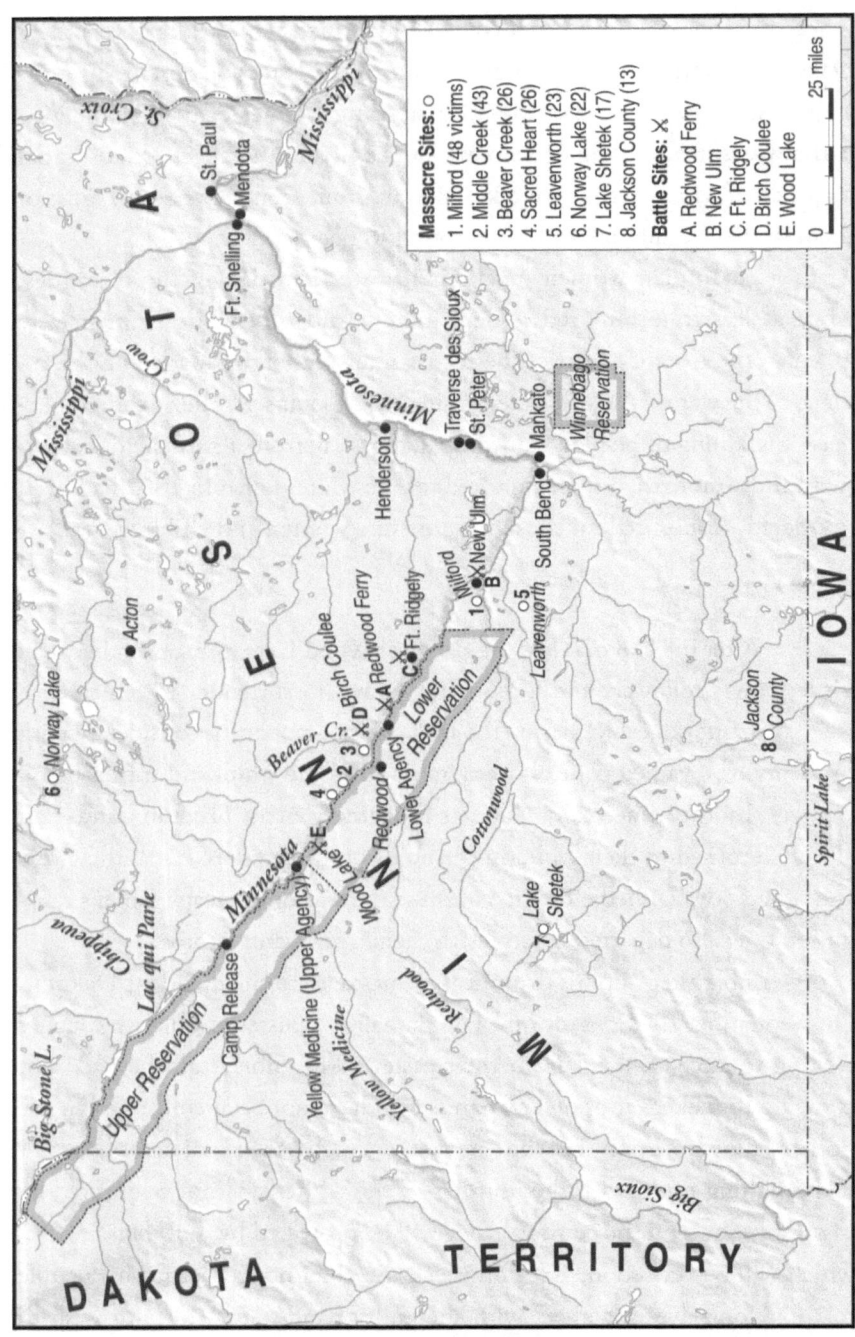

Map 2. Dakota War, 1862. Courtesy of the Pond Dakota Heritage Society.

Sibley's various parlay letters to the Dakotas enunciated solemn written principles for peace just as surely as if a new treaty had been negotiated and signed. He offered no general grant of amnesty to those who chose to surrender. The Dakotas fully understood that those within their ranks who had murdered settlers had no right to expect anything other than punishment at his hands. But Sibley also led the Indians to believe that everyone else, including men who had merely fought in military battles, would fall under his personal mantle of protection. From the standpoint of white military justice, the line Sibley drew between murderers and ordinary battle participants was consistent with the laws of war. Surrendering soldiers are entitled to be treated as prisoners of war, but that status does not exempt them from prosecution for war crimes, such as the intentional killing of defenseless civilians. Even if Sibley had not expressly warned the Dakotas that they would be subject to punishment for such murders (which he repeatedly did), he would have been acting within U.S. law to bring charges for conduct amounting to crimes of war.

Sibley awaited word that the hostages were safely separated into a conciliatory camp before giving the order to march from Wood Lake. His letter to three dissident chiefs explained the delay: "I feared that if I advanced my troops before you could make your arrangements the war party would murder the prisoners."[82]

Sibley also may have had an unexpressed rationale for holding his troops back at this stage: to prevent a vengeful massacre by his own men. One soldier described the mood: "The impetuous and indignant soldiers, after what their eyes had beheld in the region where the whites had been murdered, were determined to annihilate the [Dakota] camp, and it was almost impossible to restrain them, especially Company A, of the Sixth Minnesota, which had suffered so severely at Birch Coolie."[83] Charles Flandrau, in his history, said, "The desire of the troops to attack and punish these savages was intense."[84] Some of these men, while defending Fort Ridgely, had taken a formal pledge "upon the altar of the Eternal God" to "prosecute a war of utter extermination of the entire Sioux race" should they survive the Indians' onslaught.[85] With or without orders, these still-raw volunteers were bent on killing Indians.

Accepting the likelihood that a headlong charge into the Indian camp would result in the death of many of the captives, other soldiers expressly favored a deceit-and-carnage approach: "Many of our men insisted that Col. Sibley would be justifiable in making any treaty he could to obtain the captives, and when that was done, kill all the Indians, men, women, and children." To those who might blanch at the notion of killing children, one trooper quoted the notorious Indian fighter, Col. William Harney, that "nits make lice."[86]

On September 25 Sibley ordered his men to recommence their march toward the Dakota camp without haste, so as to prevent a captive-risking clash with hostile bands. His measured approach gave the Dakotas ample time to contemplate their two main options: surrender to Sibley or flee beyond Minnesota's western boundary. We know from later developments that a considerable number of Dakota men who were implicated in the killings of white noncombatants chose to stay behind, though unknown numbers fled westward. Why did some men who knew they might fall on the "punishment" side of Sibley's peace equation surrender nonetheless?

Bearing in mind that the eastern bands were woodland hunters with little knowledge of either the terrain or hunting haunts on the western prairies, some members concluded that their entire families would starve if they left. Missionary Thomas Williamson later explained that such men had given themselves up despite their belief that they would be executed, believing that "though we may die our wives and children will live."[87] Judging from later comments, it appears that there was also some genuine intercultural confusion about who among the Dakotas had "murdered" whites. A warrior who stood back and fired shots while others rushed in to attack with tomahawks and spears might not have viewed himself as having made a "kill," even if his bullets were the actual cause of the victim's death. Similarly, if two or more Dakotas shot simultaneously at the same intended victim, it made no difference under white principles of justice that only one person had pulled the fatal trigger; all shooters would have been equally guilty of murder. Today, such long-established legal concepts are still confusing to nonlawyers, so it is likely that the Dakotas, too, were unsure about which actions might subject them to Sibley's punishment. White law defined as murder many acts that did not qualify as Dakota "kills." The opposite was also true: many "kills" in Indian terms, such as the touching of a dead enemy, did not amount to murder in white eyes.

Some Dakota men who had killed civilians considered surrender at the urging of their leaders. Ironically, the chiefs of Dakota bands whose rank-and-file warriors committed some of the worst massacres were oriented toward the peace faction. Both Wabasha and Wakute, the Dakota leaders with whom Godfrey and his Indian relatives were affiliated, intended to surrender and urged their followers to do likewise. Finally, it is likely that some Dakotas who had killed white settlers believed they would not be punished because they left no witnesses to their deeds. As is true in almost any comparable situation, some knew they were guilty but believed that no one could prove it.

But, at least for some of the Dakotas who had joined in the massacre at Milford, the fact that few whites survived to give evidence against them would provide no solace. Their decision not to kill Joseph Godfrey would come back to haunt them.

NOTES ON CHAPTER 4

1. Heard, *History of the Sioux War*, 191.
2. See Godfrey's trial record, trial 1, Dakota Trials Records ("were all murdered"). All citations to the 1862 trial records, unless otherwise indicated, are from three rolls of National Archives microfilm of the 1862 trials, in my collection. The original trial records are found in the Center for Legislative Archives, U.S. Senate Records, National Archives. In this book the trial microfilms are cited by the trial name of the defendant and his trial number. Occasionally, due to microfilm legibility and other issues, I reference the original records, which I have also reviewed.
3. Heard, *History of the Sioux War*, 191–92; Godfrey, trial 1, Dakota trials records.
4. Germans were often referred to as *Dutch*, an Anglicized version of *Deutsch* (German).
5. Heard, *History of the Sioux War*, 192–93; Godfrey, trial 1, Dakota Trials Records.
6. Because the general history of the 1862 Dakota War is the subject of so many readily available books, this chapter does not contain extensive footnotes to document well-established aspects of the story of the war. For readers seeking a basic history, see Folwell, *History of Minnesota*, vol. 2; Carley, *Dakota War of 1862*; and Anderson and Woolworth, *Through Dakota Eyes*.
7. See Folwell, *History of Minnesota*, 2:393–400, appendix 9, for the woeful history of the wrongs done to the Dakotas in the 1858 treaties.
8. Thomas J. Galbraith's report, in *Report of Commissioner of Indian Affairs for 1863*, 286; italics in original.
9. Bachman, "Death of Ernst Dietrich," 17–19; *New Ulm Pioneer*, August 16, 1862 (from Brown County Historical Society); Nix, *Sioux Uprising*, 83.
10. See Anderson, *Little Crow*, 139–40. More pacific chiefs, such as Wabasha and Wakute, had even less influence during the hostilities.
11. Victim lists and data used in this chapter have been compiled using information gathered by Marion Satterlee: "List of the People Killed in the Sioux Indian War of 1862," MHS (1914 list); "Authentic List of the Victims of the Indian Massacre and War 1862 to 1865," MHS, (1919 list); and Satterlee, *Outbreak and Massacre*. Folwell, who also relied on Satterlee as his principal source of data on white victims, credited Satterlee's efforts as being "so nearly complete that few if any additions are likely to be made." Folwell, *History of Minnesota*, 2:392. Satterlee's lists provide names, ages, and the dates and locations of killings, but, because Satterlee did not count a casualty unless he had a source record, his methodology almost certainly understates the total number of killings. By comparing Satterlee's data with the known information about captives, one can also readily determine the Dakotas' different killing patterns at different locations, a subject that has largely been ignored in the literature. Captive lists are from NA, RG 393, Dept. of NW, 1862–65, Headquarters, E3449, pt. 1, Unentered Letters; and Satterlee, *Outbreak and Massacre*, 90–94.

12. The misconception that the Dakotas mostly took white women and children as captives rather than killing them is often repeated in the war literature. Folwell may have given rise to this error when he said the Dakotas "shot the men, made captives of the women, and indifferently butchered the children or let them follow their mothers." *History of Minnesota*, 2:111. Anderson and Woolworth embraced this notion and carried it a step further: "The Dakota warriors almost always killed the men and carried women and children into captivity." *Through Dakota Eyes*, 69. Carley is more accurate: "In some instances, whole families were wiped out, while in others the men were shot and the women and children either killed or taken prisoner." *Dakota War of 1862*, 21.
13. Compare Satterlee victim lists with lists of captives in NA, RG 393, Dept. of NW, 1862–65, Headquarters, E3449, pt. 1, Unentered Letters.
14. Godfrey testified that he was among a band of about fifteen Dakotas that left the reservation, but it appears that the number of attackers swelled to about thirty to forty between that point and the late-afternoon attack on the Patoille wagon. Godfrey, trial 1, Dakota Trials Records; Heard, *History of the Sioux War*, 193. An eyewitness to the ambush on the recruiting party estimated that twenty to thirty Indians were involved. *New Ulm Review*, September 12, 1946. Max Zeller was fatally shot at Milford when he stepped out of his house to give the Dakotas some bread. See [Schilling], "Nine Year Old Girl's Experiences," 9–10.
15. One of the Massopust girls was reported to have been beheaded. See Satterlee, "Indian Massacre in Brown County," 2–3. The spelling of the family's name varies in historical accounts; *Massopust* is taken from the spelling adopted by descendants.
16. Three-year-old Magdelena Mey, found alive by Sheriff Roos's posse, bore the tomahawk's "ugly scar across her forehead" until her death sixty-six years later. See *Brown County Journal*, July 27, 1928, reporting the death of Lena May Frappler, daughter of Sebastian May.
17. Three of the children of Anton Henle, the owner of the Travelers' Home, were killed, though his wife managed to run to safety. Martin Henle, age twelve, became a virtual poster boy for Indian brutality as he, severely slashed from repeated sword swipes, was transported via New Ulm and St. Peter to St. Paul. See *St. Paul Pioneer and Democrat*, August 26–27, 1862, and *St. Paul Press*, August 26, 1862. Martin died in St. Paul two weeks after the Milford killings. *St. Paul Pioneer and Democrat*, September 3, 1862. See also Satterlee, *Outbreak and Massacre*, 40–41. The "horribly mutilated" Joseph Messmer was the man spotted at the side of the road by the recruiting party. Satterlee, "Indian Massacre in Brown County," 3. He died on August 19.
18. Godfrey, trial 1, Dakota Trials Records; Heard, *History of the Sioux War*, 194–95.
19. *The American Heritage Dictionary* defines massacre as "the act or an instance of killing a number of human beings indiscriminately and cruelly"; the *Merriam-Webster Dictionary*, "killing a number of usually helpless or unresisting human beings under circumstances of atrocity or cruelty." Places at which thirteen or more people were massacred during the 1862 war include Milford (forty-eight victims), Middle Creek (forty-three), Beaver Creek (twenty-nine), Sacred Heart (twenty-six), Leavenworth (twenty-three), Norway Lake (twenty-two), Lake Shetek (seventeen), and Jackson County (thirteen). A total of 221 whites were killed at these locations, while only 1 Dakota warrior is known to have been slain (at Lake Shetek) during these massacres. See Satterlee's 1919 victim list, "Authentic List of the Victims of the Indian Massacre and War 1862 to 1865," MHS, which sets forth known victims by locations of killings.
20. Godfrey, trial 1, Dakota Trials Records. Godfrey testified that "all the Indians got drunk" at Travelers' Home.

21. Dietz, "Henry Behnke"; Fridley, Kellett, and Holmquist, *Flandrau and the Defense of New Ulm*, 34.
22. Heard, *History of the Sioux War*, 196–97; Godfrey's testimony in trial of Wazekootay, trial 213, Dakota Trials Records. In their warfare with the Ojibwes, the Dakotas had followed the practice of tearing the clothes from female victims. See Frazer, *Iron Face*, 7–8. It is likely that this practice was misinterpreted by whites in 1862 as proof of sexual assault, but the raping of female victims at the scene of attack was not a Dakota custom.
23. "Reminiscences of Mary Schwandt Schmidt as told to Mrs. Edna Sandford Ward," 1913, 23, and "The Story of My Captivity," October 30, 1935, 3–4 (three men killed in Patoille attack), both in Schwandt Schmidt Papers, MHS, M581.
24. Heard, *History of the Sioux War*, 198, quoting Godfrey.
25. Account by Schwandt Schmidt *in St. Paul Pioneer Press*, May 12, 1912.
26. Pond, *Dakota or Sioux in Minnesota*, 129.
27. Schwandt testimony in Godfrey, trial 1, Dakota Trials Records. Also see Schwandt Schmidt, "The Story of My Captivity," October 30, 1935, 4 ("demon"), and "Reminiscences of Mary Schwandt Schmidt as told to Mrs. Edna Sandford Ward," 1913, 23 ("sweetest voice"), both in Schwandt Schmidt Papers, MHS. In her 1913 account Schwandt also implies that Godfrey was wearing a string of victims' scalps, a claim never mentioned in her trial testimony or any of her numerous earlier versions of her story. Schwandt appears to have embellished some of her later accounts. The idea that she saw Godfrey wearing human scalps but told neither the court nor anyone else about it for more than fifty years is illogical, not credible, and inconsistent with other evidence. Mattie Williams, another eyewitness, made no such claim. Relatively few scalps were taken from whites in 1862. For these reasons, this claim by Schwandt is not included in the text.
28. Schwandt Schmidt, "The Story of My Captivity," October 30, 1935, 5, Schwandt Schmidt Papers, MHS. The first account attributed to Schwandt essentially claimed that she had been gang-raped. Bryant, *History of the Great Massacre*, 340. The fact that she gave no trial testimony that she was raped raises doubts about whether Bryant either misunderstood her statements or added his own interpretations to her story. Schwandt's many later accounts not only omit any claims that she was sexually attacked but explain her whereabouts and treatment in ways that appear to be inconsistent with such assaults. Because of these uncertainties, the possibility that Schwandt was sexually assaulted is not mentioned in the text.
29. Schwandt Schmidt, "The Story of My Captivity," October 30, 1935, 7, Schwandt Schmidt Papers, MHS (Tazoo was "ugly looking, and horribly pockmarked"). In the trials Tazoo was convicted of rape and also of aiding in the murder of Patoille and Mary Anderson. Tazoo, trial 4, Dakota Trials Records. Later claims that Williams had been gang-raped would appear to have no foundation in fact. Compare the gang-rape claims by Minnesota senator Morton Wilkinson (obviously referring to Mattie Williams as one such victim) with the trial transcripts. Contrary to Wilkinson's assertions on the Senate floor that Williams had identified her multiple rapists before Sibley's court, she named only one man: Tazoo. For Wilkinson's claim, see *Congressional Globe*, 42nd Congress, December 5, 1862, 13.
30. Pond, *Dakota or Sioux in Minnesota*, 129.
31. Ibid., 127.
32. Carley, *Dakota War of 1862*, 16.
33. Pond, *Dakota or Sioux in Minnesota*, 128–29.
34. Ibid., 130.

35. Ibid., 133–34.
36. Testimony by David Faribault Sr. (mixed-blood trader) and Mary Woodbury (mixed-blood captive), in Godfrey, trial 1, Dakota Trials Records; Sweet, "Mrs. J. E. DeCamp Sweet's Narrative," 366.
37. Recently Dakota scholar Elden Lawrence claimed that Godfrey was given the name Many Kills due to the number of men sent to the gallows by virtue of his postwar testimony in trials against the Indians. Lawrence, *Peace Seekers*, 135. This assertion is mistaken, for two main reasons: (1) Godfrey, the first man to be tried, was identified as Otakle (Many Kills) in the caption of his case, at a time when no one knew he would give state's evidence; and (2) Godfrey himself explained during the trials that he was given his name as a consequence of his presence among those who killed the settlers at Milford. Godfrey was named for his involvement in killing whites, not for the "killing" of Indians through testimony.
38. Sweet, "Mrs. J. E. DeCamp Sweet's Narrative," 367–68.
39. In addition to the specific threats to kill him on August 18, Godfrey testified that his life was again threatened on the way to the Fort Ridgely. Godfrey testimony, trial 1, Dakota Trials Records.
40. Theodore Carter to Agent, Santee Indians, August 18, 1909, Carter Papers, MHS, box 2.
41. Satterlee, "Comments on the Trials of Dakota Indians," Folwell Papers, MHS, box 80: "It is not probable that he [Godfrey] ever killed anybody, his 'Nigger' prattle to the contrary." Elsewhere Satterlee discounted reports that Godfrey was the "devil incarnate" that early histories made him out to be: "As a matter of fact [he] was a 'scared stiff nigger.'" Satterlee, *Outbreak and Massacre*, 39.
42. Heard, *History of the Sioux War*, quotes Godfrey as saying he had one child, but a Dakota source refers to a second child. The text therefore refers to two children, though it is possible that the second child was born later in 1862. See discussion in chapter 12.
43. See NA, RG 75, E529, Miscellaneous Sioux Reserve Papers (marriage of William Barnes to Sarah Thompson and birth of their daughter, Mary Elizabeth Barnes, in 1855); 1860 Minnesota census, Shakopee, Scott County (William Barnes, age sixty-one, born in England, shown with his wife, Sarah, and their two children, Mary E., five, and William, two, listed immediately beneath the James Thompson family with son George, sixteen. Sarah is erroneously double-counted in this census, both as Barnes's wife and as Thompson's daughter). William Barnes's whereabouts after 1860 are unknown; he may have died before 1862, or he may not have accompanied his wife to the agency that summer. In the first list of captives freed at Camp Release, "Mrs. Sarah Barnes, of Shakopee" is named (but not her husband), along with her three children: May [*sic*] Elizabeth (7), William Henry (4), and Lucy Emma (2). Sarah's brother, George Thompson (18), is also on that list. See NA, RG 393, Dept. of NW, 1862–65, Headquarters, E3187, pt. 1, Unentered Letters.
44. Only one mixed-blood man, Francois LaBathe, was killed by the Dakotas. Satterlee, *Outbreak and Massacre*, 15.
45. George Spencer was the only white man living on the Lower Reservation to be taken captive by the Dakotas and survive the war. He was grievously wounded on August 18 but was then taken under the protection of Chaska, or Wakinyantawa, his Indian koda (an unusual relationship, similar to a blood brother). Samuel Brown's account lists three métis men who also survived captivity. See Anderson and Woolworth, *Through Dakota Eyes*, 225, 265n3.

46. George C. Tanner, "Miss West's Narrative," in "Indian Missions—for the Women's Auxiliary," manuscript, n.d., Episcopal Church Diocese of Minnesota Papers, MHS. See also Heard, *History of the Sioux War*, 67–68; and Satterlee, *Outbreak and Massacre*, 38. Taylor's death dealt a major setback to historians' efforts to document the role played by St. Paul's black community in aiding slaves brought to the region. Taylor must have known a great deal about the slaves brought to Minnesota by army officers and private citizens during the 1850s and about efforts to help them flee to freedom. But that crucial knowledge was lost when he was slain on August 18. Taylor's nephew, Joseph Farr, gave an interview in the late 1800s that is the best single source of information about Minnesota's Underground Railroad. But Farr's account makes it clear that William Taylor would have been far more knowledgeable on the subject. See Swanson, "Joseph Farr Remembers."
47. The untold story of the Thompson family's involvement in the Dakota War is pieced together from several sources. (1) Thompson's trial testimony, trial 362, Dakota Trials Records, suggests that his wife and daughter remained behind when hostilities broke out, but that Thompson was not at his house when the Dakotas came to kill him. (2) The lists of people who took refuge in Fort Ridgely during the war include "Jones Thompson, 57, born in Virginia, Redwood, wife and 6 children prisoners." Norman K. Culver, list of Fort Ridgely survivors, MHS, entry 200. James Thompson was born in Virginia and was approximately fifty-seven to sixty-three (his age differs in various census accounts). "Redwood" is another name for the Lower Agency. Carrie R. Zeman, who prepared an analysis of Culver's list, noted the discrepancy of "Jones" Thompson saying he had a wife and children in captivity although "they are not listed among captives freed at Camp Release or on Satterlee's compiled list of deaths." Zeman, *Population of Fort Ridgely*, appx. C. These inconsistencies are explainable once one realizes that Thompson's full-blood Dakota wife would not have been included on a list of captive whites and mixed-bloods and that his daughter, Sarah, and her three children were listed under her married name, Barnes. Thompson's eighteen-year-old son, George, was listed as a captive. NA, RG 393, Dept. of NW, 1862–65, Headquarters, E3449, pt. 1, Unentered Letters (published in *St. Paul Pioneer and Democrat*, October 3, 1862). (3) A December 25, 1862, letter from Jane Williamson to Mary Riggs, Riggs Family Papers, MHS, box 1, offers further proof that "Jim Thompson's" son was with his mother during the war. (4) A letter from Capt. John Kennedy to Henry Sibley, October 10, 1862, refers to the transport of "half breeds and negroes" (Thompson's family) from Camp Release to a point near Yellow Medicine on or about October 5. The Thompson family members were in a wagon apparently headed for Fort Ridgely (where they were presumably reunited with James Thompson). See Court Martial of John Kennedy, NA, RG 153, Records of Judge Advocate General, Courts Martial file no. KK 516, exhibit B. (5) Notes in the handwriting of Thomas S. Williamson, written sometime between 1865 and 1868, indicate that Makanahtakay (trial 362) claimed to Williamson, years after his trial, that Thompson's family were his "near relatives" and that he came to the Thompson home to protect them, not to kill Thompson. Stephen R. Riggs Papers, MHS, box 2.
48. The attempt to kill Thompson is recorded (albeit as hearsay testimony) in James Thompson's trial evidence against Makanahtakay, trial 362, Dakota Trials Records.
49. Jane Williamson to Mary Riggs, December 25, 1862, Riggs Family Papers, MHS, box 1. I have added some punctuation, which Williamson used sparingly.
50. Satterlee, *Outbreak and Massacre*, 20–22.

51. Godfrey's testimony, trial 1, Dakota Trials Records. Godfrey said he remained at home for two days after the Milford assault, and thus he was not at the first New Ulm battle on August 19.
52. Testimony of Godfrey, trial 1, and David Faribault Jr., trial 134, Dakota Trials Records.
53. Though it is sometimes claimed that the Dakotas targeted Germans and not other immigrant groups, the Kandiyohi killings suggest otherwise. It would be more accurate to say that the Dakotas killed white settlers of all ethnicities who happened to live near the Lower Agency. The claim, for example, that Swedes were spared because they had treated the Dakotas more kindly than the Germans is not borne out by the victim data. In Kandiyohi County Swedes represented about 35 percent of the population, but they made up about 70 percent of the Dakotas' victims. Few Swedes or Norwegians were killed in the main killing areas (Brown and Renville Counties) because virtually none lived there. I am not suggesting that Swedes were targeted, but these killing patterns help to dispel the notion that the ethnicity of immigrant groups was a significant factor in the Dakotas' decisions about whom to kill. The predominant Dakota cry was "kill the whites," and no ethnic group was spared. Contrast Lawrence, *Peace Seekers*, 47–49, with 1860 census data for Kandiyohi (Monongalia), Brown, and Renville Counties and Satterlee, *Outbreak and Massacre*, 55–58.
54. Flandrau, *History of Minnesota,* 278–80. Flandrau, in his much later confession about the whiskey-poisoning incident, which he then conceded was "cowardly," claimed that he had had a change of heart and ordered that the tainted whiskey be poured out. Two other sources, however, suggest that the poisoned whiskey was left behind. See *Mankato Semi-Weekly Record,* August 30, 1862 (refers to poisoned whiskey, sugar, and flour, which, "we regret to say," the Dakotas did not consume); and account of John G. Hicks, Hennepin County Historical Society, Minneapolis, 4 (claims Indian scouts saw the whiskey being poisoned and thus did not drink it).
55. *St. Paul Daily Union,* December 22, 1862 ("Mrs. Didrich and four children" listed in pre-Christmas appeal to the public to render assistance to twenty-three Dakota War widows and sixty-one children who were then living in St. Paul attics and cellars and "receiving aid from the State refugee fund").
56. Heard, *History of the Sioux War,* 201.
57. Godfrey testimony, trial 1, Dakota Trials Records.
58. Victim data is from Satterlee, *Outbreak and Massacre,* 63–67.
59. Sibley to Malmros, September 13, 1862, *Minnesota in the Civil and Indian Wars, 1861–1865* (hereafter, *MCIW*), 2:228–29.
60. The exchange of messages between Sibley and Little Crow is found in Heard, *History of the Sioux War,* 147–49. See also Folwell, *History of Minnesota,* 2:171–72.
61. Wabashaw and Taopee to Sibley, September 10, 1862, in Heard, *History of the Sioux War,* 149.
62. Sibley to Wabashaw and Taopee, September 12, 1862, in Heard, *History of the Sioux War,* 150.
63. Sibley to Malmros, September 13, 1862, *MCIW*, 2:228–29.
64. Sibley letter, September 13, 1862, *MCIW*, 2:229.

65. Speed Butler to William Butler, October 5, 1862, Gen. John Pope letters, Chicago Historical Society. Pope wrote wild and brooding letters after his arrival in Minnesota, suggesting that Lincoln was no longer in control of the government and was about to be removed in a putsch. See Pope to Richard Yates, September 21, 1862; Pope to William Butler, September 22 and 26, 1862; and Pope to Halleck, September 30 and October 20, 1862, ibid. See also Pope to Horton, November 1, 1862, Pope Letters, New York Historical Society, War, 1861–65, box 5, MS Dept.
66. *Mankato Semi-Weekly Record,* September 20, 1862, reporting Pope speech given in La Crosse, Wisconsin.
67. On September 19, 1862, the *St. Paul Press* reported that the extension of the telegraph line to the hotel would permit Pope to communicate "directly with the War Department at Washington."
68. Pope "proposes . . . extermination of the Sioux race," *Mankato Independent,* September 20, 1862; "Extermination is Pope's policy," *Mankato Semi-Weekly Record,* September 20, 1862; "This officer [Pope] . . . intends to exterminate the vermin," *St. Cloud Democrat,* September 25, 1862 (from Stearns History Museum).
69. Initially, Secretary of War Edwin Stanton promised Pope that his demand for ten thousand troops would be granted, but further consideration in Washington led to the conclusion that such a large military allocation was not necessary. See Stanton to Pope, September 18, 1862, NA, RG 393, E3450, pt. 1, Telegrams Received, Department of NW.
70. See Pope to Stanton, September 29, 1862, NA, RG 393, E3436, pt. 1, LS, Letters Sent and Received, Department of NW, Headquarters.
71. *The Minnesota State News,* September 13, 1862, noted that Pope's arrival "will relieve the State of much of the burden and cost of the Indian war."
72. See Big Eagle's account and Victor Renville's account in Anderson and Woolworth, *Through Dakota Eyes,* 234–39.
73. Casualty figures from Satterlee, *Outbreak and Massacre,* 71–72 (seven white and fourteen Dakota deaths), as supplemented by Satterlee's list of "Dakota Indians Killed in the Outbreak of 1862," in "Dakota Indians Hanged at Mankato, Dec. 26, 1862," MHS (seventeen Dakota deaths).
74. Sibley to Ramsey, September 23, 1862, *MCIW,* 2:240–42; Pope to Sibley, September 28, 1862, *MCIW,* 2:257.
75. Samuel J. Brown's recollections in Anderson and Woolworth, *Through Dakota Eyes,* 223.

76. Word of Sibley's promotion reached Minnesota via a September 29 telegram to Pope from General-in-Chief Henry Halleck. Published versions of this message report that Sibley was promoted for his "judicious fight" at the Wood Lake battle, but the original copy shows that the more logical phrase, "Indian fight," was actually used. Compare NA, RG 393, E3450, pt. 1, Telegrams Received, Department of NW (original) with *MCIW*, 2:258 (incorrect copy). Pope sent news of the appointment in a dispatch to Sibley on October 2. NA, RG 393, E3436, pt. 1, LS, Letters Sent and Received, Department of NW, Headquarters. Though Sibley at one time apparently believed that Pope was responsible for his promotion to brigadier general (Sibley to Pope, October 7, 1862, *MCIW*, 2:267), he was almost certainly mistaken. There is no evidence that Pope recommended Sibley for the post; Pope, at the same time, was touting his own candidate for promotion to brigadier general, Capt. A. D. Nelson. See Pope to Stanton, September 22, 1862, telegram, NA, RG 393, E3436, pt. 1, LS, Letters Sent and Received, Department of NW, Headquarters. On October 6 Halleck replied by telegram to Pope, in effect informing him that his candidate could not be promoted: "no more brigadier generals can be assigned to your department." *War of the Rebellion*, 13:714–15. Pope's disdain for Sibley's lack of military experience and for his Indian-trading background makes it even more unlikely that he would have recommended Sibley. Finally, the content of a letter Pope sent to Sibley on October 6 was so condemning that it is virtually impossible to reconcile with the notion that Pope might have supported Sibley's promotion. Pope to Sibley, October 6, 1862, NA, RG 393, E3436, pt. 1, LS, Letters Sent and Received, Department of NW, Headquarters.
77. The analysis of white deaths follows the approach of Folwell's history, which in turn was based on Marion Satterlee's lists ("List of the People Killed in the Sioux Indian War of 1862" [1914 list]; and "Authentic List of the Victims of the Indian Massacre and War 1862 to 1865," [1919 list], both at MHS). See Folwell, *History of Minnesota*, appendix 8, 2:391–93, including illustration.
78. Satterlee is also the best source for Dakota casualties. See Satterlee, *Outbreak and Massacre*, 107–8. His list includes thirty Indians, but one, an infant, was killed six weeks after the cessation of hostilities and is discussed in chapter 9.
79. The Satterlee lists show that more than one hundred white children age sixteen or younger were killed during the conflict. The count of white women killed also comes from Satterlee's lists. I am aware of no source suggesting that any Dakota woman or child was killed by whites during the period extending from August 17 until about November 10. Killings of Dakota women and children, starting in November, are discussed in chapter 9.
80. Folwell, relying on Satterlee's lists, concluded that 357 whites were "killed in massacre" and 90 were killed in "military operations." Folwell, *History of Minnesota*, 2:392. I believe that Folwell's "massacre" figures were about 15 percent too high, mainly because he included some civilians killed in battle-like settings as "massacre" victims. But Satterlee's overall statistics, based on victims whom he was able to identify by name, probably significantly understate the total number of both white and Dakota victims.
81. Sibley to Tatankanazin, September 24, 1862, *MCIW*, 2:250. See also Sibley's similar letter written the same day to three Dakota leaders. Sibley to Mazakatame et al., September 24, 1862, *MCIW*, 2:249–50.
82. Sibley to Mazakatame et al., September 24, 1862, *MCIW*, 2:249–50.
83. Connolly, *Minnesota Massacre*, 144.
84. Flandrau, *History of Minnesota*, 174.

85. See "Let the Sioux Race Be Annihilated," *Stillwater Messenger,* September 2, 1862.
86. Heard, *History of the Sioux War,* 187.
87. Williamson to Griffith, April 10, 1863, NMM, MHS, box 21. Williamson applied this principle to the relatively small proportion of Dakota men who were later hanged at Mankato. Such men, according to Williamson, saw the whites as "merciful" for sparing their families, even as they faced the gallows themselves.

CHAPTER 5

Camp Release

Godfrey, like many Dakotas, decided to take his chances with white justice. As Little Crow and others who chose not to surrender headed for points beyond Minnesota's boundaries, Godfrey, his father-in-law, and their families all stayed in the Dakota camp to await Sibley's arrival.

By September 24 mixed-blood messenger Joseph Campbell had delivered Sibley the news that most of the hostages were safe, and Sibley promised the Dakota chiefs, "I shall move to-morrow, so that you may expect to see me very soon."[1] With a moderately brisk march on the twenty-fifth, Sibley's forces could readily have covered the twenty-four-mile distance from Wood Lake to the captives in a day. Instead they marched less than halfway, stopping to construct a camp for the night near the site of the Indian mission known as Hazelwood.

Indian scouts from the "friendly" camp, impatient for Sibley to arrive, watched with incredulity as the troops dug sentry pits and erected their tents as though they were on a military exercise. And then, to cap off a relatively leisurely day, Sibley ordered a grand dress parade. It has been suggested that this spit-and-polish drilling while the captives awaited their salvation was designed to "impress" the Indians or to "raise the soldiers' morale."[2] But Sibley's hotheaded army was more in need of a tedious diversion akin to a cold shower than an ego-boosting parade. His worry that the men would run amok once they spotted the Dakotas is the most likely explanation for this military spectacle.³

The second half of the army's deliberate, disciplined march ended by noon on the twenty-sixth. The Dakota tipis were clustered on the high prairie about half a mile south of the Minnesota River, opposite the mouth of the Chippewa River. Sibley directed an approach route that skirted the Indian camp as far to the north as the river would permit. To the handful of soldiers desperately hoping to learn the fate of wives or other family members, the delays seemed interminable.

Things were no less tense among the captives. Late on the last morning of their captivity, young Pauline Urban and her friend, twelve-year-old Minnie Buce, scanned the plateau to the east for the long-awaited soldiers. "Look at the stars!" Pauline exclaimed, as the parade-shined bayonets sparkled in the late-morning sun on the distant flatlands even before the infantry columns came into view. Minnie had been snatched into captivity near her Middle Creek home on August 18, the same day she witnessed her orphaning. She had watched in horror as a Dakota man fired both barrels of a shotgun at close range into her father, who was cradling baby Bertha in his arms. The same Indian then promptly killed her mother and two-year-old Caroline, who was sitting in her mother's lap.⁴

But the captives' joy at sighting the glistening bayonets of their saviors turned to puzzlement when the army bypassed them almost half a mile to the north and then, incredibly, encamped to dig latrines and hoist tents before making any effort to approach the Dakotas or their prisoners. Again, Sibley was taking no chances either that the Indians would flee in fright or that his troops would wreak undisciplined revenge. And as he occupied his men with humdrum military tasks, he sent a message to the captives, ordering them to remain in their tipis until he came to fetch them.⁵ To avoid any miscalculation of his resolve or his power over the Indians, Sibley placed his howitzers along the southern edge of the new camp, aiming them at the densest clusters of Dakota lodges.⁶

The Indians had garlanded their 150 tipis with white cloths of truce, some of them strips torn from plundered bedsheets. Many of the white women were still wearing the Indian clothes their captors had compelled them to don. Others underwent a sartorial transformation when Indians pulled stolen settlers' dresses from piles of booty.[7] Sarah Wakefield, the plump and mercurial wife of the Upper Agency physician, was given a gingham dress she recognized as one she had helped to make: it had belonged to "Mrs. Dr. Humphrey," wife of the Lower Agency physician, who had been killed with her family while attempting to flee to Fort Ridgely.[8]

At 2:00 p.m., Sibley, his aides, and just two companies of soldiers marched to the tempo of drums and fifes to the clearing at the center of the Dakota camp, where they formed a hollow square of uniformed men.[9] Sibley summoned the Dakota chiefs and headmen to this enclosure and, when they had assembled, told them of his "determination" to pursue all "guilty parties."[10] He repeated the murderers-will-be-punished theme of his earlier written messages, assuring the Indians that "no harm" would come to the rest of them.[11] Among the Dakotas, there was not a murmur of dissent to this announcement: the prosecution of murderers was fully expected. Indeed, the principal Lower Sioux chiefs, Wabasha and Wakute, later emphasized that they would have been willing to "deliver up" the warriors who had committed murders, had Sibley only asked them to do so.[12]

Several of the chiefs responded with their own speeches, summarized by Sibley in his dispatch to Pope the next day: "They [the chiefs] severely condemned the war party and denied any participation in their proceedings and gave me assurance that they would not have dared to come and shake my hand if their own were stained with the blood of the whites." Sibley apparently made but one immediate demand of the Dakotas: to deliver the captives to him "instantly."[13] As the captives were accompanied to the scene of their deliverance by their Dakota protectors, hands were shaken and the Indians' names were taken. Sarah Wakefield introduced Wechankwashtodopee, also known as Chaska, to Sibley, effusively praising him for his kind treatment of her.[14]

The sun was nearing the horizon when Sibley returned to his separate camp with the freed captives. At his direction, Stephen R. Riggs, the expedition's chaplain, prepared a list of those who had been brought over to the soldiers' camp, which was promptly dispatched to General Pope.[15] Riggs was ideally suited to the task, for he had labored in Minnesota for twenty-five years as a missionary to the Dakotas. At the outset of the war he and his family had escaped via a grueling flight across the prairie from their home at Hazelwood above the Upper Sioux Agency. Riggs's acceptance of Sibley's invitation to serve as spiritual counselor to the soldiers sent out to subdue the Dakotas was a decision that, inevitably, was fraught with a long series of conflict-of-interest dilemmas. Riggs's sympathies were continually torn between those of his erstwhile Dakota parishioners and the functions that Sibley asked him to perform. By straddling both sides, he endeared himself to few.[16]

Riggs's list of captives gave the names of 111 people: 40 women, 70 children, and 1 man. It included their places of residence and, in most cases, the ages of the children. He and Sibley noted that ninety-one of those named were "pure whites."[17] Susan Frenier Brown, the wife of former Indian agent Maj. Joseph R. Brown, her children, and others in the Brown mixed-blood family made up twelve of the twenty mixed-bloods on the list. Ultimately the captives list was expanded to include the names of more than 100 whites and about 150 mixed-bloods.[18]

Though Riggs's initial list of released captives was widely published in the press and was greeted with great exultation, no one noted then (or later) that five of those enumerated were the African American descendants of former slave James Thompson. Of course, none of them fit neatly into the "pure white or half-breeds" paradigm. Sarah Thompson Barnes, her three young children, and her brother, George Thompson, all were counted as captives.[19] Thompson's wife, Mary Thompson, almost certainly accompanied her family when they evacuated the Indian camp on September 26, but her name was omitted on Riggs's list because she, as a full-blood Dakota, did not fall within the requisite racial typologies.

To claim that the Thompson family members were "captured" by the Dakotas, as some have done, is probably erroneous.[20] In all likelihood, they simply remained throughout the conflict with Sarah and George's mother, in the company of her relatives. As we have seen, George was sought out to join the Indian soldiery. There is no evidence that any members of the Thompson family were harmed. They were never traumatized or forcibly seized by captors, as were Sarah Wakefield, Mary Schwandt, Mattie

Williams, and many other white captives. The fact that they kept safe on the Indian side of the conflict, apparently without ill effects, affirms the wisdom of James Thompson's decision to seek sanctuary at Fort Ridgely while leaving behind everyone in his family who had any Indian blood.

Curiously, one white male survivor, George Spencer, was not included on Riggs's released captives list, most likely an oversight arising from the fact that he was lodged separately from the women.[21] Spencer was the only white man among the captives who entered the soldiers' camp on September 26.[22] He had been visiting the Lower Agency on August 18 and was one of the first to be shot. Grievously suffering from bullet wounds to his right arm, chest, and abdomen, Spencer was taken under the protection of his Indian koda (a kind of blood brother), Wakkeintawa, also known as Chaska. Spencer was the only white male taken into captivity by the Dakotas during the early, most bloody stage of the conflict. Spencer undoubtedly soon made Sibley aware that he credited Chaska with saving his life and nursing him during his recovery.[23]

At day's end Riggs noticed that a few whites known to have been taken captive were not on his tally. He was especially concerned about the absence of Josephine Huggins, the widow of Amos Huggins (killed near Lac Qui Parle on August 19). Amos was the son of Alexander Huggins, the man who had given Godfrey sanctuary when he fled from slavery. Josephine was reported to be with the amicably inclined band of Spirit Walker, some ninety miles to the west. Sibley readily consented when Riggs proposed that a party of four "reliable Indians" who would be known to Mrs. Huggins be sent to retrieve her and her children. Robert Hopkins, one of Riggs's Dakota parishioners, also named Chaska, was a member of this small, handpicked rescue band.[24] In fact, there were quite a few surrendering Dakotas who answered to the name Chaska, three of whom had a white advocate: Riggs for Hopkins, and Sarah Wakefield and George Spencer for their respective Dakota protectors. Confusion about the identities of the various men called Chaska would later result in tragedy for one of them.

For as long as Sibley remained near the Chippewa River, the Indians were kept in a separate encampment, which was vacated by those whites and mixed-bloods who considered themselves liberated. The men immediately dubbed the soldiers' encampment to the north Camp Release. Most but not all of the freed captives were overwhelmed with joy, and "tears ran down many cheeks."[25] Some of the younger white children, grown used to their Dakota mothers, had to be pried away with mutual tears.[26] Other youngsters were frightened by the din of the soldiers' cheering as they entered Camp Release.[27] Some expressed gratitude to the Dakotas who had saved and protected them; others told tales of abuse and fear. Some relished their first taste of "white cooking" in more than a month (a late lunch of applesauce and biscuits, followed by a dinner of rice, hardtack, meat, and coffee); others, including Sarah Wakefield, grumbled that the culinary presentments had been better on the Dakota side. Sleeping accommodations in army tents also met with differing opinions. Wakefield complained that the straw-and-blanket beds made her miss the comforts of tipi life.[28]

On the morning of September 27 those in the Dakota camp may have marveled at their fortunate circumstances. The vanquishing white soldiers had neither killed nor abused any Indians. Sibley seemed to accept their professions of friendship and the explanation that all the "bad Indians" had run away. Despite all the killings, he had been willing to shake the hands of their chiefs and of those who delivered captives. Aside from the removal of the white captives, the Indian camp was intact and unmolested. Sibley was making good on his word to protect them as a people and not to punish those who had not taken part in the murders of settlers.

Nor did this mood change the next day, when instructions were issued that no one was to depart from the Indian camp without a special permit from the commander. After this decree, "any Indian could come into this camp, but none ever got out."[29] Sibley also demanded that the Dakotas turn over the arms and ammunition stolen during the war. Military loot from the stores and government warehouses—guns, lead balls, and powder—was promptly brought forth.[30] But the Indians must have wondered at the narrowness of the demand: they were not required to relinquish their own guns, ammunition, or other weapons of war.

Even the arrests of Godfrey and fifteen other men over the next two days—September 27 and 28—were most likely comforting to some Dakotas. All along, Sibley had pledged to punish those guilty of murder. In a camp numbering about twelve hundred Indians and mixed-bloods, with about one hundred to two hundred fighting-age men, the orderly apprehension of only sixteen suspects shortly after the surrender was eminently reasonable, a minor police action.[31] Sibley's men were not making indiscriminate arrests, and the Indians could see that most of those seized were among the minority within their ranks who had killed white settlers. At this stage it appeared that Sibley was making a good-faith attempt to isolate and punish the worst offenders.

Once the sixteen suspects were in custody, there were no summary executions or corporal punishment. Instead, soldiers merely escorted the men over to the military camp, where they were manacled and held for trial. To the Dakotas, who were accustomed to meting out immediate retributive justice to their enemies without regard to individual guilt, such limited measures and delays may have been misread as signs of leniency. Relatives of the arrested men could still hope that the suspects might be freed once white justice had run its course.

The strongest expression of outrage at these early arrests came not from the Dakotas but from Sarah Wakefield, whose captor, Chaska, was among the sixteen detainees. Wakefield, who lobbied unremittingly for her protector, had reassured a "much frightened" Chaska on the twenty-seventh that she had received word from an officer that he "should be pardoned on account of his kindness to me and my children."[32] But he was soon taken to jail.

Likely few tears were shed when Godfrey was arrested. Rumor and fact swirled around the camp, averring that Godfrey was one of the worst culprits. He was reputed to have killed "more than any Indian," to have been the "most brutal in atrocity" and the "bravest and foremost in battle." To top it off, Godfrey had repeatedly bragged of his bloody deeds.[33] Within the ranks of freed captives, according to Wakefield, "every one knew [Godfrey] was guilty."[34] Among all those who had surrendered in the Indian camp, he became the "object of most bitter malediction."[35] A crescendo of enmity now spurred many soldiers to want to deal with "the negro" more summarily than Sibley intended: "These statements [about Godfrey] favored the natural prejudice against his color, to a white heart, and he would have been lynched, when we caught him with the Indians, at Camp Release, had the soldiers been permitted to act, as citizens would have acted."[36] Incarceration may have saved Godfrey's life, but it did not quench the continuing desire for lynching.

Determined to keep the lid on his cauldron of vengeful troops, Sibley issued an order on September 27 creating a military commission to try Godfrey and the other men being brought to a makeshift log jail. He initially appointed three of his most respected officers as judges: Col. William Crooks, Lt. Col. William R. Marshall, and Capt. Hiram Grant. Sibley, as he reported to Pope, ordered this commission to "sift the antecedents" of all the Indian men and mixed-bloods who had surrendered and to see that the guilty were "properly dealt with," adding, "I have no doubt we will find some."[37]

The "sifting" process began on the twenty-seventh, when Crooks and Marshall assembled the white women captives, announced the formation of the military court, and began interrogating potential witnesses. With Victorian obliqueness, the commissioners announced that any women who had "anything more of a private nature to relate" should speak privately with Reverend Riggs. A puzzled Sarah Wakefield did not at first grasp the point: rape victims were being invited to confer in confidence with a cleric.[38]

At this time (though not in connection with the rape inquiries) female captives came forward to point an accusatory finger at Godfrey. Painted for war, they said, he was among the Dakotas who attacked Patoille's fleeing wagon. And his open boasts to the Indians about killing many whites at Milford had been overheard by several potential witnesses.

The second day after the surrender, the scheme for Indian justice was fully in place. On September 28 Sibley's Order No. 55 expanded the membership of the military commission to five officers, adding Capt. Hiram S. Bailey and Lt. R. C. Olin. It also defined the scope and purposes of the commission: "A Military Commission . . . will convene . . . to try summarily the Mulatto, and Indians, or mixed bloods, who may be brought before them, by direction of the Col. Commanding and pass judgment upon them, if found guilty of murders or other outrages upon the whites, during the present state of hostilities of the Indians, the proceedings of the Commission to be returned to these Head Quarters immediately after their conclusion for the consideration of the Col. Commanding. The Commission will be governed in their proceedings by Military Law and Usage."[39] "The Mulatto," of course, was Godfrey.

Sibley's order specified the crimes to be tried before the commission as "murders or other outrages." That murder would be considered the main crime to be prosecuted was simply a fulfillment of Sibley's many previous messages and statements. But what did he intend to include within the broad and vague term "other outrages"? At the barest minimum, it encompassed rape, as evidenced by the immediate announcement that female captives could speak privately with Riggs about sexual abuses. "Outrages against women" was the most common euphemism for rape at the time, and the crime was a capital offense under both civil and military laws.

If Sibley's court limited its prosecutions to murder and rape, there was precedent under military law for its actions. During the Mexican-American War, Gen. Winfield Scott had used military commissions to try American adversaries for those offenses. Moreover, at a time when Union soldiers were being executed for rape, it would have been unthinkable for Sibley to omit that offense as perpetrated by an enemy.[40] But the term "other outrages" was not defined in Sibley's order, and only time would tell how far it would be stretched to cover other acts.

Sibley's order sculpted the basic shape of his new tribunal. The commission, using "military law and usage," was to act "summarily."[41] Later, Sibley likened the trials, as he envisioned them, to drumhead courts-martial, abbreviated in-the-field-of-battle trials whose hasty tenor implied conditions so extreme that the only flat surface available to the court was the head of a drum.[42] Whether a commission acted with extended deliberation or "summarily" depended mainly on the discretion of the commander in the field.

Use of a military commission was required because only mustered soldiers could be subjected to a court-martial. In times of war military commissions were used to try people who were not subject to the jurisdiction of a court-martial and to prosecute cases such as murder or rape that ordinarily would be heard by a civil court.⁴³ Such commissions were also occasionally used in the Civil War for cases that did not fit neatly into military justice categories. Union soldiers who murdered, raped, or robbed civilians were sometimes tried in this manner.⁴⁴ Sibley was the first commander to use a military commission to try Indians.

Sibley's Order No. 55 also reflected and enshrined the rigid racial cast imposed on the conflict. In addition to Godfrey, the "mulatto," the commission was directed to try "Indians" and "mixed-bloods" for crimes against "whites." Sibley simply could have ordered, without reference to race, that those persons suspected of crimes in the recent hostilities against Americans were to be tried. But his use of racial labels was entirely consistent with Minnesotans' view of the uprising as a race war. That he literally intended to limit the victim list to "whites" seems unlikely; it is entirely possible that Sibley was then unaware that a black man and a mixed-blood man had been slain. Whatever he knew, Sibley's choice of racial terms, not status- or conduct-driven language, deserves underscoring.

Sibley followed military practice for general courts-martial when appointing his commission. The sixty-fourth Article of War called for a court of from five to thirteen officers, with the highest ranking as president. All members were required to be commissioned officers.⁴⁵ The five members Sibley appointed would today be characterized as blue ribbon and bipartisan. Especially considering the remoteness of Camp Release, the military commission was a distinctive court. The ranking officer, thirty-year-old Col. William Crooks, commander of the Sixth Minnesota, had spent two years as a cadet at West Point and was one of the few frontier residents with formal military education. Moreover, Sibley had longstanding, close ties with Crooks's father, Ramsay Crooks, who had been his boss, mentor, and supporter in the American Fur Company starting in the 1820s. Colonel Crooks was both respected and affable, though no one ever accused him of being a deep thinker. He later was elected to serve in both houses of Minnesota's legislature.⁴⁶

Next to Sibley, Col. William Marshall was the most prominent Minnesotan among the soldiers on the expedition. Then thirty-six years old, Marshall had already served stints in both the Wisconsin and Minnesota territorial legislatures. He was among the founding leaders of Minnesota's Republican Party in 1855, placing him high in the opposite political camp from Sibley. Citing Marshall's ardent opposition to the extension of slavery, Folwell later gave him the highest encomium: "Minnesota had no citizen who more ardently loved justice and freedom." A successful St. Paul businessman, Marshall had founded the most important Republican newspaper in the state, the *St. Paul Press*, just a year before the war. He had already distinguished himself on the battlefield, commanding his Seventh Regiment at Wood Lake and, earlier, at Birch Coulee, relieving the men besieged there. His subsequent Civil War career took him to the heart of Mississippi, the Battle of Nashville, and the advance on Spanish Fort in Alabama, where he was wounded. For his service at Nashville, he was commissioned brevet brigadier general in 1865. At war's end, returning to Minnesota as a hero, Marshall immediately reentered the political fray and was nominated and elected as the state's governor, a post he held for two terms.[47]

The other members of the commission were competent, if not as distinguished. Capt. Hiram Grant's main claim to historical fame comes from his ill-fated selection of the campsite at Birch Coulee, plus his insistent quibbling later that he, not Maj. Joseph R. Brown, had been in command at that battle.[48] Capt. Hiram Bailey (no relation to Alexis Bailly) and twenty-two-year-old Lt. Rollin C. Olin rounded out the commission's membership. Though it is unclear what legal training he had, Olin was appointed to serve as the commission's judge advocate—its prosecutor. Olin later served as Sibley's acting assistant adjutant general and was thus the pipeline through which the commander corresponded with his subordinate officers.[49] Both the caliber of the writing in these letters and the fact that Sibley was a stickler for precision in correspondence indicate that Olin possessed strong verbal skills and probably was well educated. To assist the commission, Sibley appointed Isaac Heard as "recorder" and asked Chaplain Riggs to give out-of-court help in dealing with the trials. These two lesser appointments were ultimately to prove crucially important to both the course of justice and subsequent assessment of the workings of the court.

Heard, just twenty-eight years old, was already the premier criminal prosecutor in the state. Born and educated in New York, he moved to the still-rough frontier town of St. Paul at age eighteen. After clerking with private lawyers, he was appointed city attorney in 1856. In 1857 he was appointed, and then elected, to the post of county attorney; he was reelected in 1859 and 1861. Both city and county attorneys prosecute criminal cases in Minnesota, there being no separate district attorney's office. Heard had thus prosecuted criminals in the state's largest city, and then in its most populous county, for six years before he volunteered for military service in 1862.

Heard was a bookish, quiet, unprepossessing man. Despite his courtroom experience, he became nervous when speaking, his mouth twisting in a peculiar manner. But however halting his presentation, he projected a powerful combination of knowledge, sincerity, and conviction. Heard's sensitive nature must have played to mixed reviews on the rough-and-ready military front. One acquaintance later said he had "the delicate sympathy of a woman." That he commanded the utmost respect from the members of the military commission, however, is beyond doubt. During the course of the trials Heard's role and stature mushroomed, albeit without change to his title. As the trials progressed the commission asked him to replace Olin as prosecutor even while he continued recording the testimony.[50]

The judges very likely leaned on Heard's expertise in bringing charges, weighing evidence, and determining sentences. Minnesota Supreme Court Justice Charles Flandrau, when writing about Sibley's commission, said that Heard was "the most important feature in the composition of this most extraordinary court."[51] This was a classic, if extreme, example of experience and competence overshadowing rank: there can have been few, if any, other court proceedings of any nature in which the official scribe is later acknowledged as the most important participant.

Heard would also prove, without exception, to be history's most valuable source of information about Joseph Godfrey. In 1863 he published what is still recognized as the best of the early books about the war, *History of the Sioux War and Massacres of 1862–1863*. His coverage of Godfrey's story is the longest ever to appear in print until now. It is evident that Heard relied not only on his own trial transcriptions but also on out-of-court interviews of Godfrey.

Reverend Riggs's name was not mentioned in Order No. 55, nor does it appear in any official documents of the military commission. But from September 27 until mid-November Riggs devoted much of his time to the behind-the-scenes workings of the court. His role commenced narrowly, with the private interviews of possible rape victims. He presumably reported his findings so that formal charges could be brought against the Dakotas accused by the women. Then Riggs's involvement expanded to include interviewing potential witnesses and helping to record the Dakota names of witnesses and defendants in court papers.

Riggs's deep familiarity with the Dakotas from twenty-five years of service as a missionary made him a logical candidate to play a part in the judicial process. Better than any other white man in camp, he knew the Dakota language and customs and, in some instances, was acquainted with the suspected men and their families. He had helped to develop a system for writing the Dakota language and, in 1852, had edited the first Dakota grammar and dictionary, which was published by the Smithsonian Institution.[52] He had helped prepare the first translation of the Bible into Dakota and assisted in composing the first textbooks in the language.[53] He was thus well equipped to interview the Dakotas and translate their stories into the parlance of the whites' system of justice.

Riggs later sought to minimize his role in gathering evidence for the commission: "In no sense was I the *accuser* of the Indians." As he described his limited acts: "Having had considerable practice in writing Indian names, it fell to my lot to make out a list of the names of the men as they were chained two and two. Then it became necessary that I should fill in the names of these men in the papers, made out at Headquarters, as charges on which they were to be tried by the Commission. I did also append the names of witnesses whenever I could find any."[54] To the extent that Riggs was simply ascertaining Indian names and recording them correctly on court papers, his function was purely ministerial. But he also admits that it was he who "found" witnesses to possible crimes and then "appended" those names to the written charges. In this latter respect, Riggs was no more neutral than a cop investigating a crime.

Riggs "found" most of his witnesses by interrogating the white captives and, later and more extensively, Indians and mixed-bloods. He presumably urged those with Dakota blood to testify against their kinsmen, for the system he described would not have worked had he failed to do so. Riggs may not have been the Indians' formal accuser, but his own description of his role leads to the conclusion that he acted as the tribunal's principal police detective. Whether he liked it or not (and, mostly, he did not), Riggs was in the thick of screening the potential evidence to be brought against his prospective converts.

One of the oldest protections of American law—the priest/penitent privilege—shields clerics from being summoned as witnesses to testify about one-to-one statements made in a religious setting. The privilege is obviously intended to promote and protect the sanctity of communications with clergy acting as spiritual advisers. What precise role Riggs was playing at any given time is almost never evident; at many junctures it would have been impossible for the Dakotas to know whether he was a trusted minister or the instrument of a criminal justice system.

The final member of the court's cast of characters was Antoine Frenier, a half-blood man who served as the commission's official interpreter.[55] Ordinarily the only attributes necessary in a court interpreter are a facility with two languages and the absence of a personal stake in or bias concerning the outcome of the proceeding. Frenier's linguistic skills are not in dispute: he was described as "highly educated," he had been employed as the official government interpreter at the Upper Agency, and his published letters reflect a high level of proficiency in English.[56] But both prior reports about Frenier and subsequent statements made by him raise questions as to whether he was too prejudiced against the Dakotas to remain neutral in his job.[57]

From the Indians' viewpoint, the most disquieting feature of the court's composition was that all of its judges had just fought a bitter war against the potential Dakota defendants. They, or the men they commanded, had dodged bullets shot by the very men whose fates they would now determine. Captain Grant had lived through the harrowing siege at Birch Coulie. All of the judges presumably knew men who had been killed in the battles. The Battle of Wood Lake, in which every member of the new court participated, had been fought less than a week before the trials began. If the Dakotas' tactics had succeeded, many or all members of the court would have died at their hands.

In this important respect, the judges were unlike those who sat on general Civil War–era courts-martial panels or on other military commissions: court members in those proceedings were not called upon to decide the fate of defendants *who had hoped and intended to kill them*. Even if the Dakota trials had been limited to the prosecution of murders of civilians unrelated to and unknown by the members of the court, the knowledge that the defendants were among those who tried to kill the presiding judges in a recent military battle would cast a cloud of possible injustice over the proceedings.

This criticism of the inherent biases of the court would probably not have fazed Sibley, who was himself, as the court's creator, subject to all of the same conflict-of-interest allegations. He was determined to pursue immediate and summary punishment of the Dakotas, and he appointed the best men available to carry out that task. Necessity, Sibley would have argued, trumped what might otherwise be construed as conflicting interests. And he would likely have added that these men were *so* accomplished and *so* evenhanded that they could rise above any such criticism.

From Godfrey's unique perspective, the composition of the court that would judge him could hardly have been better. Crooks had the independence of a professional soldier, and Marshall was a leading force in antislavery politics in Minnesota. The other court members, as far as can be discerned, had not crossed paths with Godfrey before the war and had no known reason to be biased against him. But Godfrey's case would be heard not just by the court. Sibley, as the commanding officer, would have the last say about who was convicted. And Sibley, as we have seen, had known Godfrey since childhood and was close to the men and women who had held him in slavery.

Moreover, Sibley surrounded himself at Camp Release with a kind of kitchen cabinet of former Indian traders. William Forbes, whom Sibley appointed as provost marshal, had served as Sibley's right-hand man in the fur-trading business for many years.[58] One of his functions at the Dakota trials was to usher Indian prisoners from the jail to court and back.[59] Stephen Fowler was married to Emily Faribault, a daughter of Jean Baptiste Faribault, whose family had held Godfrey in bondage; Fowler himself signed the charges that led to the prosecution of Godfrey and many others. David Faribault Sr., one of Sibley's most trusted fur traders, was among the captives liberated at Camp Release; he was to play a crucial role as a witness throughout the trials. Faribault's brother, Oliver, had been Godfrey's last master, and David Sr. had taken over the Shakopee trading post shortly after Godfrey fled to freedom. He could hardly have been expected to be well disposed toward the black man. Rounding out this group was Joseph R. Brown, the former fur trader and Indian agent, who assumed the position of assistant adjutant at Camp Release and was later made superintendent of the Indian jail.

Sibley may have appointed worthy and independent men to his military commission, but it is likely that these old cronies from his trading days would have his ear as he reacted to the court's findings. And Sibley's kitchen cabinet, in contrast with the court itself, was about as bias prone a group, from Godfrey's vantage point, as could have been assembled at the time. Most of its members had lived in the region when slavery was still thriving, and some of them had vested interests in keeping that fact quiet. The two members of the Faribault family were especially unlikely to look with favor on Godfrey, whom they must have regarded as a fugitive from their servitude. Nor was Sibley himself removed from such potential bias, since he had apparently used Godfrey's services as a slave and had been close to Godfrey's masters, Alexis Bailly and the Faribaults. None of these men would have seen Godfrey's flight to freedom as an act of heroism; they are more likely to have viewed it as a crime.

We must also consider the dramatic national political events unfolding at that time. As a Minnesotan, Sibley knew that this was no time to be soft on Indians, but he also knew that the status of blacks was on everyone's minds. He was, after all, a Democrat, in an era when that party opposed Lincoln and the Republicans. On September 26—the very day Sibley triumphantly entered Camp Release—the Emancipation Proclamation was reported in the Minnesota press, although it would not take effect until January 1, 1863, and then only in Southern states.[60]

Most Minnesotans opposed any extension of slavery to the Northern states, but they were much more divided on the question of whether emancipation should be forced on the South. Many Democrats and other critics of Lincoln supported the war effort but rejected what they saw as the extremist abolitionists' goals. In October the Blue Earth County Democratic Convention unanimously resolved, "We are in favor of the Union as it was, the Constitution as it is, [and the] niggers where they are."[61] The "niggers," of course, were enslaved at the time. Some Minnesotans, including many of Sibley's closest political allies, wished them to stay there.

By September 28, just two days after Sibley's triumphal procession into Camp Release, the military commission was fully in place and prepared to hear cases. The first sixteen suspects, including Godfrey, were closely guarded in the makeshift jail. The precise form of the "summary" trials ordered by Sibley would soon unfold, but the penalty for anyone convicted was preordained and would be swiftly carried out. As Sibley reported to Pope on the twenty-eighth, "If found guilty they [the suspects] will be immediately executed, although I am somewhat in doubt whether my authority extends quite so far. An example is, however, imperatively necessary, and I trust you will approve the act, should it happen that some real criminals have been seized."[62] In his postscript to a letter he sent the same day to Judge Flandrau, Sibley again acknowledged that on-the-spot executions "will perhaps be a stretch of my authority," adding, "if so, necessity must be my justification."[63]

Only Sibley's insistence on firm discipline had spared Godfrey from a lynching on the twenty-sixth. But Sibley intended neither to hold long trials nor to grant the nicety of appeals. The night before the trials began, Captain Grant predicted to Sarah Wakefield that the first batch of "devils" scheduled for trial would "swing" the very day of their trials: "Before to-morrow night they will hang as high as Haman."[64] When the new court commenced hearing cases on September 28, the first prisoner in the dock was Joseph Godfrey.

NOTES ON CHAPTER 5

1. Sibley to Mazakatame et al., September 24, 1862, *MCIW*, 2:249–50.
2. Carley, *Dakota War of 1862*, 65.
3. Connolly, a soldier in 1862, candidly described the bloodlust toward the Dakotas, saying "it was a miracle" that the soldiers did not kill all the surrendering Dakotas. Connolly, *Minnesota Massacre*, 144.
4. Wilhemina Buce (also spelled Busse or Buse) Carrigan's account, in Curtiss-Wedge, *History of Renville County*, 1:169–95 (recently republished in Tolzmann, Schwandt, and Carrigan, *German Pioneer Accounts*, 27–59). See also account of Mrs. N. D. White, in Curtiss-Wedge, *History of Renville County*, 1:214–15.
5. Account of Mrs. N.D. White, in Curtiss-Wedge, *History of Renville County*, 1:214–15.
6. Schultz, *Over the Earth I Come*, 239.
7. Account of Mrs. N. D. White, in Curtiss-Wedge, *History of Renville County*, 1:215–16; McConkey, *Dakota War Whoop*, 214 ("stolen bed sheet" used as flag of truce); Folwell, *History of Minnesota*, 2:185.
8. Wakefield, *Six Weeks in the Sioux Teepees*, 110–12.
9. Account of Mrs. N. D. White, in Curtiss-Wedge, *History of Renville County*, 1:215.
10. Sibley to Pope, September 27, 1862, *MCIW*, 2:254–56.
11. Account of Mary Schwandt, undated, 59–63, Schwandt Schmidt Papers, MHS (Sibley promised that "no harm" would come to anyone except those who hurt women or children or committed murder).
12. Wabasha gave formal testimony in 1868 acknowledging that he had surrendered due to Sibley's messages. He claimed, however, that at Camp Release Sibley promised a future parlay with him and the other chiefs but broke his word: "If Sibley had told the truth, and counseled with us as he had promised, we could then have delivered up to him the Indians who committed the murders . . . and all the guilty could have been punished; but instead of that, he imprisoned all our men and sent the women and children to Fort Snelling, and though we wished to tell him, he refused to counsel with any of us." Both Chief Wakute and Chief Big Eagle, also speaking under oath, joined in Wabasha's version of these events. See *Papers Relating to Talks and Councils*, 90–94. These accounts confirm the conclusion stated in the text that the Dakota chiefs not only accepted but agreed with the notion that murderers in their midst would be punished; their complaints arose later, when the net of justice was thrown to encompass much more than murderers and when Sibley refused to counsel with them.
13. Sibley to Pope, September 27, 1862, *MCIW*, 2:254–56.
14. Wakefield, *Six Weeks in the Sioux Teepees*, 111.
15. The original list, dated September 26, 1862, is in Stephen R. Riggs's handwriting. NA, RG 393, Dept. of NW, 1862–65, Headquarters, E3449, pt. 1, Unentered Letters. See also Sibley to Pope, September 27, 1862, *MCIW*, 2:254–56.
16. Riggs had ministered primarily to the Upper Dakota bands—the Sissetons and Wahpetons—while the majority of the surrendering Dakotas were Mdewakantons and Wahpekutes. Riggs's primary sympathies thus lay mainly with a small proportion of the men who were tried, but it is difficult to assess the impact of that distinction on his role in the trials.

17. Sibley to Pope, September 27, 1862, *MCIW*, 2:254–56. I compiled the breakdown of women and children using Riggs's list in NA, RG 393, Dept. of NW, 1862–65, Headquarters, E3449, pt. 1, Unentered Letters; captives under sixteen years of age were counted as children. Because ages for a few children were not written on the list, the figures given for women and children may vary from the exact totals by as many as five persons. George Thompson, age eighteen, discussed later in the chapter, was the only male captive on the list who was at least sixteen years old.
18. Sibley's September 27, 1862, letter reporting to Pope from Camp Release says in a postscript, "The number of half-breeds who were retained by the hostile Indians as prisoners and now under my protection will considerably exceed 100, but the exact number cannot now be given." *MCIW*, 2:254–56. On September 26 Riggs had estimated that the final total of released captives would be more than 100 whites and 150 "half-breeds." See original Riggs list, NA, RG 393, Dept. of NW, 1862–65, Headquarters, E3449, pt. 1, Unentered Letters.
19. *St. Paul Press* and *St. Paul Pioneer and Democrat*, both October 3, 1862. Sarah Barnes is called Sarah "Burns" in both newspapers.
20. Satterlee, *Outbreak and Massacre*, 90, says Barnes was "captured at Lower Agency."
21. McConkey, *Dakota War Whoop*, 215 (Sibley took "the only adult male captive [Spencer]" to "his own quarters").
22. Most accounts say that Spencer was the only white man freed at Camp Release. See, for example, *MCIW*, 1:746. Three other white men who remained on the Dakota side during the war may have entered the camp later or may not have been counted because, as métis, they were not perceived as "pure whites." Samuel J. Brown's recollections, in Anderson and Woolworth, *Through Dakota Eyes*, 224–45.
23. See George Spencer's account, *St. Paul Weekly Pioneer and Democrat*, April 17, 1863, published the day before Wak-ke-in-ta-wa (Wakinyantawa) was tried by a military court at Fort Snelling, where Spencer was a crucial witness helping to gain his acquittal. See discussion in chapter 11. Years later, Spencer's protector was described as "one of the noblest Indians that ever lived" in the context of decrying the failure of the government, at the request of Sibley, Heard, and others, to grant his widow a pension. Newson, *Pen Pictures of St. Paul*, 13.
24. S. Riggs, *Tah-koo wah-kan*, 312–18. Riggs reported that the mission was a success. Mrs. Huggins, her two children, two "German girls," and a "half-breed boy" were brought back to Camp Release.
25. S. Riggs, *Tah-koo wah-kan*, 312–18.
26. Connolly, *Minnesota Massacre*, 143.
27. Carrigan account, in Curtiss-Wedge, *History of Renville County*, 1:188.
28. Wakefield, *Six Weeks in the Sioux Teepees*, 112–13; account of Mrs. N. D. White, in Curtiss-Wedge, *History of Renville County*, 1:216.
29. Thomas A. Robertson reminiscences, in Anderson and Woolworth, *Through Dakota Eyes*, 230.
30. Gabriel Renville's memoir, in Anderson and Woolworth, *Through Dakota Eyes*, 232.
31. Folwell, *History of Minnesota*, 2:192.
32. Wakefield, *Six Weeks in the Sioux Teepees*, 113.
33. Letter from "H" [Isaac Heard], *St. Paul Pioneer and Democrat*, November 15, 1862. For bragging claims, see testimony in Godfrey's trial, trial 1, Dakota Trials Records.
34. Wakefield, *Six Weeks in the Sioux Teepees*, 114. Given her penchant for exaggeration and rash judgments, it is possible that some captives did not share Wakefield's views. In general, Wakefield is a colorful but potentially unreliable source.

35. Heard, *History of the Sioux War*, 189.
36. Letter from "H" [Isaac Heard], *St. Paul Pioneer and Democrat*, November 15, 1862.
37. Sibley to Pope, September 27, 1862, *MCIW*, 2:254–56.
38. Wakefield, *Six Weeks in the Sioux Teepees*, 113–14.
39. Order No. 55, September 28, 1862, is available in the Dakota Trials Records, hand-copied in the transcript of every case held by the tribunal.
40. For a general discussion of military commissions at the time of the 1862 trials, see Coppée, *Field Manual of Courts-Martial*, 104–6. Coppée noted that: (1) military commissions are to be used for persons not triable by courts-martial; (2) their proceedings are exactly the same as those in a court-martial; (3) cases that ordinarily would be tried by a civil court can be submitted to a military commission "in time of war"; and (4) military commissions were used in the Mexican-American War under General Scott for prosecution of adversaries for crimes including murder and rape. Twenty-three Union soldiers were executed for rape during the Civil War; see chapter 5, note 44.
41. Heard, quoting Order No. 55 in his history, italicized the word *summarily* for emphasis. See Heard, *History of the Sioux War*, 251.
42. Sibley to Whipple, December 7, 1862, Whipple Papers, MHS, box 3. An undated article by Sibley suggests that his model for the 1862 trials may have been the actions of the British during the War of 1812. "When . . . a Sioux Indian murdered two Canadians, inhabitants of Prairie du Chien, then in the possession of the British, a detachment was sent in pursuit of the criminal who was apprehended . . . , tried by a drum-head [court] martial, convicted, and the same evening executed in the presence of many hundred Indians. No more murders were committed while the British held the country." Sibley Papers, MHS, M164, roll 1, frames 16–18.
43. Coppée, *Field Manual of Courts-Martial*; Fisher, "Military Tribunals," 11–14.
44. National Archives records indicate that Union soldiers were executed during the Civil War for the crimes of murder (seventy-three), rape (twenty-three), and robbery or pillage (five). See "List of U.S. Soldiers Executed by United States Military Authorities during the Late War," undated, NA, RG 94, M1523, reel 1. The summary figures are taken from the case data contained in this file. Some soldiers were charged with multiple offenses (e.g., desertion and rape), and I have counted those under the more specific crime (rape). Of 267 Union soldiers who were executed during the Civil War, at least twelve were tried by military commissions and two by a drumhead court-martial. See "Proceedings of U.S. Army Courts-Martial and Military Commissions of Union Soldiers Executed by U. S. Military Authorities, 1861–1866," 1988, NA, RG 94 (pamphlet describing microfilm 1523), 1.
45. "Proceedings of U.S. Army Courts-Martial and Military Commissions of Union Soldiers Executed by U.S. Military Authorities, 1861–1866," 1988, NA, RG 94, 2.
46. Folwell, *History of Minnesota*, 2:149n4, 177n50; West, *Ancestry, Life, and Times of Sibley*, 53; and Upham and Dunlap, "Minnesota Biographies," 151.
47. Baker, *Lives of the Governors*, 147–59; Folwell, *History of Minnesota*, 1:375–76; and *MCIW*, 1:707–8.
48. Folwell, *History of Minnesota*, 2:156, 387–90.
49. *MCIW*, 1:180, 458, 720.
50. Biographical information about Heard is from Newson, *Pen Pictures of St. Paul*, 346–49. Newson accurately described Heard as the "Acting Judge Advocate" for the military commission.
51. Flandrau, *History of Minnesota*, 176.
52. Meyer, *History of the Santee Sioux*, 53.

53. *Iapi Oaye—The Word Carrier*, September 1883, quoting Riggs's obituary from the *St. Paul Pioneer Press*, August 25, 1883.
54. Riggs's review of Heard's book, *St. Paul Press*, December 17, 1863; italics in original.
55. Some scholars, relying on inaccurate secondary sources, have identified Rev. Stephen Riggs or others as the interpreter for the 1862 Dakota trials. But Isaac Heard, the court recorder who participated in every trial, said that Frenier served as the tribunal's interpreter. Heard, *History of the Sioux War*, 252.
56. *Stillwater Messenger*, February 24, 1863 ("highly educated"); *St. Paul Pioneer and Democrat*, December 14, 1862 ("official interpreter"). For Frenier's letter-writing proficiency, see *St. Paul Pioneer and Democrat*, August 23, 1862, and December 14, 1862.
57. Frenier was one of the mixed-blood members of the Renville Rangers. See letter from "S," *St. Paul Pioneer and Democrat*, December 18, 1862. Disguised as an Indian, he claimed to have reconnoitered the regions as far upriver as the Upper Agency, and his wildly incorrect reports that all of the whites at that location had been slaughtered were sent in an official letter to Governor Ramsey and then published in the press. See *St. Paul Pioneer and Democrat*, August 23, 1862, and *New York Times*, August 24, 1862. He specifically (and incorrectly) reported that the missionaries and other whites who later surfaced unharmed had been killed. At that point his earlier report was called a "gross fabrication." *St. Paul Pioneer and Democrat*, August 24, 1862. Frenier was equally unreliable and biased after the trials, when he took extreme public positions about the Indians' guilt. See Frenier's letters to the *St. Paul Pioneer and Democrat*, December 14, 1862, and the *Stillwater Messenger*, February 24, 1863. At one point a newspaper cited the unnamed "highest local military authority" to rebut Frenier's claims as being "utterly without foundation." *St. Paul Press*, February 20, 1863.
58. Heard, *History of the Sioux War*, 252; Gilman, *Henry Hastings Sibley*, 69.
59. Letter from "H" [Isaac Heard], *St. Paul Pioneer and Democrat*, December 11, 1862.
60. *St. Paul Press*, September 26, 1862.
61. *Mankato Semi-Weekly Record*, October 25, 1862.
62. Sibley to Pope, September 28, 1862, *MCIW*, 2:256.
63. Flandrau, *History of Minnesota*, 175–76; also in *MCIW*, 1:746. Flandrau incorrectly gives September 25 as the date of Sibley's letter, but its contents (e. g., the arrest of sixteen Indians at Camp Release) establish that it could not have been written before September 28.
64. Wakefield, *Six Weeks in the Sioux Teepees*, 114.

CHAPTER 6

Godfrey's Trial

The venue of Godfrey's trial was rather exotically but accurately recorded at the top of the September 28 written charges against him: "Camp Release, opposite the Mouth of Chippewa River." To add to the rustic flavor of the setting, the "courtroom" was a tent.[1] There were no buildings at Camp Release until a crude wooden jail pen was built to house Godfrey and the other suspects.

It is likely that the trials were held in one of the expedition's large, tipi-like military Sibley tents, ironically named for the tent's patentee, Henry Hopkins Sibley, the distant relative of Minnesota's Sibley. The "other General Sibley," the officer whose brother-in-law had brought slaves to Fort Ridgely, would have become rich from patent royalties during the Civil War had he not joined the secessionists.[2]

In the standard manner specified for courts-martial, the formal allegations against Godfrey were divided into charges (the basic offense) and specifications (the details supporting the charge).[3]

> The Military Commission was then duly sworn and O-ta-kle or Godfrey, a colored man connected with the Sioux tribe of Indians, was arraigned on the following charge and Specification

Viz:

Charge—Murder

Specification 1st. In this that the said O-ta-kle or Godfrey a colored man, did at or near New Ulm, Minn., on or about the 19th day of August 1862, join in a War Party of the Sioux tribe of Indians against Citizens of the United States and did with his own hand murder seven white men and women and children more or less, peaceable Citizens of the United States.

Specification 2nd. In this that the said O-ta-kle or Godfrey, a Colored Man, did at various times and places between the 19th day of August 1862, and the 28th day of September 1862, join and participate in the Murders and Massacres committed by the Sioux Indians on the Minnesota Frontier.[4]

Antoine Frenier probably informed the judges that "Otakle" translated as "Many Kills."

From today's vantage point, the declaration of August 19 as the starting date for the Dakota War seems jarringly incorrect, for histories now accurately recite the fact that large-scale killings commenced on August 18. This small discrepancy, though legally irrelevant (given the customary legal usage "on or about"), betrays the commission's relative unfamiliarity with the extent of the war on its first and bloodiest day. Knowing that the initial assault on New Ulm came on August 19, they may have mistakenly inferred that date for Godfrey's alleged murders (all of which occurred on August 18).

Before his trial, Godfrey had been manacled by one ankle and chained to a similarly restrained Indian prisoner.[5] We don't know if a link in the chain connecting the two men was hammered off to permit Godfrey to attend court without his jail mate. But the metal ring fetter probably remained on his ankle during his testimony.

As Godfrey entered the tent-cum-courtroom, his appearance did not match that of a ruthless killer. He had abandoned his breechcloth in favor of white dress, with the exception of moccasins on his feet. Atop his head, at an angle, was an old plush cap with a rumpled flat top and large earflaps bent upward—creating a floppy variant of a Civil War private's cap. Godfrey's curly hair jutted straight out an inch or so from the bottom edges of the cap. With both his coat and shirt buttoned to the top and with his scraggly mustache and goatee, Godfrey had a somewhat scruffy military look. He might easily have been mistaken for a diligent-looking recruit assigned to a "colored" regiment of the U.S. Army. Heard noted that Godfrey was slightly cross-eyed ("but not enough to disfigure"). Varying descriptions said he was short or of medium height, slightly or stoutly built. He was smaller than most of the Dakotas. He looked much younger than his thirty-two years, and more than one observer underestimated his age.[6]

Departing from the ordinary sequence of events in a criminal trial, "prisoner" Godfrey gave his testimony in full before the first witness against him was called. The charges against him were read. Asked if he was guilty or not guilty, he launched into a long narrative statement, rendered in "broken English." If his harmless-looking appearance had not yet made an impression on the court, his softly delivered testimony almost immediately riveted their attention. Godfrey, Heard said, had "a voice of [the] most marvelous sweetness."[7]

The beginning of Godfrey's testimony is as significant for what it omits as for its content. On the eighteenth, he was obviously surprised when a messenger brought news of the daybreak attack at the Lower Agency. He was near his home, peacefully reaping crops. He said nothing about the previous day's murders at Acton or the late-night Dakota meetings at the soldiers' lodge and at Little Crow's house.

> The first time I came in I was mowing hay and Indians let me have their team to draw hay—Wa-Ze-Ye-ta was helping me. I was close to my house and heard hallooing, I told Indian and we ran back, one Indian was on horseback, had on new hat he got at Red Wood. I asked him what was the matter. He said people at Red Wood were all murdered; he had his gun cocked. I asked him who killed them. He said Indians. He looked to me and

came near killing me. He asked which way I would go, he said it twice. I said I couldn't tell. I have my wife and children and didn't want to be killed. He said 200 Indians were behind, and I had better go in my house and get a breech clout. I did so.

Though it is only implied in this truncated trial version, Godfrey explicitly told Heard that, when he saw the Indian on horseback, "I was afraid, because he held his gun as if he would kill me."[8]

The gun-toting messenger's reports conveyed two important falsehoods. In actuality, the Dakotas had killed only the lead traders and a few other men at Redwood (the Lower Sioux Agency). Nor was it true that "200 Indians" were swooping eastward to continue the slayings. Most of the Dakotas remained closer to the agency on the eighteenth (the largest group ambushed Captain Marsh's company at the ferry) or fanned out to attack and pillage the settlements—Birch Coulee, Beaver Creek, and others—across the river to the north. But these two bogus reports, which the messenger himself may have believed, incited the Dakotas who heard them and would also have had an intimidating impact on Godfrey. If all the prominent whites and their families at the Lower Agency had indeed been killed, a call to eliminate local white settlers would have been a logical, even expected, follow-up. Not surprisingly, the Dakotas who lived near Godfrey abandoned their haymaking and other pursuits and took up the cry to "kill all the whites."

When one compares the 1862 transcript of Godfrey's trial testimony with the more complete version of his story as published in Heard's 1863 history, the summary nature of the former becomes obvious. Two possible explanations may account for this difference. Godfrey may well have made much longer statements in the courtroom, but Heard, as the court's recorder, only had time to write down their essence. Or Godfrey may have supplemented his evidence during out-of-court conversations with Heard. Some of the references in Heard's book make it clear that he continued to interview Godfrey for many weeks, even as the trials progressed. Either way, comments that are confusing or incomplete in the transcripts are often explained in the longer version in the book. In several instances, statements Heard attributes to Godfrey are not found anywhere in the trial transcript. Because the events of August 18 are so crucial—to Godfrey's story and to history—both sources will be quoted or referenced here when necessary to avoid confusion.

In his trial Godfrey briefly discussed his reluctance to join the Dakotas, saying, "I told my squaw I would try to run away. We took flour and ran into bushes. The Indians stopped me, and told me not to run down but to start up—that all the whites would be killed. He told me to follow. I did so. About 10 Indians followed us and then we all started together to kill all the Dutch farmers. I lived below the Fort and towards New Ulm. After that we crossed the creek (on the reservation this side of Cotton Wood)."

Heard's book gives more detail about Godfrey's fear and indecision:

> I went to my house and told my wife to get ready, and we would try to get away. I told my wife what the Indian told me. I told her we would try to get down the river. She said we would be killed with the white people. We got something ready to take with us to eat, and started—we got about two hundred yards into the woods. (The old man, my wife's father, said he would fasten the house and follow after.) We heard some one halloo. It was the old man. He called to us to come back. I told my wife to go on, but her mother told her to stop. I told them to go ahead; but the old man called so much that they stopped and turned back. I followed them.
>
> I found my squaw's uncle at the house. He scolded my wife and her mother for trying to get away; he said all the Indians had gone to the agency, and they must go there. He said we would be killed if we went toward the white folks; that we would only be safe to go and join the Indians. I still had my pants on. I was afraid; and they told me I must take my pants off and put on the breech-clout. I did so. . . .

> I started with him toward New Ulm, and we met a lot of Indians at the creek, about a mile from my house. They were all painted, and said I must be painted. They then painted me. I was afraid to refuse.[9]

Some Dakotas apparently viewed Godfrey differently than they viewed other non-Dakotas. No white man was similarly conscripted and painted in 1862, and Godfrey was the only participant on the Dakota side with no Indian blood.

The next part of Godfrey's trial testimony dealt with the first acts of the war party he joined:

> They [the Indians] tried to catch a buggy on the way down. They watched two teams. I was told by the Indians to go into a house and ask for Chippewas, while they waited for teams. I didn't go into the house. The Indians all went into the house. An Indian said as soon as the others brought in the team tell us and we will kill them. They shot and the Indians in the house shot them in the house. I didn't tell them. They took an ox team, and the Indian who had it told me to drive it. I did so. Half of the Indians were in the wagon—15 were in the party.

From this confusing excerpt, we learn that the Indians "shot them in the house," but we are left wondering where the house was, who was killed, and what relevance the ox-driven buggy has to those killings. And why did the Dakotas demand that Godfrey ask the people at the house about Ojibwes?

In Heard's history Godfrey's retelling answers all these questions and puts his trial testimony in perspective:

> We started down the road. We saw two wagons with people in them coming toward us. The Indians consulted what to do, and decided for half of them to go

up to a house off the road, on the right-hand side. They started, but I stopped, and they called me and told me I must come on.

There was an old man, a boy, and two young women at the house—Dutch people. The family's name was something like "Masseybush" [Massopust]. The boy and two girls stood outside, near the kitchen door. Half of the Indians went to the house, half remained in the road. The Indians told me to tell the whites that there were Chippewas about, and that they (the Indians) were after them. I did not say any thing.

The Indians asked [the Massopusts] for some water. The girls went into the house, and the Indians followed and talked in Sioux. One said to me, "Here is a gun for you." Dinner was on the table, and the Indians said, "After we kill, then we will have dinner." They told me to watch the road, and when the teams came up to tell them, and we will kill them. I turned to look, and just then I heard the Indians shoot; I looked, and two girls fell just outside the door. I did not go in the house; I started to go round the house. We were on the back side of it, when I heard the Indians on the road hallooing and shouting. They called me, and I went to the road and saw them killing white men. My brother-in-law told me I must take care of a team that he was holding; that it was his. I saw two men killed that were with this wagon. I did not see who was killed in the other wagon. I saw one Indian stick his knife in the side of a man that was not yet dead; he cut his side open, and then cut him all to pieces. His name was Wakantonka (great spirit). Two of the Indians that killed the people at the house . . . are Waki-ya-ni [Wakinyanna] and Mah-wha [Mahoowaywa]. I got into the wagon, and the Indians all got in. We turned and went toward New Ulm.[10]

The location of these events is clarified beyond any doubt by Godfrey's statement that the occupants were named "something like Masseybush," for the Massopust family was the first to be killed on August 18 in Milford. Godfrey, who was probably the only English speaker among the attackers, said he refused to convey to the Massopusts the ruse that Ojibwes were about, so the Dakotas then pretended to ask for water.[11]

At this juncture the trial transcript makes a fleeting mention of the Travelers' Home, Anton Henle's farmhouse that doubled as a tavern, where, Godfrey told the court, "all the Indians got drunk." But the trial record contains no description of any killings that occurred between those at the Massopust home and the Travelers' Home. That gap in the court record is filled by Godfrey's story from Heard's book:

> I got into the wagon [near the Massopust home], and the Indians all got in. We turned and went toward New Ulm. When we got near to a house the Indians all got out and ran ahead of the wagons, and two or three went to each house, and in that way they killed all the people along the road. I staid in the wagon, and did not see the people killed. They killed the people of six or eight houses—all until we got to the "Travelers' Home." There were other Indians killing people all though the settlement. We could see them and hear them all around. I was standing in the wagon, and could see three, or four, or five Indians at every house.[12]

While Godfrey was driving the ox-drawn wagon down the road, the Dakotas were systematically killing the Milford residents. Only a handful of warriors were needed to dispatch the unsuspecting farm families at each home.

Godfrey's trial record refers obliquely to the slayings at the Travelers' Home; he says that the Dakotas "killed all [the] folks in [the] saloon." But again, Heard's book is more complete:

When we got near the "Travelers' Home," they told me to stop. I saw an old woman with two children—one in each hand—run away across the yard. Maza-bom-doo [Muzzabomadu] . . .[13] shot the old woman, and jumped over and kicked the children down with his feet. The old woman fell down as if dead. I turned my head, and did not see whether the children were killed. After that I heard a shot behind the barn, but did not see who was shot. I supposed some one was killed. After that the Indians got in the wagon, and told me to start down the road.[14]

The "old woman" at the Travelers' Home was probably Anton Henle's mother-in-law, Mary Anne Messmer, who was with her two grandchildren, Anton and Mary Henle, ages eight and four, respectively.[15] Only the book version makes it clear that the killing of "all the folks in the saloon"—which might incorrectly conjure an image of adult male beer swillers—included the innkeeper's aging mother-in-law and two children.[16]

Until this point, Godfrey said, he had been hanging back from the Dakotas, sitting in the wagon while they carried out their rampage through Milford. But then the Indians bluntly confronted him. Godfrey testified,

After we were at the Travelers' Home, [the Indians] . . . said to me if you don't kill a white man we will kill you. I had no gun and they gave me a hatchet. . . . We passed to another house and they killed all in it. The Indians told me to go into the house first and get 3 guns there, and kill some one there. I ran into the house and the whites were taking dinner. I struck the old man with a hatchet—with the back of it, on the shoulder. A big man, two women and a child were killed, they then shot them all.

Again, the book offers more details:

> After that [the Travelers' Home] the Indians got in the wagon, and told me to start down the road. We started on, and got to a house where a man lived named Schling [Adolph Schilling]—a German—an old man. The Indians found a jug in the wagon, and were now almost drunk. They told me to jump out. I jumped out and started ahead, and the Indians called me to come back. They threw out a hatchet, and said I must go to the house and kill the people. [Muzzabomadu] was ahead. He told me there were three guns there that he had left for some flour, and we must get them. I was afraid.
>
> I went into the house. There was the old man, his wife and son, and a boy and another man. They were at dinner. The door stood open, and the Indians were right behind me, and pushed me in. I struck the old man on the shoulder with the flat of the hatchet, and then the Indians rushed in and commenced to shoot them. The old man, woman, and boy ran into the kitchen. The other man ran out some way, I did not see how; but when we went back to the road, about twenty steps, I saw him in the road dead. He was the man I struck in the house. I heard the Indians shoot back of the house, but did not see what at. After we started to go to Red-Wood, one little Indian, who had pox-marks on his face, and who was killed at [the battle of] Wood Lake, said he struck the boy with a knife, but didn't say if he killed him. He told this to the other Indians.[17]

By striking "old man" Schilling with the blunt edge of the hatchet, Godfrey made the kind of direct contact with an enemy that the Dakotas would have viewed as a "kill" (even if the blow led to no injury), despite the fact that Schilling was then actually slain by the Dakotas.[18]

At this point, after most of the population of Milford had been killed, Ernst Dietrich and the wagons filled with the unarmed Civil War recruiters from New Ulm appeared on the horizon. The trial version of

Godfrey's story provides only a bare outline of that encounter. "After that we met some four teams, and ran back to a creek. They saw the Indians in the grass, a bugle then played and they started on. The Indians killed all. After that they killed two men. They told me to seize the horses. I did so, didn't kill any after the two men. Two Indians took the team from me."

The mention of four wagons, Indians hiding in the grass, and the bugle can refer only to the ambush of the recruiting expedition. But Heard's book gives many more specifics in confirmation:

> We saw coming up the road two wagons, one with a flag in it.[19] The Indians were afraid, and we started back, and went past the "Travelers' Home." We got to a bridge, and the Indians got out and laid down in the grass about the bridge. I went on up the road. The wagons, with the white men, came on up and stopped in the road, where there was a dead man, I think; then they sounded the bugle and started to cross the bridge, running their horses.
>
> The foremost wagon had one horse, of a gray color; three men were in it, and had the flag. Just as they came across the bridge, the Indians raised up and shot. The three men fell out, and the team went on. The Indians ran and caught it. The other wagon had not got across the bridge. I heard them shoot at the men in it, but I did not see them. After the Indians brought the second wagon across the bridge, three Indians got in the wagon.
>
> After that all of them talked together, and said that it was late (the sun was nearly down), and that they must look after their wives and children that had started to go to Red-Wood. Many of these Indians lived on the lower end of the reservation. The two-horse team that they had just taken was very much frightened, and they could not hold them. They told me I must take and hold them, and drive them. I took the team, and then they all got in. We then had four teams. We started from there, and went on up.[20]

Godfrey's account is the only detailed description of the deaths of the recruiters from the Indians' perspective. The "dead man" by the side of the road was most likely the all-but-dead Joseph Messmer, Anton Henle's brother-in-law, whom the recruiting party initially mistook for a drunk. Messmer's multiple wounds soon proved fatal. The three men whom Godfrey described falling out of the wagons were Dietrich, Julius Fenske, and John Schneider. (A fourth recruiter, Adolph Steimle, died later from his wounds.)[21]

It is perfectly understandable that Godfrey and the Indians were alarmed at the sight of the all-male wagon train, the flag, and the "bugle" (probably a trumpet). They believed they were ambushing a contingent of soldiers coming to combat them.[22] From the Dakota perspective, this was one of two battles with white troops on August 18, the other being the ambush of Captain Marsh at the Redwood ferry. The encounter with the recruiters at Milford must have strengthened the Dakotas' belief that white men, even bands of soldiers, could be killed with ease.

Can Godfrey's description of the recruiting party ambush and his professed role as a reluctant warrior be reconciled with the official dispatch that Sheriff Roos sent to St. Paul late on the night of August 18, reporting a "negro leading" the murdering Indians at Milford? By examining the two reports, we can see that the differences between them lie not in factual premises but in diverging perceptions—conflicting interpretations from witnesses of the same scene. Godfrey admitted that he was standing in the road near the bridge at the time of the recruiting party ambush, but he evidently made that statement in an attempt—one of many—to separate himself from the actions of the Indians during the Milford massacre. Just as he was in the road during most of the house-to-house killings in the village, he did not join the Dakotas who hid themselves in the ravine in preparation for ambush. But his visibility (and probably his black-man-in-breechcloth uniqueness) caused the whites to see him as a ringleader. That the Indians' fusillade poured forth from the very spot where Godfrey had stood in the road, hatchet in hand, must have underscored that notion. The Dakotas, on the other hand, almost certainly did not see Godfrey as their leader, though they viewed him as a willing participant.

As another author has noted, Godfrey's detailed story of the killings at Milford "mirrors almost exactly" the independently created white accounts of those same events.[23] But how does Godfrey's story stack up against the Dakota version? We will apparently never know, since Dakota history, significantly, is virtually silent on the subject of Milford. Of the sixty-three known Indian or mixed-blood narratives collected by Gary Clayton Anderson and Alan Woolworth that tell the Dakotas' side of the 1862 conflict (gathered for their classic 1988 book, *Through Dakota Eyes*), only Godfrey's covers the Milford massacre.

As the Dakotas backtracked from Milford to the reservation, keeping to the road with their plunder-laden wagons, they came upon the Patoille (anglicized in the trial records as Patwell, Patville, or Patrick) wagon, filled with six whites fleeing east to hoped-for refuge at New Ulm. Godfrey's abbreviated rendition at his trial was the earliest-recorded account of this attack: "Near the creek 15 miles from the fort [Ridgely] an Indian saw some persons and said someone had better run ahead and see who they were. An Indian said whip up the horses and I went ahead. Patwell was in the wagon going down. They killed the man, smashed the trunks (5 I think). [I] saw no women's clothes in the trunk."

Again, a more complete version appears in Heard's book:

> We saw, far away, a wagon coming toward us. When it was only two miles from us we saw it was a two-horse wagon, but the Indians didn't know if it was white people. When it came nearer they told me to go fast. The Indians whipped the horse and hurried them on. Two Indians were ahead of us on horseback.
>
> Pretty soon we came near, and the team that was coming toward us stopped and turned around, and the Indians said it was white men, and they were trying to run away. The two men on horseback then shot, and I saw a white man—Patville—fall back over his seat; and after that I saw three women and one man jump out of the wagon and run. Then those in the wagon with me jumped out and ran after the women. We got up to the

wagon. Patville was not dead. The Indians threw him out, and a young Indian . . . stuck a knife between his ribs, under the arm, and another one, who is with Little Crow, took his gun and beat his head all to pieces.[24] The other Indians killed the other white man near the little lake, and brought back the three women—Mattie Williams, Mary Anderson, and Mary Swan [Schwandt].

Patville's wagon was full of trunks. The Indians broke them open and took the things out; there were some goods in them (Patville was a sort of trader on the reservation). They put one woman in the wagon. I drove. The other two were put separately in the other wagons. The one in my wagon (Mary Swan) was caught by [Muzzabomadu]. Tazoo had Mattie Williams.[25]

Because Mary Schwandt and Mattie Williams survived their captivity and were freed at Camp Release, the court would soon hear more about the Patoille wagon and the plight of Williams as Tazoo's captive.

The final portion of Godfrey's August 18 saga covered the last leg of his journey back to the reservation, driving one of the wagons stolen from the recruiting party. In the bare bones of the trial transcript, Godfrey said,

> After that we started away and put this girl (Mary Swan) in the wagon. This girl asked me where we go. I said I didn't know. I said I have been taken prisoner.— This was before the fight. I said maybe we would go to Red Wood, she said John Moore was there in the morning and said the whites were killed. We got at Red Wood late at night. I told Wakantu [Chief Wakute] to take this girl in the house. He said he [already] had two [girls]. The girl went into Wakantu's house—I found my folks at Little Crow's house. We stopped there two days.

At the end of the day, Godfrey delivered captive Schwandt to Chief Wakute, who headed his father-in-law's band. He found his family "at" (probably camping near) Little Crow's house.

Other than an oblique mention of the "two girls" already in captivity in Wakute's house, Godfrey's trial testimony contains no reference to Mary Anderson, the third young woman taken captive from Patoille's wagon. But Heard quoted Godfrey's report of an interesting interlude involving Anderson:

> We then went on [after the Patoille wagon attack], and stopped at a creek about a mile ahead to water the horses. Then they called me to ask the woman that was wounded [Mary Anderson] if she was badly hurt. She said "Yes." They told me to ask her to show the wound, and that they would do something for it. She showed the wound. It was in the back. The ball did not come out. She asked where we were going. I said I didn't know, but supposed to Red-Wood. . . . I told her I heard that all the whites at the agency were killed and the stores robbed. She said she wished they would drive fast, so she could have a doctor do something for her wound; she was afraid she would die. I said I was a prisoner too. She asked what would be done with them. I said I didn't know; perhaps we would all be killed. I said maybe the doctor was killed, if all the white people were.[26]

Godfrey was again called upon by the Dakotas to translate. He revealed that the Indians shot Anderson in the back, a detail confirmed many years later by Schwandt, who also documented the two agonizing days spent by the grievously wounded young woman in a dusty loft at Wakute's house and her death on the third day of her captivity.[27] If we credit Godfrey's version of his conversation with Anderson, it is unfortunate that she did not live to testify; she would have been in the best position to confirm his assertion that he too considered himself to be a prisoner on August 18. Godfrey's talk with Anderson also highlights the fact that he (and presumably all of the Dakotas who were at Milford) continued to believe, until late in the day on August 18, the false report that all the whites at the agency had been killed.

The Dakotas saw the three women in Patoille's wagon in the same light as they viewed females from enemy tribes. This is obvious from Godfrey's naming of the individual Dakotas who claimed the two women who survived: Muzzabomadu took Schwandt and Tazoo claimed Williams. (A later trial identified Anderson's captor, Chankahda.)[28] Just as in intertribal hostilities, it was up to the warrior who first approached a woman to decide whether she lived or died, to kill her or to assert his ownership of her as a captive.

This interpretation also helps explain another otherwise perplexing detail: why were the Milford attackers, who had slain so many people with such abandon, later solicitous of the injured Anderson, offering to "do something" for her wounds? The answer, apparently, flows from Chankahda's decision to claim her as his captive, thereby instantly transforming her into his potential new wife and someone who, to some extent at least, merited protection. Of course, as Williams soon discovered, the captor was free to treat such a woman as he wished.

Another crucial conversation that took place on August 18 is omitted from the transcript of Godfrey's trial testimony. Near the end of his narrative, apparently in response to a question from the court, he identified his father-in-law as Wahpaduta. But the account in Heard's book tells more: "We started up the road [after the Milford killings], and stopped at a creek about a mile farther on. We waited for some of the Indians that were behind. While we were there we saw a house on fire. When the Indians came up they said that [Wahpaduta], my father-in-law, shot a woman, who was on a bed sick, through the window; and that an old man ran up stairs, and the Indians were afraid to go in the house; they thought he had a gun, and they set fire to the house and left it."[29]

Since this deeply incriminating statement against Wahpaduta is not found in the trial records, we cannot tell when this information was given to Heard (and hence to Sibley's court). But the fact that Wahpaduta was brought before the judges on October 7—not long after Godfrey's trial—suggests that Godfrey himself may have furnished the allegations that led to his father-in-law's arrest. Godfrey, after leaving Milford, also said he was "waiting" for Wahpaduta, who was "behind." This explains why everything Godfrey told Heard about his father-in-law's deeds at Milford was secondhand, for the two of them were not together. The men had been in each other's company on the reservation, but we do not know when they separated. As we shall see, the probability that Wahpaduta was not in a position to see Godfrey's acts at Milford will assume more importance later.

Before turning to the rest of Godfrey's trial, it is worth noting that his testimony relating to August 18 makes up more than half of the transcript of all the evidence he gave. In Heard's book that emphasis is even greater: almost eight full pages of the chapter about Godfrey are devoted to the events of August 18, while the other weeks of the Dakota War consume just three pages.[30]

But if one looks only at the official record of the testimony Godfrey gave, it is not even clear where the Milford killings took place. It is a striking fact that Sibley's court's records—for Godfrey's trial and all subsequent cases—never refer to Milford by name or even indicate that the site was seven miles distant from New Ulm. In the transcripts, the killings there were "on the road to New Ulm," or near the Travelers' Home, or simply at the homes of the "Dutch farmers," who are only occasionally identified by name. Only by piecing together all available historical information does it become clear that the events Godfrey described took place at Milford and that the killings at that location were separate from the New Ulm battles that began the next day.[31] This lack of clarity is part of a broader problem that recurs throughout the trials, for the rushed judges often failed to ascertain dates, places, and names that would be a standard part of any ordinary criminal trial testimony.

Most of the balance of Godfrey's testimony dealt with his presence at four battles: Fort Ridgely, New Ulm, Birch Coulee, and the final engagement at Wood Lake. He portrayed himself as a reluctant soldier and minimized his participation in the fighting. A couple of days after the Milford killings, Godfrey said, Little Crow announced a plan to attack the fort. The chief insisted that "all must go," including "half-breeds." Again, Godfrey, who was apparently seen as having skills as a teamster, was conscripted to drive a team of horses, as had happened with the oxcart and recruiters' wagon at Milford.[32] Godfrey told the judges that his life was threatened by a Dakota soldier with a knife while he was driving the team toward the fort, indicating his continuing jeopardy, even after August 18.

Godfrey himself supplied ample evidence of his participation in battles. He and David Faribault Jr., Godfrey acknowledged, stole horses from the stable at the fort; he admitted firing five shots at the second assault on New Ulm; he fired into the tents of the sleeping soldiers at daybreak at Birch Coulee; and he was present at the last battle, at Wood Lake. But Godfrey repeatedly claimed that he was an unwilling conscript. His story is laced with references to Dakota threats and coercion (those who failed to join the Birch Coulee war party "should be killed," Godfrey claimed; twice he used the expression "all must go" to describe conscription announcements).

Near the end of his testimony Godfrey must have been asked a few pinpoint questions by the court. Someone apparently inquired if he had bragged about killing people, to which he replied that he "never boasted I killed white people." How, if he denied killing anyone, had he acquired the Dakota name meaning Many Kills? "They gave me my name on account of many being killed where I struck the man with the hatchet," Godfrey said. Finally, someone must have asked him who killed Patoille, for his final words to the court identified another suspect: "All the Indians said his people killed Patwell—We-a-ta-tow [Wyatahtowah] is his Indian name."[33]

At this stage of the trial, after Godfrey had completed his story, six witnesses were called against him. Any criminal defense lawyer would note the overwhelming disadvantage created by this procedural sequence. In American jurisprudence, one of the major advantages for a criminal defendant is the chance to hear the prosecution's full case before responding in any way, if at all. But Godfrey, in reply to very unspecific charges, had laid out his complete story in detail. He was, as lawyers would put it, locked into his testimony.

Not only could prosecution witnesses now undercut his version of events, but by implicating several Dakotas by name, Godfrey had exposed himself to accusatory salvos from men he had essentially accused of murder. They could retaliate by claiming, truthfully or not, that it was he who had committed the murders with which they were charged. That Godfrey not only spoke first but was the first to be tried placed him in an extremely precarious position: he could not modify his story in response to later testimony *and* he faced retributive countercharges from men he had implicated. For a criminal defendant, going first is worst.³⁴

The first three witnesses against Godfrey were women who had been held captive. Mary Woodbury, a mixed-blood woman, testified,

> I was at the Lower Agency when I was taken by the Indians on Monday, the day of the fight.³⁵ I know the prisoner. I saw him among the Indians. I saw him first at Little Crow's village two or three days subsequently. He painted his legs and face for a war party and put on his breech clout. They said they were going to New Ulm, he started off with them—he was willing to go, he was whooping around. He was very happy with the Indians. He appeared to be as willing to go as any of the Indians, and took as prominent a part. When they came back there was a Wakpaton [Wahpeton] named Kunckkatrinme [who told me that] the Negro was the bravest of all—that he led them into the house and clubbed them with a hatchet.³⁶ I was standing in the prisoner's tent door [and] the Indians asked him how many he killed, and he said only seven. I saw him have a hatchet, a gun and a knife when he started.

While Woodbury did not witness Godfrey killing or harming anyone and had no contact with him until a few days after the Milford slaughter, her evidence damaged his cause on two fronts. First, she portrayed him as a willing, even enthusiastic, member of the bands that departed to fight battles. Even worse, she completely undermined his claim that he had not boasted of killing whites. On the other hand, her hearsay report of the hatchet incident tended to support Godfrey's claim that the worst act he had committed at Milford was striking a man with the blunt edge of a hatchet.

Mary Schwandt, who gave evidence next, was one of two witnesses who saw Godfrey on August 18, albeit only during and after the attack on the Patoille wagon. She said,

> I was taken captive by the Indians about 15 miles this side of New Ulm, on Monday the first day they commenced killing the people—Miss Williams, Mr. Patrick [Patoille], Mr. Lee, Mary Anderson and a Frenchman were with me. We were on the road in a wagon going to New Ulm. A large party [of] over 40 captured us. They came up as the prisoner says and they shot Mary Anderson, Mr. Patrick, Mrs. Lee, and the Frenchman, and took me and Miss Williams prisoners. They also took Mary Anderson but she died afterwards. The prisoner was of the party. He was driving the horses, but I didn't see him have any arms. I didn't see him lay his hands on any of the persons. He acted to me as if he was there willingly, he acted just the same as the Indians did, when I asked him questions he kind of grinned as if he was glad of it. The Indians were drunk—he was not. I rode with him to Wakunta's [Wakute's] house at the Lower Agency. It was then 6 o'clock when we started and 8 o'clock when we got in. I asked him if they had been to New Ulm and he said "no." He appeared to me to be in with the Indians, and to act as they did. About a week ago at Red Iron's village he told me to run away, that the Indians wouldn't know. Never saw prisoner treat any one harshly.

Schwandt's use of the phrase "as the prisoner says" strongly suggests that, rather than being sequestered in the ordinary fashion outside the courtroom, she (and perhaps other witnesses) had listened to Godfrey's testimony. This situation created yet another disadvantage for Godfrey, for Schwandt could have pounced on any discrepancy between his story and her recollections. Her testimony was helpful to Godfrey's defense of a murder charge, but she too depicted him as a willing ally of the Dakotas.[37]

Unfortunately, Sibley's court did not create a now-standard question-and-answer transcript of the trials. All of the case records follow the same summary narrative format. Even assuming that Heard accurately entered the substance of the testimony, much is lost by this method. It is impossible, for example, to know whether the prosecutor or a judge was asking the questions or even if testimony was in response to a question or was volunteered. Moreover, the absence of the questions makes the assessment of witness credibility (always difficult from a written page, even under the best of circumstances) more difficult. To judge whether a witness is straightforward or evasive, it is extremely important to compare the queries with the responses given. Eliminating the questions tends to make all witnesses sound equally credible, unless they contradict themselves or make foolish statements. Furthermore, we cannot tell if the answers were given in response to questions or rendered in language chosen by the witnesses. The practice of recording testimony in narrative fashion was not uncommon in military courts at the time; it was sometimes used even in capital cases against Union soldiers.[38] But it always detracts from the value of the extant record.

The third witness was Mattie Williams, the eighteen-year-old woman who, like Schwandt, was captured from Patoille's wagon. She identified Godfrey as being among the wagon's attackers but made no claim that he hurt anyone. She also noted no reluctance on his part: "He appeared to be a willing member of the party and to act like the Indians." On the other hand, he had reassured her that "we are not going to kill you."

The next witness, David Faribault Jr., the first mixed-blood man to appear before the court, did no damage to Godfrey's case. Godfrey had already told the court that he and Faribault had been together at the Fort Ridgely battle (where they both stole horses from the stable) and also at the second assault on New Ulm. But Faribault was vague and evasive on the stand: "I know the prisoner. I have been with the prisoner sometimes, but don't know what he did. I was with him first at the war party at the fort. We started from Red Wood. I saw him first at the Fort. I saw him first after the Indians came back to their camp a mile from the Fort after the attack had been made. He was dressed like an Indian. I saw him next at New Ulm. He was painted I think like an Indian[. I] know nothing further. Don't remember whether he was painted."[39] Faribault obviously sought to distance himself from Godfrey, claiming almost no recollection of his actions at the fort or New Ulm, despite his admission that he was "with" him "sometimes." Perhaps he feared—with justification, it turned out—that he would find himself in the prisoners' dock and did not want to incriminate himself or alienate Godfrey.

The next witness, Bernard LaBatte, offered even less than Faribault. Another mixed-blood man, LaBatte admitted that he knew Godfrey but claimed he did not "know anything about" his actions during the conflict. LaBatte's appearance was an early indication of the slapdash investigation that had preceded the trials. Usually the police or prosecution would have winnowed out such know-nothing witnesses so as not to waste the court's time. The failure to follow this simple procedure—repeated many times in subsequent cases—suggests both Riggs's inexperience at playing detective and the rushed nature of the proceedings.

If David Faribault Jr. was one of Godfrey's pals, the same could not be said for his father, David Faribault Sr. Lucy Bailly's brother pulled no punches in his testimony:

> I know the prisoner. He has told me [he] was in war parties with the Sioux. He said he had killed about seven men. This was in the beginning, he said he had killed them this side of New Ulm in the road. He said he killed them with the tomahawk. He said he went in with the Indians and they laughed—and speak—and kill[ed] them.
>
> He said he killed some more—children, but that he didn't consider this of any account. There were Indians

present. He was telling it to all of us. This was three or four days after he came back.

Faribault clarified what was fuzzy in Mary Schwandt's testimony: that the Milford killings were the subject of Godfrey's boasts ("in the beginning . . . this side of New Ulm"). He continued,

> [I] saw him at New Ulm. He was there in the fight acting in the battle. I also saw him at the Fort before this, at the battle. He was shooting there with the others. I saw him. He was shooting with the rest. He never told me he was forced into it. I had two horses in the stable and I took one of mine. The prisoner took a mare and he gave it to an Indian. He was also in the first battle at the fort, he was also in the battle of Birch Coolie, I was told. At the fort he had a bow and arrow. [I] didn't see him have a gun. He was also in the battle at Wood Lake.

Faribault described Godfrey as an active participant in the four battles (thereby admitting his own presence too). He also undercut Godfrey's assertions that he was coerced, mainly with his recital of his ghoulish boasts of child-killing but also by saying, "He never told me he was forced into it."

From Heard's book we know that either Heard or the court confronted Godfrey at some point with the ample evidence of his braggadocio in the Dakota camp and that he then withdrew his initial denial. Godfrey admitted the boasts to Heard but said that he only "spoke of killing in the Indian acceptation of the term" and that he had done so "in order to keep the good will of the Indians."[40] This interrogation most likely took place shortly after the prosecution's witnesses testified at Godfrey's trial, but it was never recorded in the transcripts. Whenever it happened, by his acknowledgment Godfrey sought to retract—if belatedly, and if believed—the biggest discrepancy between his story and that told by the witnesses against him.

When the prosecution's case was closed, the evidence against Godfrey fell into three parts: his own statements that he had killed seven or more people with a hatchet or tomahawk at Milford; his admitted, if reluctant, participation in the Milford massacre; and his involvement in four battles. While there was no direct evidence that he had murdered anyone "with his own hand," Godfrey's own boastful words could be taken as a confession to the first allegation against him if the court did not believe his belated explanation for those statements. Similarly, the judges could find him guilty of "joining and participating" in the Milford killings unless they concluded that he acted under duress. Finally, if the court believed that shooting into the tents at Birch Coulee or at a house in New Ulm constituted a crime, it did not need to go any further than Godfrey's own statements to find him guilty.

But the military commission, which was soon to display its iron resolve against many defendants and could scarcely be accused of softheartedness, was flummoxed by Godfrey and by the evidence in his case. Heard, in a newspaper article published after the trial, said, "He [Godfrey] entered upon many . . . details, and with such an air of candor that those who heard him, instead of retaining their feelings of detestation became prepossessed in his favor."[41] Heard used similar words in his book to describe the court's transformation: "He [Godfrey] had such an honest look, and spoke with such a truthful tone, that the court, though prejudiced against him in the beginning, were now unanimously inclined to believe that there were possibilities as to his sincerity. His language was broken, and he communicated his ideas with some little difficulty. This was an advantage in his favor, for it interested the sympathetic attention of the listener, and it was a pleasure to listen to his hesitating speech." And so the court decided not to decide, at least not yet. Instead, the judges "held his case open for a long time, and, while the other trials were progressing, asked every person who was brought in about [Godfrey's deeds]."[42] The proof or disproof of his story would come by comparing it with the evidence of future defendants and witnesses.

Heard, with his prosecution experience, may have pointed out the benefits of such a delay. Godfrey's story was so specific, and he had implicated so many Indians who would be called before the court to give their versions of the same events, that any lies would likely be unmasked as the trials went forward. Godfrey, whose trial had begun in an atmosphere of almost universal prejudice, was momentarily spared. The noose had not tightened around his neck, but it would hover over his head until the judges made up their minds.

NOTES ON CHAPTER 6

1. Letter from "H" [Isaac Heard], *St. Paul Pioneer and Democrat,* November 15, 1862.
2. For the use of Sibley tents, see Stephen R. Riggs to Mary Riggs, September 8, 1862, Riggs letters, CCHS. For the tent patent story, see "Henry Hopkins Sibley," *Wikipedia,* at http://en.wikipedia.org/wiki/Henry_Hopkins_Sibley, accessed June 9, 2006. A patent was issued to Sibley for the tent in 1856.
3. The format of charges and specifications was the same as was then used in court-martial trials. See Coppée, *Field Manual of Courts-Martial,* 19–20, 104–6.
4. Unless otherwise noted, all quotations from the trial proceedings and testimony are from the Dakota Trials Records. Trial testimony is reproduced verbatim. I have sometimes added punctuation and paragraphing for clarity.
5. Heard, *History of the Sioux War,* 189. Later in his incarceration Godfrey was chained alone. *St. Peter Tribune,* November 1, 1862.
6. The sources for Godfrey's physical description are Heard, *History of the Sioux War,* 189–90; Robert O. Sweeny, sketch in the collections of MHS, published in Anderson and Woolworth, *Through Dakota Eyes,* 86; and Sweeny letter, March 27, 1886, *St. Paul Dispatch, March 28, 1886.* Sweeny's sketch is the only known likeness of Godfrey. Sweeny took Godfrey to be several years younger than he was, as did Egbert. S. B. Egbert to Carter, February 3, 1910, Carter Papers, MHS, box 2.
7. Heard, *History of the Sioux War,* 190.
8. Ibid., 192.
9. Ibid., 192–93.
10. Ibid., 193–94. Godfrey is quoted as saying that "Waki-ya-ni" and "Mah-hwa" "have been convicted," indicating that Heard either based portions of his statement on Godfrey's later testimony as a witness or interviewed Godfrey long after his own trial so as to offer his readers a more complete account of Godfrey's story. To avoid confusion about the sequence of events, in quotes from Heard's book in this chapter I have omitted references to later convictions, instead discussing them in the notes. Godfrey was referring to Wakinyanna (trial 383) and Mahoowaywa (trial 382), who were both tried and sentenced to death near the end of the trials. I have not been able to identify Godfrey's brother-in-law, although if he surrendered, it is likely that he was one of the men tried for participating in the Milford massacre.
11. There are conflicting reports about the identity of the two men killed in the wagons. Fritsche says they were teamsters hauling goods to the Lower Agency, though he does not name them. Satterlee makes no mention of the teamsters but does refer to the killing of two farmers (Carl Heuyers and Joseph Emery) from the neighboring village of Leavenworth who were delivering loads of hay to Milford. Fritsche, *History of Brown County,* 162, 189; and Satterlee, *Outbreak and Massacre,* 41–42.
12. Heard, *History of the Sioux War,* 194.
13. The phrase "who was convicted" has been deleted at this point to avoid confusion. The record of Godfrey's trial testimony tells of the killing of this woman and her two children, but it does not mention Muzzabomadu (trial 10) by name.
14. Heard, *History of the Sioux War,* 194–95.
15. Satterlee, *Outbreak and Massacre,* 40–41.

16. The trial transcript contains a clause—"one killed an old woman and children"—that must have been a reference to Muzzabomadu (trial 10), but it is unclear in that context where the killing took place, how many children there were, or who committed the murders.
17. Heard, *History of the Sioux War*, 195.
18. Adolph Schilling, like Joseph Messmer, survived his injuries for a short time. Both injured men were placed in the wagons of the recruiting party that returned to New Ulm. See Fritsche, *History of Brown County*, 193. The fact that Schilling and Messmer were far enough east to be picked up by the retreating recruiters strongly confirms the sequence of events described by Godfrey, who refers to the "dead man" (Messmer) and to the attack on the Schilling house as both occurring beyond (to the east of) the ambush on the recruiting party at the ravine.
19. The reference to two wagons is probably a mistake in Heard's book, since Godfrey specifically testified at his trial to seeing four wagons and other accounts verify that the recruiting party had more than two wagons. Heard may have confused the earlier attack on two ox-driven wagons at Milford with the recruiting party story, or he may have been confused by Godfrey's mention of capturing two wagons earlier and seeing four wagons in the recruiting party, yet having only four wagons to take back to the agency. The rest of the recruiting party wagons were not taken by the Dakotas.
20. Heard, *History of the Sioux War*, 195–96.
21. See the introduction for citations to accounts of the ambush of the recruiting party.
22. In a later trial Godfrey referred to the members of the recruiting party as "soldiers on the bridge." Trial of Muzzabomadu, trial 10, Dakota Trials Records.
23. Paulson, *Franz Massopust*, 14–18, compares the Spelbrink account with Godfrey's testimony.
24. To avoid confusion, the words "sentenced to be hung" have been deleted from the quote. They may have been inserted at a later date by Heard, or they may indicate that an interview with Godfrey took place after the conclusion of the trials. Late in the course of the trials Godfrey gave evidence against the "young Indian" referenced in the text, Oyatayakoo. Trial 377, Dakota Trials Records.
25. Heard, *History of the Sioux War*, 197–98.
26. Ibid., 198–99.
27. "Reminiscences of Mary Schwandt Schmidt as told to Mrs. Edna Sandford Ward," 1913, 9 (shot in back); and "The Story of My Captivity," October 30, 1935, 5–7 both in Schwandt Schmidt Papers, MHS.
28. See trial of Chankahda, trial 359, Dakota Trials Records.
29. Heard, *History of the Sioux War*, 197. The sickbed killing of Caroline Stocker and the attempt to burn her husband alive in their house are described in [Schilling], "Nine Year Old Girl's Experiences." See also Fritsche, *History of Brown County*, 190–91. Instead of hiding in the attic, Joseph Stocker and nine-year-old Cecelia Ochs survived the attack by first taking refuge in the cellar and then digging their way to an escape from the burning house. See also Satterlee, *Outbreak and Massacre*, 41, who identifies the woman shot by Wahpaduta as Mrs. Stocker.
30. Heard, *History of the Sioux War*, 191–99 (events of August 18), 199–201 (the rest of the conflict).

31. The court's lack of clarity continues to confuse scholars. Professor Carol Chomsky, in her excellent law review article about the Dakota trials, says about two of the convicted defendants (Muzzabomadu, trial 10, and Wakinyanna, trial 383), "It is unclear from the evidence given whether these were isolated attacks not part of a general battle or actually part of the united attack on New Ulm." Chomsky, "United States–Dakota War Trials," 89n475. But when the trial records are placed in the context of Godfrey's complete statements and when collateral historical evidence is considered, no reasonable doubt remains that these two men (and several others implicated by Godfrey's testimony) were convicted for participating in the Milford massacre, not for joining in the battles at New Ulm.
32. The repeated references to Godfrey being called upon to drive wagons suggest that he, unlike most of the Dakota traditionalists, who were unaccustomed to using wagons, was skilled as a teamster. Perhaps he learned about wagons and horses during his slave days, though he also could have picked up the skill doing teamster work on the reservation. Later Godfrey did work formally as a teamster, and one of his descendants told me that Godfrey had been a horse trader. See chapter 12. All of these references suggest a knowledge of and skill with horses and horse-drawn wagons.
33. See trial of Wyatahtowah, trial 5, Dakota Trials Records.
34. Heard mentioned that Godfrey testified "before witnesses were called." As an experienced prosecutor, he would have realized both the exceptional nature of this sequence and the huge disadvantage it was to Godfrey. *History of the Sioux War*, 253–54.
35. Mary Woodbury, a Dakota mixed-blood, was married to a white man, Warren Woodbury. See Woodbury affidavit, #66, Scrip Rolls.
36. In Heard's book the word "clubbed" is italicized, apparently as his way of emphasizing that Godfrey did not use lethal force. *History of the Sioux War*, 253.
37. Schwandt's testimony is difficult to reconcile with portions of her later accounts, which also cannot always be reconciled with one another. In recollections recorded fifty to seventy years after the war, she made varying claims about Godfrey's conduct, the most damning of which was a reference to seeing him wearing watches stolen from Milford victims and telling her, "I have killed the owners and it was great fun." *St. Paul Pioneer Press*, May 12, 1912. In another account she said, "He boasted that he had killed seventeen persons that day, and said that it was great fun to kill the whites for they made no resistance whatever." Schwandt Schmidt, "The Story of My Captivity," October 30, 1935, 4, Schwandt Schmidt Papers, MHS. In another version, she described Godfrey as the "foremost demon of the bunch" at the Patoille attacks and implied that he was wearing "many scalps" when she first saw him. "Reminiscences of Mary Schwandt Schmidt as told to Mrs. Edna Sandford Ward," 1913, 24, Schwandt Schmidt Papers, MHS. If indeed Godfrey had been wearing scalps, had expressly told her that he had killed the owners of the watches, or had bragged of killing seventeen people, it seems almost inconceivable that Schwandt would have told none of these "facts" to the judges. The (comparatively) bland nature of her trial testimony, the inconsistencies among her own later accounts, and the long delay in recording her recollections strongly suggest that Schwandt later misremembered or embellished her stories about Godfrey. Yet even she made no claim of seeing Godfrey harm anyone.
38. See "Courts-Martial and Military Commission Proceedings against Union soldiers, 1861–1866," NA, RG 94, M1523.

39. It is interesting that Heard, despite covering every other witness against Godfrey, omits the testimony of David Faribault Jr. in his book. *History of the Sioux War,* 252–53. Since Heard did include another witness against Godfrey who said even less than Faribault (LaBatte, who said he knew nothing), it is possible that he was purposely downplaying the role of the mixed-blood family that was close to Sibley. By the time Heard's book was published, Faribault had already received an extraordinary pardon—with Sibley's help. See chapter 11.
40. Heard, *History of the Sioux War,* 254. Heard implies that this exchange took place during the trial, but it is possible that it took place out of court. In either event, it seems likely that the judges knew of Godfrey's change of position before they made a final decision in his case.
41. Letter from "H" [Isaac Heard], *St. Paul Pioneer and Democrat,* November 15, 1862.
42. Heard, *History of the Sioux War,* 254. The trial transcript does not recite the commission's decision to keep the case against Godfrey open, but one small slip of the pen appears to corroborate Heard's account. Immediately following the testimony of the last witness, the words "And therefore" appear, indicating the recorder's intention to write the verdict. The next paragraph repeats the words "And therefore," which are crossed out. It looks as though Heard started to write the verdict, then stopped writing and returned at some later time.

CHAPTER 7

Chained Alone

For a military court ordered by its commander to try defendants "summarily," the commission began the Camp Release trials at a rather deliberate pace. Because Sibley's court seldom noted the dates on which cases were tried, we do not know exactly how long Godfrey's trial lasted. But Sarah Wakefield later voiced her view that Godfrey got more time in the courtroom than he deserved: "The first man tried was the negro and several days were passed in bringing in testimony, when every one knew he was guilty."[1] Even making allowances for Wakefield's penchant for exaggeration, it is likely that Godfrey's case consumed at least a day or two.[2] Meanwhile, Wakefield and other women in the pool of released-captive witnesses grew restive with the delay that compelled them to stay tent-bound on the prairie while waiting to testify, postponing reunions with their families.

By twenty-first-century standards, even a two-day criminal trial in a capital case—military or civil—would be considered ludicrously short. The very brevity of the proceedings would form a basis for appealing any guilty verdict, and if the death penalty ensued, for probable reversal by a higher court. But standards were very different during the Civil War, when many Union soldiers were executed following courts-martial trials lasting two days or less.[3] Trials that might appear hopelessly abbreviated today were not uncommon at the time, especially in military courts.

As the military commission heard its first batch of cases at Camp Release, Sibley stayed aloof from the proceedings. He focused instead on hardtack and forage, on the welfare of the surrendered Dakotas and the released captives, and on his continuing strategy to entice more Indians to surrender.

Apart from the arrest of a relative handful of men, daily life was remarkably unchanged in the Dakota camp. Families remained together in their tipis, just where they had erected them before Sibley's arrival. Security checkpoints of military guards ringed the camp, their presence bringing much-needed protection from the vengeance of troopers. The only ironclad rule was that no one got in or out without a permit.

The undecided Dakotas lingering in the area could see, or hear from messengers sent to them, that no pogrom was in progress. The clinching fact that may have convinced many Dakota doubters to travel the one-way path to surrender was Sibley's decision not—at least, not yet—to disarm the Indians. To warriors and hunters, nothing could have been more reassuring than the knowledge that their kin in camp still kept not only their lives but also their guns and ammunition, their tomahawks, spears, and knives.

Following his trial, Godfrey was returned to the crude jail. As the days passed there still were no mass arrests in the Dakota camp. In addition to the sixteen men who had been taken into custody earlier, another thirteen were apprehended based on information furnished by Godfrey and others. Still, at twenty-nine, the total number of men arrested during the first two weeks at Camp Release was relatively low—far less than the increases to the Indian camp numbers by those who were late to surrender.

Wahpaduta, Godfrey's father-in-law, was one of those now arrested, probably because Godfrey had named him during his testimony. Wyatahtowah, Muzzabomadu, and Dowansa, also chained in the small wooden jail, were likely arrested due to Godfrey's evidence.[4] Sharing close quarters with men he had implicated could not have been a pleasant experience.

The invitation to the white female captives to have a private chat with Chaplain Riggs apparently yielded two of the three cases that followed Godfrey's. Tehehdonecha (trial 2) was charged with having "forcibly ravished" Margaret Cardinal after she was taken captive near Beaver Creek, north of the river. Tazoo (trial 4), who claimed Mattie Williams as his captive after the Patoille wagon attack, was accused of raping her. Both men were convicted and sentenced to be hanged.

Williams would soon capture the attention of the highest officials of the state, General Pope, and many Minnesotans as a virginal white icon symbolizing the Dakotas' supposed rapaciousness. Her sexual mistreatment was not only exaggerated but widely (and mistakenly) presumed to have been the lot of almost all of the female captives. Lurid reports that Williams and other white women were subjected to gang rapes by hordes of Dakota men find no support in the trial records, which contain just two sexual assault cases, each involving a single rapist.

Since each of the two rape victims had been claimed and taken back to her captor's home, it is likely that these instances of sexual assault—as whites viewed them—would not have violated traditional Dakota proscriptions against raping enemy women during warfare. In a society in which marriages were sometimes arranged without the woman's consent and in which female captives could be killed, sold, used, or abused at the discretion of their captors, Dakota men may not have seen nonconsensual sexual relations with a captive woman as violating tribal norms.

From Tazoo's perspective, his actions in saving Mattie Williams's life were paramount: "If this woman is living now and is about to see her relatives, I am the cause of it," he claimed. But once he admitted to the court that he had "ravished" Williams, he had, in white eyes, confessed to subjecting her to a fate worse than death. Godfrey had named Tazoo as being present at the attack on the Patoille wagon, but he was not called as a witness in Tazoo's trial. At the conclusion of Tazoo's testimony, the judges apparently questioned him about Godfrey's involvement. He replied simply, "The Negro was in the middle wagon with my party [during the attack on Patoille's wagon]." Those words did not help the court make a decision in Godfrey's case, for they merely confirmed part of his story.

Similarly, though Godfrey in his own trial had identified Wyatahtowah (trial 5) as present at the Patoille attack, his testimony was not necessary to convict Wyatahtowah of killing Patoille, directly or by "participation." Informing the court that his chief, Wabasha, had told him to surrender at Camp Release, Wyatahtowah then offered this evidence: "It was never my intention to kill any one, but what I did was done under the influence of evil spirits. . . . I saw the Indians fire at Patoille. I shot at him but don't know whether I hit him, or not. I was near when I shot at him. A good many shot. I aimed at the crowd when Patoille was shot. I shot at the crowd when they were in the wagon."

Given the Dakota concept of a "kill," Wyatahtowah probably did not believe that he had committed a murder: he was one of many men who fired at Patoille. But to Sibley's court his admissions were tantamount to a confession, for when two or more people shoot at an intended victim all are equally guilty of homicide. Wyatahtowah's name was added to the hanging list. The judges also obviously quizzed him about Godfrey's involvement, and he replied, "The Negro was of the party [that attacked Patoille]. I never saw the Negro man kill any whites. . . . Don't know that the Negro killed anybody." By the end of the first week of the court's docket the Godfrey case was still undecided, and no one had supplied more incriminating evidence against him.

The paucity of provisions and the hardship conditions at Camp Release now started to have a substantial impact on the pending trials, for Sibley was forced to send his best potential witnesses—the white women captives—back to safer environs. Beginning on October 4 at least ninety of the released captives were escorted more than one hundred miles to St. Peter, the nearest town that had not been destroyed in the war.[5] At the same time that some of the Indians who had at first refused to surrender were coming into Camp Release, the witness pool was seriously diminished.

On the same day that most of the white captives were sent away, Sibley also ordered the relocation of virtually the entire Dakota camp—about 1,250 people—twenty miles downriver to Yellow Medicine. This move, too, was necessitated by the shortage of provisions. The unharvested corn and potato fields planted by Dakota farmers near the Upper Agency offered the only available sustenance to feed the Indians—and, unless supply trains soon arrived, the white soldiers. Godfrey's wife and children were undoubtedly part of this group. With the exception of Godfrey and twenty-eight Indians held in manacles and chains at Camp Release, Sibley also sent all the adult Dakota men—almost three hundred—to Yellow Medicine.[6]

Sibley dispatched a military guard of 150 soldiers, under the leadership of Capt. J. C. Whitney, to the new camp.[7] Sibley was careful to respect the authority of Indian agent Thomas Galbraith, who accompanied the Dakotas to Yellow Medicine. In separate letters given to Galbraith and Whitney, Sibley said that Galbraith was to "take charge of the Indians," while Whitney was to "render such aid to the Indian agent as he may require."[8] At Yellow Medicine the still-armed Dakotas outnumbered white troops by almost two to one.

Meanwhile, back at Camp Release, Godfrey's first appearance providing state's evidence, in the case against Muzzabomadu (trial 10), segued naturally from the testimony he gave in his own trial. Having already identified Muzzabomadu as being among the Milford and Patoille attackers, Godfrey would have had little choice other than to appear as a witness, for he still needed to convince the judges of his truthfulness.

Typically, Riggs wrote the names of potential witnesses near the bottom of the formal charges, and "Godfrey (Negro)" was listed to support the charge that Muzzabomadu killed "an elderly woman and child in a garden near New Ulm." The notation of Godfrey's race in the court's record was not irrelevant under the law of the times. It was not a foregone conclusion that even a free black man would be considered a competent witness whose testimony would be accepted in court. Whether blacks were entitled to citizenship (the Dred Scott decision said they were not), could vote, could serve on juries, or could offer testimony in court all were disputed points and in constant flux in Northern states.[9] Neither the military commission nor any contemporary commentators questioned Godfrey's capacity to serve as a witness, but it is entirely possible that his testimony was permitted only because this was an extraordinary military court and because the defendants were Indians, who were not seen as entitled to the protections given to white defendants. In any event, Godfrey was often identified in the court's record as a "Negro."

Muzzabomadu testified in his own defense, denying that he was guilty of the murders charged: "I call God to witness that I have not killed or shot at a white man." He claimed he was cutting bark for tobacco (kinnikinnick) near New Ulm when he heard of the outbreak. He implied, in his direct evidence, that his first contact with the hostilities was when he came upon the Patoille wagon on his way back to the Lower Agency. Arriving after those shootings, Muzzabomadu claimed he saved the lives of Mattie Williams and Mary Schwandt.

Amplifying the eyewitness testimony he gave in his own trial, Godfrey then took the stand and said, "I know the prisoner. This Indian killed an old woman and two children. They were going into a garden when he fired on them. It was near the Traveler's Home near New Ulm. I saw the Indians fire on the old woman and saw her fall. He then jumped into the garden and kicked the children down. I didn't see him kill the children. I was in the wagon at the time. This took place on the first day they commenced killing the whites. I saw him again, but he didn't say he had killed any whites."[10] The reference to the Travelers' Home and to "the first day" of killings reconfirm that Godfrey was describing killing scenes at Milford.[11]

Muzzabomadu retook the witness stand to rebut Godfrey. "What Godfrey said is not true. I met Godfrey at the Travelers' Home. I heard Godfrey had not killed any. I met Godfrey and his party near the Travelers' Home. I didn't stop with them but went up near where they killed Patwell. I had no whiskey. I had a bad gun when we met soldiers on the bridge and it didn't go off." By admitting his presence at the Travelers' Home, Muzzabomadu put himself in the thick of the Milford massacre (which he omitted from his opening testimony). His isolated statement that "I heard that Godfrey had not killed any" was probably in response to a question by the court, seeking evidence, pro or con, to help them decide Godfrey's case. The judges found Muzzabomadu guilty of murder and sentenced him to hang. This court had no qualms about relying on a black man's testimony.

The next case was against Wahpaduta (trial 11), Godfrey's father-in-law. The transcript begins with his opening statement:

I am not guilty. At the time of the outbreak I was among the settlements and the Indians came down and that was the first news I heard of it. I was living with the Germans near New Ulm. They built a house for me. I did not go to New Ulm. I was at the battle this side of the Cotton Wood River—at New Ulm. I had no gun and was a good ways off—had not even a knife. Have not been with any other war party—have kept myself at home. I am telling the truth. I and my German neighbors were great friends. I was not at the Lower Agency when the murders were committed there.

I have killed no white men. I was going into a house and a white man presented his gun to my breast and I shot him. Some of the Indians said I had shot another white man, but it is not true.

The first paragraph appears to contain Wahpaduta's denial of any participation in the New Ulm battles. But Colonel Crooks and other members of the court must have reeled in surprise upon hearing the last portion. Though the time, place, and victim identity are missing, Wahpaduta admits trying to enter a white man's house, then shooting one of his "great German friends," a settler who confronted him with a gun.

David Faribault was then called as a witness.[12] "I was at the prisoner's lodge the day after the troops came here and he told me he killed 2. Have seen him often at battles—at New Ulm, at the Fort, and at the last battle. He said the persons he killed were 2 cooks. I thought he meant Myrick. He said he shot one in the head and one in the body. His wife was present. The place he mentioned was where Divoll and Myrick were killed."

If Wahpaduta had indeed boasted about killing two cooks at the place Faribault surmised, he still would have had a valid alibi defense to such a murder charge, for Divoll and Myrick were traders killed at the Lower Agency during the first hour of the war. According to both Godfrey and his father-in-law the latter was at his home, miles away, at that time, and he then headed east, toward Milford, rather than to the agency, in the opposite direction. Of course, it is possible that Faribault correctly reported the defendant's boasts but got the location and identity of the victims wrong. Under either view, Faribault's testimony is weak.

But then Wahpaduta stepped into the breach to fill any holes left by his earlier admissions: "All the Dakotas have killed whites. If the guilty are punished, there will be none left.... The man I shot was near New Ulm. ... It was an old man that I shot with a white head of hair. I shot him and he fell. The Negro was with the party at the time but was not present.... I shot at the man because he attempted to shoot me first."

If taken literally, Wahpaduta's claim that "all the Dakotas have killed whites" is the single most damning statement in hundreds of pages of trial testimony. But the assertion that "everybody did it," while perhaps true of small groups of Dakotas such as the one at Milford, was surely not true of the whole tribe. All historical evidence points to the fact that a relatively small number of Dakota warriors (a speculative guess would be between one hundred and two hundred men) were involved in killing white settlers. Wahpaduta's attempt to portray his shooting of the old white man at Milford as an act of self-defense would have held little weight in the context of the systematic, house-to-house killings that had preceded it. The fifty-two to zero death totals at Milford make it clear that any isolated defense attempts by whites were both feeble and futile.

Wahpaduta next turned his sights on Godfrey. Whether the defendant was releasing his own bile or answering questions from the court, one can almost feel the venom in his words:

> The negro is my son-in-law. I heard he was a brave man.... It was below the Fort near a stream where the nigger killed people with a hatchet. There is another stream near this one. The negro killed 4. I was always with him at the start but I was left behind. When I overtook them they told me the others killed 12. He had a gun and a hatchet with him....
>
> The colored man went of his own free will with us. I was living with my son-in-law when the outbreak

commenced. We started away together but he left me and went on with the young men. [Taopi] brought us word that the Indians were all going below to New Ulm—that they had killed all at the agency, that they were going to kill all the whites. The Negro was cutting hay at the time. I heard the black man hallooing that the Indians were coming. I then saw him take his gun and go towards the Indians. The Negro went because he was willing to go.

This testimony contradicts Godfrey's on several critical points: whether he acted under duress or willingly, whether he was armed from the outset, and most important, whether he killed anyone. On the last issue the testimony is tantalizingly vague. Though Wahpaduta claims that "the negro killed 4," he also says that Godfrey "left me and went on with the young men" and that he "heard" about Godfrey's deeds, suggesting that this crucial evidence is all hearsay. It is also not clear if he is using "kill" in the Indian sense of touching coup. No matter what interpretation is given Wahpaduta's broadside against Godfrey, however, there can be little doubt it was delivered in anger. He was the only witness throughout all the trials to use the epithet "nigger."[13]

That Wahpaduta was convicted and sentenced to death should come as no surprise. His own words afforded the evidence to send him to the gallows. But for our purposes, the key question is, What did the commission make of Wahpaduta's testimony against Godfrey? Fortunately, the ambiguities inherent in the record are clarified somewhat by Heard, the court's recorder, who wrote in his book, "The court . . . could find no person who *saw* him [Godfrey] kill any one, although the Indians were indignant at him for having disclosed evidence against a number of them, and would be desirous of finding such testimony."[14] However we interpret his father-in-law's statements against Godfrey, Heard's comments show that the judges took them for something less than an eyewitness account of murder. It is also very likely that Wahpaduta, who mixed his professions of boundless friendship for his German neighbors with his chilling admission that he killed an old man with white hair, departed from the courtroom tent with something close to zero credibility.

Godfrey appeared as a witness only once more in the remaining seventeen cases in the first group of trials. Dowansa (trial 22) was charged with killing three men and two women in the massacre near Swan Lake "on or about August 23."[15] At trial the defendant entered no plea and said nothing, at first, in reply to the allegations. Godfrey testified,

> The prisoner told me he went to Swan Lake. He saw teams going along and ran after them and killed white men, that when he overtook them he killed three white women and two men—that he intended to take one good looking young woman home and her mother interfered. That he was leading the young woman away and her mother ran after her to take her away and the Indians told him to shoot the mother.
>
> That he shot the mother and wounded the daughter, that he went away and one of the Indians saw she wasn't dead and he ran and pulled up her clothes and she jumped up and another Indian took his tomahawk and struck her in the head and killed her. I know him perfectly well. I heard these facts from him. He came to my lodge and told me of his doings. The prisoner told me that the party was made up of five besides himself.

At first glance the case here looks similar to that against Godfrey, resting entirely on evidence of the defendant's boasts. But Dowansa was far more specific: he bragged of having shot the mother of the woman he hoped to take as a captive and then apparently started to rape the daughter, an act that was interrupted when she, while attempting to flee, was killed by another Indian's tomahawk.

At this point the defendant responded, admitting that he had been a member of the war party near Swan Lake and that those Indians had killed three women and one man. He added, "What Gus [Godfrey] says about the party is true. But I killed no one." Later Dowansa said, "I told

Gus what he says only I didn't killed a white man." With these words he affirmed everything in Godfrey's testimony. However one interprets the evidence, therefore, this case offers no dispute between Godfrey and the defendant, whose defense was, in essence, that his boasts to Godfrey were untrue. The commission sentenced Dowansa to hang.

Godfrey was called as a prosecution witness in just three of the twenty-nine cases that made up the first batch of Dakota trials. If the trials had ended at this point his evidence would have been seen as crucial to the prosecution's efforts in those three instances, but his importance as a witness would have paled in comparison to that of David Faribault Sr. Faribault testified in eight of those cases, most of which ended in the imposition of the death sentence.[16]

Nor was Godfrey the only defendant who turned state's evidence in the first group of trials. Tazoo, who was given the death sentence in trial 4, testified against Hapan in trial 24. Hapan had helped Tazoo take Mattie Williams as a captive, and the court sentenced him to death for his presence at the Patoille killings. In addition to Godfrey, the prosecution called a large number of other witnesses. A total of thirteen of the released white captives testified in eleven cases in the first group of trials. Nine mixed-bloods, including the busy Faribault, gave evidence in fourteen cases. And five full-blood Dakotas testified against their kinsmen in seven cases.[17]

Even as the court queried witnesses and Dakota defendants for more evidence relating to Godfrey, newspapers started to convict him before the jury of Minnesota public opinion. The press, relying on Sheriff Roos's dispatch of August 18, had previously identified him only as "a negro." On October 4 the *Mankato Record* published a report brought back by Joseph Lagree, an infantryman in Captain Jerome Dane's company of Blue Earth volunteers. The account, in which Godfrey's name appeared in print for the first time, was an archetype of the biased press coverage he would receive:

A NIGGER MURDERS 23 WHITES.

Jos. Lagree informs us that among the prisoners taken by Col. Sibley, was a half-breed Negro, named Augustus Godfrey, who has taken an active and prominent part in the massacres, led the attack on New Ulm, and exults in the fact that he killed seventeen whites one night, and twenty-three in all. Joe has known him for a number of years, and has repeated to us the following conversation with him:

Joe. Gus, I saw you at New Ulm.

Nigger. Yes, I was there, and I tried my best to send a ball to you.

Joe. Why did you do this?

Nigger. I was forced into it. I had to do it.

In reply to an inquiry whether he killed many whites in the battle, he said that he did not know.

Joe says he afterwards learned from Indians that this nigger came in one night and said he had killed seventeen whites. Little Crow boasted to Red Legs that nigger Gus had killed in all twenty-three whites, and would kill many more.[18]

A few days later this article was republished verbatim in the *St. Paul Pioneer and Democrat,* exposing the residents of the state's then-biggest city to the "facts" about Godfrey.[19]

Later newspaper accounts about Godfrey were not always prejudicial to his cause. But this first report deserves note for it established four themes subsequently repeated, even after Godfrey was dead. First, those who sought to depict Godfrey as a devil incarnate often led (as did the headline of the *Record*'s article) with a racist slur. Even after the reader is told his full name, the colloquy is recited between Lagree and "Nigger." Reference to Godfrey as a "half-breed Negro" more subtly informs the reader that Godfrey is half Indian, since "half-breed" was then used almost exclusively to refer to persons with some Native ancestry. Those who have demonized Godfrey have often since attempted to deny, or define away, his half-white bloodline.

Second, the *Record* portrays Godfrey not only as an archcriminal but also (as Sheriff Roos did) as a leader of the Dakota war. While reporting Godfrey's statement that he was "forced" to go to New Ulm, the newspaper lends it no credence, flatly telling its readers that he was "prominent" and "led the attack on New Ulm." This distortion is an exclusively white perspective, for no Dakota has ever claimed that Godfrey was a leader at any site.

Third, a specific—and huge—number of white victims are laid at Godfrey's feet. Though Godfrey had been charged by the military commission with killing seven whites (all without witnesses, so far as the commission had been able to determine), the *Record* confidently proclaims that he committed twenty-three murders. The apparent chain of sources for this assertion was Little Crow to Red Legs to unidentified "Indians" to Lagree to the *Record*'s editor. By the time this specific "news" reached the reader, it was hearsay *at least* five times removed from the source. Yet it is this bloody "fact" that made the headline. Ironically, the supposed originator of this particular falsehood, Little Crow, was widely regarded by white Minnesotans as the most treacherous villain of the war.

Finally, it was not sufficient to label Godfrey a mass murderer. He had to *enjoy* the killing. Or, as the *Record* puts it, Godfrey "exulted in the fact." And, again citing the long chain of hearsay, the black man's alleged slaughters are coupled with Little Crow's gleeful prediction that he "would kill many more."

The trials were conducted in the strictest secrecy, with neither reporters nor observers allowed in the courtroom. But that did not prevent newspapers from publishing "authoritative" accounts about them. The first such report appeared on October 5, 1862, in the *St. Paul Pioneer and Democrat* under the headline "Indians Convicted." The article opened, "We understand the military commission instituted by Col Sibley, have convicted eight Indians of murders and other crimes, and sentenced them to be hung, which sentence has probably been carried into effect before this. One of the convicted was the negro, who was prominent in the attack on New Ulm."

In this instance the assertion that Godfrey had been convicted would have been news to the commission members, who had made no decision and were still questioning witnesses about him.

On October 11 the *St. Paul Pioneer and Democrat* updated its readers on Godfrey and the Dakota trials with a one-sentence report: "Twenty Indians have been convicted, including the negro, who confessed that he killed eight in one family." The same paper, just four days before, had revealed the "truth" that Godfrey had killed twenty-three whites. But he apparently had "confessed" to killing only eight.

One of the interesting features of these early press accounts about the trials—a pattern that would continue until they were complete—is that Godfrey (after years of total anonymity as a slave and fugitive slave) is the only defendant identified by name. All the others charged or convicted are referred to simply as "an Indian" or "the Indians." This puzzling void cannot be explained solely by the secrecy of the trials but is probably linked to the utter dehumanization of the Dakotas and to the racially driven curiosity evoked by the specter of a black man rising up with them.

The time had come for the commission to render its decision in Godfrey's case. The judges' querying of subsequent defendants had not furnished them with smoking-gun answers to key questions regarding Godfrey's guilt. Two main issues were still open: Had he actually murdered anyone? Was he a willing participant in the Dakotas' killings, or had he acted under life-threatening duress?

The court's dry decision in Godfrey's case was frustratingly succinct: "Therefore the court found the prisoner guilty on the charge, and second specification, and not guilty on the first specification." With those brief words Godfrey was found *not guilty* of murdering anyone himself (the first specification) but guilty of "participation in the murders and massacres committed by the Sioux Indians" (the second specification). The court thus accepted Godfrey's claim that his boasts about murders were untrue. But it was also unwilling to treat duress as a full defense, for it found him guilty of "participation."

The sentence for this mixed verdict was similarly divided: "[The court] . . . sentenced him [Godfrey] to be hung by the neck until he is dead (a mitigation of the sentence to imprisonment for ten years is recommended)." Thus the court decided that the facts justified hanging Godfrey and imposed that sentence. But, in the next parenthetical clause, the judges recommended to Sibley, without explanation, that he reduce the penalty to ten years in prison. Though Godfrey's testimony had already led to the conviction of two of the worst-offending Indians, it is impossible to determine the impact that his role as a prosecution witness would have had on the court's judgment. He had been a helpful witness, but it seems most likely that the judges rested their findings primarily on their overall assessment of his guilt.

Two later sources furnish support for the interpretation that the court was prompted to recommend leniency for Godfrey because it believed he acted under duress. Robert O. Sweeny, relying in part on conversations with William Marshall, one of the judges in Godfrey's case, said that he gained "the impression that [Godfrey] . . . was compelled by the Indians to join in the massacre."[20] And Theodore G. Carter, a soldier who became acquainted with Godfrey while he was in custody, wrote many years later, "The evidence showed that no one saw him [Godfrey] harm any one, but that he boasted of killing people, which the prisoners (white) and Indians testified to. But he claimed that he was told that he must take an active part in the outbreak, and that he so managed as to make them believe he was killing people while he did not hurt anyone."[21] In a newspaper article Carter added, "The Indians were suspicious of Gussa [Godfrey] and told him that he must identify himself with them. Considering his situation, he did what he was obliged to do, to save his life and that of his son."[22] While Carter did not claim to reflect the opinion of any members of the commission, his view that Godfrey acted under threat of death was probably shared, to some extent, by the judges.

In the first group of twenty-nine cases, twenty-eight men had been either acquitted or sentenced to hang. Godfrey's was the only case in which the court coupled a hanging verdict with a recommendation for leniency.[23] As the trial transcripts were submitted to Sibley in the second week of October, it was evident that he, not the judges, would decide whether Godfrey ascended the gallows.

All along, Sibley had secretly planned to arrest most of the late-surrendering Dakota men at Camp Release. Not illogically, Sibley believed that the Indians who had hung back and waited to see how he treated those who surrendered had done so because they had something to hide. At least initially, he viewed most of those in the larger, early surrendering Dakota group sent to Yellow Medicine as less guilty, and he had no plans either to disarm or to apprehend them. But starting on October 6 Sibley began receiving direct orders from General Pope instructing him to disarm the Indians and send all of them (women and children included) down to Fort Snelling, where the balance of the trials and executions would take place under Pope's scrutiny. By issuing orders to deliver all of the Dakotas to a military fort far from the reservation, there to be subject to his authority, Pope showed his total disregard for the federal Indian agency. His orders to Sibley now placed all of the surrendering (or later captured) Dakotas under direct and continuing military control.[24]

In one blistering letter Pope offered scathing criticism of Sibley's arrangements for the Dakota people's surrender: "I only regret that you ever permitted a flag of truce to be used with them." In the same communique Pope said he had received reports that former Indian traders in Sibley's camp were attempting to prevent the type of draconian postwar punishment that Pope wanted to implement. He threatened to prosecute those men for treason (for which the penalty was death). Any Dakota should be executed, Pope adamantly declared, who was guilty of "any sort of complicity in the late outrages."[25]

Promptly responding to Pope's orders, four companies of Sibley's army surrounded the Dakotas at Camp Release on the night of October 11 and, with the interpreting help of Chaplain Riggs, seized all weapons and took all the men into custody. The Indians put up no resistance, asking only why the soldiers had not come for them in the daytime. The men were promptly manacled, chained, and jailed in a log jail hastily expanded to accommodate one hundred prisoners.[26] As soon as it was ready, Godfrey would also have been relocated to that jail.

Since Pope's disarmament orders made no exceptions, Sibley immediately sent a directive to Captain Whitney at Yellow Medicine, commanding him to take all weapons from the Dakotas. This was a radical shift from Sibley's earlier intentions, but Pope left him no choice. Pope's surprising demand that all of the Dakotas be transported as prisoners to Fort Snelling was so sensitive and so likely to cause unrest among the Indians that Sibley ordered Whitney not even to disclose that order to other officers.[27]

To cope with Pope's new regimen, at Yellow Medicine Whitney and Galbraith devised a scheme that presaged modern-day "sting" operations. They instructed Samuel J. Brown, the well-educated mixed-blood son of the former agent, to go to the Indian camp and tell the Dakota men to report the next morning to be registered for an annuity roll. Responding to the dangled bait of their unpaid annuities, virtually the entire group showed up as directed, outside the warehouse designated as the payment center. Brown, Galbraith, and Whitney went through the charade of pretending to conduct a full-blown registration, promising each man that the guns, tomahawks, and knives he deposited into a barrel would be returned to him shortly. In this fashion every Indian man was taken into custody without resistance, although forty-six were soon released when Galbraith certified that they were "above suspicion." That left 234 men held at Yellow Medicine and about 100 (and rising, with Dakotas still surrendering) at Camp Release.[28]

Until this point no Dakota man had been arrested without some basis for pressing a charge against him. Suddenly and without forewarning, Pope's explicit orders led to mass arrests, without any pretense of case-by-case justification. If nothing was known about a man, he was taken into custody. Only a small percentage of (mostly older) Dakota men were exempted from this sweep. Sibley probably felt that Pope's orders left him with no other option. But Sibley still bore the responsibility for the wholesale disregard of his promises to "protect" those Dakotas not implicated in murders.

For Godfrey and the convicted Dakotas, there was one short-term beneficial (if unintended) consequence of Pope's orders. In his urgent quest to wrest control over the Dakotas by bringing them to Fort Snelling, Pope also temporarily reprieved Godfrey and those convicted by the commission from immediate execution at Camp Release (as Sibley originally planned).

Sibley wrote to Pope, "As the order is imperative to send all below [to Fort Snelling], I shall suspend the execution of the sentenced Indians, about 20 in number, and dispatch them with others whom I shall arrest in the neighboring camp."[29] Godfrey's day of reckoning was thus postponed. But Pope's directives did not bode well for Godfrey in the long run, for Pope was consistently demanding that Sibley take the harshest possible stance in administering postwar justice.[30]

Given Pope's pressures, Sibley's approval of the death sentences meted out by the commission in its first twenty-nine cases was not surprising. Sibley ratified the verdicts of the nineteen Dakotas whom the judges had, without qualification, recommended be hanged. Most of the condemned men had been implicated in murders or rapes, but Sibley also approved the execution of a few men who joined in battles or urged others to fight. With this action Sibley broke his promise to punish only those Dakotas who were guilty of murder. By letting the judges know that he was willing to hang ordinary soldiers, Sibley also ventured well beyond previous legal precedents. Prosecuting warriors whose only "crime" was joining in a battle flagrantly disregarded their rights as prisoners of war.

As Sibley reviewed each separate transcript from the first group of trials, he apparently noted his approval simply by writing a check mark beneath the court's recommended verdict. But given the court's plea for clemency for Godfrey, Sibley was required to say more in his case. On Godfrey's file, immediately beneath the words "Sentenced to be Hung," a check mark appears. Then, in words so faintly penciled that they are illegible on the National Archives microfilm of the trials, this note appears: "Recommendation for commutation of punishment not adopted. H. H. Sibley."[31] Godfrey's was thus the only case among the first twenty-nine in which Sibley did not approve the recommendation of his court. Subject only to Pope's review (a foregone conclusion) and the president's sanction, Godfrey would be hanged.

Until late on October 15 Sibley was still operating under Pope's orders and therefore contemplating no more in-the-field trials. Then new orders arrived. Pope now directed that, instead of bringing everyone forthwith to Fort Snelling, Sibley was to launch military expeditions westward to try to capture more Dakotas. He also wanted Sibley to determine "all who are guilty (whatever be the number) . . . of any complicity," assuring him that they would be hanged. Pope also changed the plan for the executions, adding a macabre twist: he demanded that Sibley bring the convicted Dakota men to the Lower Agency, where he intended to intimidate the Dakota and Winnebago tribes by forcing their members "to witness the punishment."[32]

Thus Sibley was instructed, on short notice, to try all of the Dakotas who had been taken into custody (with the assurance that Pope would rubber-stamp his actions). A court that had disposed of just 29 cases in about two weeks would now somehow have to preside over at least 300 more trials (those of the 80 untried Indians jailed at Camp Release plus another 234 at Yellow Medicine), with that number likely to swell even higher with the expected capture of more Indians.

To resuscitate his dormant court, Sibley immediately issued an order to fill the vacancy created by the departure of one of its judges, William Marshall, whom he had appointed to command an offensive expedition to round up more defendants. His Order No. 65, dated October 15, named Maj. George Bradley as the successor judge.[33] Bradley brought distinguished credentials to the commission. Speaker of the Minnesota House from 1858 to 1860—the years when Sibley served as governor—he had, said Heard, "long been rated among the first lawyers of the state."[34]

To deal with its daunting new caseload within the constraints of time and conditions, Sibley now directed his judges to streamline the proceedings. Henceforth they should proceed in a case only until they were satisfied as to a man's "voluntary participation" in the war and should do so in "double quick" time.[35] With these orders Sibley authorized his court to pursue a legally unjustifiable course: to convict and give the death penalty to regular Dakota soldiers.

Back in St. Paul, Pope was determined to hang as many Dakotas as possible, but he decided to protect his bureaucratic backside by telegraphing to Washington, "Do I need further authority to execute Indians condemned by military commission?"[36] On October 16 he received a reply: "The law requires that sentence of death to be approved by the President. This can be done by telegraph."[37] Pope relayed that message to Sibley, asking him simply to send the names of the condemned men once the trials were concluded.[38] Sibley, who otherwise would have held earlier hangings, responded to Pope, "I shall suspend the executions until the pleasure of the president is known."[39]

This protocol is significant, as it was to place Godfrey's life in jeopardy down the road. Sibley and his commission were supposed to complete the trials and forward a list of the condemned men to Pope in St. Paul. Pope would then telegraph the president to obtain his approval. The president, Pope believed, would reply by telegraph, to be followed by a dispatch from Pope back to Sibley. With the instructions from Washington, another link had been added to the chain of events required before Godfrey could be executed. Sibley now knew that only Lincoln himself could authorize putting "the mulatto" to death.

When Sibley's court commenced hearing its massive new caseload on October 16, Godfrey was listed as a potential witness in each of the first six trials (trials 30–35). Aside from a rare appearance by a white soldier, the other prosecution witnesses in those cases were all mixed-blood men. The white captives had departed, and the remotely situated court now had little choice but to rely on willing witnesses who were still around.

Stephen Riggs, who continued to screen potential witnesses and list them in the court papers, now characterized Godfrey as a prosecution enthusiast. On October 20 Riggs wrote his wife, "I don't know whether I told you about the negro Godfrey. . . . [He] has become an Indian to all intents and purposes. He was convicted among the first batch. But he was everywhere in all the battles and now he wants to convict everyone else."[40] But Riggs was not in the courtroom, and the transcripts of the many cases heard at Camp Release after October 15 belie any claim that Godfrey strained to convict all the Dakotas. As often as not Godfrey's evidence actually helped a defendant's cause, and in some cases the man charged embraced Godfrey's version of the events. Indeed, the records of the 110 trials in the second docket of cases (trials 30–139) reveal that Godfrey's testimony was the strongest evidence given against only one of the scores of men convicted. If one were to excise his words from all of the other trials in that group of cases, it appears that the outcome of each case would have been the same.

The first five cases established this pattern. After two mixed-blood witnesses (David Faribault Sr. and Thomas Robertson) testified against Tatayebomboo (trial 30), Godfrey was not called to the stand. The admission of the defendant himself clinched the outcome of this case (under the court's new, stricter standard) when he testified that he "fired [a shot], but fired over the heads of the whites" at a battle. Godfrey's testimony, whatever it might have been, was unneeded.

Similarly, Godfrey was listed as a witness but not called in the trial of Wamdetanka (trial 34). John Magner was present with Captain Marsh's company at the ferry ambush on August 18. In a rare personal identification of an Indian battle adversary, Magner said Wamdetanka was "the first man who fired a gun at me." The defendant denied being present at the ferry ambush, but he admitted firing four shots "in the direction of the tents" at Birch Coulee. He too was given the death penalty without any testimony from Godfrey.

Three witnesses—mixed-bloods Jack Frazier and Faribault, plus Godfrey—testified briefly against Toonkanahanmane (trial 31). The sum total of Godfrey's input was, "I saw the prisoner above the Fort. Didn't notice whether he had a gun there. Saw him in the road below the Fort. I saw him at New Ulm. Saw him going there in a wagon. Never heard that this Indian did anything. He is a farmer." It appears that this defendant was convicted on the strength of his own statement, in which he acknowledged the theft of a mule at the Lower Agency (because "I had a large family and needed it") and also said, "I went to the Fort without a gun and another Indian loaned me his. The Indians were firing at random and I thought I might do the same. I tried to fire but the gun wouldn't go off." As far as the newly steeled commission was concerned, attempting to fire was as bad as firing, so they added Toonkanahanmane's name to the list of those sentenced to death.

Godfrey's testimony in the next trial, against Hoopahotakaycha (trial 32), was even weaker: "I saw the prisoner at Birch Coolie. I saw him with a gun. Didn't see him fire. I never saw him do anything, or know of his doing anything." Faribault gave slightly stronger testimony, saying that the defendant "was engaged" in the battles of New Ulm and Fort Ridgely. But again, it was the defendant who uttered the fatal words that he "fired one shot" at the last battle and that he had "fired [his] gun over the whites at Birch Coolie." Despite his claim that he was conscripted under threats ("the Indians said they would kill anybody who didn't fire"), the court also sentenced him to be hanged.

Godfrey contributed no more telling evidence against the next defendant, Hoonthan (trial 33): "I never saw the prisoner in any of the fights. Saw him coming home from the last fight. He had a gun." Once again, both Robertson and Faribault offered slightly more incriminating testimony, but then the defendant sealed his own fate when he admitted, "I fired one shot at the Fort." In accordance with the court's new policy—one shot equals one noose—he too was given the death penalty.

Among the multitude of cases heard by the military commission after October 15, these three are routine and unexceptional. But they, and many more cases to come, offer a glimpse of an important aspect of Godfrey's role as a witness. In these cases Godfrey stated precisely what he saw, heard, and knew—and apparently no more. Toonkanahanmane was a farmer Indian, he said, and Godfrey "didn't notice" if he had a gun when he saw him at the fort. Hoopahotakaycha was armed at Birch Coulie, but Godfrey "didn't see him fire" and, more broadly, never saw or heard of him doing "anything." And Godfrey saw Hoonthan coming home from the Wood Lake battle with a gun but never witnessed his participation in any battle. If Godfrey's brief testimony had been the only evidence offered against these three defendants, they surely would have been acquitted.

Moreover, the variations in Godfrey's testimony in these three routine cases have a ring of truthfulness. He clearly is not straining to convict the defendants. Every prosecutor loves to hear a witness concede that he or she "can't recall," "didn't notice," or "wasn't in a position to see" some things, even if they are important things, for such concessions are the mark of a credible witness. Small but significant details also lend verisimilitude to testimony, bolstering a jury's or court's impression that a witness is describing what he actually saw instead of simply reciting what he thinks the prosecutor wants to hear or what will make him look good. By making it clear that some of the Dakotas were—as far as he knew—relatively harmless and on the fringes of the affray, Godfrey raised the value of his stock as a witness. Riggs may have been correct in saying that Godfrey was eager to testify, but his intention seems to have been to report the facts as he recalled them regardless of whether they helped to "convict everyone else."

Godfrey also testified against the next prisoner, Shoonkaska (White Dog; trial 35), a case that interrupted the shot-fired-ergo-guilty routine. The charges alleged that White Dog "[gave] the command to fire on Capt. Marsh's command at the river near the Lower Agency on the 18th day of August 1862." Marsh had rashly marched fifty soldiers from Fort Ridgely toward the Lower Agency when he learned of the outbreak. Accounts differ as to what happened before Marsh's men were ambushed, but all report that White Dog, standing on the opposite shore of the river and holding a long tomahawk/pipe, was the only visible Dakota and that, through interpreter Peter Quinn, Marsh carried on a conversation with him for a few minutes.

The court heard testimony from White Dog, soldier John Magner, and David Faribault Sr. before Godfrey was called to the stand. The sometimes inexact trial record appears to support the conclusion that White Dog engaged Marsh in a diversionary conversation while Dakota soldiers surreptitiously surrounded the white troops. Faribault also implicated the defendant in firing a shot at the Fort Ridgely battle. Godfrey's testimony was essentially Indian camp scuttlebutt: "I heard at Red Wood on the day Marsh was killed that White Dog had a council with Capt. Marsh—that he told him to cross the river. Capt. Marsh through Quinn asked White Dog why they were killing the whites and White Dog told him to come over. That while they were talking the Indians crossed over [the river]. I heard the Indians say that White Dog was the leader and had more influence than anyone there and that it was through them that the whites were killed." Godfrey, who started with "I heard," did not claim he was an eyewitness to the ambush at the ferry. Again, his testimony added little to the other evidence already arrayed against White Dog. The death penalty outcome almost surely would have been the same without Godfrey's participation.

Godfrey gave evidence a few cases later in the trial of Makamanewashechoon (trial 41). But first, Robertson and Faribault both testified that the defendant had fired his gun at one of the Fort Ridgely battles. Only then was Godfrey called to the stand, and he simply identified the prisoner as the man who had forced him to give up the horse he had stolen from the fort stable. "After the fight at the fort was over . . . , I was standing near a spring at the fort and the Indians told me to go and see if they were taking all the horses out of the stable. I went down the hill with a mare I had taken out of the stable and the prisoner told me to give it up and I was afraid and gave it up. I saw him have a gun there." Then the defendant, taking the stand for the final time, offered his endorsement: "Godfrey told the truth." The court rendered a hanging verdict, but once again, not because of any evidence given by Godfrey.

The last full-blood Dakota against whom Godfrey testified at Camp Release was Payzhihota (trial 62). The defendant sealed his fate when he admitted to the court that he "fired 3 shots at Birch Coolie." The record simply noted that Godfrey "knows nothing of his own knowledge" that would implicate Payzhihota.

Toward the end of the trials at Camp Release the court scheduled cases against nine mixed-blood defendants.[41] Even a quick glance through these trial transcripts makes it obvious that the court employed very different procedures when trying "half-breeds." The transcripts are longer and more detailed, and they record the testimony of more witnesses per case than do those of full Dakotas tried during the same period. There are three obvious reasons for this double standard. First, the accused men were descendants of well-known white traders, so the court must have felt the need to document the grounds for any punishment with greater care. Second, the judges could hardly have ignored the many stories of threats made against the mixed-bloods by some factions of Dakotas—which rendered their claims of duress, like Godfrey's, more credible. And third, the mixed-blood defendants presumably all spoke English, and thus the court could easily listen to longer stretches of their testimony without consuming precious time in translation.

Godfrey testified against Henry Milord (trial 115), the first of this group of mixed-blood defendants. In some detail, he described Milord's active participation in the battle at Fort Ridgely, where, he said, Milord fired "a great many shots" and repeatedly ran up with the Indians to shoot and then pulled back. At this stage of the proceedings many Dakotas had already been sentenced to hang on the basis of far less concrete evidence. But then witness after witness was called, each of whom incriminated Milord in the killing of a white settler during a cattle-stealing foray. The mixed-blood Baptiste Campbell admitted that he, along with Milord, Hypolite Auge (another mixed-blood), and a Dakota man, participated in this killing.

Milord's uncle, David Faribault Sr., delivered the coup de grace. In testimony that was anything but avuncular, he recounted a conversation between Milord and a Dakota confederate in which both men claimed to have killed the white man but Milord insisted that he had been the killer. Milord's group, according to Faribault, had also killed a woman at the same scene ("The woman and man were fixing a stack of oats when they killed them"). Faribault had chastised his boastful nephew: "I said he oughtn't to have done it." To which, Faribault said, Milord replied that he "had killed one any way." By the end of the trial Godfrey's shots-fired-at-battle testimony was the least of Milord's worries.

Milord's trial apparently opened the court's eyes to the possibility that some of the mixed-blood men who had initially been viewed as captives—Milord appeared on the Riggs list of captives at Camp Release—might themselves have been perpetrators. David Faribault Jr. and Thomas Robertson, also listed among the freed captives, had each testified on several occasions as prosecution witnesses. But as the Camp Release trials neared their conclusion, both men found themselves in the dock as defendants.

Godfrey gave testimony in both Faribault's and Robertson's trials, but what he said was more helpful than harmful to their defense. David Faribault Jr. (trial 134) testified first in his own case and, in the eyes of the court, offered his "confession." He admitted firing two shots at New Ulm ("at the wind mill") and "two or three" at Birch Coulie ("over the tops of the tents" and at a dead horse behind which a soldier was hiding). Godfrey confirmed that Faribault was at New Ulm and Birch Coulie, where he was "among the other Indians who were firing." But, though he saw Faribault point and reload his gun, he had not actually seen him fire a shot, Godfrey claimed.

Then Faribault retook the stand. Responding to Godfrey, he said, "What witness says is true. There were a few shots fired from the wind mill. The Indians asked me to fire and I fired. I went down because I was afraid. I went down with the witness [Godfrey] because I was asked to go." In view of accusations that were made later on Faribault's behalf, two facts about his case deserve emphasis: Faribault himself furnished the court with the most incriminating evidence against him, and he volunteered that Godfrey's testimony was truthful. This trial was not, in any sense, a confrontation between Godfrey and Faribault.

According to Riggs, charges were brought against Robertson on the basis of Godfrey's claim that Robertson "boasted of having killed a man at Fort Ridgley."[42] But at Robertson's trial (trial 135), Godfrey said his evidence was based on hearsay, that he "heard an Indian say after the fight Tom had shot a white man alongside of the cannons inside the fort." But he couldn't remember the name of the Dakota, and he added about the hearsay, "I believed it to be true when I first heard it. I don't believe now that it is true because no Indian saw him fire." He then gave a character reference for Robertson: "I don't think Tom is a bad man. I believe he was forced to go." With Godfrey's help, Robertson was acquitted.

The last case heard at Camp Release was against another mixed-blood man, Louis Labelle (trial 139). Unusually, seven witnesses gave evidence in this case. Though Labelle admitted firing his gun at the last battle, he claimed that he had not loaded it with shot. But the most serious aspect of the case hinged on whether Labelle had scalped a white solider at Wood Lake and then claimed a wampum reward for the first "kill" of a white man at that battle. Godfrey's testimony on this point was the most specific: "He came towards us with a piece of scalp in his hand. He threw it down. An Indian said who struck the first white man should get the wampum. Another Indian claimed it and this man said it ought to be his as he struck the dead body first. It was a scalp of an old man." A Dakota named Dawasin corroborated Godfrey: "I saw prisoner with a white scalp in his hand. I saw him strike the body with his war lance." Another Indian, Weanku, offered another version: "Perhaps defendant didn't kill anybody. The Indians gave this young man the wampum. When wampum is put up it is given to the person who strikes a dead body first. He struck it with a lance. He did not take the scalp."

Labelle's was another case in which the Dakota definition of a "kill" potentially conflicted with the white conception of murder. But a panel of judges who had all fought on the other side at the Wood Lake battle was disinclined to split hairs in the defendant's favor. Evidence that he had brandished a piece of the scalp of one of their comrades was enough to sentence him to death.

Though Godfrey's testimony in eleven of the post–October 15 cases at Camp Release led to only one conviction (Labelle's, and even that result most likely would have been the same without Godfrey), the Dakotas chained within the log prison must have viewed him with deep suspicion. He was the only inmate to shuttle so frequently in and out of the jail for courtroom appearances, and the combination of those trips and his earlier evidence against two of the Milford killers must have marked him for vengeance. One observer's letter to his hometown newspaper gives us an image of Godfrey's isolated uniqueness. Writing about the 130 Indians confined in the "rude log prison" at Camp Release, "chained two and two," he said, "The negro who has made his name notorious by his atrocities is chained alone."[43] It is likely that the guards segregated Godfrey from the Dakota prisoners for his own protection.

As we have seen, the vast majority of the 110 Indians prosecuted at Camp Release after October 15 were convicted and sentenced to hang on the basis of evidence other than Godfrey's. Several other witnesses were far more helpful to the prosecution. This second batch of cases was markedly different from the first twenty-nine trials, during which most of the convicted defendants had been found guilty of murder or rape. There was still a sprinkling of murder cases (such as those of Henry Milord and his three confederates), but most of the men now sentenced to hang were ordinary soldiers who had participated in one or more battles against white troops. And, in striking contrast with the proceedings in the first case group, no witnesses appeared against the majority of these warriors. Relying on Sibley's assurances that only murderers would be punished, these men had no idea that their acknowledgment of firing a shot at a battle would be considered sufficient proof to justify a hanging verdict. They were essentially tricked by Sibley and his court into "confessing" that they had fought as soldiers.

As the roster of Indians sentenced to death grew at a pace of about ten per day after October 15, Godfrey's chances of dodging the noose became worse with each new conviction. Many of the Dakotas now being sentenced to hang merely for waging war had been less involved in the war than Godfrey.

NOTES ON CHAPTER 7

1. Wakefield, *Six Weeks in the Sioux Teepees*, 114.
2. Chomsky's conclusion that "it appears that the Commission tried sixteen men" on the first day, September 28, is almost certainly incorrect. Chomsky, "United States–Dakota War Trials," 25. She apparently confused the dates the men were charged (listed on the charge sheets) with the trial dates. If Chomsky had been correct, Godfrey's case could not possibly have taken more than an hour or two—a virtual impossibility for a trial with his lengthy testimony and the evidence of six witnesses. The court numbered the trials as they were heard in sequential order, and in trial 5 the charge is dated October 5, strongly suggesting that the court heard only a handful of cases during its first week of deliberations.
3. See "Courts-Martial and Military Commission Proceedings against Union soldiers, 1861–1866," NA, RG 94, M1523. This compilation of the cases of Union soldiers who were tried and executed during the war reveals many cases that were tried in only a day or two. Though some cases took much longer, a considerable number of Union soldiers were executed on the basis of court records not much more extensive than those of the longest trials that were held before Sibley's court. The majority of the Civil War courts-martial cases appear shockingly incomplete and unfair by modern standards. Quite a few trials consisted of little more than an eyewitness pointing the finger of guilt at an alleged rapist or murderer, with only a brief defense (if any) by the accused. Many of the soldiers who were executed had no lawyer at their trial.
4. Wyatahtowah (trial 5) was apparently the man Godfrey identified in his trial as Patoille's killer ("We-a-ta-tow"). Godfrey named Muzzabomadu (trial 10) and Dowansa (trial 22) either before the court or during his discussions with Heard. See discussion of Godfrey's trial in chapter 6.
5. Sibley to Folsom [two letters], October 4, 1862, NA, RG 393, Dept. of NW, 1862, E3480, pt. 1, LS; for distances, see Pope to Sibley, October 3, 1862, *MCIW*, 2:261–62.
6. Samuel J. Brown's recollections, in Anderson and Woolworth, *Through Dakota Eyes*, 225.
7. Ibid.
8. Sibley to Galbraith and Sibley to Whitney, October 4, 1862, NA, RG 393, Dept. of NW, 1862, E3480, pt. 1, LS.
9. See Green, "Minnesota's Long Road to Black Suffrage," 69–84.
10. Trial of Muzzabomadu, trial 10, Dakota Trials Records.
11. See Satterlee's notes on this case in Folwell, Satterlee, and Brown, *Court Proceedings*, 15; Satterlee, *Outbreak and Massacre*, 40–41; and Satterlee, "List of the People Killed in the Sioux Indian War of 1862," MHS (1914 list), 12, 18. Earlier Satterlee gave conflicting versions of the identity of the victims of Muzzabomadu. Citing Godfrey's testimony, he said they were members of the Mey family. But Godfrey makes no mention of the presence of Mr. Mey, and Mrs. Mey, a young mother, does not fit the "old woman" description. Satterlee, "Indian Massacre in Brown County," 3.
12. The trial records often do not distinguish between David Faribault Sr. and his son, David Faribault Jr. I believe that the unspecified appearances were most likely made by Faribault Sr.
13. Trial of Wahpaduta, trial 11, Dakota Trials Records.

14. Heard, *History of the Sioux War*, 254. Heard made his own copy of the testimony given at the first group of trials (278).
15. Heard said that Godfrey provided the facts that led to Dowansa's arrest. *History of the Sioux War*, 282.
16. See Faribault testimony in trials 1, 11, 12, 18, 19, 26, 28, and 29, Dakota Trials Records. Of these cases, only two men, Wahpaduta (trial 11) and Wahohna (trial 12) were ultimately hanged. Again, it appears this evidence was most likely given by the elder Faribault. His son, when called against Godfrey, proved a singularly forgetful and unhelpful witness, while Faribault Sr.'s evidence was so detailed that it led to many hanging verdicts.
17. White captive witnesses: Mary Woodbury, Mary Schwandt (2 cases), Mattie Williams (4), Margaret Cardinal, Harriet Tallant (Valiant), Sarah Wakefield, Lydia Blair, Augustus Gluth (2), Sophie Loomis, Pauline Urban, Louis Getzmann (Kitzmann), Wilhemina Eldfeld (Inhenfeldt), and George Spencer. Mixed-blood witnesses: David Faribault Jr., David Faribault Sr. (9), Angus Robertson, Antoine Frenier, Ellen Brown, Henry Milord, Thomas Robertson, Gabrielle Renville, and Marion Hunter. Dakota witnesses: Wakanwashtay (Andrew Good Thunder; 3), Lorenzo (Lawrence; 3), Paul (Mazakutemani), Moushan, and Tazoo.
18. *Mankato Semi-Weekly Record*, October 4, 1862.
19. *St. Paul Pioneer and Democrat*, October 7, 1862.
20. *St. Paul Dispatch*, March 28, 1886.
21. Carter to McIntyre, Superintendent, Santee Indian Agency, November 30, 1909, Carter Papers, MHS, box 2.
22. *St. Peter Herald*, December 20, 1912, in Carter Papers, MHS, box 3.
23. A letter from Riggs indicates that the court once considered whipping and hair shaving as possible punishments for the Indians but that he (Riggs) recommended against such penalties because those punished in this fashion would be likely to "take revenge." See Riggs to Mary Riggs, October 15, 1862, Riggs letters, CCHS.
24. Pope's intention to assume military control over every Dakota person is clearly shown by his letters. On October 6, 1862, Pope demanded that all the Dakotas be brought to Fort Snelling ("I will take care of them here for the winter"); on October 7: "I desire you to disarm, and send down to Fort Snelling, all the Indians men women and children . . . upon whom you can lay your hands. I shall keep and feed for the winter such as are not hung"; on October 10: "[A]ll the Sioux must be brought to Fort Snelling as prisoners." Pope to Sibley letters, NA, RG 393, E3436, pt. 1, LS, Letters Sent and Received, Department of NW, Headquarters.
25. Pope to Sibley, October 6, 1862, NA, RG 393, E3436, pt. 1, LS, Letters Sent and Received, Department of NW, Headquarters. This scathing letter has never before been referenced in any publication. Perhaps due to the extremely personal general-to-general criticism it contains, the letter was omitted from the published collections of official Pope-Sibley correspondence. Yet the letter is crucial to an understanding of the major shifts in the trials that occurred following its receipt; the decision to convict and sentence hundreds of ordinary Dakota soldiers to death was clearly within the scope of Pope's orders. Pope deserves far more responsibility for the course of postwar military justice than he has received, for Sibley was following Pope's orders.
26. Riggs to Mary Riggs, October 13, 1862, Riggs letters, CCHS.
27. Sibley to Whitney, October 12, 1862, NA, RG 393, Dept. of NW, 1862, E3480, pt. 1, LS.

28. Samuel J. Brown's recollections, in Anderson and Woolworth, *Through Dakota Eyes*, 225–26. For numbers held at Camp Release, see Sibley to Pope, October 13, 1862, MICW, 2:274–75. Folwell, who did not have the benefit of access to some of Pope's letters to Sibley, asked two questions when discussing the "sting" operation at Yellow Medicine: "(1) Why had the Indians not been disarmed at the time of their surrender? (2) Why was a 'ruse' needed under the circumstances?" Folwell, *History of Minnesota*, 2:194–95n8. The answer to both questions comes from Sibley's changes of plans in response to Pope's letters. The evidence suggests that Sibley had no plans to disarm the Indians at Yellow Medicine, let alone take most of them prisoner, until Pope required him to do so.
29. Sibley to Pope, October 11, 1862, *MCIW*, 2:273–74.
30. See Pope to Sibley, October 6, 1862, NA, RG 393, E3436, pt. 1, LS, Letters Sent and Received, Department of NW, Headquarters. Some of Pope's directives to Sibley were cast in the form of suggestions, but not his orders for draconian postwar justice. Those, he insisted, here to be followed "strictly." See discussion of Pope to Sibley, October 20, 1862, in chapter 8.
31. Folwell's notes from his 1909 examination of the original Dakota trial records indicate that the notation on Godfrey's trial record (which Folwell identified as being "in Sibley's hand") was even then "faint." Folwell Papers, MHS, Box 80. After receiving permission from the Senate archives librarians, I examined the original trial transcripts carefully in 2003. After holding the document up to the light and deciphering Sibley's note, I concur with Folwell that Sibley's words are those quoted in the text. It is possible that Sibley added these words only after the commission renewed its request for clemency for Godfrey, but it seems more likely that he noted his decision at the outset and then simply left it unchanged on the court record.
32. Pope to Sibley, October 10, 1862, NA, RG 393, E3436, pt. 1, LS, Letters Sent and Received, Department of NW, Headquarters.
33. Order No. 65, October 15, 1862, Sibley's Orders Book, Sibley Papers, MHS, M164, roll 32.
34. Upham, "Minnesota Biographies," 71; Heard, *History of the Sioux War*, 268.
35. Sibley to Usher, December 19, 1862, NA, RG 393, Dist. of MN, E343, pt. 3, Letters and Telegrams Sent; Riggs to Mary Riggs, October 15, 1862, Riggs letters, CCHS ("double quick").
36. Pope to Halleck, telegram, October 13, 1862, *MCIW*, 2:274.
37. Halleck to Pope, telegram, October 16, 1862, NA, RG 393, E3450, pt. 1, Telegrams Received, Department of NW. I have found no history or other account that cites this telegram, though Folwell inferred its contents from Pope's subsequent dispatch to Sibley. Folwell, *History of Minnesota*, 2:195. Duane Shultz incorrectly claimed that "no answer had been received" and then misinterpreted Pope's later decision to telegraph the names of the convicted Indians as a product of his impatience and irritation at the lack of response. See Schultz, *Over the Earth I Come*, 252. In fact, Halleck made a timely reply and specified telegraph as the means by which approval of the executions might be sought.
38. Pope to Sibley, October 17, 1862, NA, RG 393, Dept. of NW, Headquarters, entry 3436, pt. 1, LS.
39. Sibley to Pope, October 21, 1862, *MCIW*, 2:281–82.
40. Stephen R. Riggs to Mary Riggs, October 20, 1862, Riggs letters, CCHS.

41. The nine mixed-blood defendants were Henry Milord (trial 115), Louis Freniere (trial 131), Antoine Provincalle (trial 132), Francis Ray (Roy; trial 133), David Faribault Jr. (trial 134), Thomas Robertson (trial 135), Charles Crawford (trial 136), Joseph Provincalle Jr. (trial 137), and Baptiste Campbell (trial 138).
42. Riggs to Mary Riggs, October 20, 1862, Riggs letters, CCHS.
43. Letter from M. Grover, *St. Peter Tribune,* November 1, 1862.

CHAPTER 8

The Cookhouse Trials

Still plagued by shortages of food, forage, and cold-weather equipment, on October 23 Sibley ordered a mass repositioning of his entire encampment forty-five miles down the Minnesota River. By moving from Camp Release to the ruins of the Lower Sioux Agency, he considerably shortened crucial supply lines.

Sibley's men arrived at the fire-scarred remains of the Lower Agency on October 24. Dakota soldiers had razed most of the agency buildings, including the houses that had been built for their farmer kin. As Sibley's forces settled in, the soldiers' hearts were hardened further by reports from their work parties sent into the surrounding countryside. Woodcutters and others returned with tales of more bodies of slain settlers, some reduced to skeletons by scavenging dogs and pigs. Throughout the whole region, "desolation reigned supreme."[1]

Isaac Heard, perhaps recalling the Indians' peaceful prairie surrender on September 26, reacted viscerally to the camp's melancholy setting: "A flag of truce would not have saved the murderers had they made their appearance on that scene of inhuman butchery."[2] Here, at the epicenter of the killings, surrounded by everyday reminders of the victims' shattered lives, those Dakotas who had not yet appeared before the military commission would face trial. It was hardly a scene conducive to dispassionate justice.

One of the Lower Agency's few surviving log buildings, formerly used as a kitchen, was soon commandeered as a courthouse. This cookhouse had belonged to trader Francois LaBathe, who had been killed in the first outbreak of violence on August 18. Even the courtroom was stained with blood: one of the Dakotas soon to be brought before the court would face charges of killing a man within the confines of this "quondam kitchen." At the close of each day's testimony the building doubled as cozy nighttime accommodations for Heard and two other officers; Sibley referred to it as their "den."[3]

The soldiers soon dubbed the place "Camp Sibley," but their commander did not use the term in his communiqués to General Pope, fearing that it would "savor of vanity."[4] Pope's last surviving letter from this time, dated October 20, arrived just as Sibley was settling into the new camp.[5] Unwavering in his demands for the harshest possible treatment of the Indians facing trial, Pope reminded Sibley that "no leniency must be shown to these savages." That order, he insisted, "I wish carried out strictly."[6]

If Sibley had private reservations about Pope's sanguinary orders, he must have been doubly shocked by a letter he soon received from Judge Charles Flandrau. Sibley had written Flandrau on September 28, informing the judge of his formation of the military commission.[7] Though Sibley was obliged to yield to the orders of Pope as his superior officer, there was probably no one in Minnesota whose judgment on law-related issues he would have respected more than Flandrau's. On October 25 Sibley showed the judge's reply to Chaplain Riggs. Riggs's summary is the only surviving record of the letter: "I have just read a letter from Judge Flandrau to Gen. Sibley which greatly astonishes me. He goes in for killing all off—men women and children—thinks that all have been engaged in these massacres except the young children, and they will only grow up like their fathers. Flandrau holds himself personally responsible for winning a feather for every person who was killed in the battles of New Ulm."[8]

There is no evidence that Sibley was ever inclined to adopt this Indian-exterminating policy, but Flandrau's letter probably had a profound effect on him nonetheless. If even a bright, accomplished former Sioux agent and fair-minded Minnesota Supreme Court justice, writing privately and not pandering to the public for acclaim or reelection, favored killing all the Dakotas without so much as a nod to judicial niceties, Pope's stringent orders were obviously embraced by virtually the entire state. In the rabidly anti-Indian atmosphere that pervaded Minnesota in the autumn of 1862, Sibley's intention to try and then execute hundreds of male warriors was actually a voice of relative moderation amid the broader genocidal clamor.

During the Lower Agency proceedings, Godfrey was catapulted in status from a lesser-ranking witness to the preeminent one. In the first 139 cases his testimony had provided the strongest evidence in the trials of only three convicted defendants: Muzzabomadu, Dowansa, and Louis Labelle.[9] In contrast, he was the premier witness in no fewer than twenty-eight of the trials held at the Lower Agency.[10]

What accounts for the dramatic rise in Godfrey's status as a witness? It does not appear to reflect any change in willingness on his part or an altered approach by the court. Though it is difficult to verify, the most probable explanation stems from the fact that the Dakotas surrendered in bands. Bands associated with Wakute and Wabasha (who lived at the eastern end of the reservation) surrendered when Godfrey did, at the urging of their chiefs. But only a few of those men were arrested and tried in the first twenty-nine cases; the rest were sent to dig potatoes at Yellow Medicine and were in that camp (and then, after mid-October, in jail) until all Dakotas were moved to the Lower Agency.

With some exceptions (mainly mixed-bloods), the men tried in the second batch of cases at Camp Release (trials 30–139) were those who had surrendered to Sibley after the others had departed for Yellow Medicine. Since they were from other Dakota bands, Godfrey did not know them as well and had not associated with them during the conflict. Only when the trials were moved to the Lower Agency did the court hear most of the cases against the early-to-surrender Dakotas. Among them were the men whom Godfrey knew best, including participants in the Milford killings and the attack on the Patoille wagon. This explanation also underscores the general reliability of Godfrey's evidence: far from trying to convict everyone (as Riggs suggested), Godfrey told what he knew about the acts of men he could identify.

During the cookhouse trials the commissioners began to permit and encourage Godfrey to assume a role—virtually unprecedented for a witness in Anglo-American legal proceedings—of prosecutor/inquisitor. Since the transcripts omit all questions, they offer no hint that Godfrey ever stepped into the shoes of the judge advocate. But court recorder Heard is unmistakably specific in describing Godfrey's novel stance, and the results:

> It was a study to watch him [Godfrey], as he sat in court, scanning the face of every culprit who came in with the eye of a cat about to spring. His sense of the ridiculous, and evident appreciation of the gravity which should accompany the statement of an important truth, was strongly demonstrated. When a prisoner would state, in answer to the question of "Guilty or not guilty," that he was innocent, and Godfrey knew that he was guilty, he would drop his head upon his breast, and convulse with a fit of musical laughter; and when the court said, "Godfrey, talk to him," he would straighten up, his countenance become calm, and, in a deliberate tone, would soon force the Indian, by a series of questions in his own language, into an admission of the truth.[11]

Godfrey was likely the only person in the court other than the official interpreter, Frenier, who could communicate with both Indians and judges. But his direct questioning of "culprits" also had the unorthodox advantage of permitting an eyewitness to confront defendants directly, without going through the usual intermediary: the state's prosecutor. Frenier presumably provided an ongoing translation to the court during Godfrey's dramatic face-to-face interrogations. After weeks of laboriously translated questions and answers, these exciting and faster-moving interrogations probably provided edge-of-their-seats theatrics for the weary judges. Over the course of the next two weeks they came to respect, then to admire, Godfrey—and, perhaps even more important for their erstwhile convict/prosecutor, to believe in his truthfulness.

While Godfrey was emerging as the star witness in the cookhouse trials, the pace of the judicial assembly line accelerated even further. The court, which had already heard 139 cases, now faced an overwhelming docket of more than 250 jailed Dakotas. Riggs calculated that it would take several weeks to try the remaining Indians, but Sibley ordered his court to conduct expeditious trials and told Riggs that the cases would all be finished in two weeks—an estimate that proved to be correct almost to the day.[12] Referring to this judicial whirlwind with gross understatement, Heard later conceded that the court's "business has been dispatched with celerity."[13]

Once the judges had settled into their new quarters and organized the remaining cases, they began hearing trials in the cookhouse on Monday, October 27, 1862.[14] Over the course of the next ten days the tribunal heard 253 cases and sentenced the majority of Dakota defendants to die. No American court before or since has ordered the death penalty for so many people over so short a period of time. The judges heard an average of more than twenty-five cases per day. At the peak of their breakneck proceedings, they decided forty cases on a single day (October 30), with most of them ending in the extreme sanction.[15] To speed the process, the Indian defendants were not only left chained to their jailmates but groups of manacled pairs of defendants, "eight at a time," were ushered into the cookhouse together for their trials.[16] Presumably this practice allowed the court to read the standardized charges—"participation in murder, robberies, and outrages"—just once to all eight prisoners.

While all defendants knew that murders would be punished, the only charged "crime" that could theoretically have fit the conduct of most ordinary soldiers was the vague term "outrages." Use of that deceptive charge was one of the ploys Sibley's court used to hoodwink Dakota warriors into "confessing" to their battlefield deeds. The Indians, however, were unaware that the judges would treat any active involvement in a military battle as a capital-offense "outrage."

Since Godfrey rose to his greatest historical prominence during this two-week judicial blitzkrieg, however, it is crucial to look more carefully at his overall role in the hurried, slipshod, and often unfair trials. Paradoxically, it is possible to both overstate and to understate Godfrey's importance as a witness. Despite Heard's implication that Godfrey scrutinized "every culprit," even a cursory glance at the transcripts reveals that he did not give evidence in the vast majority of cases. In the cookhouse trials, where his involvement was greatest, Godfrey testified in fewer than 20 percent of the cases (43 out of 253 trials).

Even this statistic overstates Godfrey's impact as a prosecution witness, however, because it includes cases in which he gave testimony that was inconsequential or favored acquittal. Subtracting those cases, we find that Godfrey's evidence led to the conviction of slightly more than 10 percent of the defendants who were found guilty at the Lower Agency. Other mixed-blood and Dakota witnesses, collectively, gave evidence at the cookhouse leading to more convictions than did Godfrey.[17] But, as had been true of the second batch of cases at Camp Release, the majority of the accused men were convicted due to their own in-court "confessions" that they had joined in a battle—without the appearance of a single witness against them.

On the other hand, a mere numerical analysis could lead one to understate Godfrey's role, for, more than any other witness, he identified Dakotas who had killed defenseless civilians. In stark contrast with the first twenty-nine trials, only a small minority of the hundreds of cookhouse cases contained any reference to acts that might be called murder, but Godfrey appeared as the central witness in more of those trials than did anyone else.

Godfrey gave his most damning cookhouse evidence in five cases that dealt with the Milford massacre and three that related to the attack on the Patoille wagon. From Godfrey's own trial and from other cases they had heard at Camp Release, the judges were already familiar with the carnage in Milford and knew the full story of the Patoille attack. To some extent the later trials merely offered a forum in which Godfrey could identify individual defendants who participated in those killings.

Godfrey was the only witness against Wakantanka (trial 210):

> I saw the prisoner down among the Dutch settlements, where they were killing the whites. On the way to New Ulm, we met 2 wagons coming towards us and the prisoner and two others said they would lay in wait for the

> wagons. I and the other Indians went to a house and prisoner and other Indians went to where the wagons were. I went to where his comrade was standing and found prisoner there. When I got there I found a white man dead in the wagon and prisoner took out his knife and stabbed the white man. I saw him do it. I heard the guns but did not see the man shot.
>
> Prisoner and others then asked me to drive the team. I did so.
>
> He took out his knife and showed it to me and said his brother had died lately, and he had now avenged his death.

The defendant then responded, "I did fire on the whites as Godfrey says, but didn't kill anyone."

The "Dutch settlements" and "on the way to New Ulm" obviously refer to Milford, and the testimony that follows describes not the ambush of the recruiting party but the earlier attack on two farm wagons (see chapter 4). Wakantanka's admission was tantamount to a confession that he had joined an ambush in which two men were killed. Whether his bullets hit their marks or not, this Godfrey-prompted statement was a solid (if incredibly abbreviated) basis for a murder conviction.[18]

Two other Milford cases are likely candidates for trials in which Godfrey greeted the defendants' assertions of innocence with "a fit of musical laughter" and then gave critically damaging testimony. According to Heard, Wakinyanna (trial 383) had been identified by Godfrey as having killed people in the Massopust family at Milford.[19] The defendant professed his total innocence to the judges, claiming that he was sleeping near Fort Ridgely as the gun and cannon battle raged and cooking food while his compatriots besieged New Ulm: "I was at the Fort at the last battle. I was asleep, because I didn't like it because the other Indians were firing. At New Ulm, I was roasting beef all day."

But Godfrey responded, most likely with derision, "At the commencement of the outbreak at New Ulm [meaning Milford], when they were killing the people, I saw him rush in a house near the Travelers' Home where they killed an old man and two young girls.[20] I did not see him do anything. After he came home I heard him say he killed two boys—killed them with his war lance."

Wakinyanna then responded to Godfrey's claim that he had admitted killing two boys: "I might have done it, but it was not with my lance, but with my flute. I touched him with it. He was outdoors and ran upstairs." Wakinyanna's defense was that he was "touching coup"—that he merely tapped a boy with a musical instrument and that such a "kill" in Dakota terms did not rise to the level of a white man's murder. He did not, however, deny his part in the murder of the "old man and two young girls." The contrast between his initial alibis and Godfrey's accusations of child killing in two separate instances could hardly have been greater: Wakinyanna was sentenced to hang.

Godfrey also testified in the prosecution of Mukatenajin (trial 254). The transcript of this trial is muddled. It begins with the defendant's statement that he was "at New Ulm" but "had no gun." Godfrey contradicted this claim, adding that Mukatenajin urged younger warriors to join the attack: "I saw the prisoner with a gun at New Ulm. I didn't see him do anything. I heard the prisoner encouraging the young men to fight." Up to this point the case record appears to deal solely with the battle at New Ulm. But then Mukatenajin said, "I had my son's gun coming down. I saw him when the Indians fired on whites who were in a wagon with a flag. I did not fire. I dissuaded the young men from fighting." The "whites . . . in a wagon with a flag" reference fits only one scene in the New Ulm/Milford theater of the war: the ambush of Ernst Dietrich and the other recruiters. So we know that this defendant was in the thick of the Milford massacre, with a gun (which he admitted carrying when "coming down," that is, coming downriver, or eastward).

Then Godfrey gave his rebuttal: "On our way to New Ulm prisoner was along when they were killing the whites and he was encouraging the young men. He said they were young—to go in—that they had nothing to fear." Again, "on our way to New Ulm" must refer to Milford, a conclusion clinched by the phrase "when they were killing the whites." In this context,

Godfrey said, the prisoner was "encouraging the young men."

While the record is far from lucid, the most probable interpretation is that Mukatenajin actively fomented young braves to kill white settlers at Milford. Had the court been inclined to press the distinction between murders and battle killings, Godfrey could surely have clarified this point through further questioning. Instead, we are left with snatches of evidence from which to decipher the facts. In any event, Godfrey wrested telling admissions from Mukatenajin that, from the judges' viewpoint, were sufficient for a hanging verdict.

The trial record of Aechaya (trial 327) is even more cryptic. In its entirety, it reads,

> Prisoner states—
> At the battle of the Fort, I fired 2 shots at the houses. I was at the battle of Birch Coulie. I fired once at a horse.
> Godfrey, sworn, says—
> I saw prisoner in a house where the Indians killed an old man and 2 girls.
> Prisoner says—
> I was there, but I don't know who shot them.

Despite Aechaya's opening "confession" of having fired shots at battles, the court took a few extra minutes to hear Godfrey's recollections, without bothering to ascertain the location or circumstances of the deaths of the "old man and 2 girls." This case may be another reference to the killing of Massopust and his daughters in Milford, about which Godfrey gave testimony in his own trial.[21]

The defendant's admission that he fired shots had already fixed his fatal sentence as far as Sibley and the judges were concerned. But Godfrey's evidence, though it was limited to proof that Aechaya was present in a house where three persons were killed, implicated him in the Dakota killings at Milford—a much stronger justification for treating his acts as a capital offense. Whatever the court's reasoning, the judges added Aechaya's name to the ever-growing execution list.

Godfrey probably had another of his fits of laughter when Mahoowaywa (trial 382) professed his complete innocence to the court:

> Prisoner states—
> I wasn't at the battle of the Fort.
> I was wounded this side of New Ulm. I had to go down. I had no gun. I went down with a pipe and did nothing.

Again the vague reference to "this side of New Ulm" appears, at least initially, to refer to one of the battles in the town of New Ulm. But Godfrey had implicated this man in his earlier testimony, placing him in the middle of the Milford massacre. Now he leaped upon Mahoowaywa's denial:

> It's not true about his not wanting to go. They were all very much pleased with the troubles and ran to the Dutch settlement [Milford]—first killed a lot of white people and then came to a load of wheat. Prisoner had a double barreled gun. He said he took the gun from a house in the German settlements [Milford]. They all made a rush at the wagon loaded with hay—two white men were in it—about. The Indians all fired on them. I did not see them afterwards. They were all scattered along the road going to New Ulm. I afterwards met him coming home to Crow's Village and he was wounded. I afterwards heard he had been away two nights. I asked him and he said it was so. I asked him if he was wounded and he said "Yes". I asked him how it happened and he said he shot a white man and ran towards him and the white man shot him with a pistol. That he fell and lay there a long time, and when he came to, the white man was dead.
> He made rush with others where an old man and two girls were killed, this side of the Travelers' Home.

Godfrey thus incriminated Mahoowaywa in three different killing scenes at Milford: the attack on the two farmers in the hay wagon at the Mey farm, the killing of "old man" Massopust and his two daughters, and the shooting of one unidentified white man who was armed with a pistol. This story of a mortally wounded settler firing his pistol at Mahoowaywa is the only record of any Milford resident offering effective resistance on August 18. Despite the Dakotas' killing of fifty-two people (and wounding of several others), Mahoowaywa's injury is the only known Dakota casualty there.[22]

Reading Godfrey's indignant burst of accusations against Mahoowaywa, one gets a sense of his exasperation with the litany of Dakota denials. Not only did Godfrey flatly contradict the defendant's claim that he was a reluctant warrior, he also declared that *all* the Dakotas were "very much pleased" at the outbreak of hostilities and enthusiastically "ran to the Dutch settlement." This was one of the last trials, and it appears that Godfrey had now lost all reluctance to lash out at the men who had forced him to join in the Milford massacre. He had transcended the role of a mere witness and, as Heard wrote, had become the court's most effective "instrument of justice."[23]

That we must deduce the location of the acts described by Godfrey in these five Milford cases helps to highlight one of the major flaws in the trials: the court's failure to introduce inquest-type evidence of the killing scenes. Sheriff Roos and the members of his posse who visited Milford on August 18 could have given graphic testimony about the victims slain there, including their number, ages, sex, and apparent causes of death. Such death-scene evidence is standard in any homicide trial.

But the decision to hold rushed and secret trials in the field, and the failure to reach out to potential witnesses elsewhere, left the transcripts strangely devoid of such routine evidence. While it is easy to see that slapdash trials were unfair to defendants, one of the salient and unusual features of Sibley's regime of military justice was that it was also unfair to the Dakotas' victims, most of whom were not even enumerated, let alone identified, in the trials. If Sheriff Roos or anyone else who had seen the aftermath of the massacre at Milford had described that frightful scene in court, the net effect would have been devastating to the defense of the Dakotas.

Because Mary Schwandt and Mattie Williams, the only survivors of the Patoille wagon attack, had long since departed with the other white female captives, it now fell to Godfrey to give evidence against three more Dakotas in connection with those killings. The first Patoille defendant to step into the cookhouse dock was Oechagay (trial 186), who told the court that he had entered into none of the hostilities: "I staid with the squaws all the time. I never had a gun." But Godfrey placed him at Milford ("at the time whites were killed, on the road to New Ulm") with a gun in hand, "dressed like a savage and painted." And, he added, "I saw him at the place where Patoille was killed." Despite the defendant's denials, the court found him guilty. But, apparently because there was no evidence that he had killed anyone or fired any shots, he was sentenced only to three years in prison.[24]

The trial of Chankahda (trial 359), who was part of the group of Dakotas at the Patoille attack, offers another indication that Godfrey was not determined to cast all Indians in a negative light. By the standards of the military court the defendant first sealed his own fate by admitting that he fired a shot, "at a horse," at one of the battles in New Ulm. But this case departed from the norm when Chankahda also admitted that he "took one wounded woman prisoner" following the Patoille attack. Godfrey then testified in a way that seems to mitigate the evidence of guilt: "I saw prisoner present when [Patoille] was killed. The Indians wanted to kill Mary Anderson, but this Indian saved her." Though it appears that Godfrey was intending to vouch for Chankahda, the judges looked askance at the idea of any Indian "saving" a white woman who was hauled off into captivity. They apparently assumed that Anderson, had she not died, would have suffered a worse fate. Despite Godfrey's endorsement of his good intentions, Chankahda was sentenced to die.

In one of the last trials Godfrey gave graphic testimony against another of Patoille's killers. Offering evidence against Oyatayakoo (trial 377), he said, "When [Patoille] was killed prisoner was present. [Patoille] was shot but was not dead. He was thrown upon the ground and prisoner stabbed him before he was dead."

The defendant, rather lamely, said, "I do not remember stabbing [Patoille]." But he also corroborated Godfrey, in part: "I was standing by when he [Patoille] was killed." The court imposed the death penalty.

One striking feature of these eight Milford/Patoille cases is that all of the defendants (usually after being confronted by Godfrey) either expressly or tacitly admitted their presence at the scenes of the killings. Though they sometimes disputed Godfrey's version of their deeds, not a single one offered an alibi or claimed that Godfrey had identified the wrong man (as was later alleged by some Dakotas against other prosecution witnesses). Especially with respect to the events in Milford, such acknowledgments were virtually conclusive evidence of participation in murders.

It is fair to infer that there were no innocent Dakota bystanders at Milford. Indeed, were the same trials to be held today with all modern legal safeguards, simple proof of the basic facts of the Milford massacre, coupled with a Dakota defendant's admission that he was present at that bloody scene, would be sufficient to sustain a conviction for murder. Since the defendants all acknowledged during their trials, in essence, that they were at Milford, their guilt—both legal and historical—is established by their own words and does not hinge on Godfrey's credibility.

Whatever evidentiary weight one gives to those admissions, they undeniably show that every one of the eight convicted men had been in a position to see Godfrey either at Milford or during the Patoille wagon attack. If Godfrey had killed anyone, one or more of them would have been eyewitnesses. By placing himself in the extraordinary position of acting virtually as the court's prosecutor, Godfrey also became uniquely vulnerable. Any Dakota among the many he confronted as witness/inquisitor at the Lower Agency trials could have retaliated with his own version, whether true or not, of Godfrey's evil deeds. If Godfrey had deceived the court when he earlier denied killing anyone, these eight defendants would have been in the best position to contradict him. Yet no new facts damaging to Godfrey emerged in the cookhouse trials. Though we could produce all the standard arguments against lending credence to any state's evidence witness, there is no reason to doubt Godfrey's testimony about the Milford and Patoille attacks.

Even when he appeared in non-murder cases, Godfrey's role in the cookhouse trials was often dramatic. Time and again, far more than any other witness, he exposed defendants' lies and prompted them to recant or change their original story. These relatively routine battlefield cases must have riveted the judges' attention, for nothing matches the courtroom drama of a witness caught in the act of deceit.

Recalling these cases, Heard paid tribute both to Godfrey's uncanny memory and to its impact on the trials: "His observation and memory were remarkable. Not the least thing had escaped his eye or ear. Such an Indian had a double-barreled gun, another a single-barreled, another a long one, another a short one, another a lance, and another one nothing at all."[25] Godfrey did not simply recite incriminating facts; he vigorously cross-examined defendants, a practice any ordinary tribunal would not have permitted. Because questions are missing from the transcripts, we can only infer his techniques from the defendants' responses. But by comparing the dry trial record of a particular case with Heard's rendition of it, we get insights into the spellbinding effect Godfrey must have had on the judges.

There was nothing particularly noteworthy about the prosecution of Haypee (trial 366). As was true of most of the cookhouse trials, the defendant was first asked to tell his story. He testified, "I was at the last fight at the Fort. I was at New Ulm, with the same party. I found an old gun, and had that with me. I haven't fired for 2 yrs. because I have a lame arm. I was at Birch Coolie. I had no gun there."

The record then indicates that Godfrey was called to the stand: "Godfrey, sworn, says: I saw the prisoner fire. I was in a clump of trees and saw this man try to drive in a pair of colts. There was a young Indian killed. He took his gun and fired it. He then borrowed my gun—shot twice with it—told me to load it and fired again. This was at New Ulm."

Finally, the transcript reports Haypee's reaction to Godfrey's testimony: "It is true what Godfrey says. I was sitting along side of a dead Indian lighting my pipe." This official record contains no suggestion that Godfrey did anything other than offer his testimony in the ordinary fashion. It is evident that his words prompted the prisoner to reverse part of his initial stance, but nothing implies a more direct confrontation.

Contrast that with Heard's description of the same case, which he cited as a prime example of the way Godfrey employed his total recall of detailed facts: "To another [defendant], who said he had a lame arm at

New Ulm, and couldn't fire a gun, and had such a bad gun that he could not have fired if he desired, he [Godfrey] replied, 'You say you could not fire, and had a bad gun. Why don't you tell the court the truth? I saw you go and take the gun of an Indian who was killed, and fire two shots; and then you borrowed mine, and shot with it; and then you made me reload it, and then you fired again.'"[26] Thus Haypee, when he admitted that Godfrey told the truth, was actually responding to accusations hurled during his court-sponsored cross-examination. It was the witness Godfrey—not the designated military prosecutor—who effectively took charge of the case.

Heard noted that cases such as Haypee's were not exceptional: "I might enumerate numberless instances of this kind, in which [Godfrey's] assumed recollection would cause his truthfulness to be doubted, if he had not been fully substantiated." He also reported the stunning statistic that "in every instance but two [cases]," Godfrey's dramatic confrontations of defendants ended with "his testimony being substantiated by the subsequent admissions of the Indians themselves."[27] (Heard exaggerated here, for often the admissions were only partial acknowledgments, not full-blown confessions.)

Once one grasps this dynamic, the otherwise arid trial transcripts spring to life. Toonkanmane (trial 218), for example, initially claimed he was armed only with arrows (shorthand for bow and arrows) at the battle of Birch Coulee. But after Godfrey said he saw him with a double-barreled gun, the defendant suddenly remembered that he had been "lent" the gun. Similarly, Etayechasnamane (trial 240) told the court he had not been at the Fort Ridgely battles. Godfrey then challenged him by claiming that he saw him "with a gun at the bottom of the hill at the fort," to which the defendant rather lamely responded, "I had forgotten I had a gun I borrowed from another. I returned it before the battle." Tawapahajata (trial 248) flatly stated, "I was not at Birch Coolie." But immediately after Godfrey took over the case, the court record notes, the defendant not only recanted but admitted firing "four times" at Birch Coulee.

At one point in the trials Godfrey prompted three defendants in a row to modify their stories. He caught Pantaninneyay (trial 258) in multiple lies. Initially telling the court he went only to the Wood Lake battle and never had a gun, Pantaninneyay switched defenses after Godfrey put him at all four of the principal battle sites, actively riding around with a gun. The prisoner than unconvincingly asserted, "I have sore eyes and didn't shoot." Otaheyaya, or Chaskaydan (trial 259), admitted he was at New Ulm but led the court to believe he had not joined in the battle. When Godfrey said Otaheyaya had charged into the melee on horseback and been repulsed only by a gun slug in his leg, the defendant not only admitted the injury but showed the court the wound. Finally, confronted by Godfrey with the fact that he carried a sawed-off shotgun at New Ulm, Washechoonsapa (trial 260) reversed his initial claim of being unarmed. He then asserted a bad-gun defense: "The gun I had was a short gun. It misses fire."

In these three cases and many others the court would have been in a position not only to hear Godfrey implicate witnesses through their own deceit but also to observe their demeanor. Even making allowances for the language and cultural barriers that separated judges from prisoners, it must have been apparent to all that these defendants were floundering in their attempts to ameliorate the impact of Godfrey's fact-laden accusations.[28]

In every one of these trials in which Godfrey prompted a reversal, the court entered a conviction. In some cases the bottom-line evidence was weaker than the court typically required for a death penalty sentence, since there was no testimony or admission that the defendant in question had fired shots. But especially in cases in which defendants were trapped in lies about their presence at or participation in battles, the court apparently inferred that such deception was proof that they were concealing the full extent of their involvement.

The fact that Godfrey was vindicated as a witness, however, does not make these prosecutions of ordinary soldiers fair. Nor is there any reason to believe that prisoner Godfrey knew, any more than the accused Dakotas did, that mere proof of battle participation would lead to a hanging verdict. Responsibility for the profound injustice of bringing hanging verdicts against men who fought at battles lies with the judges, not with Godfrey.

Because the judges kept their verdicts secret, both Godfrey and the Dakotas remained ignorant of their sentences. Nonetheless, one can readily imagine the hostility that Godfrey's in-court confrontations must have engendered among his fellow prisoners. Whatever difficulties the Dakotas faced in comprehending the proceedings, many surely grasped that Godfrey was their accuser, their nemesis, their scourge. Dakotas directly implicated in murders would probably have reacted most angrily, but those whose lies had been revealed or stories contradicted would also have simmered in anger at having been so embarrassingly exposed. At the end of a day in court Godfrey would have been marched back to the large communal jail. Even in his chained isolation, he must have faced angry slurs and threats from his fellow inmates.

As was true at Camp Release, Godfrey's testimony was not always incriminating in the cookhouse trials. In several cases that ended in acquittals, he told the court that he knew nothing about the defendant's conduct.[29] Sometimes, as he had done in the cases against David Faribault Jr. and Thomas Robertson, Godfrey went further and offered an endorsement of the defendant. When Wazekootay (trial 213) admitted that he had been "down below at the commencement of the outbreak" but denied being at battles, Godfrey placed him at Milford ("this side of Travelers' Home"), but he also reminded the judges that Wazekootay had given ameliorating counsel to the younger Dakotas: "He told the Indians . . . that they should not cut their [whites'] heads off." Following Godfrey's general endorsement ("He always gave good advice"), the judges found Wazekootay not guilty.

Once one realizes that many of the Dakotas did not disagree with the thrust of his testimony against them, Godfrey's motives for giving state's evidence assume less historical importance. Whether he simply wanted to save himself or whether he might have had other motivations makes little difference in assessing the cases in which his testimony was acknowledged by the accused man, in whole or in substance, as true.

Dee Brown, in *Bury My Heart at Wounded Knee,* claimed that Godfrey "became a willing informant" when he "learned . . . that the court would be willing to commute his death sentence if he would identify [Dakotas] guilty of participating in the attacks."[30] But there is no direct evidence of any such promises, negotiations, or arrangements. Godfrey himself never disclosed the reasons that prompted his cooperation. Writers who claim to know what he was thinking and feeling or who assert that his sole incentive was self-interest are making a leap that reflects their own viewpoint.

Conceding that the entire exercise is a matter of speculation, it does seem likely that someone connected with the tribunal said something to encourage Godfrey to carry on as a witness. Ordinarily, state's evidence is procured through some such enticement from the prosecutor. Heard, who had private discussions with Godfrey, may have told him that the judges greatly appreciated his contributions and that they would do their best to recommend that his efforts be recognized in some way.

But unlike many prosecutors who are empowered to make virtually binding agreements with cooperative witnesses, both Heard and the judges themselves had limited authority under the realities of military procedures. From Sibley's previous denial of the court's request that Godfrey be shown leniency, Heard must have realized that the best he could offer him was some form of nonbinding recommendation by the judges on Godfrey's behalf—assuming, of course, that his veracity held up until the end of the trials and that no new evidence surfaced making his own legal case worse.

Even if one posits that such a conversation took place, Godfrey may have had motives besides avoidance of the death penalty. He could have been angry, even outraged, at the Dakotas, who, he testified, repeatedly threatened his life and forced him to join in the Milford massacre. Or he could have been spurred to testify by feelings of guilt. At Milford he saw the slaughter of utterly helpless old men, women, and children. Memories of bludgeoned babies, a beheaded woman, and victims with limbs hacked off could well have prodded pangs of remorse, even if he was a reluctant participant.

Godfrey's race suggests another possible motive. Given that he was slurred as a "nigger" by one Dakota witness, it seems likely that he would have been the target of other racial epithets while he was jailed with the Indians. He would not be the first or the last black man to testify against former coconspirators as a consequence of racist insults.

Other motives are possible, too. Godfrey may have been seeking the approval of an appreciative crowd: the members of the court. Praise can be a powerful motivator, especially when one is suffering the hardships of jail. Or he may have exulted in the pure pleasure of exposing a deceitful witness—a heady experience, as any trial lawyer can attest. Had anyone asked, Godfrey probably would have offered a mixture of such motivations for giving state's evidence. We can only offer educated guesses as to what was in his mind.

As the trials ground to their conclusion in early November, it appeared that three issues would determine Godfrey's fate. First, if his life was to be spared, both the court and the chain of command had to find that he had not killed anyone. On this point Godfrey's stock had risen during the cookhouse trials, for no new murder evidence had surfaced against him. Second, Godfrey could be granted clemency for his important role as a prosecution witness. The third issue was the defense of duress, which could have been resurrected despite Sibley's initial finding that Godfrey should be hanged notwithstanding his claims of coercion. Godfrey's standing on this point received a powerful boost near the end of the trials, when both he and former slave James Thompson took the stand in the same case.

Long before the trial of Makanahtakay (trial 362), the judges had adopted an overtly racial policy toward the duress defense. According to Riggs, "It was held [by the court] that a half-breed might be forced to go to these battles, but not a pure Indian."[31] While the court never entered any such "holding" into its records, the transcripts tend to show that Riggs's understanding was correct. Few mixed-blood men succeeded with a duress defense, but the much-longer trials they were routinely accorded underscored the fact that the court was making such a racial distinction.[32] But Godfrey fit into neither of the court's established racial categories. With no one else to compare him to, the court would have had difficulty weighing his claims that the Dakotas treated him with suspicion and hostility, let alone evaluating the seriousness of the threats on his life.

The first portion of the trial against Makanahtakay was a routine confrontation between Godfrey and the defendant, who admitted he was in New Ulm but claimed he was "lying down with the belly ache." Godfrey depicted a far more vigorous participant: "At New Ulm two horses were running off and this Indian caught them. An Indian took them away from him. He said he would get them again. At Wood Lake I saw his son on one of the horses and I asked this Indian about it and he said he got the horses by giving a yoke of oxen for them." Like many of his predecessors, the defendant then modified his story, admitting that he had not been too sick to run after the horses: "At the [New Ulm] windmill I took the horses which were running away."

Then James Thompson was called to the stand. Other than Godfrey, he was the only black man to testify in the trials, and this was his only appearance. He said, "Prisoner told my wife he came to my house to kill me. He didn't find me but took all the things out of my house and burned them. He told this to my niece and daughter." Leaving aside the fact that Thompson's evidence is 100 percent hearsay, these three short sentences offer a chilling insight into the Dakotas' intended treatment of a man who was situated almost identically to Godfrey. Thompson's evidence squarely confirmed the notion that the life of a black man—even one who lived with the Indians, spoke Dakota, was married to a Dakota woman, and had mixed-blood children—was deeply imperiled when the war broke out.

The court sentenced Makanahtakay to hang.[33] For a court accustomed to lumping defendants into racial categories, Thompson's dramatic tale must have cemented the significance of the fact that Godfrey stood alone among the trial defendants in having no Indian blood—and that he thus deserved the benefit of doubt as to the "voluntary" nature of his participation in the conflict.[34]

When the last case was decided by the court on November 5, the military commission was poised to take one last look at Godfrey's plight. As their final act, the judges now drafted and signed a new plea to Sibley that Godfrey be granted a reprieve from execution. In an extraordinary document to which they all affixed their names, the judges wrote,

> General—
> The members of the Military Commission before closing their session at this Station, would respectfully beg leave to renew their application for a commutation of the

sentence of Otakle or Godfrey, a colored man, who has been tried before the Commission and condemned to death.

His testimony has been invaluable to the State, for without it a large number of men of the very worst character would have gone unpunished. It would have been impossible in many cases without his evidence—which has always proved truthful both by corroborative evidence and the acknowledgements of the prisoners themselves—to have discovered the guilt of parties who were not only instrumental in exciting the revolt, but the most bloodthirsty and cruel in carrying it out.

Believing that his services to the State have been such as would warrant the exercise of judicial clemency, we would respectfully recommend that it be extended to him.[35]

Godfrey was the only defendant among almost four hundred for whom the court prepared a separate mercy application to Sibley.[36] The petition was founded mainly on Godfrey's contribution as a witness for the state. But the judges' ringing endorsement of his honesty was almost as important a basis for their plea. For the purpose of assessing Godfrey's place in history, that aspect of the document is certainly the most crucial.

One of the time-honored concepts of jurisprudence, applied with great regularity by appellate judges, is that either jurors or, in nonjury trials, trial judges are in the best position to judge the credibility of witnesses. This doctrine of deference to the trial fact finders rests on a solid foundation of common sense, in addition to countless legal precedents. Even a transcript that reports every syllable of the words spoken in court cannot possibly capture the myriad other sounds, sights, and impressions registered by an attentive person who is present in the courtroom. The same conclusion applies with much greater force to the transcripts of the Dakota trials, which are, at best, rough summaries of the actual proceedings.

Those present in court are in the best position to assess what lawyers call the witnesses' "demeanor," a catchall term that covers infinitely varying human behaviors and reactions. Was an answer given firmly or hesitantly? Did the witness show surprise, anger, sullenness, or some other emotional reaction when confronted with potentially incriminating evidence? How did the witness react when caught in an apparent lie? What hand gestures, facial expressions, or other body language accompanied the testimony? Even in a verbatim record, these and many other important clues to credibility are missing.

Thus it is impossible to overstate the significance of the commission's conclusion that Godfrey, after appearing in more than forty-five cases, "always proved truthful." In many ways historians who write about the Dakota trials are in the same position as appellate judges: no matter how many sources we gather and how carefully we analyze them, we will never be in a position as favorable as were the judges themselves to assess credibility. Their conclusion that Godfrey gave truthful testimony is the best evidence we will ever get—*could* ever get—of his honesty as revealed during the trials.

Note, too, the judges' citing of the same point made by Heard (and confirmed by the transcripts): that Godfrey's truthfulness was affirmed by "corroborative evidence and the acknowledgements of the prisoners themselves." The judges wanted Sibley to know that they were not relying merely on their own observations. In effect, they were telling their commander, whenever we could check out Godfrey's story, it turned out to be true.

Interestingly, the judges' plea is silent on the subject of duress. They do not claim that Godfrey's sentence should be reprieved because his life was threatened or because he was forced to join the Dakotas. Most likely, they knew that Sibley had already rejected that argument by denying the court's initial plea for clemency, so they emphasized Godfrey's role as a witness. But their strong belief in his honesty more than likely led them to conclude that Godfrey was, as he said, a coerced participant.

When Sibley received the judges' petition, he was completing his review of the trial transcripts. Though he had sent some cases back to the court for further consideration, virtually all of them had been decided to the mutual satisfaction of the commander and judges by November 5. In the end, Sibley accepted almost every finding made by his court.

Only thirty-nine days had elapsed since the start of Godfrey's trial at Camp Release. Subtracting some Sundays, a short lull before October

16, and three days off for moving camp, the commissioners actually conducted trials for no more than thirty days. During that time they heard and disposed of 392 cases. More than three-fourths of the defendants, 303, had been sentenced to hang. Another 20 had been given prison terms of one to five years. The remaining men, and one Dakota woman, were either found not guilty or the charges against them were "not proven," though most of them were nonetheless kept manacled in jail with those found guilty.[37]

Before the final list of condemned men was forwarded to Washington, however, Sibley decided to review one case on his own initiative. Oyataykokejaje (trial 381) was the brother of Ampatutokacha (Ampetutokeca), known as John Other Day, a full-blood Dakota Christian who had become a hero in white eyes during the conflict. Married, quite unusually for the times, to a white woman, Other Day had enlisted in the cause of protecting whites and, later, fought his own people. On November 5 Sibley, accurately noting that the evidence in Oyataykokejaje's case was slim, granted him an extraordinary death-penalty reprieve, which Sibley acknowledged was based on the "earnest solicitation of his noble brother," Other Day.[38]

That partial pardon did not represent a clash between Sibley and his judges, for it was a response to a hero's plea for mercy rather than a rejection of the court's findings. Considering Sibley's overall approval of the acts of his distinguished judges, the transcript documentation of Godfrey's extraordinary role in the trials, and the strength of the court's petition on his behalf, it seems the most likely outcome would have been that Sibley would approve the judges' request and remove the noose hovering over Godfrey's head. But Sibley did not.

Once Sibley had approved the death penalties imposed by his court, it fell to Riggs to prepare the official tally of the condemned men. On November 3 he wrote his wife, "I have been very busy today in writing out a list of the prisoners as they have been tried by the Military Commission. This list is to go down to Gen. Pope and probably on to the President. In each case is the name and the caste (Indian or half breed) the crime and the sentence. And really my heart has been made sick with writing 'To be hanged by the neck until he is dead.'"[39] On November 5 Riggs again wrote of his unpleasant task to his wife, ruefully reporting that he had made "a list of a bundle of thirty papers on the nineteen twentieths of which were written 'Sentenced to be hung.'" Having no desire to witness the "bitter end" of the executions, Riggs requested leave to return to his family. But Sibley turned him down.[40]

No later than November 6, Riggs's list of men sentenced to death was ready to be dispatched to Pope in St. Paul. At this point Sibley expected to hold the hangings by about November 16, apparently calculating that the logistics required—overland passage of the execution list to and from St. Paul and an exchange of telegrams between Pope and Lincoln—could be accomplished in ten days.[41] The procedures outlined by Pope called for Sibley to send him a written communiqué with the list of death-row names, which Pope would in turn submit to a telegraph operator for transmission to Washington. Though some of the correspondence is missing from the records, we do have the "United States military telegram" from Pope that arrived in Washington on November 8, addressed to the president. First on the list of some three hundred men is "Otaka or Godfrey, Caste Negro."[42]

The White House telegram proves that Sibley had decided to reject his court's petition on Godfrey's behalf. But, more significant, the telegram says absolutely nothing about that commission's unanimous plea for mercy. Either Sibley or Pope—almost certainly Sibley—had decided to ask for the president's approval of Godfrey's execution without telling him that all of the judges who had imposed Godfrey's death penalty wished it to be reprieved.[43]

To twice reject his court's requests for mercy for Godfrey, as Sibley did, was extraordinary. Godfrey's was the only case out of 392 in which the commander and his judges were at loggerheads with one another. Still, Sibley's actions, while singular, could be justified as a valid exercise of his discretion. But his failure to disclose the court's clemency plea to the president raises more serious questions. Why would a man as thorough, cautious, decent, and intelligent as Sibley withhold the court's clemency plea from Lincoln? And why was Sibley more determined than any of his judges to execute Godfrey?

Sibley's behavior is so uncharacteristic that the answers probably lie in facts and circumstances that go beyond the court record. In the only statement he ever made that sheds any light on the question, Sibley told a newspaper reporter in 1886, "The evidence was sufficient to hang him [Godfrey], and he was known to be a rascal, anyway. The Negro . . . was a bright, smart scoundrel."[44] Sibley's claim that Godfrey was "a rascal anyway" supports the inference that he may have denied him clemency for reasons that go beyond the events of 1862. Sibley's apparent reliance on out-of-court behavior, coupled with his highly unusual disagreement with his judges and his unfair withholding of the court's plea from Lincoln, all justify consideration of Sibley's potential motivations.

Was Sibley aware of some earlier wrongdoing by Godfrey, the details of which have been lost to history? Did he see Godfrey as a "rascal" for having run away from enslavement? Was Sibley concerned that Godfrey might reveal facts about his own involvement with slavery? Or did Sibley simply believe that Godfrey was as deserving of the death penalty as most of the Dakotas whose executions he was then recommending? All of these questions arise from pure conjecture. But Sibley's harsh and unprecedented treatment of Godfrey invites them.

Both Sibley and Pope expected the president to approve all of the executions in short order. Immediately after Pope sent the telegram to Lincoln, Pope's aide notified Sibley that he anticipated a quick and favorable response: "The Major General directs me to acknowledge the rec[eip]t of your dispatch enclosing list of the Indians condemned by the Military Commission which has been transmitted to the President and his confirmation is hourly expected."[45] This expectation was shared by those under Sibley's command. Before departing from the Lower Agency for Fort Snelling, Colonel Marshall sent a letter to the *St. Paul Press,* assuring the public that "some 300" of the "*guilty Indians* . . . are to be executed."[46] It might take a week or more for Lincoln's orders to reach the planned site of the hangings, but, as Pope led Ramsey and Sibley to believe, the outcome was a foregone conclusion.

If everything went according to plans, the convicted Indians would be hanged before the end of November. And Godfrey would be dead before anyone knew that Sibley had withheld the court's clemency petition from Lincoln.

NOTES ON CHAPTER 8

1. Heard, *History of the Sioux War,* 235–36.
2. Ibid.
3. See trial 318, Dakota Trials Records; and Heard, *History of the Sioux War,* 240.
4. Sibley used "vanity" in his October 25 letter to his wife, but many years later, when he edited his correspondence, he changed it to "egotism." Sibley Papers, MHS, M164, roll 11.
5. Unfortunately, the record of the official, in-the-field correspondence from this point forward either was lost or has not yet been located. Collateral sources prove that later letters once existed. For example, Sibley's letters to his wife during this period refer to his dispatches from "Camp Sibley" (near the Lower Agency) to Pope and to the fact that he is "awaiting orders" from Pope. See Sibley to Sarah Sibley, October 25 and 28, 1862, Sibley Papers, MHS, M164, roll 11. Letters from Pope containing these orders are missing. See also the October 27, 1862, letter from Riggs to his daughter, Martha: "One day an order comes up to have them [the Indians not convicted, including all women and children] taken to Fort Snelling. In a day or two the order is changed to South Bend or Mankato." Riggs Family Papers, MHS, box 1.
6. Pope to Sibley, October 20, 1862, NA, RG 393, E3436, pt. 1, LS, Letters Sent and Received, Department of NW, Headquarters.
7. Sibley to Flandrau, September 28, 1862, *MCIW,* 2:258.
8. Riggs to Mary Riggs, October 25, 1862, Riggs letters, CCHS. Flandrau's advice to kill all the Dakotas (including women and children) was first published in 2004, in Gilman, *Henry Hastings Sibley,* 186.
9. Trials 10 (Muzzabomadu), 22 (Dowansa), and 139 (Louis Labelle).
10. Lower Agency cases in which Godfrey's testimony was crucial for conviction or was the strongest evidence given are trials 186, 210, 218, 240, 248, 254–55, 258–60, 268, 272, 277, 290–92, 298–99, 313, 327, 338, 344, 359, 366, 377, 382–83, and 385.
11. Heard, *History of the Sioux War,* 267.
12. Riggs to Mary Riggs, October 25, 1862, Riggs letters, CCHS. In an earlier letter to his wife Riggs said that Sibley wanted to conduct the trials in a "double quick" manner. Riggs to Mary Riggs, October 15, 1862, Riggs letters, CCHS.
13. Letter from "H" [Isaac Heard], *St. Paul Pioneer and Democrat,* November 15, 1862, in which "celerity" is misspelled as "celerily."
14. Two facts indicate that the trials recommenced on October 27: that is the earliest date on any of the newly charged cases, starting with trial 140; though most trial records are undated, "27th Oct." was written in the margin of the transcript of trial 140. Riggs, who had previously argued against holding court on the Sabbath, may have prevailed on Sibley to defer the start of the trials until Monday the twenty-seventh.
15. Riggs to Mary Riggs, October 28 and 30, 1862, Riggs letters, CCHS; refers to thirty-five trials on October 29 and forty on October 30.
16. Letter from "H" [Isaac Heard], *St. Paul Pioneer and Democrat,* November 15, 1862.
17. By my count, Godfrey was the main witness in twenty-nine cases at the Lower Agency that led to convictions, while other witnesses gave evidence leading to the conviction of forty-eight defendants.

18. This case probably dealt with the killing of two farmers delivering hay to Milford. See Satterlee, *Outbreak and Massacre,* 41–42. The version of this case attributed to Godfrey in Heard's book is more detailed in some respects, stating that one of the victims was still alive when Wakantanka "cut him all to pieces." Heard, *History of the Sioux War,* 193–94.
19. Heard, *History of the Sioux War,* 193–94 ("Waki-ya-ni").
20. The reference to the Travelers' Home removes any doubt about the fact that Godfrey was referring to Milford.
21. No killings of the sort described in this case occurred in New Ulm, and Godfrey's eye-witness account is consistent only with a Milford location. Other killings that might fit this description occurred elsewhere during the war, notably in communities north of the Minnesota River. But there is no evidence that Godfrey was present at any of those places, where many of the killings were simultaneous to the Milford massacre. Satterlee concurs in this conclusion, saying that these victims "must have been" Massopust and his daughters. Satterlee's note to trial 237, in Folwell, Satterlee, and Brown, *Court Proceedings,* 65–66.
22. Though the record is unclear, Wahetaymaza (trial 130) may also have been injured at Milford. At his trial he said that a white man shot him and wounded him in the arm "on my way down to New Ulm."
23. Heard, *History of the Sioux War,* 267.
24. The result in this case is a good example of the harsher standards to which defendants were held as the trials progressed. Makatanajin (trial 9), one of the first Indians tried at Camp Release, was identified by Mattie Williams as "one of the party who killed Patville [Patoille]," though she said she did not see if he "took an active part." Despite his admission that he was at the scene with a gun, he was acquitted and freed. Oechagay (trial 186), in contrast, was convicted and sentenced to prison on the basis of very similar evidence.
25. Heard, *History of the Sioux War,* 266.
26. Ibid.
27. Ibid., 266–67.
28. Other examples of cases in which Godfrey prompted defendants to revise their stories include those against Oyatatonka (trial 290), Wakandape (trial 299), and Makanashota (trial 385).
29. See trials of Mahpeyakahoton (trial 246), Joseph Allord (trial 334), and Wasoohdehayya (trial 358).
30. Brown, *Bury My Heart,* 59. Brown's book has many footnotes, but he offers none to support this claim.
31. S. Riggs, *Tah-koo wah-kan,* 334.

32. Riggs's conclusion about the court's preferential treatment of mixed-bloods may have been based on a trio of cases in which he took a personal interest. Three men who were together in a Dakota war party were tried in tandem. The evidence against all three was very similar. The court acquitted the mixed-blood man (who was given a longer trial) and convicted the two full-blood Dakotas. Compare the trials of Magatonka, or Narcisse Freniere (trial 236), with the trials of Eyojanjan (trial 237) and Tahohpewakan (trial 238). Riggs later requested that the two men found guilty be pardoned. See "Petition of S. R. Riggs for Clemency on Behalf of Four Sioux Indians" to Sibley, April 7, 1864, Southern Minnesota Historical Center, Minnesota State University, Mankato, originals in NA, RG 153, Records of the Judge Advocate General (Army), Shakopee, NN3132. Magatonka is not identified as Narcisse Freniere in the trial transcript, but the record describes him as a "half-breed" and a separate page in his trial records gives both names. The Riggs petition confirms this identification.
33. Despite the evidence of Godfrey and Thompson against Makanahtakay, the court initially gave him a five-year prison term rather than the death penalty. Perhaps the judges lowered the weight of Thompson's evidence because it was solely hearsay. But after Sibley reviewed the transcript and "suspended" the decision of the tribunal, the court then apparently overcame any evidentiary qualms and changed its sentence by simply crossing out the prison sentence and writing above it, "[To] be hung by the neck until dead." This sequence of events suggests that Sibley too believed that Thompson's life was in peril.
34. The judges were unaware, it appears, that one of the defendants was a young white man who had been raised from infancy by the Dakotas. See discussion of the hanging mistakes in chapter 11.
35. The November 5 application on Godfrey's behalf is in the Dakota Trials Records, microfilm roll 1, preceding the transcript of his trial.
36. The judges' wording that they were asking Sibley to "renew their application" virtually clinches the conclusion that they had already been notified that Sibley had rejected their earlier plea (contained within the transcript of Godfrey's trial) that his sentence be reduced from death to ten years' imprisonment. Both the formality of the November 5 application and the fact that it was communicated in a separate document also support this conclusion.
37. Folwell incorrectly reported 307 death sentences and 16 prison terms, as did Carley. Folwell, *History of Minnesota,* 196–97; Carley, *Dakota War of 1862,* 69. A careful examination of the notes taken by Folwell when he reviewed the trial records in 1909 (his notes are in summary, not verbatim, form) shows that Folwell's erroneous total was the result of mistakes he made in noting the verdicts in a handful of cases. See Folwell's original notes in Folwell Papers, MHS, box 80. Many other sources make similar errors. The only Dakota woman tried was Echagoheyayaywin (trial 384); she was acquitted.
38. Sibley's reasons for granting this reprieve were written on the original court file, beneath the caption.
39. Riggs to Mary Riggs, November 3, 1862, Riggs letters, CCHS. Neither the Riggs list nor any cover letter sent by Sibley to Pope has ever been found. Riggs's is the most complete extant description regarding the preparation of the list.
40. Riggs to Mary Riggs, November 5, 1862, Riggs letters, CCHS.
41. In his November 3 letter to his wife Riggs refers to Sibley's ten-day estimate. Riggs letters, CCHS. Riggs himself thought it could take until December 1 before a reply was received.

42. Abraham Lincoln Papers, Library of Congress, microfilm roll 42. Though 303 men had been sentenced to die, only 298 names were on the list that arrived at the White House. The telegram appears to enumerate the names of 300 men, but closer examination shows that two numbers (telegrams 212 and 217) were skipped. It seems that in one instance a telegraph operator blended two adjacent and similar Dakota names from the original list into one garbled combination of the two: the names of Maypehaypeya (trial 285) and Mayhpeyahota (trial 286) in the original records appear as number 216 on the telegram, spelled "Mahpetaypriahota." The other four men "missing" from the original list of 303 condemned men are Oyataykokejaje (trial 381), Other Day's brother, whom Sibley pardoned; Wakinyanhde (trial 300), who had died in jail; and two men whose names were omitted for unknown reasons, Mahoowaywa trial 382) and Wakinyanna (trial 383).
43. Because I have not located the pertinent correspondence from Sibley to Pope, it is possible that Sibley informed Pope about the court's plea for clemency for Godfrey in that communication. But since Pope had no involvement in the trials, did not have any of the trial records, and was merely relaying the information given to him by Sibley, that scenario seems unlikely. Even more remote is the possibility that a telegraph operator omitted the Godfrey disclosure. I believe all available facts point to Sibley as the person responsible for withholding the information from the president.
44. *St. Paul Dispatch,* March 26, 1886.
45. Selfridge to Sibley, November 8, 1862, NA, RG 393, E3436, pt. 1, LS, Letters Sent and Received, Department of NW, Headquarters.
46. Excerpts of letter from Colonel Marshall, *St. Paul Press,* November 8, 1862 (emphasis in original).

CHAPTER 9

Waiting for Lincoln

The large camp at the Lower Agency was broken up shortly after the trials concluded. Following Pope's orders, Sibley dispatched most of the Dakotas (almost all of the women and children, the mixed-bloods, and the men who had not been tried) on a late-season overland trek to Fort Snelling. Some of the older Indians rode in wagons, but most of the sixteen hundred people trudged on foot 110 miles to the fort. The line of weary and bedraggled walkers stretched for four miles. Godfrey's wife, Takanheca, probably walked with her son; she either was pregnant or carried her infant daughter. This group departed on November 7, accompanied by a detachment of soldiers led by Col. William Marshall.[1]

Once sufficient oxcarts and wagons had been requisitioned to transport the shackled prisoners, Sibley led a second retinue, including Godfrey and about 375 Dakota men, out of the camp. Headed toward South Bend, a turn in the Minnesota River just west of Mankato, this group left early on the morning of November 9 under a strong military escort.[2] When the prisoners reached the eastern end of the reservation, their route followed the road through Milford taken by Godfrey and the Dakotas on August 18. They passed Henle's Travelers' Home and the ruined farmhouses of the slaughtered residents. Their wagons rumbled over the small bridge where Ernst Dietrich and the other members of the recruiting party died.[3]

As the pinioned Indians passed near New Ulm on November 10, a mob of angry citizens burst forth from the town to assault them. (An artist's evocative depiction of that scene, showing an all-female, stone-throwing assemblage dressed primly in hoop skirts, later appeared in *Harper's New Monthly Magazine*.)[4] The chained Dakotas could see the attack coming, and many of them hunkered down. Godfrey, perhaps the most visible participant in the Milford massacre, crouched in a wagon and covered himself with a blanket.[5]

The official published report of this assault, written by Minnesota's adjutant general, simply states that the Dakotas "were set upon by some of the inhabitants of the town, and many of them pelted and beaten with stones and sticks, in spite of the guard accompanying them."[6] But that watered-down version hardly tells the tale. The weapons used by the outraged vigilantes ran the gamut: butcher knives, pitchforks, clubs, axes, hatchets, pots full of scalding water, bricks, table knives, and scissors.[7]

One "very large German woman" slipped through the cordon of soldiers guarding the Dakotas and pounded a prisoner in the face with a large stone until he fell backward out of the wagon. Chained to another prisoner, he was dragged along the ground for "about five rods," until the military escort lifted him back into the wagon.[8] Female assailants also fractured one Dakota's skull and "cleft the jaw" of another with a hatchet.[9] Describing the scene or another, similar attack, Heard reported that a prisoner's jaw was broken.[10]

Writing his wife a few days later, Sibley said that "some fifteen" of the "shackled wretches" were seriously injured near New Ulm, as were "some of the guards," the soldiers who sought to defend them.[11] Though Sibley never reported the fact, two Dakota men died of their injuries in the weeks following the attack. Thomas Williamson, the elder missionary colleague of Reverend Riggs, reported that the deaths "were attributed to wounds inflicted by a mob as they were brought past New Ulm in chains."[12]

To his wife, Sibley reported that he arrested fifteen to twenty of the New Ulm attackers. He also supplied details of their "punishment" for spearheading the murderous mob. Some men "were arrested, and made to march on foot, twelve miles to the spot, where we encamped for the night, where, after being reprimanded for the insult to the U.S. flag committed by them, and their female associates, they were released, and compelled to walk back the entire distance to New Ulm."[13]

This letter offers a fascinating glimpse into the workings of Sibley's mind. Though one of his prisoners had a fractured skull, another a hatchet-cleft jaw, and many others had been seriously bludgeoned, he took greatest offense at the "insult to the U.S. flag." Given the veritable civil insurrection he faced in New Ulm, Sibley would have been acting within his powers to have convened a military commission and summarily tried the offending members of the mob. Or he could have taken them in chains to Mankato to await trial for assault or attempted murder. But, probably recognizing that an outcry would have followed any effort to punish the men, he gave them a lecture and sent them home.

Though nothing excuses the conduct of the New Ulm townsfolk, we are left to wonder if they would have resorted to mob violence had they not been excluded from Sibley's judicial proceedings. Many New Ulm residents and the few survivors of the Milford attacks could have given highly relevant testimony that would have added strength to the prosecution's case, and allowing them to appear in court would have offered them a legitimate outlet for their fury.

The much larger train of Fort Snelling–bound Dakotas also encountered violent hostility from whites along the way. Samuel J. Brown, the son of former Indian agent Joseph R. Brown, accompanied them and later wrote a graphic account of the reception given them by residents of the river town of Henderson on November 11:

> We found the streets crowded with an angry and excited populace, cursing, shouting and crying. Men, women and children armed with guns, knives, clubs and stones, rushed upon the Indians, as the train was passing by, and before the soldiers could interfere and stop them, succeeded in pulling many of the old men and women and even children from the wagons by the hair of the head, and beating them, and otherwise inflicting injury upon the helpless and miserable creatures.

I saw an enraged white woman rush up to one of the wagons and snatch a nursing babe from its mother's breast and dash it violently upon the ground. The soldiers' instantly seized her and led or rather dragged the woman away, and restored the papoose to its mother—limp and almost dead. Although the child was not killed outright, it died a few hours after.[14]

Brown also saw a Henderson man "half crazed with drink" attempt to shoot Charles Crawford, a mixed-blood man who was the only defendant tried twice (and acquitted both times) by the commission. But Colonel Marshall rushed up on horseback and struck down the gun with his saber, "thus saving a life at the risk of his own."[15] Another Indian witness, Wicahpewastewin, or Good Star Woman, recalled her terror as an eight-year-old huddled beneath buffalo robes on a travois on the trek to Fort Snelling. She remembered the soldiers' efforts to ward off attacks on the Dakotas as they passed through towns along the way. She said "some Indians" died from the attacks, one of whom was secretly buried beneath the ashes of the evening campfire "so the whites would not find his body."[16]

Missionary John Williamson, the son of Thomas Williamson, also accompanied the Dakotas on the march. He reported that Marshall "exerted himself to the utmost to assist and protect his helpless charges" but that notwithstanding the guard of soldiers, they "received sundry salutations in the form of stones and sticks, to say nothing of the curses that were heaped upon them from the doorways and hillsides."[17] There is no exact count of the Dakotas who were killed or injured on the road to Fort Snelling. Whatever the number, no one was punished for those crimes.

While Pope and Sibley awaited Lincoln's response to the telegram seeking authority to hang three hundred men, consensus was building among the Minnesota public, its elected officials, and the press on three topics related to the convicted Dakotas. The first, which needed almost no expression within the state, was best captured by the *New York Times*:

"The people of Minnesota, to a man, are in favor of their immediate execution."[18] Perhaps the *Times* overstated the unanimity of the citizens' sentiments, but not by much.

Second, the erroneous belief that all three hundred of the condemned men were "convicted murderers" gained currency. On November 12 the *St. Paul Press* flatly declared that "over 300 were proved to have actually participated in the massacres, or attempts to massacre our people" and then both misinformed the public and lectured Lincoln: "They were found guilty of murder. Now, it might as well be understood at Washington first as last, that the *penalty for murder by the laws of the State is DEATH*."[19]

Third, outraged Minnesotans were in no mood for talk about legal technicalities. They wanted blood for blood, and it mattered little to them whether the fine points of proof of homicides had been met by the court or not. The *St. Paul Press* ranted against the "hated race": "This [hanging of all convicted Dakotas] is no longer the petition of the people of Minnesota. It is their demand. . . . They will not stop to measure justice by the rule and square, and make a nice adjustment of the account of blood. They are not in a temper for a delicate balancing of evidence, or a judicial discrimination of the degrees of guilt."[20] In other words, eye-for-an-eye retribution justified three hundred hangings, whether the evidence did or not.

On Pope's orders, Sibley was headed toward South Bend so that his military commission could try fourteen Winnebago Indians languishing in a jail in a large tent erected on the levee in nearby Mankato.[21] Pope had also directed that the condemned Dakotas be hanged in front of the assembled members of the Winnebago tribe.[22] Sibley's advance team had selected a beautiful, well-sheltered camping ground near the mouth of the Blue Earth River, coincidentally situated beneath a large hill named Sibley's Mound, or more grandiloquently, Mount Sibley.[23] This "eminence," as Sibley called it, had acquired its name when someone filed a claim to the land on his behalf; the moniker stuck even though the claim was "jumped" before he took title. The soldiers, perhaps hopeful that flattery might assure a quick presidential approval of the mass hangings, immediately dubbed the place Camp Lincoln.[24]

Once the camp had been established a steady stream of curiosity seekers and visitors came from Mankato, located just a mile and a half downriver.[25] Godfrey, whom the *Mankato Record* continued to brand as a mass killer ("It is alleged [he] killed twenty-three white persons"), was the "greatest attraction with visitors" and "the greatest object of curiosity as well as aversion."[26] All the area's inns were soon filled with people coming to gawk at the Indians and Godfrey, "ladies as well as gentlemen."[27]

Godfrey evoked extreme reactions. One reporter said, "He appears sullen and downcast and on the whole presents a very repulsive appearance. He is a molatto, rather dark."[28] Another visitor claimed he had met "a German who said he (the Negro) had murdered his wife and three children; the man could hardly be kept from attacking him."[29] The most likely interpretation is that the unnamed German hailed from Milford and was angered by reports that Godfrey had been sighted at the scene of the massacre there.[30] None of the eyewitness accounts published later verifies this murder accusation.

But if Godfrey's guilt was exaggerated by visitors to Camp Lincoln, so was his contribution to the trials. He was credited by one observer not only with giving the "best evidence" but also with convicting "over two-thirds" of the Indians."[31] Another said that Godfrey gave evidence "implicating over three hundred" and that "principally upon his testimony, most of the guilty have been convicted."[32] Thus the myth that Godfrey was single-handedly responsible for all (or almost all) of the Dakota death sentences took root.

The prisoners, still manacled at the ankles and chained in pairs, were housed in a long, L-shaped wooden shed hastily constructed of rough boards. The jail's earthen floor, "probably frozen when they arrived," was covered with a thin layer of straw. Half a dozen fires provided the only heat in the hundred-foot-long structure against the advancing Minnesota winter.[33]

Between the white onlookers and the vengeful Indian inmates, Godfrey occupied a woeful position at Camp Lincoln. Lt. Theodore Carter, who helped run the military jail, linked his beleaguered status to his race: "[P]oor Godfrey had black blood in his veins. He had no friends, white or copper-colored. All looked down and despised him."[34]

The fact that Godfrey's name was first on the execution list then in Lincoln's hands and that word was expected at any time authorizing his hanging did not preclude using him as a witness in more trials. Almost immediately after arriving at Camp Lincoln, Sibley ordered the same military commission that had tried the Dakotas to hear the evidence against the fourteen Winnebago suspects. The Winnebagoes had been arrested because they had been implicated by one of their kinsmen. Otanka (trial 13), the only Winnebago man prosecuted in the earlier trials at Camp Release, had been acquitted. But since Otanka had named other Winnebagoes as having joined the Dakotas, he had been held in jail as a material witness. His accusations led to the arrest of the members of his tribe now awaiting trial.

The people of southern Minnesota had been trying the Winnebagoes in the press throughout the autumn of 1862. Mankato residents were exceedingly nervous about the tribe's presence on a reservation only a few miles south of the town. Whites feared that the Winnebagoes would join forces with the Dakotas, just as Little Crow had hoped and predicted.[35] Local citizens were prepared to slaughter them at the first provocation. As the *Faribault Central Republican* graphically warned,

> Winnebagoes had better, by all means, refrain from making arrests, or killing any oxen, for the people hereabouts have determined that on the first outrage committed by the greasy devils, they will take their case into their own hands, and, regardless of Generals Pope, Sibley, or anybody else. Mr. Little Priest, Mr. Big Priest [Winnebago chiefs] and all other priests and big men will have to travel to their happy hunting grounds, or go under; and there'll be no humbug Military Commissions to try offenders . . . to interfere in the matter. . . . Henceforth death or submission, and death first, is in order for all our Country's foes.[36]

Even with minimal evidence of hostile intent on the part of the Winnebagoes, a groundswell consensus developed for removing the entire tribe from Minnesota, fueled partly by fear and partly by lust for their rich, centrally located lands. Arguments that now strike us as strained rationalizations were advanced in all seriousness to justify summary eviction of the Winnebagoes, the Dakotas, and all other Indians from the state. One theory reasoned that the Indians, as wandering hunters and gatherers, were "wasting" the productive potential of the land. The *Mankato Record* posed the Winnebago removal issue to Lincoln in these stark terms: "Our rich and fertile prairies must either be the abode of thrift, industry and wealth, or the hunting ground of a barbarous and worthless race. Which shall it be, Mr. President?"[37]

Jane Swisshelm, the fiery abolitionist editor of the *St. Cloud Democrat,* put forth an elaborate argument that purported to link three villainous classes of people: Indians, Southern slaveholders, and European aristocrats. These wildly disparate groups, she believed, each were violating God's plan for the world through their profligacy: "The Indian and the Slaveholder have been the aristocrats of American society. They have been fostered and fed and kept in idleness like a den of rattlesnakes and cage of pet panthers until grown strong and insolent they have simultaneously broken loose to sting and tear those who have fed and fondled them. Both races must be exterminated or learn the art of working for a living, and find some other occupation for their activity, than in plotting and executing treason and murder."[38] In 1860s Minnesota, no newspaper editor was more strident in his or her antislavery idealism than Swisshelm. Once the Dakota conflict began, no other editor was as virulent in demanding the "extermination" of the Indians.[39]

Some Minnesotans did argue the Winnebagoes' cause. A Winona editor said that the members of the tribe in that region "are quite as peaceably disposed as the white people themselves, and a great deal wiser than some of the latter."[40] When a settler killed a Winnebago man, the same newspaper proclaimed that the deed was "no better than murder."[41] The editor even decried the decision to withhold powder and lead from the Winnebago tribe, noting with sympathy that these items were essential for their fall hunt.[42]

In this highly charged anti-Indian atmosphere, the trials of the fourteen Winnebagoes began on November 12. According to the *Mankato Re-*

cord, Major Balcombe asked Sibley if he could retain attorneys to represent the accused men, but "the General very respectfully but firmly replied that these were 'military trials,' intimating that the request would not be complied with."[43] Though neither the Dakota nor the Winnebago trials make any mention of a request for counsel, this report is fully consistent with Sibley's concept of the Indian trials, which he viewed as summary proceedings.[44]

Since the same judges conducted both the Dakota and the Winnebago trials, it is not surprising that their transcripts follow the same format and that the Winnebago trials appear similar to the Dakota cases. But there were a few differences. This time around Reverend Riggs did double duty. He wrote his wife that he was kept very busy on November 12 because "I had to interpret for the Dakota witnesses besides preparing the cases."[45] And there were even fewer witnesses available for the Winnebago trials, for almost all of the "friendly" Indians and mixed-bloods who gave testimony in the earlier cases had been sent to Fort Snelling.

The first Winnebago defendant at Camp Lincoln was a chief, Hungkonetah, commonly known as Little Priest. The Winnebagoes' accuser, Otanka, in his Dakota trials testimony in October, had claimed that Little Priest had fired shots both at the initial outbreak at the Lower Agency and also at the battle of Birch Coulee.[46] The first to testify, Little Priest (Winnebago trial 1) admitted that he was at the Lower Agency on the day the outbreak began but said he had no gun and fired at no one: "I started home next day after the traders were killed . . . [with] 8 Winnebagoes." Five others of his tribe, he said, had departed on the first day. He claimed he had not even seen Captain Marsh's company, let alone shot at the soldiers. After his arrival back at his home near the Winnebago agency, apparently on August 20, Little Priest hadn't been "anywheres," he said.

Otanka was listed as the sole witness against Little Priest, but his testimony was mixed. He claimed that the chief had fired a gun at soldiers in Captain Marsh's company near the ferry on August 18. But, essentially recanting his previous testimony that he had seen Little Priest "with my own eyes at the battle of Birch Coolie" and "seen him fire," he now said he had not even heard that Little Priest was at that attack.[47] Godfrey was called as the second witness, despite the fact that his knowledge was based on not much more than Indian camp rumors. He said, "It was common report among the Indians that the prisoner finished Myrick after he was shot—that he finished him with a knife."

Andrew Myrick, a trader whom the Dakotas detested for his refusal to extend credit to them so that they could buy food, had been one of the first men killed at the Lower Agency on August 18.[48] If a chief of the Winnebagoes, rather than a Dakota warrior, had actually "finished" Myrick, it would have been a noteworthy involvement by that tribe at the start of the war. But Godfrey, who was at Milford the whole day of August 18, could offer only a hearsay account of the Dakotas' finger-pointing. Little Priest did not reply to his accusation, and the court did not press the point.

Based on this tenuous record the commissioners found Little Priest guilty and sentenced him to hang. But they must have had misgivings about doing so, for the whole case depended on the credibility of Otanka's testimony about the attack on Marsh's company. If the star Winnebago witness performed with similar inconsistency in the balance of the trials, their verdict in this case would be hanging by a slender thread.

The second Winnebago to be accused was Monekasdayhekah (Winnebago trial 2). He told the court he had not been at the Lower Agency on August 18 but had been at Long Lake—"two days' hard travel" from there—where he had gone upon hearing that his grandfather had died. He claimed that when he later learned of the conflict he stole a horse and started home, but he "got lost and was nine days coming down."

The court then called two men as witnesses, both of whom were standing in the shadow of the gallows. Godfrey was the first. He testified that he had seen the prisoner for the first time at the Birch Coulee battle, sitting on a horse with another Indian, to which the defendant replied, weakly, "I don't recollect of being there." Godfrey then said he had also seen Monekasdayhekah at the Wood Lake battle but "didn't see him do anything." He added, however, "I heard that he had one of two scalps brought in at that fight." The defendant, according to Godfrey, "disappeared" when there was a report of the troops coming up "and I heard he ran away."

After Monekasdayhekah denied all involvement in battles, a Dakota inmate, Wechankpedoota, was called.[49] He corroborated Godfrey by saying that he had ridden together on the same horse with the defendant while coming away from Birch Coulee. But he offered no further evidence of Monekasdayhekah's acts during the battle.

Overall, the evidence in this case was as compelling (and flimsy) as that used to convict many of the ordinary-soldier Dakotas. Monekasdayhekah had evidently lied about getting lost on the way home and had instead gone to two battles. Though he told the judges that "Godfrey lies," they had long since established Godfrey's credibility. Moreover, Wechankpeduta had largely confirmed Godfrey's version of events. The court convicted Monekasdayhekah and sentenced him to hang.[50]

The case for the prosecution, however, went steadily downhill during the balance of the Winnebago trials. Though Godfrey had gotten stronger as a witness as the Dakota trials had progressed, the opposite occurred with Otanka. With each new case it became more obvious that the state's key witness was collapsing. Called to repeat his Dakota trial testimony that he had seen several Winnebagoes fire their guns at Marsh's company, Otanka now waffled or recanted. Against Kunchahooka (Winnebago trial 4), Otanka said, "I presume he was with the party who fired at Marsh's command, but didn't see him." And so it went for the rest of the trials. Otanka said one Winnebago had a gun and was painted at the Lower Agency, another had a gun and took blankets from the stores, and another was armed with a war club.[51] But he did not describe them as either taking part in battles or killing anyone. Of another defendant, he said simply, "I know nothing about this Indian except that I saw him at the agency."[52]

With the exception of his testimony against Little Priest, Otanka never gave evidence sufficient to convict a single man. And, unlike the Dakotas, the Winnebago defendants did not fill in the evidentiary gaps by admitting that they fired shots. Instead, most of them confirmed Little Priest's statement that they had left the Dakota reservation shortly after the uprising began and gone straight home. Godfrey was not called again as a witness.

By the end of the Winnebago trials the judges could only have concluded that Otanka was a totally unreliable witness. When facing his tribesmen in court, he had failed to repeat virtually any of the damning statements he had made against them at Camp Release. It is not surprising, then, that at some point the judges revisited their verdict in the case against Little Priest. Deciding to acquit him, they simply crossed out the last words in the transcript—"and sentence him to be hanged by the neck until he is dead"—and inserted the word "not" in front of "guilty."[53] With those alterations, the court finished its docket of Winnebago cases in one day by acquitting fourteen defendants and finding only one man guilty. The most important witness in that single conviction case had been Godfrey.

On November 12, the day of the Winnebago trials, Sibley wrote his wife that he was "hourly expecting a decision of President Lincoln involving the fate" of Godfrey and the other prisoners on the death list.[54] Unbeknownst to Sibley, Lincoln had already sent a reply to Pope's execution list telegram. By telegram dated November 10, the president wrote, "Your dispatch giving the names of 300 Indians condemned to death is received. Please forward as soon as possible the full and complete record of their convictions; and if the record does not fully indicate the more guilty and influential of the culprits, please have a careful statement made on these points and forwarded to me. Send all by mail."[55] The last instruction was a none-too-subtle dig at the cost Pope had incurred for his hanging list telegram—$400, a substantial wartime expense that the *New York Times* said "ought to be deducted from Gen. Pope's salary."[56]

Pope reacted with agitated consternation to Lincoln's refusal to immediately approve mass hangings. He viewed the president's reply as reflecting the same woeful shortcomings of the commander in chief that he had seen earlier: Lincoln, he thought, was well intentioned but weak and ineffectual. Pope's upset was surely aggravated by the fact that he had already climbed out on a limb by telling Governor Ramsey and Sibley that he was "sure" Lincoln would not "forbid" the hanging of the Dakotas.[57] So long as Lincoln was reviewing the records in Washington, however, neither Godfrey nor any of the Dakotas could be hanged.

Sometime between November 12 and 15, word of the president's decision reached Sibley at Camp Lincoln. Though Sibley's initial reaction to the news is not recorded, he must have been deeply disappointed with the delay—and with the implied possible disapproval of some or all of his court's decisions. At Pope's insistence, Sibley had prodded his judges to complete their caseload quickly, with the expectation that most of the Dakotas he held in custody would be executed before he departed for home.

But, with winter approaching, Sibley saw immediately that Lincoln's review would upset his plans to keep his expedition intact until the execution date. To comply with Lincoln's demand, he entrusted Riggs with the 392 transcripts, which filled the chaplain's carpetbag. Riggs caught a stage to Minneapolis, arriving in the dead of night. After reuniting with his wife, who was living in a rented house in St. Anthony, Riggs delivered the trial records to Pope's St. Paul headquarters.[58] Pope then forwarded the transcripts to Lincoln with a bare-bones cover letter, dated November 15.[59]

The transcript of Godfrey's trial was in the pile of papers Pope sent to Washington. This time the plea from the military commission to grant Godfrey clemency was not omitted. Impressively written on fancy blue paper watermarked "Kent Mills—1856," the petition stood out from the white notepaper used for the transcripts of the early trials.[60] It was (and is today in the U.S. Senate's archives) the first court record in the voluminous files.[61] If Godfrey's fate had been jeopardized by Sibley's earlier failure to include the clemency plea, his fortunes now were bolstered by the primacy of that document in the files the president received.

On November 15, the very day that Pope dispatched the transcripts to Lincoln, Isaac Heard offered the first insider's disclosures about the Dakota trials in a letter that appeared in the *St. Paul Pioneer and Democrat*.[62] Writing under the pseudonym "H," Heard presented a very readable (if decidedly prosecution-biased) description of the secret proceedings in the "blood-stained surroundings" of LaBatte's cookhouse courtroom at the Lower Agency. Accurately, he estimated that "in at least two-thirds of the cases, the prisoners admitted that they fired [shots]." But, of course, he said nothing about the fact that those Indians made their "confessions" without any knowledge that joining in a military battle was considered a capital offense. Heard acknowledged the brevity of the trials but offered a defense: "Perhaps this may seem, to those who were not on the ground, an unjustifiably summary mode of proceeding; but it was as lengthy an examination as necessity would permit, and 'whatever necessity requires, it justifies.' Besides, no individual injustice is probably done, as ninety-nine-hundredths of these devils are guilty, and witnesses in their favor would be about as useless as teats on a boar." This justification sounded two themes reflecting Sibley's approach to the trials: the Spartan, in-the-field conditions under which the trials were conducted created the "necessity" that they be rushed and abbreviated; and the legal form followed made little practical difference, since almost all of the Dakotas had actively joined in the conflict and would have been found guilty under any form of judicial procedure.

Heard mocked the efforts of the Dakotas to downplay their involvement. One, he said, admitted stealing a horse but said it was only "a very little one." Another explained his theft of two oxen by saying his wife "wanted a pair." The older Indians, he said, claimed they "were too grey to go into battle," while the eighteen- to twenty-five-year-olds said they were "too young, and their hearts too weak to face fire." Further, Heard contended, "A small army avowed that they had crept under a wonderfully capacious stone (which nobody but themselves ever saw), at the battles of the Fort, and did not emerge there from during the fights; and a sufficiency for two small armies stoutly called on the Great Spirit . . . to witness that they were of a temperament so phlegmatic, a disposition so unsocial, and an appetite so voracious and greedy, that, during the roar of each of the battles . . . they were alone, within bullet-shot, roasting and eating corn and beef all day." While trial records support the notion that some Indians claimed to be hiding or eating rather than fighting, Heard expanded their numbers into "small armies." Lest anyone misread his sentiments, Heard ended his letter with a report of the discovery of some blackened bones of more victims of the Dakotas in the former settlements across the Minnesota River from the Lower Agency. The last words in Heard's letter are, "Death to the Sioux, say I."

Heard had written this letter on November 7, just two days after the trials concluded, during the period when Sibley had sent the list of names to Pope and expected approval of the mass hangings within ten days.

For the most part, Heard offered a kind of layman's brief in favor of the executions. Spliced into his anti-Dakota version of the trials (and later repeated in his book), however, was a remarkable defense of Joseph Godfrey. Heard declared that Godfrey was "the greatest institution of the Commission," "a providence" whose "observation and memory were remarkable." He frankly admitted the prejudice that had preceded Godfrey into the courtroom but then described the judges' change of heart as witness after witness corroborated his honesty.

But Heard also sounded one disquieting caveat: "It is not at all improbable that he [Godfrey] may be guilty as the worst. It is rumored that there is other evidence against him at New Ulm, but if there is none, imprisonment is severe enough in view of the great services he had rendered the Commission in their investigation." (Though no concrete new evidence against Godfrey has ever surfaced, Heard's statement confirms that members of the German community were not included in the trials.)[63]

Heard was obviously smitten with Godfrey, to the point that he failed to mention a single other prosecution witness at the trials. Given the importance of his authoritative account, that omission was crucial, for it led many readers (as well as future historians) to exaggerate Godfrey's role in convicting defendants and to ignore the many Dakota, mixed-blood, and white witnesses. Heard's letter evidently provoked widespread interest, for it was reprinted in at least two other Minnesota newspapers and in the *New York Times*.[64]

Interestingly, Heard made no mention of the military commission's plea to spare Godfrey's life, even though he wrote his letter just two days after that document had been submitted to Sibley.[65] As a gifted advocate, he surely must have known that this formal petition represented the most potent argument in his pro-Godfrey brief. Yet he simply told his readers that, if no further evidence against Godfrey surfaced, imprisonment would be "enough" of a punishment. Most likely Heard was silent on the clemency plea because any reference to it would have compelled him to tell of Sibley's disapproval, thus exposing to Minnesotans a rare disagreement between Sibley and his court and potentially stirring the commander's ire. To a public in no mood for leniency toward anyone connected with the war, news that Sibley opposed clemency would have stacked the deck against Godfrey. Seen in this light, Heard's silence on the subject was shrewd, offering a glimpse at his capacity for lawyerly finesse.[66]

But Heard did not issue Godfrey a stamp of pure innocence. While concluding that there was no evidence that he had murdered anyone, Heard did not eliminate that possibility. And, though he accepted Godfrey's contention that he initially joined the Dakotas with reluctance, Heard was troubled by reports that Godfrey showed great enthusiasm for the Indian cause during the war. Perhaps he had heard the tale of Godfrey's proud display of watches stolen from Milford victims. These concerns were—and still are—clouds on the horizon of Godfrey's legacy.

On November 15 Sibley issued a final order from Camp Lincoln before he and his closest officers departed for home. He designated Col. Steven Miller, a Pennsylvania native with Civil War experience who had joined him at Camp Release, to command the camp "in the absence of the Brig. General Commanding." Sibley ordered Colonel Miller to "take special charge of the Indian prisoners until instructions shall be received by him as to the disposal of them from Headquarters in St. Paul."[67]

As they waited for Lincoln to decide the fate of the convicted Dakotas, Minnesotans' wrath against Indians festered and grew. Everywhere they saw or heard reminders of Dakota perfidy. Almost every Minnesota town was giving aid to injured or homeless refugees, some of them maimed or scarred children. Other survivors told harrowing tales of hiding in swamps, running barefoot across prairies, or feigning death to avoid being killed. Desiccating remains of more victims were still being found.[68] Funeral services, delayed until bodies could be returned to their homes, were held as late as November.[69] One-third to one-half of the occupied regions of Minnesota had temporarily been cleansed of white inhabitants. The war left frontier counties without functioning stores, law enforcement, transportation, or other forms of rural infrastructure. Because no newspapers were being published in Brown County, probate notices for New Ulm–area victims (including Ernst Dietrich) appeared in the *Mankato Independent* on November 15.[70]

Many thousands of Union soldiers were dying on Civil War battlefields, but those military deaths failed to provoke even a fraction of the deep-seated anger Minnesotans felt toward the Dakotas, whom they viewed as savage rapists and murderers, not soldiers. When Minnesotans learned that three hundred Indians had been sentenced to death, virtually all of them united in demanding that the executions take place immediately, just as Sibley and Pope desired. It was in this charged atmosphere that the news of Lincoln's refusal to rubber-stamp the hanging verdicts was announced in mid-November. In Minnesotans' state of white-hot animosity, even a few weeks' delay was intolerable.

Most of the state's newspapers did more to incite than quell this rabid mood. Throughout Minnesota editors published stories answering the question on everyone's mind: What if Lincoln won't hang all of the Indians? They shuddered to think that their compassionate president might release large phalanxes of "convicted murderers" back into their midst.

From the perspective of dispassionate hindsight, the most disturbing feature of the Minnesota press in November and early December 1862 is its open call for lawless mob violence. The Republican *St. Paul Press* veiled its opinion only slightly: "There is not military force enough in the Northwest to save these infernal rascals from the vengeance of the people of Minnesota."[71] Jane Swisshelm also raised her strident and articulate voice, wanting "to see to it that every Sioux found on our soil gets a permanent homestead 6 ft. by 2." Should Lincoln free the condemned men, Swisshelm thundered to her readers, "Get ready, and as soon as these convicted murderers are turned loose, shoot them and be sure they are shot dead, *dead*, DEAD!"[72]

With almost the entire state waiting in a vengeful frenzy for Lincoln's decision, the biggest immediate risk to Godfrey and the Dakota prisoners now came from the kind of mobs that had attacked the Indians in both New Ulm and Henderson. Though Colonel Miller was determined to protect his jailed charges, citizens were plotting to take the law into their own hands.[73] The lynching schemes came to a head on the frigid night of December 4, when Miller learned that "large numbers" of men from St. Peter and Traverse des Sioux were "filling up with beer to gain courage" before coming to kill the Indian prisoners.[74] He immediately dispatched messengers to summon reinforcements available to him in the vicinity. Within hours he had increased his troops from the 196 men stationed at the camp to about 500.[75]

As the designated hour approached, Miller concealed his defenders in a hollow near the Blue Earth River bridge. On horseback at the head of his hidden men, the colonel was the first to confront the rabble as they approached. "Who comes there?" Miller asked. A voice from the dark replied, "We have come to take the Indians and kill them." Miller responded, "Well, you will do nothing of the kind." At this point Miller's reinforced cavalry emerged to the vigilantes' rear, and their courage quickly "oozed out." Miller delivered a lecture to the disheartened upstarts, telling them to return to their homes. Then he arrested a group of ringleaders, placing them in the charge of Lieutenant Carter.[76]

Miller wrote his official report of this attempted attack to Sibley at 5:00 a.m. on December 5:

> Several hundred citizens from St. Peter etc. reached Mankato early in the evening and 150 to 200, armed with clubs, hatchets, knives, etc. attempted to pass into my camp at 11 o'clock last evening. I promptly surrounded and arrested the whole of them by the assistance of Capt. White's Company of Cavalry, and after disarming the leaders and receiving their promise of good behavior let them go back to Mankato. They strongly begged for permission to pass to South Bend, but I had seized the Bridge and river and would not let them pass. They frankly admitted that they intended to murder the Indians.[77]

None of the reports of this serious affray mentions Godfrey, but there is little doubt that he would have been murdered with the Dakotas if the mob had prevailed.

NOTES ON CHAPTER 9

1. Samuel J. Brown says that the male prisoners and the group comprising mainly women and children departed from the Lower Agency "at the same time." Anderson and Woolworth, *Through Dakota Eyes*, 227. Brown was mistaken about the timing of the departures. The women's group, which was bound for Fort Snelling, left a day or two earlier than the train of male prisoners headed toward Mankato. See letter from "H" [Isaac Heard], *St. Paul Pioneer and Democrat*, November 15, 1862; John Kingsley Wood diary, entry for November 6, MHS; and *St. Paul Press*, November 9, 1862. Colonel Marshall led the soldiers escorting the women's group; Sibley led the larger contingent of soldiers that accompanied the prisoners' train. While the prisoners' route took them near New Ulm, the women and children traveled to Henderson via Fort Ridgely (located upstream and across the Minnesota River from New Ulm) and did not go through or near New Ulm. See also Mary Bakeman and Alan R. Woolworth, "The Family Caravan," in Bakeman and Richardson, *Trails of Tears*, 53–78, esp. the map of both routes on p. 78; and Monjeau-Marz, *Dakota Indian Internment*, 22.
2. Brown reports that "392 condemned Indian men" were taken to Mankato, but that was the total number of trials, and some of those acquitted had been released. Anderson and Woolworth, *Through Dakota Eyes*, 227. As stated in the text, I estimate that Sibley must have transported about 375 men.
3. See Lois Glewwe, "The Journey of the Prisoners," in Bakeman and Richardson, *Trails of Tears*, 79–106.
4. *Harper's New Monthly Magazine*, June 1863. The *Harper's* sketch is reproduced in Carley, *Dakota War of 1862*, 71.
5. Heard, *History of the Sioux War*, 243.
6. "Report of Adjutant General," reprinted in Bryant, *History of the Great Massacre*, 454.
7. Eyewitness accounts of the New Ulm attack can be found in Heard, *History of the Sioux War*, 240–43; Connolly, *Minnesota Massacre*, 158–61; Richard Mott Jackson letter, October 1903, Dakota Conflict Collection, MHS, box 5; Sibley to Sarah Sibley, November 12, 1862, Sibley Papers, MHS, M164, roll 11; and Amos Watson account, MHS, M582, roll 3. See also Gabriel Renville's memoir, in Anderson and Woolworth, *Through Dakota Eyes*, 233; and Flandrau, *History of Minnesota*, 177.
8. Amos Watson account, MHS, M582, roll 3. Watson reports only that "the poor fellow had a very sore head."
9. McConkey, *Dakota War Whoop*, 241.
10. Heard, *History of the Sioux War*, 243.
11. Sibley to Sarah Sibley, November 12, 1862. Sibley Papers, MHS, M164, roll 11.
12. Thomas Williamson to Treat, December 1, 1862, Northwest Missions Manuscripts (hereafter, NMM), MHS, box 20. See also McConkey, *Dakota War Whoop*, 241, who, alone among the early historians, reported the death of one Indian (one death "in a few days"); Flandrau, *History of Minnesota*, 177 (one death); and Walt Bachman, "Deaths of Dakota Prisoners from the New Ulm Mob Attack," in Bakeman and Richardson, *Trails of Tears*, 179–80.
13. Sibley to Sarah Sibley, November 12, 1862, Sibley Papers, MHS, M164, roll 11.
14. Samuel J. Brown recollections, in Anderson and Woolworth, *Through Dakota Eyes*, 227.
15. Ibid., 228.

16. Good Star Woman, in Anderson and Woolworth, *Through Dakota Eyes,* 263–64.
17. John Williamson to Treat, November 28, 1862, NMM, MHS, box 20.
18. *New York Times,* November 9, 1862.
19. *St. Paul Press,* November 12, 1862 (emphasis in original).
20. *St. Paul Press,* November 9, 1862.
21. *Mankato Semi-Weekly Record,* October 25, 1862.
22. *Winona Weekly Republican,* November 12, 1862.
23. *Mankato Semi-Weekly Record,* November 15, 1862 (beautiful camping ground); *Mankato Independent,* November 15, 1862 (Mount Sibley).
24. Sibley to Sarah Sibley, November 12, 1862, Sibley Papers, MHS, M164, roll 11; *Mankato Semi-Weekly Record,* November 15, 1862.
25. Sibley refers to Camp Lincoln as being 1.5 miles from Mankato (Sibley to Sarah Sibley, November 12, 1862, Sibley Papers, MHS, M164, roll 11), but the *Mankato Independent,* November 15, 1862, put the distance as a "half mile above town," possibly referring to the distance from the outskirts of Mankato.
26. *Mankato Semi-Weekly Record,* November 15, 1862.
27. Letter from "D.W.E.," November 15, 1862, *Faribault Central Republican,* November 26, 1862.
28. *Mankato Semi-Weekly Record,* November 15, 1862.
29. Letter from "D.W.E.," November 15, 1862, *Faribault Central Republican,* November 26, 1862.
30. The only place where women and children were killed and Godfrey was known to have been present that might fit this description is Milford. I know of no Milford account in which a husband saw his wife and two children killed and then escaped to tell the story. Most men at Milford were the first to be killed by the Dakotas, and virtually no men escaped from that township. Most likely the German named in this story was away from Milford on the day of the killings, and others told him that Godfrey not only was present there but was (as Sheriff Roos reported) "leading" the Indians. Moreover, when white accusers came to Camp Lincoln and identified Indian murderers, their written statements were taken for use in possible future trials; there is no record of any such statement being taken against Godfrey. This fact supports the interpretation that the unnamed German was, most likely, not an eyewitness. Shortly after the German's visit, Heard wrote, "It is rumored that there is other evidence against him [Godfrey] at New Ulm." Letter from "H" [Isaac Heard], *St. Paul Pioneer and Democrat,* November 15, 1862.
31. Letter from "D.W.E.," *Faribault Central Republican,* November 26, 1862.
32. *St. Paul Pioneer and Democrat,* November 15, 1862.
33. Thomas Williamson to Treat, November 21, 1862, NMM, MHS, box 20. See also letter from "D.W.E.," *Faribault Central Republican,* November 26, 1862.
34. *St. Peter Herald,* December 20, 1912.
35. Anderson, *Little Crow,* 143 (citing account of Susan Brown); see also Godfrey's testimony, trial 1, Dakota Trials Records.
36. *Faribault Central Republican,* October 15, 1862.
37. *Mankato Semi-Weekly Record,* October 4, 1862.
38. *St. Cloud Democrat,* September 18, 1862 (from Stearns History Museum).
39. *St. Cloud Democrat,* September 11 and 18, 1862 (from Stearns History Museum).
40. *Winona Weekly Republican,* September 3, 1862.
41. *St. Paul Press,* September 2, 1862, citing *Winona Republican.*
42. *Winona Weekly Republican,* September 17, 1862.
43. *Mankato Semi-Weekly Record,* November 15, 1862.

44. Sibley's stance seems harsh by twenty-first-century standards, but it was consistent with nineteenth-century law. At that time criminal defendants were not furnished with lawyers in either civil or military courts, and a commanding officer who convened a military court had the discretion to refuse to permit a defendant to employ his own counsel. President Lincoln signed many orders during the Civil War approving the execution of Union soldiers who were convicted (usually of murder or rape) without having legal counsel. See Wiener, "*Courts-Martial and the Bill of Rights,*" 1, 22–36, 42–44 (documenting that defendants in military trials were not afforded legal counsel until after the Civil War); and "Courts-Martial and Military Commission Proceedings against Union soldiers, 1861–1866," NA, RG 94, M1523.
45. Riggs to Mary Riggs, November 11 and 13, 1862, Riggs letters, CCHS (November 13 portion).
46. I am deeply indebted to Carrie Reber Zeman, who, in 2003, discovered the transcripts of the Winnebago trials while examining records of the House of Representatives, Committee of Indian Affairs, Center for Legislative Archives, 37th Congress, H.R. 37A, E.7.8. These transcripts are not cited in any of the histories of the conflict or in any other publication.
47. The transcript of his own trial states that Otanka (trial 13) said that Little Chief fired at the battle of Birch Coulee, but it appears that he intended to refer to Little Priest. That conclusion is confirmed by the fact that Otanka gave no such testimony in the Winnebago trials against *any* defendant. Also, in William R. Robinson's testimony against Little Priest (Winnebago trial 1), Robinson refers to Little Priest as Little Chief.
48. Folwell, *History of Minnesota,* 2:233.
49. Wechankpedoota (trial 367) had been convicted and sentenced to death for his admission that he fired two shots at the battle of New Ulm. In the Winnebago trial, his name was spelled Wechankpeduta.
50. Because the Winnebago trials were held after Sibley sent the list of condemned men to Pope, it appears that the conviction of Monekasdayhekah was never reported to Lincoln. But he was imprisoned with the Dakotas thereafter. See Mankato prison list, January 12, 1863, Dakota Trials Records, microfilm roll 1, frames 16–26, where "Manakasnay" is listed as a prisoner "condemned to be hung."
51. Haynook (Winnebago trial 5); Wazaka (Winnebago trial 6); and Choonkaka (Winnebago trial 7).
52. Hayzeka (Winnebago trial 13).
53. Looking at the record alone, it is not possible to tell when the court altered its sentence. But the caption sheet of Little Priest's trial transcript includes a notation (apparently in Riggs's handwriting) "See Alteration in verdict," confirming that the court changed its decision. Otanka's collapse as a witness is obvious when one compares his Dakota trial testimony with that given in the Winnebago trials, and it seems the most likely explanation for the reversal of Little Priest's verdict from hanging to acquittal. Also, the letter of a trial eyewitness, "D.W.E.," says that the court "did not place much confidence" in the testimony of Otanka (misidentified as a Dakota). Letter from "D.W.E.," *Faribault Central Republican,* November 26, 1862. It is quite possible that a member of the court passed along the judges' impressions to this observer.
54. Sibley to Sarah Sibley, November 12, 1862, Sibley Papers, MHS, M164, roll 11.
55. Lincoln to Pope, telegram, November 10, 1862, *MCIW,* 2:289.
56. *New York Times,* November 17, 1862. The criticism is only partially valid. Pope had been told to submit the hanging names by telegraph, but no one then knew that three hundred names would be listed.

57. Pope to Ramsey, November 6, 1862, *MCIW*, 2:287–88; Pope to Lincoln, telegram, November 11, 1862, *MCIW*, 2:289–90 (Pope's anguished frustration with Lincoln's decision).
58. Though Riggs referred to the documents he brought to Fort Snelling as "rolls of condemnation," it is evident that he was entrusted with the original trial transcripts. In a letter to his home office, Riggs indicated that the documents he delivered were "sent directly on to President Lincoln." The list of names of those sentenced to death had already been telegrammed to Lincoln, and the timing of Riggs's journey coincides perfectly with the forwarding of the trial transcripts. Riggs to Treat, November 24, 1862, NMM, MHS, box 20; Riggs to Mary Riggs, November 12, 1862, Riggs letters, CCHS; S. Riggs, *Tah-Koo Wah-Kan*, 339 (refers to transcripts as "rolls"). See also *Iapi Oaye— The Word Carrier*, April 1880, where Riggs recalls, "I remember the night when, with more than three hundred condemnations in my carpet bag . . . "; and S. Riggs, *Mary and I*, 182.
59. Pope to Lincoln, November 15, 1862, NA, RG 393, E3436, pt. 1, LS, Letters Sent and Received, Department of NW, Headquarters.
60. The color of the paper and watermark are not visible on the microfilm of the trials. This description is based on my review of the original files.
61. For an explanation of the means by which the transcripts ended up in Senate records, see chapter 10.
62. Sibley has been mistakenly identified as the author of the "H" letters, but there can be no doubt that the author was Heard. Whole sections of Heard's letter were later published as part of his *History of the Sioux War*, and it is clear from the letter's content that Heard is its author. Riggs, replying to another letter from "H," identified its author as Heard. *St. Paul Press*, December 14, 1862. Moreover, when Heard used the pseudonym "H" several years later in a newspaper letter, the editor identified him as I. V. D. (Isaac) Heard. See *Mankato Weekly Record*, May 13, 1865.
63. Interestingly, Heard dropped any reference to rumored evidence against Godfrey when he published his book. That omission tends to confirm that no incriminating facts had come to the fore in the interim.
64. *New York Times*, November 23, 1862. See also *Mankato Semi-Weekly Record*, November 22, 1862; and *Minnesota State News*, November 22, 1862 (from the Hennepin County Historical Society).
65. Although Heard's letter first appeared in the *St. Paul Pioneer and Democrat* on November 15, it was written on November 7, with a postscript on November 8. The clemency petition is dated November 5.
66. I have considered and rejected two other possible explanations for Heard's failure to mention the Godfrey clemency petition in his letter of November 7, 1862. First, it is remotely possible that Heard, since he did not sign the petition, was not aware of it. But Heard was intimately involved in all of the court's doings, and it seems more likely that he was the instigator, or even the author, of the plea. Certainly he was fully aware of it when he published his book in 1863. See Heard, *History of the Sioux War*, 254. Second, it is also possible that Heard was not aware of Sibley's rejection of the clemency plea. While this interpretation cannot be dismissed as readily, the very fact that Heard did not mention the clemency plea in his letter offers the strongest evidence against it. If he had believed that Sibley approved of the clemency petition, he surely would have mentioned both the petition and that approval as part of his effort to write favorably about Godfrey to Minnesotans.

67. Order No. 78, November 15, 1862 (Camp Lincoln), Sibley Orders Book, Sibley Papers, MHS, M164, roll 32.
68. The *St. Peter Tribune,* November 20, 1862, in a story titled "Another Body Found," told of finding the remains of a man named Applebaum, who was believed to have been killed in September.
69. For example, a Masonic funeral was held in Shakopee for George Gleason (killed in the same attack in which Sarah Wakefield was taken prisoner) on November 23. *St. Paul Press,* November 22, 1862.
70. *Mankato Independent,* November 15, 1862.
71. *St. Paul Press,* November 7, 1862.
72. *St. Cloud Democrat,* November 13, 1862 (emphasis in original).
73. For a more detailed account of the plots and attempts to lynch the Dakota prisoners, see Walt Bachman, "Colonel Miller's War," in *Trails of Tears,* 107–22.
74. "Recollections of Theodore G. Carter," *St. Peter Herald,* April 13, 1906.
75. Miller to Olin, November 30, 1862 ("196 troops"), and Miller to Olin, December 5, 1862 ("500 infantry"), NA, RG 393, Dist. of MN, 1862–63, E346, pt. 3, LR.
76. "Recollections of Theodore G. Carter," *St. Peter Herald,* April 13, 1906.
77. Miller to Olin, December 5, 1862, NA, RG 393, Dist. of MN, 1862–63, E346, pt. 3, LR.

CHAPTER 10

Atop the Pile of Cases

While Colonel Miller battled vigilantes in Minnesota, a war of words was being waged in Washington. By insisting that the trial transcripts be sent to him for review before he approved any executions, Lincoln had placed himself in the center of a veritable whirlpool of conflicting opinions. Never before or since has a U.S. president pondered three hundred death sentences imposed by a court. Yet even this historic case review, which engendered heated debate, was vastly overshadowed by the two great issues of the day: the Civil War and emancipation.

In late 1862 the Union army was proceeding from disaster to disaster. Lincoln, frustrated with the defeats and refusals to fight, had replaced Gen. George McClellan (Pope's nemesis) with Gen. Ambrose Burnside as commander of the Army of the Potomac. But when Burnside's dithering and delays led to another calamitous defeat at Fredericksburg, much of the blame for it was directed at Lincoln.

Meanwhile, Lincoln's Emancipation Proclamation, purporting to free most slaves in Southern states, was set to become law on January 1, 1863. While some Northerners opposed emancipation, many others dreaded its practical consequences, whether or not they agreed with the morality of the proposition. What was to be done, they asked, with "these cumbersome legions of slaves"? Southern blacks who sought sanctuary with federal troops existed in a legal limbo—neither enslaved nor fully free—and were routinely referred to as "contraband."[1]

Lincoln opted for emancipation, but he assured white Americans that he did not favor integration. "It is better," he said, that "a separation be effected." To achieve this end, the president supported "colonization"— sending blacks to the Caribbean or Central America.[2] By November 1862 that plan had fizzled, but Lincoln was still wedded to the concept of "voluntary" colonization.

Since the Emancipation Proclamation applied only to secessionist states (as a penalty for disloyalty), the question of what should be done with Northern slaves remained unanswered. In his December 1, 1862, address to Congress, Lincoln presented and defended his detailed proposal for gradual, "compensated emancipation."[3] The Constitution should be amended, he argued, to enact a system of phased purchases of the freedom of slaves using government funds over a thirty-seven-year period. Lincoln thus contemplated the continuation of some slavery in America until the year 1900.

The controversy over the condemned Dakotas was equally vociferous, even if it was upstaged by more dramatic national debates. Petitions, letters, and "memorials" poured into the White House, expressing strong opinions on both sides of the subject. Minnesotans had voted for Lincoln in large numbers in 1860, and they howled that he should return the favor with Indian blood. St. Paul physician Thaddeus Williams sent the president a long letter filled with gruesome (and overstated) descriptions of alleged Dakota atrocities, vehemently protesting any notion of "pardoning . . . the murderers."[4] At the other extreme, a New York advocate for Indian reforms, John Beeson, entreated Lincoln to grant "justice for the Indians." Incorrectly claiming that Sibley had already hung "several of their leading men . . . as rebels" and that the Dakotas had surrendered "with the expectation of a general amnesty," Beeson pleaded that all three hundred condemned men be spared. The long-abused Indians, he said, had "struck a blow in the only possible way by which they could make themselves heard."[5]

Men of the cloth were virtually the only Minnesotans calling for any amelioration of the Dakotas' sentences, and even they did so in a muted fashion. Riggs's missionary colleague, Thomas S. Williamson, wrote to Indian Commissioner William P. Dole urging a stay of execution for "all these Indians" until the trial records could be "examined by unprejudiced judges." Writing to Riggs, Williamson entreated him to "pray and labor that these Indians should have a new trial," surely compounding the discomfiture Riggs already felt. But Williamson (who, for the next several years, would be one of the imprisoned Dakotas' most fervent advocates) understood that fair trials would lead to some legally merited hangings: "That there are murderers among them who deserve to die both according to the laws of God and man no one doubts."[6]

But Riggs had been too deeply involved in the trials to criticize them to Lincoln. Writing the president on November 17, signing as "Chaplain of the Expedition," Riggs first offered his credentials: "My long connection with these Indians, and personal acquaintance with many of them who are condemned, would naturally lead me to desire that no greater punishment should be inflicted upon them than is required by justice!" His long ministry among the Dakotas notwithstanding, Riggs then made a strongly worded plea that he almost surely regretted later: "I feel that a great necessity is upon us to execute the *great majority* of those who have been condemned by the Military Commission. . . . Justice requires that it should be done." Riggs vaguely qualified his remarks by adding, "There is room for the exercise of your clemency." But he sought mercy for only a few of his church members and for the relative handful of Dakotas who had merely joined in plundering. If Lincoln had followed Riggs's advice, the hundreds of Dakotas convicted only of firing shots at battles would have been executed.[7]

Riggs continued to pay the price for his irreconcilable conflicts of interest by incurring the suspicion, ridicule, and animosity of both sides. Williamson expressed his concerns to mission headquarters that Riggs had succumbed to the biased "atmosphere" of the military camp.[8] He told Riggs that he "was beginning to fear . . . that your sympathies for them [the Dakotas] were deadened, in some measure at least."[9] On the other hand, Riggs was belittled in the press for his starry-eyed religious idealism, for "the philanthropic experiment to which his life has been devoted."[10]

Minnesota's Episcopal bishop, Henry B. Whipple, entreated Lincoln not to hang all of the condemned men: "We cannot hang men by the hundreds." But even he drew the line at murder: "There is no man who does not feel that the savages who have committed these deeds of violence must meet their doom. The laws of God and man alike require it. The stern necessities of self protection demand it."[11] As he learned more about the conduct of the trials, Whipple proposed making a "broad distinction" between those who committed "fiendish violence, massacring women and babes" and men who plundered or "engaged in some one battle where hundreds were engaged."[12]

Godfrey is not mentioned in any of the letters, petitions, and personal pleas submitted to Lincoln. Nor is there any indication that Heard's published paean to Godfrey ever reached the president's office. Godfrey had not been a member of any church, so no missionary took up his cause. Nor, as a non-Indian, did he garner the support of the federal Indian bureaucracy. Judging from the tenor of the newspapers and political debates, it was an inauspicious time to secure clemency for a black man. Lincoln's Democratic opponents lost no opportunities to portray him, paradoxically, as both a weak-willed humanitarian and an autocrat willing to run roughshod over civil rights. At the core of his alleged weakness was Lincoln's sympathy for blacks, whether free or enslaved. One Democratic newspaper in Minnesota reduced the Lincoln Republicans' flaws to an inverted political pyramid:

REPUBLICAN PYRAMID.

Suspension of the writ of Habeas Corpus
Lincoln's Emancipation Proclamation
Destruction of the Constitution
Martial law in Loyal States
Military Necessity
Crowded Bastiles
Green Backs
Nigger
Nig[13]

Lincoln's entire presidency, some Democrats asserted, teetered on the precarious foundation of his elevated regard for "the niggers."

In his annual address to Congress on December 1, 1862, Lincoln devoted just one paragraph to the Dakota War. He noted the "extreme ferocity" of the Indians, "killing, indiscriminately, men, women, and children." The "wholly unexpected" attack killed an "estimated" eight hundred people, Lincoln told Congress.[14] But the president gave no hint of his intentions regarding Godfrey and the three hundred condemned Dakotas. He made no reference to the trials, the sentences, or the spirited public debate on the subject. In contrast, Lincoln devoted several pages of his speech to a discussion of slavery and his proposals for compensated emancipation and colonization of American blacks in foreign countries. He sought to assure troubled Northerners that former slaves would not "swarm" north in vast numbers ("people, of any color, seldom run"), even suggesting that legislation could prohibit black migration northward: "Cannot the north decide for itself, whether to receive them?"[15]

Before making a decision about the Dakotas, Lincoln considered the option of setting guidelines for executing "only a part" of the three hundred men and sending the cases back to "some officer on the ground" (Sibley, most likely) to make case-by-case designations. The president sought a legal opinion on the point from Joseph Holt, his judge advocate general. But Holt promptly advised that "the power cannot be delegated." This previously unnoticed legal interlude ended fortunately for Godfrey, for if Lincoln had been given the authority to remand the transcripts to Sibley, Godfrey's fate would have been a foregone conclusion.[16]

Lincoln's political allies in Minnesota were unremitting in their pressure to approve all the hangings. Senator Morton Wilkinson and Representatives Cyrus Aldrich and William Windom—the entire Minnesota Republican delegation to Congress—coauthored a demanding letter to Lincoln. The uprising was not a war, they wrote, but "wholesale robbery, *rape, murder.*" Repeating widespread rumor as fact, they claimed that "nearly all" of the "ninety female captives" had been repeatedly "violated." In a reference that could only be to the "refined and beautiful" Mattie Williams, they said, "She was taken, her arms were tied behind her, she was made fast to the ground, and ravished by some eight or ten of these convicts before the cords were unloosed from her limbs. This girl fortunately lived to testify against the wretches who had thus violated her."[17] The trial records in Lincoln's hands, however, showed that Williams had mentioned just one rapist.

At about the same time Lincoln received a "memorial" from the citizens of St. Paul, filled with more anonymous stories of gratified "brutal lusts."[18] Just as some Minnesotans had falsely claimed that almost all of the three hundred men had been convicted of murder, newspapers and civic leaders now argued that the transcripts would verify their assertions of wholesale sexual assaults.

At this stage Lincoln asked two aides, George C. Whiting and Francis H. Ruggles, to make a "careful examination" of all the transcripts and to identify those Dakotas who "had been proved guilty of violating females." Given Minnesotans' adamant claims of gang rapes, the president was surprised when the two men reported that "only two" rapists were identified in the transcripts. He then asked Whiting and Ruggles to make "a further examination," instructing them to identify "all who were proven to have participated in *massacres*, as distinguished from participation in *battles*."[19]

The aides soon returned with their final analysis, transcribed in the appendix to this volume. This time, screening for those "convicted of rape and murder" (the phrase used in their report to Lincoln), they identified thirty-eight more cases, bringing the overall potential execution list (including the two rapists) to forty names.[20] Whiting and Ruggles pulled the transcripts of the listed men from the much larger pile of 392 cases, laying them before Lincoln with their report. They also gave Lincoln a brief written summary of the proof against each man.[21]

The first defendant on the list given to Lincoln was "O-ta-kla, alias Godfrey, a negro." Presumably Godfrey's case record, including the military commission's clemency plea, was atop the pile of cases. In their one-sentence summary of the results of his trial, Whiting and Ruggles succinctly framed Godfrey's case for Lincoln's review: "Engaged extensively in the massacres, and, though sentenced to be hung, recommended to have his punishment commuted to imprisonment for ten years, because of the valuable testimony and information furnished the commission." But more ominously, Whiting and Ruggles sketched, in pencil, a little pointed index finger on the first page of Godfrey's transcript. The finger drew attention to

> E.
>
> SIR: Having, by your directions, examined the records of the convictions of Sioux Indians by the military commission ordered by Brigadier General Sibley, we submit the following list of those who were convicted of rape and murder, viz:
>
> No. 1. O-TA-KLA, *alias* GODFREY, a negro.—Engaged extensively in the massacres, and, though sentenced to be hung, recommended to have his punishment commuted to imprisonment for ten years, because of the valuable testimony and information he furnished the commission.
>
> No. 2. TE-HE-HDO-NE-CHA.—Engaged in the massacres; took a white woman prisoner, and *ravished* her.
>
> No. 4. TAZOO, *alias* PLAN-DOO-TA.—Convicted of participating in the murder of Mr. Patville, and of ravishing a young girl.
>
> No. 5. WY-A-TAH-TO-WAH.—Confesses to have participated in the murder of Mr. Francis Patville, and to have been engaged in three battles.
>
> No. 6. HIN-HAN-SHOON-KO-YAG-MA-NE.—Convicted of the murder of Alexander Hunter, and of having taken and had Mrs. Hunter a prisoner until she was rescued from him by another Indian.
>
> No. 10. MUZ-ZA-BOM-A-DU.—Convicted of the murder of an old man and two children.
>
> No. 11. WAH-PA-DU-TA.—Confesses that he was engaged in the massacres, and that he shot a white man.
>
> No. 12. WA-HE-HUD.—Convicted of participating in the battles, and of murder.
>
> No. 14. SUA-MA-NI.—Convicted of the murder of two persons.
>
> No. 15. TA-TE-MI-MA.—Convicted of murder, and of the capture of women and children.
>
> No. 19. RDA-IN-YAN-KUA.—Took a prominent part in all the battles, including the attack on New Ulm, leading and urging the Indians forward, and opposing the giving up of the captives when it was proposed by others.
>
> No. 22. DO-WAN-SA.—Convicted of the murder of a white woman, and of the design to *ravish* her daughter, who was wounded by him and killed by another Indian before he had carried his design into execution.
>
> No. 24. HA-PAN.—Confessed that he was in all the battles and at the murder

Fig. 5. Whiting-Ruggles report, first page. In the wake of the Dakota War, President Abraham Lincoln asked two lawyers on his staff, George C. Whiting and Francis H. Ruggles, to review the records of the military commission to identify those Dakota men convicted of rape or murder. The Whiting-Ruggles report, dated December 5, 1862, named forty men and briefly recited the evidence against them. The full text of the report is reproduced in the appendix to this volume. "Message of the President of the United States in answer to a resolution of the Senate of the 5th instant in relation to the Indian barbarities in Minnesota," 37th Congress, 3rd Session, Executive Doc. 7, Exhibit E, 1862.

these words: "See evidence against this man in the statement of his father-in-law, [Case] No. 11." The president thus was urged to turn to the testimony of Wahpaduta, who had claimed that "the nigger killed people with a hatchet" and that the "negro killed 4."[22]

If lawyers for the prosecution and defense had appeared before Lincoln at this stage, they both would have cringed at his aides' presentation of Godfrey's case. On the one hand, a prosecutor would have underscored the fact that Sibley had twice rejected the commission's clemency pleas. Yes, Sibley's comment was duly recorded on Godfrey's file, but Lincoln's aides had failed to note it in their summary, and it was written so faintly as to be all but illegible. Without prompting, a busy president could easily overlook or misunderstand the position of the commanding officer in the field.

On the other hand, a defense lawyer would have objected to the aides' cross-reference to the case file of Wahpaduta and to their failure to highlight the fact that the commission had found Godfrey *not guilty* of killing anyone. Clearly, if the judges had believed Wahpaduta's testimony that his son-in-law had killed four people, they would not have acquitted Godfrey of that charge. Again, a harried chief executive, even one who was an experienced lawyer, might well miss the actual sentence imposed on the last page of Godfrey's trial record and instead make his judgment based on a misleading summary. Perhaps the best that can be said about these imperfections in the presentation of Godfrey's case to Lincoln is that they tended to balance each other out.

Once the shots-fired-at-battles cases had been culled from the hanging roster, Godfrey's importance as a trial witness emerged with greater clarity. Though Whiting and Ruggles did not identify witnesses in their case summaries, the transcripts they pulled for Lincoln's review showed that Godfrey had given the crucial testimony against nine of the forty men on their list. Only David Faribault Sr. appeared in as many of the listed cases. Since other witnesses had also given evidence in several of those cases, however, Faribault's testimony had not proved as indispensable as Godfrey's.[23] Other than Godfrey and Faribault, no other witness was responsible for the conviction of more than two people on the list.[24] Here is Ruggles and Whiting's summary of the cases in which Godfrey testified:

> No. 10. Muzzabomadu. Convicted of the murder of an old man and two children.
>
> No. 22. Dowansa. Convicted of the murder of a white woman, and of the design to ravish her daughter, who was wounded by him and killed by another Indian

before he had carried his design into execution.

No. 210. Wakantanka. Convicted of the murder of a white man not named.

No. 254. Makatenajin. Convicted of participating in the massacre near New Ulm, and of encouraging the young men to do so.

No. 327. Aechaga. Convicted of participating in the murder of an old man and two girls.

No. 359. Chankahda. Is proven to have been of the party, and present when Patville was killed, and to have saved Mary Anderson (who had been wounded) from being killed, and to have taken her prisoner.

No. 377. Oyatayakoo. Convicted of participating in the murder of Patville.

No. 382. Mahoowaywa. Convicted of participating in the massacre at "Travellers' Home," and of murdering a man on the road near there.

No. 383. Wakinyanna. Convicted of participating in the murder, near the "Travellers' Home," of an old man, two young girls, and two boys.[25]

The Whiting-Ruggles list offered few surprises. Even today, any attorney asked to examine the trial records and identify the forty most serious cases would come up with most of the same names. Six of the nine cases in which Godfrey gave crucial testimony arose from the Milford massacre on August 18. Two involved the murders of members of Patoille's group. The case against Dowansa was based on the defendant's admissions to Godfrey of killings at Swan Lake.

Besides its emphasis on Milford cases, another striking feature of the Whiting-Ruggles report relates to child victims. Three of the six Milford defendants implicated by Godfrey had killed children; their victims were "an old man and two children," "an old man and two girls," and "an old man, two girls, and two boys." In all of the trial summaries furnished to Lincoln, only two other defendants were identified as child killers.[26] Thus

Godfrey, more than all of the other witnesses combined, had documented the Dakotas' slaughter of children. Yet these little-reported child-killing figures also highlight the price that was paid for the decision to hold hurried trials in remote locations. The court never heard evidence relating to most of the one hundred white children killed in 1862. By spending much of their limited time on ordinary-soldier cases, Sibley's judges had failed to concentrate on the very sort of offenses—murder and rape—that the commission was initially created to handle.

Listed immediately after Godfrey were the two rapists, Tehehdonecha and Tazoo. Apparently to highlight the heinous nature of their crime, the word "ravished" was underlined in the aides' report.[27]

Only two of the forty cases on the Whiting-Ruggles list do not include any evidence of rape, murder, or massacre. Rdainyankna (trial 19) was cited primarily for military deeds; the report said he "took a prominent part in all the battles" and was "leading and urging the Indians forward" at New Ulm. But he was also singled out for "opposing the giving up of the captives when it was proposed by others." In blunter words, Rdainyankna was a leader of the militant Dakota faction that in September had argued for killing the captives or removing them to long-term captivity in the West.[28] Thus he was placed on the list for his deeds not merely as a warrior but as a prime advocate for killing or mistreating the captive women and children.

White Dog (trial 35), without doubt, was on the list due to the role he played in the only military battle on August 18: the ambush of Marsh's men at the Redwood ferry. The Whiting-Ruggles report said that he "was the leader of the party that attacked Captain Marsh's company, and was the man who detained Captain Marsh in conversation until the Indians crossed the river and surrounded the command, and then gave the signal to fire." White Dog did not make the list for leading the Indians into what Lincoln's aides believed to be a massacre, however, for other Dakotas convicted of joining in the ambush were not hanged. Instead, White Dog was listed because he pretended to be a noncombatant so as to entice the enemy into an ambush—a grave war crime tantamount to approaching under a flag of truce and then opening fire.[29]

A few defendants not on the list arguably should have been. Of the three Chaskas who had been condemned, only Chaskaydon (trial 121) was listed (for "shooting and cutting open a woman who was with child"). In the trial record the evidence against another Chaska, Robert Hopkins (trial 163), appears to be stronger than that against some men whose names were submitted to Lincoln for execution. But either Hopkins's efforts to save whites in the first few days of the war or the multiple entreaties of missionaries on his behalf succeeded in gaining his reprieve.[30] Sarah Wakefield's savior, also commonly known as Chaska, was omitted from the list too, despite his conviction for murder based on evidence that he had either "finished off" or "snapped his gun at" a white man who was killed. Wakefield's fervent support most likely made the difference in his case.[31]

By following Lincoln's directive to limit their list to massacre participants and rapists, Whiting and Ruggles unwittingly identified some of the trials that were conducted most fairly. Since Sibley had announced his intention to punish Dakotas who had committed murders, it cannot be argued that most of the men on the list of forty names sent to Lincoln were tricked into surrendering under false pretenses or were ignorant of the main accusation against them during their trials. Aside from potential cultural misunderstandings about the definition of a "kill," those Dakotas found guilty of murder had received fairer trials than many who had been sentenced to death for their military deeds alone.

The trials of those on the list were more fair in other ways too. A disproportionate number—thirteen of forty—were in the first batch of twenty-nine Camp Release prosecutions. Those cases were conducted more slowly, with more safeguards, and held to a higher standard of proof than the subsequent cases. Moreover, many of the men on the list were convicted on the strength of eyewitness evidence. Though their trials were often shockingly brief, there is little reason to believe, in most instances, that longer trials would have swayed witnesses' identifications.[32] Godfrey, for one, was well acquainted with the Dakotas he implicated in the killings at Milford and in the Patoille attack. David Faribault Sr. was also very familiar with the men against whom he gave evidence, as were the white women who gave evidence against men who had held them in captivity.

Godfrey's case alone came before Lincoln with conflicting recommendations. In all other instances the president could later say that he had relied on the screening and advice of his two aides. But Whiting and Ruggles offered no guidance in Godfrey's case. They drew the president's attention to the court's clemency plea but offered no counsel on whether to accept it. Lincoln was compelled to decide Godfrey's fate himself.

On December 5 or 6 the president reviewed his aides' summary and the trial transcripts. On the sixth he personally penned his execution order to Sibley.[33] Writing in his meticulous script, carefully recording the name of each Dakota defendant together with his trial number (e.g., "No. 12 by the record"), Lincoln ordered Sibley to "cause to be executed on Friday the nineteenth day of December" thirty-nine men. Of the forty names submitted for Lincoln's review, only Godfrey's was not on the execution order. By that omission, his death sentence was reprieved.

Besides writing directly to Lincoln, Minnesota's Senator Wilkinson had sponsored a legislative resolution demanding that the president "furnish the Senate" with any documents "touching the late Indian barbarities." Lincoln responded on December 11 by forwarding the transcripts, the Whiting-Ruggles report, and other trial-related materials to the Senate. In his cover letter Lincoln referred to the list of forty and then offered a simple explanation (the only one he ever gave) for Godfrey's reprieve: "One of the number is strongly recommended by the Commission which tried them, for commutation to ten years' imprisonment."[34] Significantly, Lincoln mentioned neither Godfrey's name nor his race. With the "negro-loving" accusations filling the air, the president apparently wished to draw no extra attention to his act of mercy toward a black man.

But Lincoln could not resist aiming a subtle zinger at Wilkinson. Enclosing the lurid letter he had received from the Minnesota congressional delegates, the president wryly noted that it "contains some statements of fact not found in the records of the trials." Driving home this refutation of Wilkinson's tales of mass rapes, Lincoln explained his methods for reviewing the trials: "Anxious to not act with so much clemency as to encourage another outbreak on the one hand, nor with so much severity as to be real cruelty on the other, I caused a careful examination of the records of the trials to be made, in view of first ordering the execution of such as had been proved guilty of violating females. Contrary to my expectations, only two of this class were found."[35]

Reiterating the instructions he had given Whiting and Ruggles, Lincoln emphasized to the Senate that he had ordered the hangings only of those who had "participated in *massacres*, as distinguished from participation in *battles*."[36] In the end Lincoln drew a line between war criminals and warriors. Despite flawed trials, Lincoln's decision brought military justice back to a rough approximation of Sibley's pre-surrender promise to punish Dakota murderers—with the glaring exception of the more than three hundred Dakotas who still languished in jail despite the absence of evidence linking them to murders.

Even after Lincoln issued his decision, hard information about the trials was a scarce commodity in Minnesota. Few people were familiar with the names of (let alone the facts proved against) even the worst Dakota miscreants. The first news about Lincoln's actions did nothing to dispel this state of ignorance, since the telegraphic reports simply relayed the decision to hang thirty-nine men. Neither the Whiting-Ruggles report nor a copy of the president's order was initially available in Minnesota, so no one in the state knew which men were on the list or how they had been selected.

But the racist editor of the *Chatfield Democrat*, J. S. McKenny, apparently received word from someone in Washington confirming his suspicions that Godfrey was not on the list. McKenny wrote, "Mr. Lincoln has decided that only 30 [sic] of the Sioux murderers shall be executed. The *nigger* captain; who commanded the most ferocious party of the Indians, and who boasted of having butchered eight persons in one family, is not included in this number. Of course not. 'Cuffy' [a slang word meaning "nigger"] having proved himself a most scientific slayer of women and children, will doubtless be made a Brigadier General and sent South to assist in carrying out the emancipation scheme of our tender hearted President."

The Chatfield editor also used Godfrey's supposed murderous exploits to assail Caleb Smith, the secretary of the interior, for claiming that "evil-disposed white men," sympathetic to the Confederacy, were actually responsible for the Minnesota uprising: "The far-fetched idea that the Indians were 'led by evil-disposed white men,' is certainly news to the people of our State, as such a thing never was heard of before. If the Secretary had not been so much prejudiced in favor of the colored race, and said that the Indians were led by an 'evil-disposed' *negro*, he would have came nearer the truth."[37]

Other than the few readers of McKenny's newspaper, however, the rest of the state learned nothing about who was on or off Lincoln's list until shortly before the executions.[38] What Minnesotans did know—that the president had decided to hang "only" thirty-nine men—did not satisfy them. But at least the hanging order explicitly instructed Sibley to keep the other Indians in prison "subject to further notice," which alleviated the citizenry's worst fear: that Lincoln would release large numbers of convicted Dakota warriors back into their midst.

Some Minnesota newspapers saw Lincoln's execution order as merely the first installment. The *Mankato Weekly Record* confidently reported that the president's approval of only thirty-nine executions was part of a strategy to obtain the release of white captives still held by Little Crow. Once the captives were freed, the *Record*'s editor incorrectly implied, Lincoln would authorize more hangings.[39]

Stung by Lincoln's rebuke of most of the actions of his court, Sibley refused to believe the first report of the presidential decision, published by St. Paul newspapers on December 11.[40] He directed his adjutant to write to Colonel Miller in Mankato to tell him that he had received "nothing from the President . . . to indicate [a decision] . . . in relation to the condemned savages. . . . The newspaper reports relative to the proposed action of the President are not credited by the Brigadier General Commanding [Sibley]. He believes that the first intimation of his decision will be communicated through the proper military channels, and not to the newsmongers about the public offices in Washington."[41]

When Lincoln's order arrived in Minnesota on December 15, however, Sibley could no longer deny reports by "newsmongers." He immediately faced two unanticipated problems. Sibley's foremost concern was the date Lincoln had set for the executions, December 19, which was only four days away. Though Sibley dutifully forwarded the hanging order to Miller in Mankato, he immediately telegraphed Lincoln to request a delay. The president replied by telegram the next day, approving a postponement until December 26.⁴²

Sibley also fretted about the problem of identifying the thirty-nine Dakotas who were to be hanged. About 375 Dakota and mixed-blood men were imprisoned in Mankato. How, with the trial transcripts in Washington, could the identity of the condemned men be verified? Compounding his difficulties, Sibley soon discovered that the list of the names of the three hundred men the commission had sentenced to death was also missing from his files. He immediately sent a dispatch via special messenger to Riggs: "Have you the list of condemned Indians? I supposed it was here but it cannot be found and you probably have it." Sibley also asked Riggs either to report to him or to go directly to Mankato to help the executioners ascertain that the right prisoners were hanged. Riggs hastened to Mankato, arriving on December 20.⁴³

As Riggs later recalled, Lincoln's execution list proved to be an insufficient guide for identification, just as Sibley had feared. The president had carefully written the names and case numbers for each man. "But," Riggs said, "no one could remember which number attached to which person." Furthermore, among the men in the Mankato jail, there were "three or four *Chaskays*, two or three *Washechoons*."⁴⁴

Lincoln himself had foreseen the risk of hanging the wrong man due to the many similar-sounding Dakota names. John Nicolay, the president's private secretary, wrote to Sibley on December 9, "The President directs me to call your especial attention to the case of Robert Hopkins, alias Chaskaydon, no. 163 by the record, one of the condemned Indians now in your custody, that you may not be led by a similarity of names to confuse him with Chaskaydon, or Chaskayetay, No. 121 by the record, one of those whose sentence of death the President has confirmed."⁴⁵ As we shall see, Lincoln's concerns about hanging the wrong Chaska (or Chaskay) were prescient.⁴⁶

Lincoln's hanging order said nothing about Godfrey. Technically, the president had not signed any document commuting his death penalty. That the Minnesota military authorities understood Godfrey's status is confirmed, however, by a January 1863 record of those jailed in Mankato, which says he was "condemned to be hung but commuted and sentenced to imprisonment."[47] In this respect Godfrey's situation was better than that of the 260 or so condemned Dakotas whose names had been on Pope's telegram but not on the Whiting-Ruggles list. Though Lincoln's order to hang just thirty-nine men has commonly been misconstrued as a wholesale lifting of the death sentences of the remaining prisoners, Lincoln actually made no decision about them.[48] On the January 1863 prison list their status was uniformly recorded as "condemned to be hung."[49] With the exception of Godfrey, all of the men sentenced to execution by Sibley's court thus remained on death row, many of them for years. Contrary to widely held belief, they were not pardoned in 1862, nor were their sentences reprieved.

Support for Lincoln's decision to hang those Dakotas who had committed murder came from one source that is omitted from virtually all historical accounts. On December 17 Chiefs Wabasha and Wakute and thirty-six other Dakota leaders signed a petition to Lincoln ("Our Great Grandfather"), the thrust of which argued that the "good" Indians who took no part in the hostilities should be permitted to return to their homes on the reservation. Paraphrasing the promises Sibley made to them before their surrender, they stated that "the bad [Dakotas] ought to be punished and the good to be well treated." More specifically, they entreated, "All of the Indians who were engaged in killing the white man and women and children should be hanged."[50]

Since Lincoln's decision to hang thirty-nine men had been publicly known for almost a week by the time they signed the document, the Dakota petitioners were openly endorsing the scheduled executions. This posture is not surprising when one considers that the petition signatories were the very men who had gained the most from the government's acculturation policies. Moreover, some of these men had brought the Dakotas to the brink of a civil war through their opposition to the declarations and tactics of the soldiers' lodge. Many of them were outraged at the ruination wrought by what they viewed as a disastrous decision to go to war and to wage it in a manner that was guaranteed to bring down harsh vengeance from whites. Wabasha and the other headmen saw the execution of murderers as a necessary part of their concept of an honorable peace.[51]

Colonel Miller now turned his full attention to preparing for the hangings. On December 22 the thirty-nine condemned men were removed from the log shanty jail to a room in the nearby three-story stone Leach Building. Almost three months had passed since the trials had begun, but none of the prisoners knew who had been convicted, who had been acquitted, or what their sentences were.

Riggs and Joseph Brown, the former Indian agent, were responsible for identifying the thirty-nine men shortlisted for execution. They apparently went to the jail and called out the names on Lincoln's list. When they called the name "Chaskaydan" they must have watched, as Lincoln had directed, to be sure that Robert Hopkins did not step forward. Ironically, that presidential caution may have diverted their attention from the fact that *another* Chaska—Sarah Wakefield's savior—responded to the call.[52]

A second mistake was made when the name Washechoon (the Dakota term for "white man") was called. Later accounts indicate that the young man who responded in error, Washechoonna (trial 332), looked like an Dakota but was actually a cognitively challenged white boy who had been raised from infancy among the Indians.[53] Washechoonna, thus wrongly selected for execution, had been acquitted but was being held in jail nonetheless (as were about fifty other Dakotas who had been found not guilty).[54]

At about the same time the condemned men were called forth, Godfrey was also taken from the log jail, most likely for his own protection. When the list of thirty-nine men was announced to the prisoners, it would have become apparent that many of them were going to the gallows due to Godfrey's testimony. He was probably confined in another room of the Leach Building, though it is possible that he occupied a corner of the death-row quarters.[55]

Once the condemned men were in the Leach Building, Riggs read to them in Dakota from a script written by Miller. They were told that their "Great Father at Washington" had concluded that they were all "guilty of

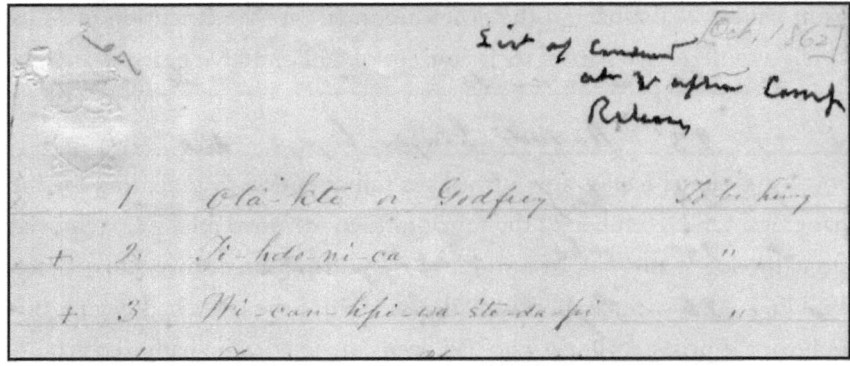

Fig. 6. In November, 1862, Rev. Stephen Riggs recorded the names, sentences, and case numbers of each of the 392 defendants tried after the war. Later, Riggs and Rev. Dr. Thomas S. Williamson used this list to record prison deaths and other facts reflecting their knowledge of each prisoner's status and fate. Generally, the missionaries indicated that a prisoner had been hanged at Mankato by placing a "+" before a man's name. In two instances, a "+" was placed before the names of men who were on Lincoln's final hanging list but were not executed as a result of mistakes by prison authorities. Defendant 3, Wi-can-hpi-wa-ste-da-pi (also known as Chaska), was not on President Lincoln's hanging list, but the "+" before his name shows that the missionaries knew that he had been hanged. The Whiting-Ruggles report in the appendix in this volume verifies that defendant 3 was not on Lincoln's hanging list. There is no "+" before Godfrey's name because he was not executed; the check mark beside his name indicates that he was still alive in the Davenport prison in 1865. Missionaries' annotated list of defendants tried in 1862, with notations through 1865, in the Stephen R. Riggs and Family Papers. Courtesy of the Minnesota Historical Society.

wantonly and wickedly murdering his white children" and that they were to be "hanged by the neck until they [were] dead." Riggs informed them (as Miller had instructed) that "there is no hope of clemency except in the mercy of God through the merits of the blessed Redeemer . . . their only remaining source of comfort and consolation." The Indians were told that "good ministers . . . both Catholic and Protestant" would be made available to them and they could "commune with them constantly" until the hanging.[56]

Three mixed-blood men among the condemned group had been baptized Catholic, but none of the other thirty-six Dakotas had professed to be Christian before their sentence was announced. Whether the other

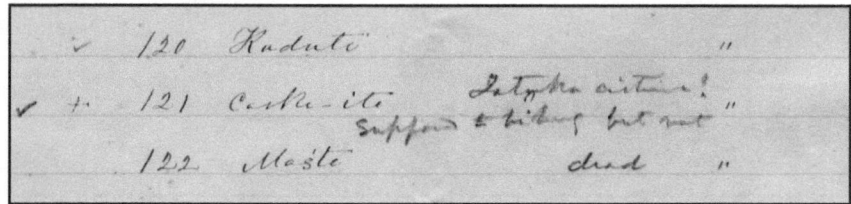

Fig. 7. This frame from the missionaries' list shows that defendant 121, Caska-ite, was sentenced to execution. The missionaries also noted that he was "supposed to be hung but not." The appearance of both a check mark and a "+" next to his name shows that he was named on Lincoln's final hanging list but was still living in 1865. He appears as "No. 121. Chaskay-Don, or Chaskay-Etay" on the Whiting-Ruggles list. Thus, the missionaries were aware of the mistaken hanging of defendant 3, Wi-can-hpi-wa-ste-da-pi, also known as Chaska (see fig. 6), in lieu of defendant 121, and they also knew that the man who was "supposed to be hung" was released from prison in 1866. Missionaries' annotated list of defendants tried in 1862, with notations through 1865, in the Stephen R. Riggs and Family Papers. Courtesy of the Minnesota Historical Society.

prisoners understood Riggs's translation of such terms as "mercy of God" or "blessed Redeemer" is unknown. But we do know that Father Ravoux, a Catholic priest, and Thomas Williamson, the Protestant missionary, immediately launched a religious tug-of-war for their souls. Over the next four days almost all of the men elected one church or the other and were baptized as Catholics or Protestants. The competing "good ministers" kept box scores of the results. Though the exact margin of victory is still in dispute (Father Ravoux said thirty-three chose the "black robe"; Riggs credited the Catholics with only twenty-four baptisms), the Protestants lost the contest by all accounts.[57]

Riggs, implying a handicap for the Protestant side, later noted that the Indians were advised that he could not be selected as their spiritual adviser because he was officially acting in Mankato as a government translator. He ascribed the Catholics' success to the influence of Baptiste Campbell, one of the mixed-blood prisoners.[58] But it seems just as likely that Riggs's active participation in preparing charges for the military court did not sit well with the condemned Indians and that they gravitated to the other branch of Christianity in consequence.

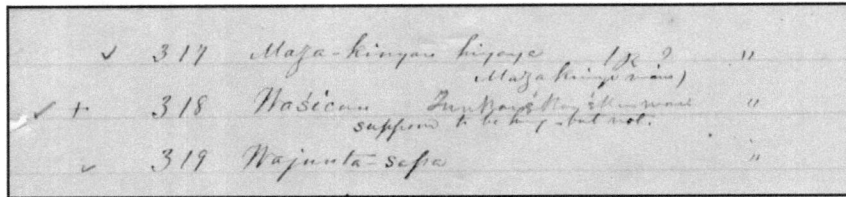

Fig. 8. The missionaries' notations on defendant 318, Wasicun, include a "+" and a check mark, indicating that he was included on President Lincoln's final hanging list but was still alive in 1865. They specifically noted that he was "supposed to be hung but not." This man appears on the Whiting-Ruggles report as "No. 318. Wa-She-Choon, or Toon-Kan-Shkan-Shkan-Mene-Hay." Acquitted defendant 332, Wasicunna (see fig. 9), was executed by mistake in his place. Missionaries' Annotated list of defendants tried in 1862, with notations through 1865, in the Stephen R. Riggs and Family Papers. Courtesy of the Minnesota Historical Society.

Nonetheless, Riggs still had around-the-clock access to the condemned Dakotas in the Leach Building. He spent his time in long conversations with almost all of them, taking careful notes that were soon published in Minnesota newspapers as their "confessions."[59] In fact, most of the statements were protestations of innocence.

Since some modern historians assert or imply that many Dakotas were convicted based on false testimony given by Godfrey, it is worth noting in the Riggs "confessions" that only one defendant (Wakantanka, trial 210) accused Godfrey of lying. When one reads the defendants' statements carefully, it appears that many of those who were to be hanged based on Godfrey's evidence did not so much contradict his words (if they offered any dispute at all) as claim that his testimony did not implicate them in killings. Understandably, the Dakotas did not grasp some elementary principles of Anglo-American justice: that joining with a group of others to shoot at victims, rushing into a house with others who do the actual killing, and urging and assisting others to kill all are actions that could lead to a murder conviction. Some of the condemned men whom Riggs interviewed must have been genuinely befuddled about how they could have been found guilty. In any event, such misunderstandings help to explain why the condemned Dakotas, with one exception, did not focus their enmity on Godfrey.

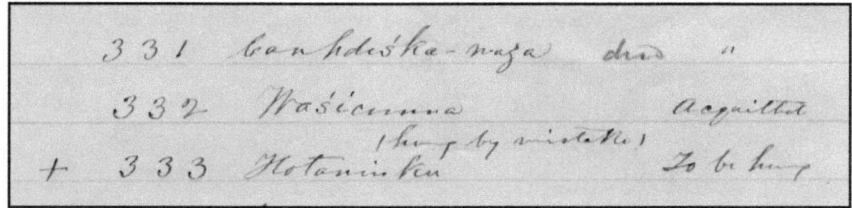

Fig. 9. This frame shows the missionaries' notation that defendant 332, Wasicunna, was "hung by mistake" despite the fact that he had been acquitted in his trial. This innocent man was mistakenly executed in lieu of defendant 318 (see fig. 8). Missionaries' Annotated list of defendants tried in 1862 with notations through 1865, in the Stephen R. Riggs and Family Papers. Courtesy of the Minnesota Historical Society.

At the Mankato prison, Riggs was torn between his desire to help the Dakotas and his duties to Sibley and to the continuing process of military justice. As far as the public and his family were aware, he was assisting those on death row by recording their comments and publishing them in a neutral and sympathetic fashion. But an obscure file in the National Archives holds a secret report to Sibley showing that Riggs also played a decidedly nonreligious, even irreligious, role in Mankato. This document reveals that while Riggs was recording the prisoners' "confessions" he was surreptitiously jotting down incriminating statements they made against other Dakotas—statements *not* included in published versions of the prisoners' statements. Riggs then consolidated his notes into a report implicating twenty-two Dakotas, called "revelations made by the Indians who were executed."[60] Typical entries in Riggs's confidential memo included:

> [Muzzabomadu] says he saw Ka-win-gay . . . kill a white man in the New Ulm settlement [probably a reference to Milford].
> Shoonkasha [White Dog] says that Chankpey-ooha commanded the Indians when they fired on Capt. Marsh's company.
> Henry Milord says that David Faribault Sr. was painted up as Indian warriors were, and shot off his gun at

Fort Ridgely. Waze also shot at the woman shot by himself.

Tatayhdedan says that Ampaynechaga killed a woman at Lake Addie.

Chankahda says Kawingay shot Mary Anderson.

These brief summaries of the condemned men's accusations may not appear to be sufficiently detailed to warrant prosecutions, but they contain precisely the type of shorthand information that led to similar cases being brought before the military commission. One does not have to be an ethicist to conclude that Riggs was blurring the positions of parson and prosecutor. His religious colleagues, especially Thomas Williamson, would have been alarmed to learn that he used information from the prisoners' pre-hanging statements to inform against other Indians. Nor was this an empty exercise, for Sibley soon launched an investigation of the allegations.[61]

The night before the scheduled executions word reached Mankato that Lincoln had reprieved Tatemima, one of the condemned men for whom Williamson and his sister, Jane Williamson, had sought clemency.[62] The missionaries had persuaded Sibley that alibi evidence cast doubt on two young German boys' identification of this Dakota, and Sibley had telegraphed Lincoln to that effect on December 22. Perhaps divine intervention deserves credit, for Tatemima had hedged his religious bets: first baptized into the Presbyterian Church by Williamson on December 22, he was also baptized a Catholic by Father Ravoux on the twenty-fifth. With Tatemima's reprieve, the execution numbers were reduced to thirty-eight men.[63]

During the last two days before the hangings, Robert Sweeny, an artist, was given access to the prisoners in the Leach Building. He had known many of the condemned men for years, and most of them greeted him warmly. Sweeny sketched nine of the death-row prisoners. He also drew a pencil sketch of Godfrey, the only known image of him. While he was at the jail, Sweeny spoke with Godfrey's jailers, and he retained a vivid recollection of those conversations:

> The negro Godfrey, Gussay, or O-ta-kia, as the Sioux called him, was not among them [the Indians slated

for execution on December 26]. I had seen him the day before in another place, and had made a sketch of him and had talked of him with Maj. Jas. R. Brown, Lt. Redmond, Gen. Wm. R. Marshall and other officers, and from those conversations I retain the impression that Gussay it was thought was compelled by the Indians to join in the massacre, rather than they being incited to the atrocities by himself. . . . The officers seemed to like the fellow, and I think it was through their recommendation he escaped the fate of the others, who were largely convicted through his aid and assistance.[64]

Sweeny's memories offer valuable confirmation of the high regard in which Godfrey was held by men who conducted the trials (such as Marshall) or served as his jailers (Brown and Redmond). No one in a position of authority at Mankato offered the least criticism of Lincoln's decision to extend mercy to Godfrey.

Sweeny also gave a physical description of Godfrey, one of the few we have: "He was light colored and seemed bright, intelligent and rather prepossessing—not appearing in the least like the bloody wretch he was said to have been in the massacres. . . . O-ta-kia was short and slight of build, looking not over eighteen or twenty years."[65] Sweeny underestimated Godfrey's age by about twelve years, but he obviously was as taken with him as Isaac Heard and Theodore Carter had been.

Large crowds descended on Mankato to view the executions. Miller issued a decree of martial law covering a distance of ten miles around the town.[66] In the days before the executions reinforcing troops poured into Mankato, until the number of soldiers massed for the event exceeded fourteen hundred.[67] On the day of the hangings Godfrey rejoined the general jail population. General Order No. 23, prescribing the sequence of events on December 26, specifically directed the provost marshal to see that "the prisoner 'Godfrey' is duly returned to the old prison."[68]

Fig. 10. Joseph Godfrey by R.O. Sweeny, December 1862. Courtesy of the Minnesota Historical Society.

A specially designed scaffold had been erected in the open area next to the jail. The massive oak structure, fourteen feet high and twenty-four feet square, resembled "an old fashioned barn frame without rafters."[69] Forty notches were carved into the top timbers of the frame, intended to accommodate ten noose ropes per side. The condemned men would stand on a sturdy four-foot-wide wooden platform (akin to a large horizontal picture frame), which was suspended from eight ropes attached to a stout twenty-foot pole erected in the center of the scaffold. These ropes, in turn, were linked via a cable and pulley to a huge two-inch-thick rope that would hold up the entire platform contraption, plus the weight of forty men.

Thus, in lieu of a trap door, the device utilized a gargantuan hollow square that would (if it worked properly) crash to the ground when someone axed the one heavy rope that held it up.[70]

As the time of the hangings neared, the shackles on each condemned man were hammered free and his arms were bound behind his back with rope. Most of the men walked the short distance from the Leach Building to the execution site with dignity and bravery, singing in unison as they ascended the scaffold stairs. One local newspaper reported that "no equal number ever approached the gallows with greater courage, and more perfect determination to prove how little death can be feared."[71]

The scaffold was surrounded by rows of uniformed soldiers, behind whom thousands of spectators crowded. When the large rope was cut (by a survivor selected for the "honor"), the gallows worked almost precisely as planned, though one Dakota's rope broke and he (though already dead of a broken neck) was strung up again.[72] Two men managed, despite their bonds, to grasp hands and hold that clasp even in death. The crowd and soldiers, after an initial hush, erupted in a "loud huzza." A few men who had not been killed instantly by the drop "kicked savagely" for up to ten minutes until they strangled.[73] The log structure where Godfrey and the Indian prisoners were chained was immediately adjacent to the execution ground, permitting those in the jail to glimpse the execution of their kinsmen through crevices in the walls.[74]

Pope had ordered the hangings to be held in Mankato to allow the Winnebagoes to witness the consequences of antiwhite rebellion. But it would have been unthinkable to assemble Indians of any tribe in the middle of the volatile hanging crowd; the only Winnebago man who attended, a chief named Baptist Lassuillier, came disguised in "citizens'" clothes. Virtually no one knew he was there.[75]

Colonel Miller exulted at the smoothness of the execution proceedings, writing Sibley that they were "an entire success."[76] Sibley telegraphed Lincoln that "everything went off quietly" and told Pope that "everything was orderly."[77] The citizens and soldiers who witnessed the Mankato hangings were conscious of the historic nature of the event, still America's largest mass execution. Newspapers quickly issued "extra" editions reporting the most trivial details of the preparation for and scene on December 26. Large printings of those papers quickly sold out. Lithographs depicting the execution, the most famous of which was published nationally in *Leslie's Illustrated Newspaper*, also enjoyed brisk sales.[78]

The bodies of the thirty-eight men were carted in four wagons to a mass grave near the Minnesota River in a forlorn, low-lying area "overgrown by swamp willows." They were stacked in a long pit and covered with sandy soil.[79] After nightfall, when the grave was no longer guarded, the sand covering the bodies was shoveled aside and the Dakota men were, to use the snide term later adopted by the press, "resurrected." Referring to the angel who brought news of Christ's birth, one paper dubbed a participant in this grave robbery "Gabriel."[80]

The most zealous "resurrectors" were cadaver-seeking doctors. Dr. William W. Mayo, best known as the father of two physicians who later founded the Mayo Clinic, was supposedly given his pick of bodies due to his valuable medical assistance during the siege of New Ulm. He was said to have selected the remains of the notorious Cut Nose, though other reports give that "distinction" to Dr. Charles Boutillier, the official surgeon assigned to the Ninth Minnesota volunteers.[81] The *New York Times* reported with a journalistic smirk, "The bodies of those buried at Mankato have nearly all been dug up and taken to the dissecting room; among them, 'Cut-Nose,' who is being 'cut up' at Saint Peter."[82] There is no evidence that Miller condoned this grave robbing, but it appears that he was less than diligent in protecting the dead. No one was punished for removing or defacing the bodies.

As the fateful year of 1862 ended, both Godfrey and the jailed Indians faced a highly uncertain future. Though reprieved from the gallows by Lincoln, Godfrey still needed to survive a ten-year prison term. White soldiers of the time who barracked in close quarters or were held as prisoners of war routinely died of illness and exposure, and the Indian prison at Mankato was no model of humane incarceration. Measles, consumption, and other commonly fatal diseases loomed as Godfrey's biggest risk.

But he also was an oddity in the prison. Besides being the only non-Dakota inmate and the only black man, Godfrey was virtually the only prisoner who had given important testimony against the Dakotas. He would have to find a means of surviving his confinement with all the other imprisoned Indians, many of whom believed that his words had sent their kinsmen to the gallows. Lincoln's reprieve had, legally speaking, spared Godfrey's life. But a unique mix of extralegal perils did not augur well for his longevity.

NOTES ON CHAPTER 10

1. *New York Herald,* November 20, 1862.
2. Lincoln's comments as published in the *St. Paul Press,* August 21, 1862. At the time Lincoln was touting Chiriqui, in the present-day country of Panama, as a colonization site.
3. "Lincoln's Annual Message to Congress," December 1, 1862, in Basler, *Collected Works of Abraham Lincoln,* 5:518–37.
4. Williams to Lincoln, November 22, 1862, Lincoln Papers, Library of Congress, microfilm roll 44.
5. Beeson to Lincoln, November 18, 1862, NA, RG 48, LR, Indian Division, Dept. of the Interior, M825, roll 20.
6. Williamson to Treat, November 21, 1862, NMM, MHS, box 20 (recites content of letter to Dole); Williamson to Riggs, November 24, 1862, Riggs Family Papers, MHS, box 1.
7. Riggs to Lincoln, November 17, 1862, Lincoln Papers, Library of Congress, microfilm roll 44. In his later writings Riggs was much more critical of the trials and praised Lincoln's eventual decision, but he omitted any reference to his own plea to hang "the great majority" of the condemned Dakotas. Riggs later falsely implied that he had favored a policy of hanging only those convicted of murder—and that Lincoln agreed with his views. S. Riggs, *Tah-koo wah-kan,* 337–40; and S. Riggs, *Mary and I,* 181–83.
8. Thomas Williamson to Treat, November 21, 1862, NMM, MHS, box 20.
9. Thomas Williamson to Riggs, December 5, 1862, Riggs Family Papers, MHS, box 1.
10. *St. Paul Press,* December 6, 1862. For other scornful references to Riggs, see *St. Paul Pioneer and Democrat,* December 9 and 13, 1862.
11. Whipple to Sen. Henry Rice, November 12, 1862, Whipple Papers, MHS, box 40. Rice promised Whipple that he would convey his message to Lincoln, but it is not known whether he did so. See Rice to Williamson, November 9, 1863, Whipple Papers, MHS, Box 3; and Nichols, *Lincoln and the Indians,* 102–13.
12. Whipple letter, December 5, 1862, *St. Paul Press.* Because Lincoln made the same distinction a day later, some writers have jumped to the erroneous conclusion that the president followed Whipple's advice. But there is no evidence that Whipple's comments reached Lincoln before he made his final decision. The president had already instructed his aides to examine the transcripts so as to separate soldiers from murderers.
13. *Chatfield Democrat,* December 20, 1862, reprinted from the *Muscatine (IA) Courier* (no date given).
14. "Lincoln's Annual Message to Congress," December 1, 1862, in Basler, *Collected Works of Abraham Lincoln,* 5:525–56. Though the precise source for Lincoln's estimate of eight hundred deaths is unknown, it was roughly consistent with an estimate of 737 deaths reported by Dakota agent Thomas Galbraith. See Folwell, *History of Minnesota,* 2:392. Satterlee's lists, discussed in chapter 4, include only victims he could identify by name and total slightly less than five hundred.
15. "Lincoln's Annual Message to Congress," December 1, 1862, in Basler, *Collected Works of Abraham Lincoln,* 5:536.
16. Lincoln to Holt, December 1, 1862, in Basler, *Collected Works of Abraham Lincoln,* 5:537–38; and Holt to Lincoln, December 1, 1862, Lincoln Papers, Library of Congress, microfilm roll 44.

17. Lincoln's Message to Senate, received December 11, 1862, appendix C, NA, RG 46, Legislative Center, 37th Congress, Senate 37A-F2, box 43. The letter by Wilkinson et al. is undated but was evidently sent early in December 1862.
18. NA, RG 46, U.S. Senate Records, 38A-H7, Committee on Indian Affairs.
19. Lincoln to Senate, December 11, 1862, in Basler, *Collected Works of Abraham Lincoln*, 5:550–51.
20. The massacres/battles distinction was set forth by Lincoln in his December 11 message to the Senate (ibid.), but the Whiting and Ruggles report (Whiting and Ruggles to Lincoln, December 5, 1862, Dakota Trials Records, microfilm roll 1, frames 9–11) refers to those "convicted of rape and murder." It appears that the terms *murder* and *massacre* were used interchangeably in Lincoln's (apparently oral) directions to Whiting and Ruggles.
21. Whiting and Ruggles to Lincoln, December 5, 1862, Dakota Trials Records, microfilm roll 1, frames 9–11.
22. Ibid.
23. Cases in which David Faribault Sr. gave testimony that were selected by Ruggles and Whiting included Godfrey (trial 1), Wahpaduta (trial 11), Wahohna (trial 12), Rdainyankna (trial 19), Toonkanechataymane (trial 67), Etayhoota (trial 68), Amdaychu (trial 69), Henry Milord (trial 115), Toonkankoyagenajin (trial 225), and Washechoon (trial 318).
24. Baptiste Campbell (trial 138) implicated Henry Milord (trial 115) and Hypolite Auge (trial 175), two of his confederates in murder who were on the list; and Thomas Robertson (trial 135) gave crucial testimony against two men on the list: Hotaninkoo (trial 333) and Chaytanhoonka (trial 342).
25. Whiting and Ruggles to Lincoln, December 5, 1862, Dakota Trials Records, microfilm roll 1, frames 9–11.
26. Mahpeokenajin (trial 96; Cut Nose) and Hdahinhday (trial 373).
27. In the final, printed version of Whiting and Ruggles's report, issued by the Senate, the names of Margaret Cardinal and Mattie Williams were deleted, apparently to protect their privacy. Compare Lincoln's Message to Senate, received December 11, 1862, NA, RG 46, Legislative Center, 37th Congress, Senate 37A-F2, box 43, with the printed version of the report in Whiting and Ruggles to Lincoln, December 5, 1862, Dakota Trials Records, microfilm roll 1, frames 9–11.
28. Heard, *History of the Sioux War*, 151–52, 158; Paul Mazakutemani's statement, in Anderson and Woolworth, *Through Dakota Eyes*, 195–96, refers to Rdainyankna as Rattling Runner.
29. Pencil notations made by Whiting and Ruggles on the case files of Tahomiinwashtay (trial 28) and Pahwashtay (trial 29) indicate that they had taken part in "the butchery of Marsh's command," yet they were not included on the hanging list. White Dog was not the only Indian defendant tried by a military commission in the nineteenth century for the war crime of feigning noncombatant status. In a formal 1873 legal opinion the U.S. attorney general, George H. Williams, authorized a trial by military commission of Modoc Indians in Oregon who had approached U.S. Army officers under a false flag of truce and then "treacherously assassinated" two men. See *Official Opinions of the Attorneys General of the United States* 14 (1875): 249–53. Dakota attackers at widely scattered massacre sites, including Milford and Lake Shetek, similarly violated the laws of war by pretending to be friendly noncombatants so as to enable them to commit murders with greater ease.

30. Riggs to Lincoln, November 17, 1862, Lincoln Papers, Library of Congress, microfilm roll 44; Thomas Williamson and his sister, Jane Williamson, also wrote letters on Hopkins's behalf, but not directly to Lincoln. See, for example, Thomas Williamson to Treat, November 21, 1862, NMM, MHS, box 20, discussing his letter to Indian Commissioner Dole on behalf of Hopkins and others.
31. Wakefield's efforts on behalf of her protector would have been obvious from reading the transcript of his trial (trial 3, Dakota Trials Records).
32. One possible exception was the court's reliance on two small German boys as witnesses in the cases against Snamani (trial 14) and Tatemima (trial 15). The latter defendant was reprieved based on alibi evidence submitted later, while the former was hanged based on the same eyewitnesses' evidence.
33. The Lincoln Order has been termed "perhaps the most valuable" document in the possession of the Minnesota Historical Society. See Lincoln, "Lincoln's Sioux War Order." For a more arcane discussion of how the original order in Lincoln's handwriting was not the actual copy sent to Sibley, see Davis, "Two Sioux War Orders."
34. Lincoln to Senate, December 11, 1862, in Basler, *Collected Works of Abraham Lincoln*, 5:550–51.
35. Ibid.
36. Ibid. (emphasis in original).
37. *Chatfield Democrat*, December 13, 1862 (emphasis in original).
38. The first Minnesota publication of the Whiting and Ruggles report, with its list of the condemned and brief descriptions of the evidence against them, did not appear until December 23, 1862, and then only in St. Paul. See *St. Paul Pioneer and Democrat*, December 23, 1862.
39. *Mankato Weekly Record*, December 20, 1862.
40. The first Minnesota report of Lincoln's decision was printed by the *Winona Republican*, December 10, 1862. The next day both the *St. Paul Press* and the *St. Paul Pioneer and Democrat* published the story.
41. Olin to Miller, December 11, 1862, NA, RG 393, Dist. of MN, E343, pt. 3, Letters and Telegrams Sent.
42. See Sibley's Special Order No. 59, December 15, 1862, attaching Lincoln's order for executions, Sibley Orders Book, Sibley Papers, MHS, M164, roll 11; and Lincoln to Sibley, telegram, December 16, 1862, *MCIW*, 2:292.
43. Sibley to Riggs, December 15, 1862, Riggs Family Papers, MHS, box 1; Riggs to Sibley, December 22, 1862, Sibley Papers, MHS, M164, roll 11.
44. S. Riggs, *Mary and I*, 184. Compounding the litany of errors before the execution, a "deeply mortified" Miller admitted that by a "remarkable oversight" he had mistakenly included his original copy of the president's order in one of his dispatches back to St. Paul. But Sibley had already noticed the error, and it was immediately sent back to Mankato. Miller to Sibley, December 18, 1862, NA, RG 393, Dist. of MN, 1862–63, E346, pt. 3, LR (including responsive note by Sibley). There is no reason to believe that this temporary absence of the official order had any impact on the later difficulties in identifying prisoners to be hanged, but the episode highlights the repeated errors that occurred in the pressured pre-hanging period.
45. Nicolay to Sibley, December 9, 1862, Lincoln Papers, Library of Congress, microfilm roll 96.
46. As far as we know from the trial records and other accounts, there were at least six Dakotas who were known by the name Chaska and were prosecuted before the military commission: trials 21, 72, 121, 163, and 259.

47. This January 12, 1863, list is published in the Trial Records, microfilm roll 1, starting at frame 16. A succinct summary of Godfrey's unique status was published by one Minnesota newspaper, though it did not mention him by name. See *Minnesota State News*, December 20, 1862.
48. See, for example, Clodfelter, *Dakota War*, 58, which incorrectly says that Lincoln, in 1862, "reduced the sentences of the other POWs to jail time."
49. Mankato prison list, January 12, 1863, Dakota Trials Records, microfilm roll 1, frames 16–26.
50. *Congressional Globe*, January 28, 1863, 514.
51. Since the names of the men to be hanged were not yet public, this petition should not be read as an endorsement of each hanging verdict. But it does demonstrate that the Dakota leaders supported the principle that Dakotas shown to have committed murders should be executed—and that they were not shocked in December 1862 to learn that as many as thirty-nine Dakotas would ascend the scaffold. Even more strongly, this petition underscores the point that the surrendering Dakotas neither expected nor favored amnesty for Dakota murderers. A knowledgeable reader of the manuscript of this book strongly suggested that, given the dire plight faced by the Dakota people at Fort Snelling, the Wabasha petition should be seen as a coerced concession rather than willing acceptance of Lincoln's decision to hold mass hangings. As discussed in the text, I strongly disagree with that position. Any suggestion that Wabasha and the other signatories were disingenuous in giving Lincoln their support for the hangings ignores the fierce opposition of these men—during the war, at Camp Release, at Fort Snelling, and many years later—to the goals and tactics of the militants in the soldiers' lodge and minimizes the anger they felt toward the "bad" men within the Dakota community. During the last weeks of the war some of the signers of the Wabasha petition had formed their own soldiers' lodge; they were willing to risk their lives to wrest the white captives from the more militant lodge. See Anderson and Woolworth, *Through Dakota Eyes*, 100, 108, 170–72, 187–88, 198–99. It is not surprising that men who had been willing to kill other Dakotas to fight for their beliefs would also favor their execution. Wabasha's appearance on the petition is consistent with his behind-the-scenes opposition to the war, with the content of his secret wartime communications with Sibley, with his conduct at Camp Release, with his decision to become an informer in January 1863 and to testify against Dakota defendants in the April 1863 trials, and with his other postwar statements and actions. As late as 1868, Wabasha reiterated that his vision of an honorable peace would have included "delivering up" all Dakota "murderers" and "instigators" of the war to white justice. See chapter 5, note 12; and *Papers Relating to Talks and Councils*, 90–94.
52. Riggs later put the "main" responsibility for selecting the thirty-nine condemned Indians on Brown. See S. Riggs, *Mary and I*, 184. But Riggs was personally involved in the process too (Riggs to Mary Riggs, December 22, 1862, Riggs letters, CCHS), and his knowledge of the charges against each man might have been superior to Brown's, given the role he played in interviewing witnesses and preparing papers for the military commission. See also Wakefield, *Six Weeks in Sioux Teepees*, 121–25 (Wakefield's reaction upon learning that the wrong Chaska was hanged).

53. See figures 8 and 9 in this volume. The four most reliable sources of this story are (1) Thomas Robertson account, MHS, M582, roll 3, 32 (eighteen-year-old white boy hanged by mistake was a "simpleton" or "idiotic"); (2) Charles E. McColley account, MHS, M582, roll 2, 1 ("innocent white boy" was hanged); (3) John P. Williamson, Hughes Papers, Southern Minnesota Historical Center, Minnesota State University, Mankato, MSS 101, box 10, folder 3, vol. 7, 93–94 ("full blooded white boy who was innocent" answered the call to his name and was hanged by mistake; gives circumstances of his adoption in infancy by an Indian woman after the death of his parents); and (4) Fred Pearsall, "*Short Stories and History of Dakota People (Sioux),*" circa 1983, MHS, 14–17 (All of the Dakotas knew of the mistaken hanging. It was widely discussed because the "rabid prejudice against the Indians had backfired . . . [when the whites hanged] one of their own number thinking he was an Indian."). There are many conflicting and incorrect accounts regarding the mistakes made in selecting those to be hanged. For example, Flandrau, *History of Minnesota,* 180, says that a "pardoned" Dakota was hanged, and Whipple, *Lights and Shadows,* 131–32, in an apparent reference to Sarah Wakefield's protector, claims that a man "acquitted for saving a woman" was hanged by mistake. In fact, only Tatemima and Godfrey were pardoned or granted partial clemency before the hangings, and neither of them was hanged. Chaska, who saved Wakefield, had been convicted and sentenced to death but was not included on Lincoln's hanging list. Whipple's assertion that Wakefield's protector (or any other prisoner) would have been released the day after the hangings is incorrect; Chaska, like all of the other convicted defendants, would have remained in prison to await further orders from the president. On Chaska, see figures 6 and 7 in this volume.
54. See figures 8 and 9 in this volume. The identity of the mistakenly hanged man, Washechoonna, comes from a missionary list of prisoners (prepared by Riggs, Thomas Williamson, and others) compiled at Davenport in 1865. Riggs Family Papers, MHS, box 1. The list indicates that the acquitted Washechoonna (trial 332) was "hung by mistake," while the man who should have been executed, Washechoon (trial 318), was "supposed to be hung but not." Similarly, the same list notes that Chaskaydon or Chaskayetay (trial 121) was also "supposed to be hung—but not" and provides an alternate name for him—Tatanka Cistina. Sarah Wakefield's protector, Wechankwashtodopee (trial 3; aka Chaska), is also indicated as having been "hung by mistake." From other records it appears that Tatanka Cistina (John Little Buffalo) was pardoned in 1866 and later became a land allottee on the Santee Reservation. See 1866 pre-pardon list, NA, RG 94, LR, Adjutant General, M619, roll 483, frame 696 (Tatonkacestinna, trial 131); and 1872 Santee allotment list, NA, Office of Indian Affairs, M175, roll 768, frame 661 ("Tatanka Cistinna; John Little Buffalo"). The 1865 missionary list verifies that Riggs and Williamson knew: that two men were mistakenly hanged; their identities; the identities of the two men who should have been hanged; that both men were still alive and in prison in 1865; and that Chaskaydon (trial 121), convicted of killing a woman and cutting out her fetus, was released in 1866. This information raises interesting questions about whether the missionaries withheld their knowledge so as to shield the two condemned men from further punishment and whether Williamson's public statements that none of the men at Davenport had been found guilty of murder were made disingenuously. See discussion of the 1866 pardon of Tatanka Cistina in chapter 11.
55. The condemned Indians occupied only a small portion of the three-story Leach Building, a back room on the first floor. Buck, *Indian Outbreaks,* 253. Troops were quartered in other areas of the building, and thus there would have been many places in the building where Godfrey might have been held.

56. A typewritten copy of the script is found at NA, RG 94, LR, Adjutant General, M619, roll 483, frame 613.
57. Ravoux, *Reminiscences,* 77; Riggs to Mary Riggs, December 23, 1862, Riggs letters, CCHS (twenty-four opted for the Catholics and fifteen for the Protestants). Religious partisans exaggerated these totals in accordance with their faith. Berghold, a Catholic, reported that thirty-six of thirty-nine became Catholic. *Indians' Revenge,* 146.
58. S. Riggs, *Mary and I,* 185.
59. Riggs himself referred to these statements as "confessions": see Riggs to Mary Riggs, December 23, 1862, Riggs letters, CCHS. The confessions were widely published. See *Mankato Weekly Record,* December 26, 1862, and *St. Paul Pioneer and Democrat,* December 28, 1862.
60. Undated report of Stephen Riggs, received at [Sibley's] headquarters on January 9, 1863, NA, RG 393, Dept. of NW, 1862–64, Headquarters, E3449, pt. 1, Unentered Letters. The only apparent reference to this report in any scholarly work is in Anderson, *Kinsmen of Another Kind,* 348n52. Anderson does not attribute the report to Riggs, and he says, incorrectly, that "no action was taken" against the implicated men.
61. Following investigation, two Dakotas on Riggs's list were prosecuted in April 1863. See NA, RG 393, Dept. of NW, 1862–65, Headquarters, E3449, pt. 1, Unentered Letters; and discussion of the 1863 trials in chapter 11.
62. Thomas Williamson supplied evidence that Tatemima was "miles away helping white folks to escape" when the murder for which he was convicted was committed. See Charles E. McColley account, MHS, M582, roll 2.
63. For the correspondence relating to Tatemima's reprieve, see Sibley to Lincoln, telegram, December 22, 1862, NA, RG 393, Dist. of MN, E343, pt. 3, Letters and Telegrams Sent; Stanton to Sibley, telegram, December 23, 1862, and Sibley to Miller, December 23, 1862, both in NA, RG 94, LR, Adjutant General, M619, roll 483. Both the Protestants and the Catholics apparently had questions about whether Tatemima was an appropriate candidate for baptism. Williamson asked Riggs to talk to Tatemima, saying Tatemima did "not feel well satisfied that he was a Christian," although the Dakota acceded to Williamson's wish to baptize him. Riggs to Mary Riggs, December 22, 1862, Riggs letters, CCHS. Ravoux, aware that Tatemima had already received a Presbyterian baptism, granted him only a "conditional baptism" into the Catholic Church. Ravoux, *Reminiscences,* 77. The official Catholic records, written by Ravoux, show that Tatemima was given the Christian name Geogh, while the "conditional" nature of his baptism is not shown. St. Peter's and St. Paul's Roman Catholic Church records, MHS. One serious problem suggested by Tatemima's reprieve is that it casts doubt on the guilt of Snamani (trial 14), who also professed his innocence and who was identified by one of the same young German boys thought to have mistakenly accused Tatemima (trial 15). Snamani was hanged.
64. Sweeny letter, March 27, 1886, *St. Paul Dispatch,* March 28, 1886.
65. Ibid.
66. Special Order No. 21, issued by Miller on December 24, 1862, was widely published in the newspapers. See *Mankato Weekly Record,* December 26, 1862, and *St. Paul Pioneer and Democrat,* December 28, 1862.
67. Exactly 1,419 troops were at the executions. Hughes, *History of Blue Earth County,* 134.

68. General Order No. 23, issued December 25, 1862, by J. K. Arnold, post adjutant, in Hughes, *History of Blue Earth County*, 132. It is also possible that Godfrey had been separated from the other prisoners at an earlier date, but the fact that he was promptly returned to the general prison population on the day of the executions suggests that he was separated from the rest on December 22 and held in another room in the Leach Building. Another possible explanation for Godfrey's separate confinement is favoritism by the jailers, due either to Lincoln's act of clemency or to the friendship shown Godfrey by the officers in charge of the prison. See Sweeny letter, March 27, 1886, *St. Paul Dispatch*, March 28, 1886.
69. *Mankato Independent*, December 26, 1862.
70. Ibid. Reference to the pulley comes from the account of soldier Julius Owen, MHS, M582, roll 2. Hughes describes the scaffold, including the "stout cable," in *History of Blue Earth County*, 132.
71. *St. Peter Tribune*, December 27, 1862.
72. *Mankato Weekly Record*, December 26, 1862.
73. Ibid.; and *Mankato Independent*, December 26, 1862.
74. S. Riggs, *Mary and I*, 185; and Nix, *Sioux Uprising*, 135.
75. *Mankato Weekly Record*, as reprinted in *Mankato Daily Review*, December 26, 1896.
76. Miller to Olin, December 26, 1862, NA, RG 393, Dist. of MN, 1862–63, E346, pt. 3, LR.
77. Sibley to Lincoln, December 27, 1862, *MCIW*, 2:292; Sibley to Selfridge, December 27, 1862, NA, RG 393, Dist. of MN, E343, pt. 3, Letters and Telegrams Sent.
78. *Leslie's Illustrated Newspaper*, January 24, 1863.
79. *Mankato Weekly Record*, December 26, 1862; *Lake City Times*, January 3, 1863.
80. *Mankato Daily Review*, December 26, 1896, reprinting article from *Mankato Weekly Record* (grave robbery as "resurrection"); and *St. Peter Tribune*, January 30, 1863 ("Gabriel").
81. Several accounts say that Mayo took the body of Cut Nose. See, for example, Porter, "Little Crow," 127; Carley, *Dakota War of 1862*, 75. Comparing the skull reported to be that of Cut Nose with his photo, a scientist later found a "good to excellent match" between the two. Hart, "Rule of the Bone." Theodore Carter, usually a very accurate source, was the officer of the day for the hangings. He reported in detail that the body of Cut Nose was taken to St. Peter, where it was dissected by Dr. Boutillier. See *Mankato Free Press*, January 25, 1937.
82. *New York Times*, January 13, 1863. Since Mayo lived in LeSueur, not St. Peter, this article tends to support the account of Theodore Carter. Further complicating this story is the fact that other human remains (a piece of tattooed skin) identified as being from the body of Cut Nose were apparently eventually donated by the family of a third physician, Dr. S. B. Sheardown, to a Michigan museum. See the *Minneapolis Star Tribune*, July 16, 2000. Since Sheardown was one of the official physicians who examined the bodies of the executed men (Heard, *History of the Sioux War*, 293), this account adds another complication to the mystery surrounding the remains of Cut Nose. Theoretically, it is possible that all three doctors were involved: Sheardown by removing a patch of skin at the grave, Boutillier by dissecting the body, and Mayo by obtaining the skeleton. But it seems more likely that these accounts offer conflicting claims among the various doctors as to which of them actually removed the body of Cut Nose.

CHAPTER 11

The Prison Years

By late December Godfrey and the Dakota prisoners had been chained in rough-hewn wooden prisons for almost three months. They had lived and slept in the same clothes for far too long, and Colonel Miller now reported to Sibley that their "garments are covered with vermin, very rotten, tattered and filthy." Miller proposed to burn their "lousy" clothing and furnish each man with a new flannel shirt and drawers. Medicines too were in short supply, both for the soldiers guarding the jail and for the inmates.[1] But Sibley was reluctant to provide new clothes for men he still hoped to hang. And any money spent from his limited military budget to clothe, feed, and give medical care to Indian prisoners reduced his ability to meet other priorities.[2]

Both in Mankato and at Fort Snelling, the military was now paying the full price for Pope's rash decision to wrest every Dakota from the jurisdiction of the Office of Indian Affairs. Angered by Pope's broadside blasts at Indian agents and the federal Indian officials who supervised them, the Washington bureaucrats who ordinarily would have looked out for Dakota interests were now content to let the army stew in the consequences of Pope's hasty words and actions: the Interior Department steadfastly refused to allocate any money to assist the military in caring for the two thousand Dakotas now interned at Mankato and Fort Snelling.[3] Again and again, the effects of this governmental infighting fell harshly upon the Dakota people.

After consulting with Pope, Sibley told Miller to provide the Indians jailed at Mankato only with such clothing as was "absolutely necessary," instructing him to keep accounts so as to enable the military to claim back against the Interior Department.[4]

At the muddy Indian camp below Fort Snelling, Sibley struggled to define the status of Godfrey's wife, Takanheca, and the other Dakotas taken there on Pope's orders. If they were viewed as prisoners of war, Sibley acknowledged, they would be entitled to receive the same full rations as rebel prisoners. But in a telegram to Washington, Sibley advised that "complete rations . . . are not necessary," to which he received an immediate reply from the War Department: "Feed Indians at discretion. Full rations not necessary."[5] By this means the military justified feeding the Dakotas less food than white prisoners would have been given.

To forestall any thought by Lincoln of issuing wholesale pardons, Sibley continued to defend the findings of his military commission. Tacitly conceding that the president was now unlikely to approve all of his court's death-penalty orders, Sibley pushed Lincoln to authorize the hanging of "at least fifty more" Mankato prisoners as a compromise. Any idea of freeing the convicted men, he told Lincoln, was "out of the question, for they would return to their prairie haunts, filled with thoughts of revenge and murder."[6]

Besides pressing Lincoln to hang more of those already condemned, Sibley sought to expand the number of men on death row by investigating new charges brought against Dakotas who had not yet been convicted. Riggs's revelation of condemned prisoners' statements provided one source of new accusations, but the most prominent person now to turn informant was none other than Chief Wabasha. Col. William Crooks, formerly the president of the military commission, was acting as commander of the internment camp at Fort Snelling. In a January 2 letter to Sibley, Crooks reported that Wabasha "sent for me" and then made incriminating "statements voluntarily through the U.S. Interpreter."[7]

The chief provided evidence against five Dakotas, accusations that Crooks summarized for Sibley. Wabasha implicated two men who had been identified with the Dakota peace faction and who had given testimony for the prosecution in the 1862 trials: Taopi was "in all the fights" and Wakinyanwashtay (Good Thunder) was "the first Indian that went into the government stable at Fort Ridgely," was "painted from head to foot with red paint" at Birch Coulee, and "was at the battle of New Ulm." In addition, Taxunkamaza, Wabasha alleged, had "killed a white man near New Ulm on the Big Cottonwood River." Wahinkpe had "killed a white man near New Ulm." Wakkeintawa, he asserted, had killed the trader Divoll, later bragging that he had "done . . . [what] he always intended to do, viz, he had killed a white man with his bow and arrow."

Sibley ordered the arrest and jailing of four of the five men accused by Wabasha, but he dismissed the charges against Taopi after personally questioning potential witnesses at Fort Snelling.[8] Significantly, none of the new complainants made accusations against Godfrey. The fact that he had already been tried did not exempt him: Wakkeintawa (Wakinyantawa, George Spencer's protector, also called Chaska) had been tried and acquitted at Camp Release, but that did not stop Sibley from ordering his rearrest and confinement at Fort Snelling to await a second trial.

In the Mankato jail, Godfrey now faced the reality that deeply entrenched Dakota cultural customs placed his life in peril. Imprisoned brothers, cousins, uncles, in-laws, and other kin of hanged men against whom Godfrey had testified traditionally would all have felt duty-bound to kill him in retribution; it would have made no difference to them if Godfrey's testimony had been truthful or not.[9] Taopi, whose testimony in the trials had been far less damning than Godfrey's, later expressed his fear of reprisals should he be forced to rejoin the Dakotas: "Taopi cannot go to his people. You hung men at Mankato, whose friends will require their blood at my hands. If I go [back to live among the Dakotas] I shall die. I shall never have a home until I sleep in the grave."[10]

Godfrey was further isolated and disadvantaged by his choice of religion. Sometime during the winter he was baptized into the Roman Catholic faith by Father Ravoux.[11] He probably made the decision to become a Catholic while being held in separate confinement with the men who were hanged. But Ravoux departed from Mankato early in 1863, after most of his converts had been executed.[12] That left Godfrey and a few of the remaining mixed-blood prisoners as the only Catholics in the jail—a distinction that probably meant little at first but was to assume much greater importance as Protestant missionaries gained religious ascendancy in the prison.[13]

Though Lincoln had said nothing at all about his plans for the 260 condemned men who had not been hanged, it was Sibley who now became the local lightning rod both for critics who favored more executions and for those who opposed more hangings. The most vocal crusaders in the former camp railed at Sibley for having started down the path of military justice. One common criticism was that he could have avoided the present legal predicament simply by summarily killing *all* the Dakotas at Camp Release. As the *Faribault Central Republican* said, "Gen. Sibley didn't half execute his duty. He ought to have shot every Indian that approached his command, for in point of fact the guilt of the recent massacres is about equally shared by the entire Sioux nation."[14]

Jane Swisshelm sounded a similar theme when she traveled to Washington to lobby for more hangings and gave invective-laden speeches. She pledged that the imprisoned Dakotas would die, one way or another:

> If justice is not done, [Minnesotans] will go to shooting Indians whenever these government pets get from under Uncle Samuel's wing. Our people will hunt them, shoot them, set traps for them, put out poisoned bait for them—kill them by every means we would use to exterminate panthers.
>
> We cannot breathe the same air with those demon violators of women, crucifiers of infants. Every Minnesota man, who has a soul and can get a rifle, will go to shooting Indians and he who hesitates will be black-balled by every Minnesota woman and posted as a coward in every Minnesota home.[15]

As Swisshelm buttonholed politicians in Washington corridors, she heard a familiar argument that landed on Sibley's doorstep:

> Why didn't you *kill* them? My—to think of the crimes you say they perpetrated and then to think of you coming here to whine and ask for justice!!
>
> Why didn't you kill them?
>
> There was enough of you to have exterminated the whole tribe and relieved the world of the presence of the monsters! Why didn't you do it? Nobody could have blamed the people of Minnesota under such provocation for killing the whole tribe. Or at worst it would have been savage killing savage; but you take them prisoners, admit them to the rights of prisoners of war and then come here and ask the Government to damn itself in the eyes of all Christendom by a wholesale hanging of these prisoners!![16]

By this reasoning Lincoln's hands were tied because Sibley had committed himself to following legal procedures (however flawed). Sibley, his critics ranted, could have accomplished his goals directly with three hundred bullets.

At the other extreme, clergymen now attacked Sibley for being too harsh on the Dakotas. Rev. Thomas Williamson was the most public thorn in his side, pointing out in the press that none of the men remaining in prison had been convicted of murder.[17] When Bishop Whipple learned of Sibley's proposal to hang fifty more Dakotas, Whipple wrote privately to him, emphasizing that the men in prison had surrendered: "The civilized world cannot justify the trial by a military commission of men who voluntarily came in under a flag of truce."[18] Sibley was unyielding in his lengthy reply to Whipple, declaring that "these wretches" should all have been hanged as soon as they were convicted.[19]

Both the anti- and pro-Indian polemicists who assailed Sibley would have been interested in—and surely have raised their eyebrows at—an unpublicized clemency petition that Sibley quietly endorsed in January 1863. David Faribault Sr. secured Sibley's written support for a presidential pardon of his convicted son, David Jr. Significantly, the Faribault pardon papers went directly to Lincoln, bypassing Pope and the normal chain of military command.[20]

Though it would have been obvious to Lincoln that David Faribault Sr. was the prisoner's father and that the signer of a supporting affidavit, Alexander Faribault, was also a relative (his uncle), the petition also included a strongly worded statement under oath by Stephen Fowler, one of Sibley's officers, who had assisted in conducting the Dakota trials.[21] Fowler represented to Lincoln that Godfrey was at fault for Faribault's plight: "The *Negro Godfrey* who was probably as deeply culpable as even the most Devilish of the Savages was brought before the Commission and tried—when in the desperation of his case and with the hope to save his own neck from the halter he turned informant and among others inculpated to a certain extent the above named David Faribault."[22]

Faribault's father joined the refrain: "All the evidence given against him as he now understands was given by a Negro man in the presence of Maj. S. H. Fowler a well known gentleman connected with the Army whose statement of the facts of the case is hereto appended and to which particular reference is made as also to the accompanying papers. . . . He could, had a defence been gone into, [have] contradicted controlled and repelled such evidence of the colored man."[23] Faribault thus claimed to have the support of an independent officer, who declared that Godfrey had given evidence to save his own skin and that a fair trial would have assured the younger Faribault's acquittal.

But Fowler falsely set up Godfrey as a straw man. David Faribault Jr. (trial *134*) had been convicted on the strength of his own admissions (made *before* Godfrey testified) that he had fired multiple shots at both New Ulm and Birch Coulee. And after Godfrey gave rather lukewarm evidence against him, Faribault responded on the record, "What witness says is true." Because there was no conflict between the trial testimony given by Godfrey and by Faribault, the claims of Fowler and Faribault Sr. were bogus. This was the first time—but by no means the last—that Godfrey was unjustly used as a scapegoat by those who asserted their innocence.

Nor did anyone disclose to Lincoln that the supposedly objective officer joining in the petition, Fowler, was also the prisoner's uncle. Since 1841 Fowler had been married to Emily, a sister of David Faribault Sr.[24] Sibley was a longtime friend and business associate of both the Faribaults and Fowler, so he would have known of their familial ties, yet neither he nor Faribault Sr. informed the president of this connection.[25] Even without knowing the undisclosed background of the Faribault petition, Lincoln must have noted the irony of Sibley's endorsement of a plea seeking a full pardon for a man he had so recently recommended to be executed. If the president were to accept Fowler's criticisms of Godfrey at face value, he might well ask Sibley how he could have supported the December hangings of men convicted solely on the basis of Godfrey's testimony. Sibley was fortunate that he managed to keep the Faribault petition a secret from the Minnesota press, for many newspapers would have relished the chance to dissect some of the arguments advanced in an attempt to free a man who was as guilty (or as innocent, depending on one's perspective) as almost every Dakota in the Mankato jail.

As winter progressed, conditions faced by Takanheca and the sixteen hundred Dakotas held in the grim Fort Snelling internment camp stockade worsened daily.[26] Epidemics of measles and mumps hit nearby St. Paul, killing some of the refugee white children who had lost one or both parents in the war.[27] Damp, overcrowded, unsanitary, and cold conditions at the fort, coupled with an insufficient allotment of food, made the Indian internees especially vulnerable to such diseases. Godfrey's infant daughter, Hapan, was among the two hundred or more Dakotas—many of them children—who perished during the winter.[28]

The Dakota men jailed in Mankato had been accustomed to spending a good part of the winter outdoors on long hunts and supplementing their annuities by trapping. Now, with manacles chafing their ankles and the shadow of the custom-made scaffold still darkening their place of confinement, they embraced en masse the offerings of the Protestant missionaries: literacy lessons coupled with religious conversion. On February 3 Rev. Thomas Williamson and Gideon Pond conducted a huge baptism ceremony in the Mankato jail to receive 274 prisoners into the Presbyterian faith.[29] Riggs was more skeptical than Williamson about the bona fides of some of the converts, noting that "deliverance from the chair" was one of their motives.[30]

The Episcopalians also joined the race to baptize Dakotas. By early

April every single prisoner had accepted the Christian sacrament.[31] As the *Mankato Record* wryly reported, some (like Tatemima at the time of the hangings) were "so liberal in their religious views" that it was "not unlikely" that they had been baptized into more than one faith.[32] Godfrey now became one of only a handful of prisoners not enrolled as either a Presbyterian or an Episcopalian.[33]

A similar competition for Dakota converts occurred at the Fort Snelling encampment. John Williamson, the son of Thomas, complained about the sharp practices of the soul-hungry Episcopalians, who offered money to one Dakota leader in an attempt to induce him away from the Presbyterian fold.[34] Takanheca brought five-year-old Joseph Godfrey Jr., the couple's sole surviving child, to be baptized as an Episcopalian by Rev. S. D. Hinman.[35]

The educational transformation at the Mankato prison was equally remarkable. Dakotas who had busied themselves with card games ("It was not unusual to witness as many as fifteen or twenty games . . . in operation at one time") now huddled in study groups to pore over their ABCs.[36] Riggs furnished one hundred Dakota-language copies of John Bunyan's *Pilgrim's Progress* to those who had moved on to the next stage of literacy, while many prisoners learned to read and write on slates and paper provided by the missionaries.[37] Riggs exulted that the Dakotas had made more educational progress in one winter's time than in the previous twenty-six years of his ministry among them. Maj. George Bradley, who had been a member of Sibley's military commission, advanced the theory that "the best way to civilize Indians is to imprison them."[38]

While the amazed and approving whites saw literary and religious instruction as prerequisites for Bible study, it is likely that some of the Dakotas at both Mankato and Fort Snelling were embracing education and conversion for other reasons. The prisoners used their newfound skills mainly for communicating with their loved ones (from whom they had been separated for months) via letters.[39] The Dakotas also may have hoped—as, in fact, proved the case—that those who most strongly proclaimed their Christianity might be favored for early release from jail.

Where was Godfrey during this frenetic period of religious and educational activity? Apparently he had been pulled from the general prison population to serve as a cook. When the editor of a Mankato newspaper was invited to dine with the officers in charge of the jail, he filed this report: "Gus., the negro prisoner, has been promoted to the position of cook to the officers in charge of the Sioux prisoners. Yesterday we partook of a sumptious [sic] dinner, at Major Brown's quarters, prepared by him. We would give the bill of fare, but fear that it might reach President Lincoln's eye, in which case Gus., would certainly be ordered to the Presidential Mansion."[40] Again, Godfrey was treated differently from the other prisoners. Most likely his jailers were trying to protect him by keeping him safely in the kitchen, apart from vengeful Dakotas, but in removing him from the daily routine they also denied him the chance to learn to read and write.

At Fort Snelling, after further investigation of the accusations forwarded to him by Riggs and Wabasha, Sibley apparently decided that there was insufficient evidence to hold Wakinyanwashtay (Good Thunder) for trial; he was released from the fort guardhouse.[41] But the general directed that the new charges merited the appointment of another military commission, which he created in April 1863. Only four Dakotas were brought before this court, which conducted its deliberations in secret at Fort Snelling.[42] Riggs served as the interpreter for these now-forgotten trials. Observing the fairer proceedings of this court, Riggs revised his opinion of the cases tried the previous autumn and became much more critical of them.[43] In April only one of the four defendants was convicted, roughly the reverse of the conviction ratio in 1862.[44]

The most celebrated and longest April case was the retrial of Wakkeintawa, George Spencer's friend, whom Spencer knew as Chaska.[45] At Fort Snelling Chief Wabasha appeared as the main prosecution witness, repeating his claim to Crooks that Chaska had admitted to him that he had shot trader Divoll on the first day of the outbreak. But Spencer got Chaska off again with a spirited defense both in the newspaper and in court.[46]

At the Mankato jail, the bodies of about ten Dakotas who died during the winter were treated with no more respect than had been those of the thirty-eight hanged men. Prisoners who expired from disease were buried in the same sandy riverside plot from which grave robbers had removed the executed men's bodies. The local press covered the disinterment of one newly deceased Dakota prisoner in the same way it had treated the post-hanging "resurrections," describing him as having reappeared "like Banquos ghost."[47] In March a St. Peter newspaper reported in codelike references the apparent dissection of a prisoner's body for medical purposes: "A GOOD INDIAN IN TOWN.—We are informed that another good Indian arrived here a few evenings since—that is, an Indian who will not do any wickedness hereafter. He . . . has already received a sharp welcome from friends, who have an interest in him. 'Peace be to his hashes!'"[48] By early April the Dakota gravesite was beyond reach of body snatchers, entirely flooded with spring rains. Dakota women who had come to pay their respects were seen "crying bitterly" at the sight.[49]

Due to continuing threats against the lives of the Dakota prisoners from white lynch mobs, Sibley and Riggs were relieved when orders came through in early April to transport them to Davenport, Iowa. At this point Riggs pleaded with Sibley to release the fifty or so Dakota men who had been acquitted in 1862 but still languished in the Mankato jail. Only after consulting with Pope did Sibley agree.[50] These men had spent almost six months in chained confinement despite the court's conclusion that they were innocent. But two of the acquitted prisoners were not set free. Washechoonna (trial 332) had paid the ultimate price for his wrongful imprisonment when he was hanged in error. And Otineyapa (trial 280), against whom no witness had testified and who had admitted nothing during the trials, remained in prison due to a clerical error: despite his acquittal, his sentence was incorrectly noted on the roster of prisoners as "condemned to be hung."[51]

On the morning of April 22 Godfrey and the other manacled prisoners were marched past the gallows between two lines of soldiers to the steamboat *Favorite*.[52] After the acquitted Dakotas disembarked at Fort Snelling, the Dakota women and children at the fort watched the boat as it steamed away with the remaining prisoners to a destination unknown. The press reported, "The most affecting scene connected with the trip from Mankato occurred while passing Fort Snelling, where were quartered 1,600 Indians—mostly the squaws and children of the prisoners. The prisoners knew not but that they were going away to their execution, and that they were for the last time beholding their wives and children."[53]

As the *Favorite* proceeded down the Mississippi, one deckhand gestured to the Indians to indicate that their fate was to be hanged and have their throats cut. But Major Brown, who supervised the prisoner transfer, assured everyone that they were not going to be executed and thus restored calm aboard.[54] On the journey to Iowa, one low-ranking white soldier who helped guard the prisoners complained bitterly about the arrangements aboard the *Favorite*. Apparently, most of the prisoners were chained below. But the sixteen Dakota women who had worked as cooks and laundresses at Mankato and the other members of Major Brown's jail staff (including a few mixed-blood men), all of whom were making the trip to Iowa, were given meals and accommodations much better than those of the white enlisted men. The indignant soldier from the Sixth Regiment protested in a letter home,

> Our soldiers have been highly exasperated since we came on board the boat. There are several Indians, half-breeds and squaws on the boat. At meal time they set down to the excellent table and good fare furnished by the boat, along side the officers. They have the ladies cabin set apart for their use, and all this is paid for by the Government, while the sick and hungry soldier on deck below must eat his hard bread or else pay 50c a meal—but as it has been four months since last pay day, not many can do that. . . . It is no wonder that the patriotism which stirred our volunteers to enlist deadens and dies, seeing this.[55]

It seems likely that Godfrey—Brown's cook at Mankato—was included in this favored group.

Upon the prisoners' arrival in Davenport, they were jailed at Camp McClellan (also called Camp Kearney). Godfrey was again placed in a position that distinguished him from the other prisoners, this time as an interpreter. The local newspaper reported, "With the Indians came three interpreters; David Ferribault [Jr.], a half-breed Sioux, who speaks English fluently and writes a handsome hand, he having received some education at school at Prairie du Chien; Antoine Provicili [Provincalle], another French and Indian half-breed, and George Godfrey, a half-breed Indian negro." (Faribault had not yet received a response from Lincoln regarding his father's pardon request, so he was sent to Davenport with the rest of the prisoners.) The same newspaper repeated the distortions of Godfrey's deeds during the war that had circulated in Minnesota. Godfrey "escaped hanging with the thirty nine who were executed last winter, by turning State's evidence, and who is under sentence of imprisonment for ten years. It is said that he alone murdered 18 men, women and children in that awful massacre."[56] The notion that Godfrey was a mass murderer, always attributed to vague or anonymous sources ("it is said"), was to plague him wherever he went.

On April 25 Iowa's Capt. B. M. Littler signed a receipt for the Dakotas transferred to his control: 272 male prisoners, 16 "Indian squaws," and 4 Dakota children.[57] Major Brown, his prison staff, and the Minnesota soldiers returned to St. Paul, relieved of their charges.

Meanwhile, wildly conflicting proposals were being floated regarding the future of the Dakotas held at Fort Snelling. No bureaucrat or politician was willing to accept Chief Wabasha's plea that the "friendly" surrendered Dakotas be permitted to remain in Minnesota. At the other extreme, responsible officials rejected the outlandish plan to evict all Minnesota Indians—Dakotas, Ojibwes, and Winnebagoes—to live or die in an isolated "penal colony" on Isle Royale, far from Minnesota's shores in icy cold Lake Superior.[58]

The Dakota Indian agent, Thomas Galbraith, favored the creation of a new reservation just beyond Minnesota's western boundary, in a "healthful" region dotted with small lakes called Coteau des Prairie. At the recommendation of the Office of Indian Affairs, Lincoln accepted a relocation site farther west, along the Missouri River within one hundred miles of Fort Randall. The president's advisers assured him that lands could be located in that vicinity with "an abundance of timber for all useful purposes, with rich and productive soil, easy of cultivation, and where they [the Dakotas] can . . . live happily."[59]

In the first week of May most of the Dakota men, women, and children who had survived the winter in the Fort Snelling stockade were crammed onto two steamships, the *Northerner* and the *Hannibal*, to begin their journey to their new home on the Missouri River. No roster of deportees was prepared, but it is virtually certain that Godfrey's wife and son were among those transported from their Minnesota home. The *Northerner* had come to the state with a cargo of mules and former slaves, all apparently destined for service as teamsters to assist Sibley and his forces in their planned expeditions against the still-hostile Dakotas. The *St. Paul Pioneer and Democrat* offered its comment on this historic diaspora of the state's original residents and the simultaneous substantial addition to Minnesota's black population: "CONTRABANDS—MULES.—The Northerner brought up a cargo of 125 niggers and 150 mules on Government account. It takes back some eight or nine hundred Indians. We doubt very much whether we benefit by the exchange. If we had our choice we would send both niggers and Indians to Massachusetts, and keep the mules here."[60] The mention of Massachusetts indirectly reminded readers of a tongue-in-cheek petition, signed by more than three thousand Minnesotans, to relocate the Dakotas to Boston Common in retaliation for the Bay State's opposition to wholesale Indian hangings. This racist desire to rid Minnesota of former slaves applied with equal force to Godfrey.[61]

A total of 1,310 Dakotas from the Fort Snelling camp were crowded onto the two steamboats. On their miserable forced transport they were fed a "pitiable diet" of "musty hardtack and briny pork." Ten Dakotas died before the boat reached its destination, Crow Creek, South Dakota, and many others were weakened or sickened by the journey. Within a month of their departure from their homeland, twenty-eight had died. Conditions spiraled downward as it became apparent that the glowing reports of the region as a lush Eden were cruelly mistaken. The risk of wholesale starvation soon loomed.⁶² The Winnebagoes, too, had failed in their efforts to remain in Minnesota. The entire tribe was forcibly removed to a reservation just twenty miles away from Crow Creek, where they were soon plunged into the same grim struggle for existence.⁶³

For the Indian prisoners, Camp McClellan was an improvement on the Mankato jail. Four buildings that had been used as barracks for Civil War recruits were designated as the Indians' new quarters. Not far away, both a military hospital and a camp for Confederate prisoners of war also operated under federal authority.⁶⁴ For a time after their arrival in Iowa, the Dakota prisoners were kept in chains. The daily routine continued as at Mankato. Dakota Presbyterian elder Robert Hopkins Chaska conducted regular Protestant religious services. The Dakota women who were brought with the prisoners prepared meals from fresh beef and corn.⁶⁵

Shortly before the arrival of his pardon papers, David Faribault Jr. served as scribe for a remarkable letter to Sibley that was signed by the leading Dakota inmates. Knowing of Sibley's plans to mount an expedition against Little Crow, the convicted Dakotas volunteered to fight on the white side in that campaign, "willing to die for the white people." Among the fourteen signers of this letter were Wamdetanka (Chief Big Eagle), Marpiyawakanhdi (son of Chief Wabasha), and Anpetuwaxte (son of Chief Red Owl).⁶⁶ Sibley was not about to permit men who had so recently taken up arms against white Minnesotans to switch sides. While almost no one held at Davenport had been found guilty of murder, virtually all had admitted their participation in battles. But Riggs was hopeful that what he termed a "noble letter" would help the future cause of the jailed Dakotas.⁶⁷

On May 11, less than a month after he had arrived in Iowa, David Faribault Jr. was pardoned by Lincoln.⁶⁸ That act of clemency was succinctly reported in one Minnesota newspaper, though without any hint of the dubious part played by Sibley and Fowler in endorsing the pardon plea.⁶⁹ Faribault's departure from Davenport removed the man who was most literate in English from the prisoners' ranks, heightening the chances that the jailers would rely even more on Godfrey for his services as a translator.

Most of the Dakotas held in Iowa were still under sentence of death, simply awaiting a yea or nay from the president as to whether they would ascend the gallows. But it appears that Lincoln, acting without any public notice, had buttressed his desire not to hang any more Dakotas with a legal opinion from his judge advocate general, Joseph Holt. As early as January 1863 Holt had been asked to review the trial transcript of a typical Dakota defendant, Toonwanwakinyachatka (trial 105). The record against this man was virtually indistinguishable from those of most of the other ordinary-soldier defendants. He had been convicted solely on the basis of his own admissions. His trial transcript, in its entirety, read, "I fired one shot at the Fort, and 2 through windows at New Ulm. Fired 3 shots at New Ulm." Holt, after looking at this skimpy trial, promptly reported back to Lincoln on January 20, "This record is altogether too imperfect to justify the Government in carrying out its sentence into execution."[70]

Most likely to avoid inflaming still-angry Minnesotans, Lincoln neither acted on nor made any reference to Holt's recommendations until after the Dakota prisoners were safely ensconced in Iowa. On May 11, the same day he approved Faribault's pardon, the president simply accepted Holt's analysis by adding the words "sentence disapproved" to the Toonwanwakinyachatka case and signing his name. Lincoln's decision was not a pardon, for it neither vacated the conviction nor freed the prisoner.[71] But this test-case review reinforced the president's wish not to hang any more Dakotas.

Since Lincoln had not officially decided whether to free or to execute the Dakotas, he was content to keep the import of his internal review of the workings of Sibley's court confidential. He released only his dry conclusion in the Toonwanwakinyachatka case but made no suggestion that it might apply to anyone else.[72] For all practical purposes, however, commuting Toonwanwakinyachatka's death sentence meant that no more Dakotas would be hanged as long as Lincoln remained in office. For the time being, the other prisoners faced no greater risk of hanging than did Godfrey. But neither they nor their jailers were aware of that fact.

Thomas Williamson, who had worked so ardently behind the scenes on behalf of the Dakota prisoners in 1862, intended to spend the summer of 1863 with the prisoners at Davenport. But the district commander, Gen. Benjamin S. Roberts, was so incensed by Williamson's insistence that the Dakotas were innocent that he banned all white missionaries from the jail. Sibley, who ruefully recalled Williamson's public criticism of his military trials, was not surprised to learn that his outspoken former minister had committed another "indiscretion."[73]

When the more diplomatic Riggs visited Camp McClellan in October 1863, he found that the "very gracious" General Roberts was willing to lift the ban against missionaries. Riggs was immediately granted access to the prison. At that point the general was supporting the pleas of the Indians to fight in the Union army in Missouri. The military had no taste for or expertise in operating an Indian jail, so it continually favored other approaches: sending the prisoners off to fight Confederates, transferring them to a penitentiary, or hanging them forthwith. Riggs endorsed the scheme but it came to naught.[74]

As the incarceration regime loosened, the Dakotas were unchained and they sometimes did prison-related chores, such as hauling water from the river, cutting wood, and cutting hay for animal feed.[75] To earn spending money, the Dakotas made articles to sell to local citizens. Bows and arrows were sold to boys in the town for four bits each; mussel shells gathered from the river were carved into rings, birds, crosses, and other ornaments. Moccasins and beadwork rounded out the Indian product lines. According to Riggs, the prisoners collectively earned as much as ninety dollars a week through these enterprising efforts.[76] As the prison routine relaxed even more, some lightly guarded Dakotas were permitted to go off on deer-hunting expeditions.[77] Their presence in the community sometimes prompted complaints from the populace, though more from unfounded fears than because of any actual wrongdoing.[78]

Visitors to the Indian prison sometimes remarked on Godfrey, and they usually distorted his heritage and deeds: "We saw the half breed negro and Indian who was proved to have slain 16 of our people. We were disposed to give him a wide berth and were disgusted with the petting he received from others. . . . The half breed turned State's evidence and thus saved his neck, thus showing himself a coward as well as a most atrocious scoundrel."[79] The observation of "petting," presumably by the jailers, suggests that Godfrey was still receiving favored treatment at Camp McClellan.

During the three years that Godfrey and the Dakotas were to spend in the Davenport prison, disease proved the biggest risk. By February 1865, 61 of the 272 prisoners had died. Most had suffered from pulmonary diseases, though a smallpox epidemic that swept through the jail in March 1864 claimed thirteen lives.[80]

Disease was even more devastating among the prisoners' families. In addition to the two hundred or more Dakotas who had perished in the Fort Snelling stockade and those who had died during the earlier forced march to the fort, ten more women and children expired on the overcrowded steamboats en route to Crow Creek. During the winter of 1863–64 another two to three hundred Dakotas (once more, mostly women and children) died in the miserable starvation conditions at Crow Creek.[81]

Though some of these totals are approximate, a conservative estimate would place the number of Dakota deaths from late 1862 through early 1864 at more than five to six hundred, exceeding the total of known white deaths during the 1862 war. The fact that most of the postwar Dakota deaths resulted from disease, exposure, starvation, neglect, or mistreatment instead of from intentional killing only marginally alters the relative measure of guilt and responsibility. Sibley, while promising to punish murderers, had pledged to protect the rest of the Indians who surrendered. That promise had not been kept.

One continuing mystery concerning the Dakotas who died at Camp McClellan is where they were buried. Dakota descendants have earnestly sought their gravesites so that any human remains can be repatriated.[82] But, given the macabre disinterment of the bodies of men who were hanged at Mankato or died in the Mankato jail, there is reason to fear that the deceased may have suffered a similar fate in Davenport.

On March 28, 1865, the *Davenport Democrat* carried an exposé offering evidence that the bodies of dead Confederate soldiers from the nearby prisoner-of-war camp had been sold to doctors for use as medical cadavers. One unnamed doctor admitted that a body he was dissecting was "a dead reb he had bought from Rock Island Barracks," and he claimed to know of five other purchases of such bodies. Adding a tragic family dimension to the story, the paper reported, "There are rumors, too, of persons coming here from the south to get the bodies of deceased friends, and, on raising the box which was supposed to contain the body, nothing but a block of wood was to be found therein."

There is no direct evidence that Dakota bodies were sold. But if the bodies of rebel soldiers were secretly bought by doctors, there would seem to be an even greater likelihood that the deceased Dakotas suffered the same illicit treatment. As a result, the search for Dakota remains at Davenport may never fully succeed.

When Godfrey and the Dakotas had been incarcerated for a year and a half, Rev. Thomas Williamson decided to undertake a serious effort to secure pardons for some or all of them. Williamson tackled the task with his usual thoroughness and tenacity. He traveled to Washington with plans to entreat Lincoln personally, but first he did his homework: he tracked down the original Dakota trial transcripts in the Senate's files and read them carefully.[83] He was apparently the last person to review and take notes on those transcripts before they were "lost" for more than four decades. Not until 1909 did historian William Watts Folwell rediscover them.[84]

Williamson learned that Lincoln was amenable to pardoning one-third, or even all, of the imprisoned Dakotas, provided that the Minnesota congressional delegation raised no objections.[85] But no Minnesota politician was willing to stick out his neck on behalf of the Dakotas, so Williamson had to pare down his pardon list to twenty-five names that he personally selected.[86] He apparently employed two standards in deciding which Dakotas should be freed: adherence to the Presbyterian faith and a trial record that showed no aggravated misdeeds in 1862.[87] On April 30, 1864, Lincoln signed what might be called the Presbyterian pardon order, which was handwritten by Williamson himself.[88] Not surprisingly, neither Godfrey nor any of the Catholic mixed-blood inmates were on the list.

To be sure, Williamson's sympathies for the Dakota prisoners never extended to Godfrey. When the *Davenport Gazette* wrote that all of those jailed were "convicted murderers," the minister sprang to their defense with a lengthy, if somewhat overblown, rebuttal letter. "I defy any person to produce evidence from [the trial] records that any Indian now here was a participator in any murder," he thundered. As to Godfrey, he said, "All the Sioux who were convicted of participating in the massacres of Minnesota were executed at Mankato. The mulatto, who had no Indian blood in him, was so convicted, but was spared at the request of the court which tried and sentenced him to be hung."[89]

Williamson somewhat overstated the Dakotas' case, since both Tatemima and Robert Hopkins Chaska had been implicated in murders before Sibley's court and were not hanged.[90] But he was technically correct with respect to Godfrey, who had indeed been found guilty of "participation" in murder. When Williamson later compared notes with Riggs about further prisoner releases, he explicitly recorded his thoughts on Godfrey's future: "I do not feel favorable to the release of Godfrey, but think he ought to be sent to some penitentiary."[91] Overall, Williamson's negative approach presaged Godfrey's later treatment by other strongly pro-Dakota writers who refuse to consider that Godfrey acted under duress and was found by the court to have killed no one. Instead, like Williamson, they vilify the man who had "no Indian blood in him."[92]

Back at the prison, Godfrey served as an interpreter at one of the most publicized events during the Davenport years. In December 1864 Gen. Nathan Baker presented his war trophy, a large "Indian lodge," to Chief Big Eagle, the highest-ranking Dakota in the prison. Baker had seized the huge buffalo-hide tipi during his punitive expedition into Dakota Territory against Dakotas who had not surrendered in 1862. The *Gazette* reported the ceremony, once again distorting Godfrey's lineage and history: "Through an interpreter, a half negro and half Indian, who claims to have murdered sixteen white people in Minnesota, the General made known to the Chief the purpose of his visit. . . . We give a full copy [of Big Eagle's responding speech], 'Ugh, ugh, ugh.'"[93]

By all rights, Big Eagle should not have been jailed in Davenport at the time of this grossly insensitive presentation of a gift derived from the conquest of his kinsmen. Almost two months earlier Lincoln had signed a unique order for his pardon, written in pencil on the back of a note of introduction for a visiting Iowa lawyer and businessman. But the Iowa jailers refused to accept the idea that any president would order the release of a federal prisoner in such an irregular fashion, so Big Eagle stayed in jail until more official paperwork could wend its way to Davenport.[94]

Godfrey was upset that he was left off the pardon lists. He complained during a "long conversation" with a *Chicago Tribune* reporter: "[Godfrey] adverted to the incident of his trial, strenuously denying the charges then made, and complaining bitterly that a chief, 'Big Eagle' and 'Little Crow's' son had been discharged from custody, contending justly that those who were leaders in the terrible massacre were permitted to depart, while the less guilty ones had to still remain in durance vile."[95] One significant kernel to be gleaned from this interview is Godfrey's steadfast denial of his guilt, notwithstanding the many published reports that he was (or claimed to be) a mass murderer.[96]

The only extant letter from Joseph Godfrey was written at Davenport in Dakota by an unknown prison scribe, addressed to Stephen Riggs, dated January 21, 1865.

> Rev. Riggs,
> I am writing you a letter to tell you how I am and I write to tell you what I want. I am recovering from an illness and feel well, as God has taken pity on me and is watching over me. So I'm writing you, my fraternal brother, and hope you are well. I heard from your mouth that God is dependable.
>
> I am a real Indian my brother. I depend on you. You know how they slandered me at Sacred Bank [Chippewa River, or Camp Release]. No one knows of the wickedness but God. I did nothing wrong and I volunteered myself and they heard me about my honesty.
>
> Therefore, my brother, I want you to help me. I am dependable and so my brother I want you to take pity on me. So, my brother, I want to hear quickly from you.

That is all I have to say to you.
> Shake my hand.
> Joseph Godferyye: It is me.[97]

Aside from a short mention of illness, the most interesting part of this letter is Godfrey's characterization of his role in the trials: "I did nothing wrong and I volunteered myself and they heard me about my honesty." Godfrey obviously viewed his state's evidence testimony against the Dakotas as inseparable from his effort to convince the judges that he was telling the truth about his own role in the war. There is no indication that Riggs responded to Godfrey's letter or that he undertook any efforts on his behalf.

By 1865 the prison regimen was so relaxed that Godfrey and the Dakotas had "almost unrestricted liberty."[98] Local racecourse promoters capitalized on the prisoners' new freedom by organizing gimmicky horses-versus-Indians races at a nearby track. Fast-running Dakotas were given stage names like Deerfoot and Fleetwing and were pitted against Chicago thoroughbreds. For a purse of $1,000, the Indians ran a distance of slightly more than four miles while the horses were required to cover eight miles. Shorter races offered prize money of $500 or $100. The *Democrat* reported that a horse won the big-stakes race but an Indian won one of the shorter contests. The *Gazette* chastised the competing newspaper's promotion of these bizarre "man against a brute" spectacles.[99]

Back in Minnesota, during the Davenport prison years only tiny enclaves of the once-powerful Dakota people avoided the forced exodus in 1863, most of them mixed-bloods or "friendly Indians" allied with the Episcopal church, like Taopi. Dakotas were essentially regarded as outlaws in the state. When isolated Dakota raiding parties returned to Minnesota in 1863, panicked state officials offered a bounty for the scalp of any Dakota warrior.[100]

Throughout the summer of 1863 Sibley led an expedition to Dakota Territory that was intended to root out Little Crow and his supporters. Riggs agreed to go along as chief interpreter, despite the opposition of Williamson, who argued that "operating with the white people in this war will make [Riggs] unpopular with the Indians."[101] But while Sibley was wandering ineffectually in the west, Little Crow slipped back into Minnesota with a small band of men. Little Crow was killed in the company of his son, Wowinapa, on July 3, 1863, though the chief's identity was not verified until later, after his emaciated son was captured in Dakota Territory.[102]

While the Dakota prisoners awaited their fate in Davenport, other men who had played key roles in the Dakota War moved into new positions. Governor Ramsey, in 1863, was elected to fill a vacancy in the U.S. Senate. Colonel Miller was elected the same year as the state's fourth governor.[103] In the 1864 election Lincoln again carried Minnesota, though by a narrower margin than in 1860.

Commission recorder Isaac Heard persuaded Harper Brothers to publish his *History of the Sioux War*, copyrighted in 1863 and published in1864. The chapter on Godfrey, which was substantially a reprint of Heard's 1862 letters to the press, exposed a wider audience to his ringing defense of Godfrey. Diplomatically, Heard omitted Sibley's unsuccessful recommendations to hang Godfrey, which meant that the point has gone unnoted in subsequent histories.

When the Civil War ended in the spring of 1865, those advocating for the Dakota prisoners were optimistic that the time was ripe to approach Lincoln again about pardoning the men remaining at Davenport. At the urging of Riggs and Williamson, George E. H. Day, a former Office of Indian Affairs special commissioner, made an appointment to see the president on Saturday, April 15. But John Wilkes Booth effectively canceled that meeting when he shot Lincoln the preceding day.[104] Godfrey and the Dakotas probably spent an extra year in prison as a consequence of the assassination.

By the summer of 1865 even Iowa congressman Hiram Price was pressing for release of the Dakotas from prison. His motives were not humanitarian, however, since he argued mainly that it was a waste of money and resources to keep them in jail: "Sooner or later these Indians must either be executed or liberated."[105]

Serious efforts to release the Dakota prisoners were not rekindled until President Andrew Johnson's administration had been in office for several months. But by then a curious problem had emerged. The authorities wanted to review the 1862 trial transcripts to decide who should be pardoned, but no one in the government remembered where they were. Diligent searches were made by military officials, at the White House, and in the judge advocate's office, but the records were gathering dust, unnoticed, in the files of the Senate. Officials apparently could not even find any of the original lists naming those who were convicted, for they asked the Iowa prison staff to compile a new one. Started from scratch, the January 20, 1866, prison list recorded the names of the remaining 177 prisoners who had not died, been pardoned, or been released when their term expired.[106] "Joseph Godfeyy" was now listed as convict number 170.

One Dakota prisoner would almost surely not have been pardoned had the authorities in Washington known what the missionaries knew: that "Tatankacestinna," number 131 on the 1866 list, had been convicted in 1862 under his birth name, Chaskaydon (trial 121). He had been sentenced to death for shooting a pregnant woman and cutting out her unborn child. After reviewing the evidence in that case, which referred to the single most heinous act of killing described to the military commission, Lincoln had ordered Chaskaydon to be hanged. But Sarah Wakefield's protector had erroneously been executed instead due to his confusingly similar name.[107]

Meanwhile, the same government that couldn't locate its own trial records had taken three years to find a more suitable reservation site than the semiarid Crow Creek.[108] A location in northeastern Nebraska was selected, at the point near the confluence of the Niobrara and Missouri Rivers.

Finally, in the spring of 1866, Godfrey, all of the Dakota inmates, and the sole Winnebago prisoner were unconditionally pardoned by President Johnson.[109] Only this action liberated the hapless inmate Otineyapa (trial 280), who spent three and a half years in prison because a scribe had incorrectly noted his acquittal as a hanging verdict.[110]

Considering the vehemence of Minnesotans' feelings toward the Dakotas in 1862–63, the reaction of the Minnesota press to the pardons was remarkably restrained. The *Mankato Record* briefly reported the news without editorial comment on May 8. Later in the month the *Record* and the *St. Paul Press* both noted the protests of local white residents of Nebraska and Dakota Territories to the plan to create a new reservation in their region for the "hostile Indians" who were "condemned to death for the Minnesota massacres." As long as the potential problems were not in their neighborhood, however, Minnesotans seemed relatively unconcerned about the release of the Dakota prisoners.[111]

In Iowa, the prisoners' departure for Nebraska in April 1866 was noted by the *Davenport Democrat,* which identified by name only "the negro Godfrey.... He goes along as he has been with the tribe since a youth and is married to a squaw."[112] When the transport ship, the *Pembina,* dropped off the pardoned men in St. Louis, Godfrey again uniquely attracted the attention of the press: "A half breed negro is amongst them—the States' evidence gentleman of the party—who is said to be, as his position before the court justifies the surmise, the biggest rascal of the lot."[113] As far as we know, this was the first time Godfrey set foot in a slave state. But he was no longer at risk, for any lingering doubts about his legal status had been erased in December 1865 with the abolition of slavery that had occurred upon ratification of the Thirteenth Amendment to the U.S. Constitution.

In St. Louis, Godfrey and the Dakotas transferred to another steamer, the *Dora,* for the final leg of their journey to Nebraska. They were confined to the lower deck, adjacent to the ship's boiler, a location that was stifling hot by day and uncomfortably cold at night. Under these conditions more and more Dakotas became ill; the sick list rose to thirty-two names before the month-long journey from Davenport ended.[114]

Godfrey himself must have had deeply conflicted feelings when he was released with the Dakotas. On the positive side, he would soon be reunited with his wife and son and would no longer suffer the privations of jail. But he must also have dreaded leaving the protective umbrella of the prison authorities, who had helped keep him alive for three years among many Dakotas who considered him a blackguard.

Godfrey and the Dakotas arrived at Niobrara on May 11, but they had to wait another four weeks before the women and children who had survived Crow Creek came down to join them. After three and a half years and about ninety deaths in the Mankato and Davenport prisons, "many women looked in vain for their husbands."[115] Godfrey was probably overjoyed to learn that both his nine-year-old son and Takanheca were still alive. But the toll on his marriage might have been even greater than that experienced by other prisoners who had been separated from their spouses for almost four years. Godfrey had pointed the finger of accusation that led to the execution of Takanheca's father in 1862. In consequence, it appears that Godfrey never again lived with Takanheca.[116]

NOTES ON CHAPTER 11

1. Miller to Olin, December 28, 1862, NA, RG 393, Dist. of MN, 1862–63, E346, pt. 3, LR.
2. Sibley insisted on consulting with Pope before ordering even "necessary clothing and medicine." Sibley to Selfridge, December 30, 1863, NA, RG 393, Dist. of MN, E343, pt. 3, Letters and Telegrams Sent.
3. Letters between Pope and Halleck document the former's repeated attempts to transfer control of (and financial responsibility for) the Dakotas back to the Interior Department. But Interior adamantly refused all such pleas. See Pope to Kelton (Halleck's assistant adjutant general), February 18, 1863, Halleck to Pope, March 23, 1863, and Pope to Kelton, March 30, 1863, in *War of the Rebellion*, 22:117, 176, and 186, respectively.
4. Olin to Miller, January 8, 1863, NA, RG 393, Dist. of MN, E343, pt. 3, Letters and Telegrams Sent. Sibley's letter to Pope noted the "anomalous position" of providing clothes to condemned men. Sibley to Selfridge, December 30, 1862, ibid. Miller apparently requisitioned clothing for the prisoners, which occasioned another admonition that only "*absolutely* necessary" garments should be provided: "All needless expense will be avoided." Olin to Marshall, February 6, 1863, ibid. *(emphasis in original)*. A similar line was drawn regarding food for the prisoners. Sibley instructed Miller to feed them "sufficiently, but not luxuriously." Miller, in his discretion, was permitted to feed the inmates less than the rations of white soldiers, but "in no case" more. Olin to Miller, March 10, 1863, ibid.
5. Sibley to Selfridge, telegram, November 29, 1862, NA, RG 393, E3450, pt. 1, Telegrams Received, Department of NW; Selfridge to Sibley, November 29, 1862, NA, RG 393, Dist. of MN, Dept. of War, 1862–66, E347, pt. 3, Telegrams Received.
6. Sibley to Lincoln, February 16, 1863, Lincoln Papers, Library of Congress, microfilm roll 49.
7. Crooks to Sibley, NA, RG 393, Dept. of NW, 1862–65, Headquarters, E3449, pt. 1, Unentered Letters.
8. See Olin to Crooks, January 6, 1863 (to jail Wakkeintawa, Taxwinkamaya, Wahinkpe, and Wakinyanwashtay), and Olin to Crooks, January 24, 1863 (to release Taopi), NA, RG 393, Dist. of MN, E343, pt. 3, Letters and Telegrams Sent. Taopi was also the subject of a written complaint sent to Sibley by four women (Mrs. L. Pettijohn, Mrs. A. Prescott, Miss J. Prescott, and Miss S. Prescott), who reported that Taopi had kicked the headless body of Philander Prescott. See Pettijohn et al. to Sibley, January 7, 1863, NA, RG 94, E173, Indian Prisoners. Sibley reported the results of his investigation of Taopi in his own handwriting: "Brig. Genl. S[ibley] made a visit to Fort Snelling on 10th inst. to investigate charges against Taopi—and other Indians. White Dog's wife, Wabasha and others were questioned and all stated that they did not know of Taopi having done any thing wrong. . . . [N]o one knew that he had committed any crime against the whites." Ibid.
9. Pond, *Dakota or Sioux in Minnesota*, 69–70.
10. Whipple, "The Bishop's Address [at Taopi's Funeral]," *Passion Week*, 1869, quoted in Welsh, *Taopi and His Friends*, 53.

11. Santee Episcopal Mission Baptismal Register, 1843–1904, 96–97, CWS; copy furnished to me by Godfrey descendant Delores Espinoza. This record is apparently based on Godfrey's later reporting of his baptism, which is listed as having taken place in Mendota in 1863. Since Godfrey was never in Mendota that year, it seems most likely that he was baptized by Ravoux during the winter of 1862–63 at the Mankato prison. No official entry of Godfrey's baptism has been found in the records of the Catholic Church in Minnesota.
12. By January 1863 Ravoux was back in Mendota, where he baptized a significant number of Dakotas at the Fort Snelling camp. Church of St. Peter, Mendota, parish registers, MHS, M263.
13. Comments by Riggs's wife, Mary Riggs, reflect the anti-Catholic attitudes among the Protestant missionaries. See, for example, her March 22, 1839, letter contrasting the Catholics' tendency to "flatter a proud and ambitious heart" with the Protestants' "simple truths of the Gospel" and her later reference to the "dark designs of Romanish priests." M. Riggs, *Bit of Bread and Butter,* 92, 143.
14. *Faribault Central Republican,* January 7, 1863. The *New York Post,* December 5, 1862, had sounded a similar theme, arguing that Sibley could have killed all three hundred men "at the moment, in hot blood" but that "no President could hang more than 300 men," adding, "It is a pity that [Lincoln] had the opportunity to interfere."
15. Swisshelm, letter from Washington, February 23, 1863, published in *St. Cloud Democrat,* March 5, 1863.
16. *St. Cloud Democrat,* April 2, 1863.
17. *St. Paul Press,* January 11, 1863.
18. Whipple to Sibley, March 7, 1863, Whipple Papers, MHS, box 40. Whipple expressed similar sentiments in a letter to the Interior Department, April 21, 1863, ibid.
19. Sibley to Whipple (marked "private"), March 11, 1863, Whipple Papers, MHS, box 3.
20. Executive Clemency Documents of David Faribault Jr., MS Collection 164, Southern Minnesota Historical Center, Minnesota State University, Mankato, from original records at NA, RG 153, Records of the Office of the Judge Advocate General (Army), Shakopee, NN3132.
21. Fowler, a lieutenant colonel in the state militia at the time of the trials, signed almost all of the charges against the Dakotas, and thus his name appears in virtually every trial transcript. He served as Sibley's assistant adjutant at Camp Release. See Dakota Trials Records.
22. Executive Clemency Documents of David Faribault Jr., MS Collection 164, Southern Minnesota Historical Center, Minnesota State University, Mankato, from original records at NA, RG 153, Records of the Office of the Judge Advocate General (Army), Shakopee, NN3132.
23. Ibid.
24. Emilie Fowler affidavit, #231, Scrip Rolls.
25. The Faribault petition is demonstrably false in other respects. In an effort to exaggerate his son's whiteness, David Faribault Sr. put forth his mixed-blood wife as the mother of David Jr. In reality she was his second wife; his first wife, a full-Dakota woman, was David's mother. Fowler offered the same deception more explicitly, claiming that David Faribault Jr. was only one-fourth Dakota. In fact, David Faribault Sr. knew that his son was five-eighths Dakota and had signed an earlier affidavit indicating that David Jr.'s mother was a full-blood Mdewakanton Dakota. See David Faribault [Sr.] affidavit, #229, Scrip Rolls.

26. Takanheca is not on any of the Fort Snelling census lists, which named only heads of families. She most likely stayed in her mother's tipi. The account of the death of the Godfreys' daughter at Fort Snelling and the record of the baptism of their son prove Takanheca's presence at Fort Snelling.
27. See *St. Paul Daily Union,* December 22, 1862. This article reports the acute suffering of some of the impoverished white widows rendered homeless during the war, including my great-great-grandmother, Pauline Dietrich. The widows, with their young children, struggled to survive on limited relief allowances in St. Paul cellars and attics. At the time the article was written, many of the children had measles and one had recently died from the disease.
28. The sole reference to Godfrey's daughter is found in the 1912 deposition of Henry Trudell, Godfrey heirship file. For an excellent discussion of the measles epidemic and medical conditions at the Fort Snelling internment camp, see Monjeau-Marz, *Dakota Indian Internment,* 54–57.
29. Thomas Williamson to Walter Griffith, April 10, 1863, NMM, MHS, box 21.
30. Riggs to Treat, March 26, 1863, NMM, MHS, box 21.
31. Williamson to Griffith, April 10, 1863, NMM, MHS, box 21.
32. *Mankato Weekly Record,* March 28, 1863.
33. Thomas Williamson et al. to J. P. Usher, September 8, 1864, in *Report of the Secretary of the Interior 1864,* 564–66: "Except a few who call themselves Roman Catholics, all who survive of the prisoners taken to Davenport in 1863 belong to the Episcopal or the Presbyterian Church."
34. John Williamson to Thomas Williamson, April 6, 1863, Thomas Williamson Papers, MHS.
35. Santee Episcopal Mission Baptismal Register, 1843–1904, pp. 96–97, CWS.
36. *St. Paul Pioneer and Democrat,* March 13, 1863; Riggs to Treat, March 10, 1863, NMM, MHS, box 21.
37. *St. Paul Pioneer and Democrat,* March 13, 1863; Riggs to Treat, March 10, 1863, NMM, MHS, box 21.
38. Riggs to Treat, March 10, 1863, NMM, MHS, box 21.
39. Many prisoner letters written in the Dakota language still exist, and I was invited to speak at symposium held in 2005 that offered translations and discussion of some of them. Dakota Letters Symposium, Sisseton Wahpeton College, Sisseton, SD, July 25–28, 2005.
40. *Mankato Weekly Record,* February 28, 1863.
41. The length of Good Thunder's incarceration at the fort is unknown, but he was never charged or tried. Ironically, there is historical evidence that supports the charges made against him in January 1863 by Chief Wabasha. Both Big Eagle and George Quinn later told of Good Thunder's active participation in military battles, and Quinn specifically corroborated Good Thunder's theft of a horse at Fort Ridgely. See Anderson and Woolworth, *Through Dakota Eyes,* 148, 157.
42. No modern history refers to these April 1863 trials; they were evidently unknown to Folwell, a main source for later historians. The trial transcripts are located at NA, RG 393, Dept. of NW, 1862–65, Headquarters, E3449, pt. 1, Unentered Letters.

43. See S. Riggs, *Tah-koo wah-kan*, 321–22, 333–40. Riggs's change of heart about the trials is also obvious from the altered tenor of his correspondence before and after the April 1863 trials. In March Riggs was still defending the 1862 trial verdicts, with few exceptions. Contrasting his views with those expressed by Thomas Williamson and Gideon Pond, Riggs said, "[M]y point of observation is different from theirs, and my convictions are different also. I could not but feel that there were many bloody hands there [among the convicted Dakotas]." Riggs to Treat, March 26, 1863, NMM, MHS, box 21. Riggs expressed a different view in a May letter: "Many of those men at Davenport were unjustly condemned by the military commission last fall. I felt that it was so then." Riggs to Alfred Riggs, May 12, 1863, Oahe Mission Collection, CWS, box 3. Though Riggs linked his change of opinion to his observation of the fairer 1863 trials, he was less than candid, both in this letter and later, about his earlier support for almost all of the 1862 trial verdicts.
44. Wiyakamani, the only defendant convicted in the April trials, was sentenced to death based on the testimony of a Dakota woman, Hapan. Wiyakamani had not been accused by either Riggs or Wabasha. He was apparently arrested when Hapan told "some half-breeds" that she had seen Wiyakamani kill a white woman. See transcript of testimony, NA, RG 393, Dept. of NW, 1862–65, Headquarters, E3449, pt. 1, Unentered Letters.
45. See trial 21, Dakota Trials Records.
46. Spencer apparently procured the publication of a newspaper article strongly praising Chaska that appeared the day before his trial. *St. Paul Weekly Pioneer and Democrat*, April 17, 1863.
47. *Mankato Independent*, February 27, 1863.
48. *St. Peter Tribune*, March 7, 1863.
49. *St. Paul Press*, April 3, 1863, reprinting a story from the *Mankato Record*.
50. Riggs to Thomas Williamson, April 13, 1863, Oahe Mission Collection, CWS, box 3.
51. For Washechoonna (trial 332), see discussion of hanging mistakes in chapter 10. Both the prison records and the missionary lists mistakenly recorded a hanging verdict for Otineyapa (trial 280). See Mankato prison list, December 31, 1862, NA, RG 393, Dist. of MN, 1862–63, E346, pt. 3, LR; and Mankato prison list, January 12, 1863, Dakota Trials Records, microfilm roll 1. For the 1865 missionary list, see Riggs Family Papers, MHS, box 1.
52. *Mankato Independent*, April 24, 1863.
53. *Davenport (IA) Democrat*, April 27, 1863; *St. Paul Pioneer and Democrat*, May 1, 1863 (forty-eight acquitted men left the steamer at Fort Snelling).
54. *Davenport (IA) Democrat*, April 27, 1863. I am indebted to John LaBatte, who furnished me with a copy of this article.
55. *St. Paul Press*, May 3, 1863.
56. *Davenport (IA) Democrat*, April 27, 1863.
57. Littler receipt, April 25, 1863, NA, RG 393, Dist. of MN, 1862–63, E346, pt. 3, LR.
58. See the proposal of pamphleteer James W. Taylor in *St. Paul Press*, October 24, 1862.

59. Commissioner of Indian Affairs William P. Dole to A. D. Balcombe, April 10, 1863, in *Report of Commissioner of Indian Affairs for 1863*, 305–7. The secretary of the interior, J. P. Usher, acknowledged the "inhumanity" of keeping the Dakotas at Fort Snelling and expressed his conviction that the Fort Randall region of Dakota Territory was, based on the "flattering" reports, a "remarkably good" site for a new Indian reservation. Usher to Doolittle, January 15, 1863, NA, RG 48, LS, Indian Division, Dept. of the Interior, M606, roll 4. These letters show that top administration officials fully intended to place the Dakotas and Winnebagoes in a favorable new environment. While the Indians paid a severe price for the reliance on incorrect reports, suggestions that an arid and forlorn place was selected as a punitive measure are not borne out by the official correspondence.
60. *St. Paul Pioneer and Democrat*, May 8, 1863.
61. *St. Paul Pioneer and Democrat*, January 16, 1863.
62. Barton, *John P. Williamson*, 72–78; John P. Williamson to Riggs, June 9, 1863, Williamson Collection, Dakotah Prairie Museum, Aberdeen, SD.
63. Carley, *Dakota War of 1862*, 76–80.
64. *Davenport (IA) Democrat*, April 27, 1863. See also *Davenport (IA) Democrat*, March 28, 1865 (Confederate prisoner-of-war camp), and *Davenport (IA) Gazette*, March 6, 1866 (hospital buildings).
65. *Davenport (IA) Democrat*, April 27, 1863.
66. The Dakota-language letter, dated May 18, 1863, is found in NA, RG 94, E173, Indian Prisoners. Riggs summarized and commented on the letter in Riggs to Treat, May 27, 1863, NMM, MHS, box 21.
67. Riggs to Treat, May 27, 1863, NMM, MHS, box 21.
68. See Executive Clemency Documents of David Faribault Jr., MS Collection 164, Southern Minnesota Historical Center, Minnesota State University, Mankato, from original records at NA, RG 153, Records of the Office of the Judge Advocate General (Army), Shakopee, NN3132.
69. *St. Paul Pioneer and Democrat*, June 5, 1863.
70. I found a typewritten version of the trial, Holt's review, and Lincoln's order regarding Toonwanwakinyachatka in the files of Alan Woolworth, MHS. It was apparently copied from a National Archives file that I have not yet located. Holt's review explains why the transcript of trial 105 is missing from the microfilm of the 1862 trials: it was not returned to the trial records that Lincoln sent to the Senate.
71. One scholar suggests that Lincoln issued a pardon in trial 105. Chomsky, "United States–Dakota War Trials," 39. But the president was very precise in limiting his decision to disapproval of the sentence: the death penalty. He issued no order for the prisoner's release. Proof of this interpretation comes from a list of Dakota prisoners still held in Iowa in 1865, prepared under the supervision of Thomas Williamson. "Tonwanwakinyan," identified as defendant 105, was still being held at that time. See handwritten list of prisoners, Riggs Family Papers, MHS, box 1.
72. Lincoln's decision in the Toonwanwakinyachatka case was briefly reported in the *St. Paul Pioneer and Democrat*, June 5, 1863, though the newspaper made no mention of the broader significance of the case.
73. Riggs to Alfred Riggs, May 12 and August 20, 1863, and Riggs to Mary Riggs, August 20, 1863, Oahe Mission Collection, CWS, box 3; Roberts to Meline, August 22, 1863, NA, RG 393, E3436, pt. 1, LS, Letters Sent and Received, Department of NW, Headquarters, in which Roberts claims that Williamson was "teaching these convicts falsely, and indoctrinating them with ideas that they are not guilty."

74. Riggs to Treat, November 7, 1863, NMM, MHS, box 21 (General Roberts had rescinded his order . . . before I reached here); Riggs to "Home," October 27, 1863 (Roberts is "very gracious indeed"), Riggs to Mary Riggs, October 27, 1863 (Indians fighting in Union army), and Riggs to Thomas Williamson, November 11, 1863 (should be sent to penitentiary if not used as soldiers), Oahe Mission Collection, CWS, box 3; and Williamson to Riggs, August 18, 1863, Riggs Family Papers, MHS, box 1 (desire to hang all prisoners).
75. S. Riggs, *Tah-koo wah-kan,* 370–71.
76. *Davenport (IA) Gazette,* June 23, 1865 (bows and arrows); S. Riggs, *Tah-koo wah-kan,* 372.
77. S. Riggs, *Tah-koo wah-kan,* 371.
78. See, for example, the complaint registered in the *Davenport (IA) Democrat,* March 20, 1865, which was followed by a ringing defense of the prisoners by the prison guards, reported in the same paper March 22, 1865.
79. *Davenport (IA) Democrat,* December 11, 1863, as published in Temple, *Camp McClellan during the Civil War,* 34–35.
80. The most reliable record of prison deaths appears to be a handwritten record prepared in about February 1865 by Thomas Williamson. See "Names of Dakota who have died at Camp McClellan near Davenport," mistakenly dated 1863, Riggs Family Papers, MHS, box 1. See also *Davenport (IA) Gazette,* April 11, 1866, reporting that most Dakotas who died at Davenport had suffered from "lung diseases."
81. Hyman, "Survival at Crow Creek," 153.
82. The repatriation of Dakota remains from the Davenport prison site is still a pressing issue in the Dakota community.
83. It appears that Williamson even made his own handwritten notations on some of the original records. When I reviewed the original files in Washington, I noted the doctor's distinctive scrawl, in pencil, mainly indicating the deaths of some of the Dakotas on their trial records. These faintly written comments are not legible on the National Archives microfilm of the trial records. Williamson was apparently the only person to make notations on the original files other than those who acted in an official capacity.
84. Williamson's notes made while reviewing the trial transcripts have not been found. For the rediscovery of the transcripts by Folwell in 1909, see "Accessions," *Minnesota History* 8 (1927): 299–300.
85. In a contemporaneous letter to Riggs, Williamson reported that Lincoln was willing to release one-third of the prisoners; later he claimed that the president would have released all of them but for the objections of Minnesota politicians. See Williamson to Riggs, April 7, 1864, and January 12, 1865, Riggs Family Papers, MHS, boxes 1 and 2, respectively.
86. Williamson met with Ramsey, who had been elected to the Senate, as well as with Representative William Windom and Senator Morton Wilkinson. He could not procure a pardon endorsement from any of them. See Williamson to Riggs, April 7, 1864, Riggs Family Papers, MHS, box 1.
87. Williamson later told Riggs that his notes on the trials reflected the "relative innocence" of the defendants, indicating the likelihood that he used such a standard. See Williamson to Riggs, January 12, 1865, Riggs Family Papers, MHS, box 2.
88. The pardon order is published in Basler, *Collected Works of Abraham Lincoln,* 7:325–26. The order in Williamson's handwriting is found in the Robert Todd Lincoln Papers, MHS.
89. *Davenport (IA) Gazette,* March 22, 1865.

90. There is little doubt that Williamson himself was convinced of the innocence of these two men, but the court had not been as charitably inclined toward them.
91. Williamson to Riggs, February 10, 1865, Riggs Family Papers, MHS, box 2.
92. Dakota elder and scholar Elden Lawrence, for example, contends that Godfrey was more deserving of being hanged than any of the men executed at Mankato. Lawrence, *Peace Seekers*, 134, 138.
93. *Davenport (IA) Gazette*, December 9, 1864, quoted in Temple, *Camp McClellan during the Civil War*, 38–39.
94. George S. C. Dow to Lincoln, November 14 and 20, 1864, Lincoln Papers, Library of Congress, available at http://memory.loc.gov/ammem/alhtml/malhome.html. See also the formal order for Big Eagle's pardon, December 24, 1864, NA, RG 94, E173, Indian Prisoners. It appears that the chief was released in early 1865.
95. *Chicago Tribune*, October 16, 1865, as reported in *Davenport (IA) Gazette*, October 23, 1865. Little Crow's son, who had been arrested in 1863 and tried, had been released sometime prior to Godfrey's interview.
96. See, for example, an earlier article in the same newspaper that said that Godfrey "claims to have murdered sixteen white people in Minnesota." *Davenport (IA) Gazette*, December 9, 1864.
97. Godfrey to Riggs, January 21, 1865, Riggs Family Papers, MHS, box 2. I am indebted to Louis Garcia, Fort Totten, ND, for translating this letter. The two-page letter, written in a neat and legible hand, has been punctuated and organized into paragraphs here.
98. *Chicago Tribune*, October 16, 1865, as reported in *Davenport (IA) Gazette*, October 23, 1865.
99. The horse-versus-Indian races are reported in the *Davenport (IA) Democrat*, October 16 and 21, 1865. Criticism of the races is found in the *Davenport (IA) Gazette*, October 18 and 21, 1865. Though it is tempting to look at the races as a purely racist promotion, the *Democrat* reported that fleet-footed white men also were part of the competition. Still, the promoters obviously played up the unusual fact that Indians would be running against horses. The *Democrat* headlined its story "Indian Races" (October 16).
100. *St. Paul Press*, July 22, 1863 (twenty-five dollar bounty for Dakota scalps); and *St. Peter Tribune*, July 27, 1863 (seventy-five dollars for killing any "hostile Sioux warrior"). The amount was later increased.
101. Riggs to Alfred Riggs, May 12, 1863, Oahe Mission Collection, CWS, box 3; Riggs to Treat, May 12, 1863, NMM, MHS, box 21.
102. Carley, *Dakota War of 1862*, 83–86.
103. Folwell, *History of Minnesota*, 2:333–38.
104. See Day to Riggs, October 27, 1865, Riggs Family Papers, MHS, box 2. Though Day's recollection was undoubtedly correct about the sequence of events, he mistakenly placed Lincoln's death one day earlier than it occurred. The president was shot on Friday, April 14, and died the following day. Thus Lincoln expired on the very day of a scheduled meeting that might have led to the Dakotas' pardon.
105. Price to Stanton, July 8, 1865, NA, LR, Adj. Gen., M619, roll 483.

106. The comedy of errors in connection with the "loss" of the trial transcripts is best documented in NA, RG 94, LR, Adjutant General, M619, roll 483. To the unending consternation of later researchers and Dakota descendants, the spellings of Indian names on the 1866 pardon list were so garbled that most of them cannot be matched with the original trial records or with the missionary lists. Moreover, an entirely new numbering system was used, since the jailers no longer had the original trial numbers. It is thus a difficult process to determine precisely which convicted Dakotas survived the Davenport prison experience or to link descendants with their ancestors who were tried.
107. On the hanging mistakes, see chapter 10, notes 53 and 54.
108. For a detailed account of the woeful story of Crow Creek, see Hyman, "Survival at Crow Creek."
109. See Day to Riggs, April 5, 1866, Riggs Family Papers, MHS, box 2; and *Davenport (IA) Gazette,* April 11, 1866. The actual pardon order has not been found. The Winnebago prisoner was identified on the 1865 missionary list as Magasan, and that was the name under which he was released.
110. Neither the jailers nor the missionaries detected Otineyapa's mistaken imprisonment, nor has it been noted in any history. "Ofiniyapa" was listed as prisoner no. 107 on the 1866 pardon list, NA, RG 94, LR, Adjutant General, M619, roll 483.
111. *Mankato Record,* May 8 and 26, 1866; *St. Paul Press,* May 19, 1866.
112. *Davenport (IA) Gazette,* April 11, 1866.
113. *St. Louis Democrat,* April 14, 1866, as reprinted in the *Mankato Weekly Record,* April 28, 1866.
114. The two-ship journey from Davenport to Niobrara is recorded in two official reports: E. Killpatrick to D. Cooley, May 19, 1866 (Davenport to St. Joseph), and Jedediah Brown to James Harlan, June 30, 1866 (St. Joseph to Niobrara), NA, M574, roll 66, file no. 235 (Indians from Davenport).
115. ABCFM Report, September 1866, NMM, MHS, box 21.
116. No document records the scene of Godfrey's reunion with his wife and son, but Joseph Godfrey, Jr. later gave testimony that his father's second marriage (discussed in chapter 12) took place not long after the Dakota survivors arrived at Santee. That evidence strongly suggests that Godfrey and Takanheca's marriage ended while he was in prison or shortly after his release.

CHAPTER 12

Life and Death at Santee

To revenge-minded Minnesotans who had predicted in 1862 that freeing the imprisoned Dakotas would result in renewed hostilities, life on the Santee Sioux Reservation from 1866 until 1900 offered a powerful rebuttal. The reservation, according to historian Roy W. Meyer, was "remarkably placid" throughout those decades.[1] The pardoned men never revived antiwhite animosities or presented any threat to their neighbors. Indeed, one of their longest-serving agents viewed them as a strategic barrier "against the incursions of the wilder Sioux." Far from taking up arms against the whites, in 1874 forty Dakotas from the reservation signed up to serve as scouts for George Armstrong Custer's first Black Hills expedition, two years before Custer's last stand.[2]

Not coincidentally, the religious flames that had been ignited in the Mankato and Davenport jails continued to burn, with the active encouragement of Protestant missions on the reservation. The Santee mission schools turned out so many Dakota ministers that some were exported to serve, in the words of one Dakota-drafted petition, as "missionaries to the wild Indian tribes."[3]

Economically, the picture was not as bright. The transition to a self-sufficient agricultural society was fraught with difficulties; for many years, very few Indians were able to support themselves by farming without government assistance. Some achieved a degree of financial independence

Map 3. Minnesota and the Santee Reservation, 1866. Courtesy of the Pond Dakota Heritage Society.

by taking up trades, such as carpentry, blacksmithing, and sawmilling. Others earned money by working on various reservation projects.[4]

Just as Godfrey had been singled out in prison to serve as a cook and interpreter, he was almost immediately hired by the Santee Indian agent for some of the scarce jobs on the reservation. In November 1866 Godfrey commenced work as a laborer, earning sixteen dollars per month. His skill in handling teams of horses and wagons soon enabled him to earn more income than most of his Dakota neighbors. During the summer of

1867 Godfrey was "driving a team . . . , hauling wood . . . , and [doing] other necessary work," for which he received wages of forty-eight dollars in three months.[5] His performance must have been satisfactory, for his pay rose dramatically in the next few years. During parts of 1869 to 1871 he earned lucrative wages by local standards (apparently the same as those paid to white agency employees) of forty-five dollars per month for his services as a hostler, teamster, and laborer.[6]

After the breakup of Godfrey's marriage to Takanheca in 1866, he soon found and married his second wife, Icazontewin, a full-Dakota woman who was enrolled as a Santee tribal member. She was recorded in the 1885 and later Santee census lists by her English name, Emma Godfrey, wife of Joseph. Emma was eight years younger than Godfrey and had had at least one child, John Smith, from a previous marriage. She and Godfrey had no children. We do not know whether Godfrey's son remained with Takanheca or lived with his father during Godfrey's first years on the reservation, but it is likely that Joseph Jr. moved in with his father and stepmother after Takanheca's death in 1873.[7]

While surely boosting his living standards, Godfrey's agency employment was not sufficiently reliable to support his family in the long run. His prosperity ultimately depended, as it did for the Dakotas as a group, upon establishing himself as a farmer. As had their Minnesota counterparts, the Indian agents assigned to the reservation pushed the development of agriculture as their highest priority. To create conditions that were conducive to stable, long-term farming, they sought to formalize the reservation boundaries. But they were impeded for at least three years because they had no assurance that the executive order tentatively setting aside the Nebraska land for a reservation would not be revoked, uprooting the tribe yet again.[8]

Things began to stabilize when the Treaty of Fort Laramie was signed in 1868, providing for allotments of land on the reservation to individual Dakotas. The next year reservation boundaries were drawn. The reservation abutted the Missouri River on the north and extended southward for an average of fifteen miles; it stretched twelve miles from east to west.[9]

From an agricultural standpoint the lands to be allotted were extremely variable, ranging from semiarid bluffs to lush parcels in valleys adjoining the numerous creeks.[10] The selection of allotments began informally in 1870 and was finalized two years later. From Godfrey's perspective, the most important single step in securing his future among the Dakotas was his inclusion on the 1872 formal "list of names of members of the tribe of Santee Sioux Indians entitled" to land allotments. That year he was assigned an eighty-acre parcel in Township 32 (later called Union Township). Godfrey's allotment was identified as number 57, with his "Indian Name" dutifully recorded as Kasa and his "English Name" as Joseph Godfrey.[11]

Whether due to luck or his prudence in selecting it, Godfrey's land allotment proved to be one of the better properties on the reservation, both as a home and for purposes of farming. It was centrally located, about six miles south of Santee Village and about five miles east of Niobrara, the closest white town. Lost Creek meandered through the property, providing fresh water. The main Santee to Niobrara road, following the creek, also bisected the Godfrey farmstead. Carl Crosley, an enrolled Santee member who bought the farm from the Godfrey family in about 1960, described it as "ideal land," part of which is still suitable for growing corn and part (low-lying and with water) for pasturing cows.[12]

The year after Godfrey's allotment was approved, the Santee agent, Joseph Webster, had to decide which of the ninety-two Dakotas who had been assigned farms would receive livestock. The essential test, as Webster described it, was whether a landholder was "capable of taking care of stock without expense to the government." In June 1873 Webster submitted a list of forty-eight men, all "members of the tribe of Santee Sioux Indians," who were qualified under the terms of the Fort Laramie treaty to be furnished with sheep or "working" cattle (oxen for plowing, apparently). Godfrey was included on this list.[13] He thus was well along the road to being integrated into the nascent Santee farming community.

One enduring mystery, however, is why Godfrey was included as a "member of the tribe" when valuable reservation allotments and other entitlements were distributed. After all, he had no Dakota blood, a condition that had precluded him from receiving annuities in Minnesota. The most likely explanation is that he was counted as a member due his marriage to a full-blood Dakota woman (Icazontewin), his mixed-blood Dakota minor son, his fluency in the language, and his adoption of Dakota customs.

To supplement the income generated by farming, regular food rations were distributed to all tribal members. When Quaker Isaiah Lightner began his eight-year term as Santee Indian agent in 1877, he faced a debate over the future of such rations in the context of a population that was moving toward agricultural self-sufficiency. In a dialogue quite similar to modern discussions of the pros and cons of welfare, the authorities in Washington and Lightner struggled to find a way to distribute rations to the truly needy without penalizing the industrious. Washington sometimes wanted the agent to discontinue distributions to the most prosperous Dakotas, but Lightner saw this policy as rewarding the "bad" or "lazy." Instead, he threatened to cut off rations to those who refused to move toward self-sufficiency, thereby "inflicting punishment" on them.[14] This policy was a spin on the Indian agency's decisions about treaty annuities that had provoked the 1862 war, but this time it led to no unrest. (The different reactions were understandable, given that the 1863 abrogation of the Dakotas' treaty rights eliminated claims of entitlement.)

By 1878 Godfrey had accumulated an above-average menagerie of domestic animals on his farm, which Lightner duly inventoried in a report to Washington: "2 cattle; 1 cat, 1 cow, 1 dog, 2 oxen, 2 ponies." Lightner reminded his superiors that canines, too, were livestock: "For a change, they eat the dogs, considering their flesh quite a delicacy."[15] In 1880 Lightner, following orders from Washington, compiled two lists of Dakotas. List A named those who "can do considerable towards supporting themselves," and List B identified those "who will not be able to support themselves." Lightner did not want to eliminate all food rations to members of the more prosperous group; he asked for authority to make distributions to them every two to four weeks, at his discretion. Godfrey's name appeared on List A.[16]

But Godfrey's status as a full-fledged member of the reservation community did not translate into acceptance by the Dakotas. For as long as he lived, most of the Indians regarded Godfrey with scorn. To what extent these feelings were motivated by his 1862 testimony and to what degree they were prompted by racist feelings toward possibly the only black man on the reservation is difficult to determine. A toxic mixture of prejudice and vengefulness evidently rendered him a virtual outcast.[17] Godfrey was actively shunned by some Dakotas. Santee tribal member Cornelia Frazier recalled being driven as a young girl in her family's horse-drawn wagon along Lost Creek through the Godfrey farm. Her mother, spotting Godfrey, instructed her, "Don't look at him. He's a bad man."[18] Another Dakota woman always spat to the side in disgust when telling her relatives about Godfrey.[19]

Nor was the Dakotas' conduct limited to insults and snubs. Minnesota historian Thomas Hughes said, "The negro Godfrey, who had turned state's evidence . . . was shot at several times by the Indians who always believed that he swore away the lives of several of their relatives."[20] George Rouillard, a Santee tribal member, recalled that Godfrey "lived on a farm . . . and never sat at the window of his house—not even when eating. Afraid that somebody would take a potshot at him, Godfrey always lived in a corner."[21]

The Santee Sioux Reservation formalized and expanded the allotment of lands to its enrolled members in 1885, two years before the passage of the Dawes Act extended quasi-homestead land ownership to most Indians throughout the western reservations. Godfrey was issued a full quarter-section allotment, a parcel that included his original eighty acres as well as another eighty acres to the west. He then received title to this 160-acre parcel, though he and the Dakotas were prevented by law from selling their allotments for a period of twenty-five years. In the interim the federal government held the title to the land in trust.[22]

This expansion brought Godfrey's property even closer to the banks of the Missouri River; it now virtually touched the water at its northwest corner. The addition also enlarged the section of the Santee to Niobrara road that snaked through the parcel, guaranteeing that local residents would pass through the farmstead frequently. Even today the well-known site is referred to as "Godfrey Corner" or "the Godfrey land."[23]

Whatever the reasons that agents awarded land and other benefits to Godfrey, he appears to have used them to fruitful ends. Over the years he gained a reputation as a dedicated and progressive farmer, contributing more than his share to the development of the reservation.[24] A Santee superintendent, writing in a formal report in 1905, reported that "Joseph

Godfrey . . . is unquestionably at present and has been for many years one of the best farmers on this reservation."[25] Family oral history suggests that he also had a sideline business that capitalized on his equestrian expertise: he was a horse trader.[26]

During his second marriage Godfrey apparently took an interest in organized religion for the first time, for records of the Episcopal Church indicate that he was confirmed as a member in 1879.[27] The next year his twenty-one-year-old son, Joseph Jr., married Louise Stone, a Dakota woman who was a member of the same church. In 1881 Joseph Jr., who had attended the local government school rather than the missionaries' historic Santee Normal Training School, also became a confirmed church member.[28] At the age of fifty-four Godfrey became a grandfather when Anna Godfrey was born in 1884. Because her birth came before the 1885 land allotments, little Anna apparently received her own property, subject to the control of her parents while she was a minor.[29] Godfrey's descendants multiplied as three more children were born to Joseph Jr. and Louise: Esther (1887), Cecelia (1891), and Edward (1892).[30]

Godfrey passed along his agricultural skills to his son, who also became one of the best farmers on the reservation. Joseph Jr.'s allotment was located in Hill Township, about seven miles east of his father's property.[31] The reservation authorities consistently noted the "excellent manner" in which Joseph Jr., one of "our best people," farmed his land. His livestock holdings exceeded those of most other reservation residents. By the early 1900s Joseph Jr. owned ten horses, twenty cattle, forty hogs, and an unspecified number of chickens. In 1904 he raised one thousand bushels of corn, eleven hundred bushels of oats, and thirty tons of hay, bumper crops by local standards.[32]

In 1895 Godfrey's wife, Icazontewin, died at the age of fifty-six.[33] For the next three or four years, Godfrey lived alone. He was unmarried when he turned sixty-five. Isolated on his farm, he must have enjoyed visits from his son, daughter-in-law, three granddaughters, and grandson.

Godfrey married again at the age of sixty-eight. Jennie Goodteacher, the eighteen-year-old daughter of William and Maggie Goodteacher, became his third full-Dakota wife in 1898.[34] Jennie Goodteacher apparently lived with her parents until she married Godfrey.[35] Given her age and circumstances, the marriage may well have taken place without her parents' approval, for she was said to have significant mental impairment. A neurological episode suffered at the age of three months ("she was dead about one hour") had left her "kind of weak-minded."[36] Later reports about Jennie Godfrey said that she "did not have the intelligence of a 10 year old child" and referred to her as "feeble-minded" or "suffering from some sort of nervous disorder." Though there was a long period during her childhood when she did not talk at all, she could converse as an adult, but not very effectively. Jennie was, however, reputed to be a good housekeeper.[37]

In the spring of 1900 Godfrey and Jennie had their first child, a boy they named John Joseph. At the time of John's birth Godfrey's grandchildren ranged in age from seven (Edward) to sixteen (Anna).[38] Anna was thus sixteen years older than her infant uncle John. Over the next eight years Godfrey and Jennie had two more children: Sally, who died in May 1905 at only three months of age, and James, born in 1907.[39]

Why would an impaired young woman decide to marry a man fifty years her senior rather than continue to live with her parents? We will never know, but multiple later reports indicate that William Goodteacher mistreated his daughter. A Santee government employee wrote that he had "frequently" been informed that Jennie was "abused by" her father. Even John Godfrey later claimed that his mother "is not treated right by her father" and that "she was afraid of him."[40] Godfrey, who had been beaten and mistreated as a slave, may well have identified with this young woman if she sought refuge, through marriage, from her father.

Quite early in Godfrey's tenure on the Santee Reservation, the Dakotas enacted a major change in their form of government. Though hereditary chiefs had continued to lead them since their arrival in Nebraska in 1866, by the 1870s there was growing sentiment in favor of elected leaders. The scales in this debate tipped when the principal hereditary chief, Wabasha, died in 1876.[41]

That Wabasha, despite his actions in 1862–63, remained in power for fourteen years after the war deserves note. The chief had favored the surrender of his people on Sibley's terms in 1862, had written Lincoln to support the hanging of Dakota murderers, had informed against other Dakotas in January 1863, and had given state's evidence testimony in April 1863. Yet Wabasha was recognized as the hereditary leader of the Dakotas at Santee until his death.

In January 1878 the reservation held a plebiscite to determine how many people were "in favor of abolishing the present form of Government," chieftainship. Joseph Godfrey was number 34 on the list of 155 eligible voters. Since proponents of the hereditary system boycotted the referendum, all of the votes cast favored the proposition. Nonetheless, as the Indian agent noted in his report, the voters outnumbered all of the abstainers, and thus a clear majority favored a move toward republican government.[42] Whether Godfrey actually cast a ballot in this election cannot be determined, but the mere fact that he was an eligible participant is one more indication that the government viewed him as a full member of the tribe.

Another sign of Godfrey's integration into Dakota culture at Santee may be that he and his children were given Dakota names. During his years in Nebraska Godfrey never used the name Otakle (Many Kills), given him by the Indians during the 1862 war. At some point he was given the name Tatankanajin (Standing Buffalo).[43] His oldest son, Joseph Godfrey Jr., was dubbed Wanjuhedan (Little Feather Ornament). His son John, from his marriage to Jennie Goodteacher, was called Pejihokxidan (Medicine Boy).[44]

Surrounded by his family members and other Dakota speakers, Godfrey almost surely used Dakota as his principal language for the last decades of his life. But, unlike his tribal peers, the special treatment he had received in prison, ironically, denied him the opportunity to become literate. Those who sought to portray Godfrey as a villain insisted that he could read and write in several languages. That claim made it more plausible to believe that he was a mastermind of the 1862 war or (as some Indians and whites believed) that he had been well equipped to con Sibley's judges, the prison authorities, and the reservation officials who repeatedly protected him.[45]

Godfrey's lifelong illiteracy is wholly consistent with his having spent his childhood and adolescence in slavery. A routine document created in 1867, the year after his release from the Davenport prison, offers the earliest solid evidence of Godfrey's inability to read or write. After driving a team of horses and performing other odd jobs, he was asked to sign his name to a government receipt. The official who witnessed Godfrey's placement of "X, his mark" added this explanation: "The above [receipt] was explained to Joseph Godfrey by me before signing." Throughout his life, Godfrey always signed official records with an "X."⁴⁶

Back in Minnesota, many new settlers were learning their state history by attending John Stevens's traveling presentations of his spectacular panorama of oversized paintings of the "Indian Massacre" of 1862. As audiences watched with morbid fascination, images from a 6-foot-high, 222-foot-long translucent canvas scroll were rolled out, backlit by oil lamps in the darkened theater. Near the end of the blood-drenched and melodramatic tale of "white innocence" and "Indian savagery," one of the twenty-one paintings featured Godfrey, shown in the act of tomahawking a blond girl as her mother, on her knees, pleaded for mercy.⁴⁷

"The Negro Godfrey," the narrator intoned, "of full-blooded African descent," had left "the civilization of the whites" to take an Indian "maiden" for a wife. Living with the Indians, he acquired their "bloodthirsty proclivities." He was a "foremost performer" in the slaughter of innocents, a villain "with a heart blacker than his face." Reporting that Godfrey's life had been spared, the narrator predicted that he would be a "prominent actor in other scenes of blood and carnage" during his exile.⁴⁸

As Minnesotans' memories of 1862 faded, Godfrey's fate was sometimes misreported. In an 1886 letter to the *St. Paul Dispatch*, A. T. Lindholm, claiming to have been present at the Mankato hangings, swore that he was "very positive" that Godfrey was hanged next to Cut Nose on the Mankato scaffold, adding that Godfrey "attracted as much attention from spectators as any of the lot."⁴⁹ Before publishing this supposed eyewitness account, however, the *Dispatch* sent a reporter to interview the aging Henry Sibley about his recollections of Godfrey. Since Sibley made few comments at any time about Godfrey, his words are worth quoting in full:

Fig. 11. This oil on canvas depiction of Godfrey is the nineteenth panel in Rochester, Minnesota, painter John Stevens's "Panorama of the Indian Massacre of 1862," exhibited throughout Minnesota around 1870. While the audience viewed this scene, a narrator read aloud from a script: "The chief actor in this scene, ladies and gentlemen, is Negro Godfrey, of full-blooded African descent, who leaving the civilization of the whites dwelt a long time with the Indians one of whose maidens he had taken for a wife. He seemed to have all the blood-thirsty proclivities of the Indians. This man with a heart blacker than his face was one of the foremost performers in this awful tragedy. This Negro boasted of having killed thirteen women, and as for the little children, he did not think them worth counting. This Negro, dyed deep in the blood of innocent women and children, was not executed, but exiled with those who were less guilty to the Missouri reservation, where no doubt he will be a prominent actor in other scenes of blood and carnage." Courtesy of the Minnesota Historical Society.

> Gen. H. H. Sibley stated to a DISPATCH reporter this morning, however, that to the best of his recollection, the negro Godfrey, was not hanged. The papers which were forwarded to Washington for the president's approval showed conclusively that Godfrey was much the most valuable witness in the case, and this, the general thinks, may have induced the authorities at Washington to exempt the negro from execution, although the evidence was sufficient to hang him, and he was known to be a rascal anyway. He made such clear, decisive statements on the witness stand, and questioned the Indians so closely regarding their evidence, that they were forced to speak the truth. The negro, the general said, was a bright, smart scoundrel.[50]

Sibley, as usual, got the story essentially right: Godfrey had not been hanged and owed his life to a reprieve of his death sentence by "the authorities at Washington." But, just as Heard had omitted the fact that Sibley had twice overruled the court's pleas for leniency to Godfrey, so Sibley now excised his 1862 stance recommending Godfrey's execution. No reader of Sibley's words would realize that he had refused to accept the pleas of his own judges and done everything in his power to see that the trials' "most valuable witness" was hanged. Sibley also omitted any reference to Godfrey's enslavement, an approach that was consistent with his studious avoidance of that touchy subject in his writings about early Minnesota history.

That Godfrey faced insults and threats from Dakotas while he was living at Santee is understandable. But several reports indicate that he was also the target of white vigilantes, apparently including residents who lived near the reservation as well as Minnesotans. Daniel Buck, who fought as a private in 1862 and later sat on the Minnesota Supreme Court, published his Dakota War history, *Indian Outbreaks,* in 1904. He believed that justice had been cheated when Godfrey was not hanged, a view that may have been influenced by his racial outlook as set forth in the first chapter of his book: "The master race of the world is the Caucasian."[51]

Buck recited the efforts of white Minnesotans to kill Godfrey during his years at Santee:

> He [Godfrey] has never left the reservation since he took up his residence there, and the reason given for that is that he was afraid of being killed by some of the white people who resided near the reservation for his participation in the massacre. . . .
>
> It has been stated that two or three men went from Minnesota to Springfield [South Dakota, across the river from Santee] and took up their residence there many years ago for the very purpose of killing this negro at the first opportunity when he was off the reservation, and he has never dared trust himself in Springfield nor any other community of white people.[52]

While Buck's assertion that Godfrey never left the reservation is dubious, there is no reason to doubt the story that vigilante Minnesotans had gone so far as to camp out in Springfield in hopes of killing him when he was off the reservation. Dakota sources also describe the threats to Godfrey's life from incensed whites. Archie Redfox, who was a boy when Godfrey was living at Santee, reported that Godfrey once escaped angry whites who caught him while he was across the river at Springfield: "Somehow the whites got word that he had confessed to crimes. Many years later . . . [he] took a bull boat and crossed the Missouri to a town [Springfield]. He was recognized there [by the whites] and fled for his life."[53] Another Dakota story had Godfrey running all the way from Mankato to the Nebraska reservation, pursued by white soldiers the entire time. In Springfield Godfrey "jumped into the river. Soldiers shot at him as he swam. Godfrey made it over to Santee, where the Indians felt sorry for him and he lived the rest of his life there."[54]

A 1910 letter from Santee agent Frank E. McIntyre confirmed that "[Godfrey] was treated like a fugitive from justice by both Indians and whites, and many attempts were made to kill him, and his life was undoubtedly prolonged by the intervention of Major Stone, Acting Indian Agent, who told the Indians that any one who killed Godfrey would be hung. On this account no attempts were made on his life while on the reservation but as soon as he was off they were after him and he had many narrow escapes."[55] In reporting that "no attempts" were made to kill Godfrey while he was on the reservation, this account differs from another that mentions shots taken at him "several times."[56] Perhaps the Dakotas ceased their on-reservation assaults once the agent threatened them with hanging.

Though conflicting details of these varying stories of white efforts to lynch Godfrey cannot be reconciled, the similarity of their themes strongly suggests that they contain kernels of truth about the perils he faced. They also place in perspective the continuing slurs and threats that Godfrey faced from Dakotas on the reservation. As unpleasant as his existence may have been at Santee, Godfrey was probably safer there than he would have been elsewhere. Godfrey's inclination to stay at Santee also may have been related to his childhood experiences. After all, until he sought refuge with the Dakotas as a teenager, he had known nothing but enslavement. Whatever the drawbacks of living in the Indian community, it had given him his first taste of freedom. His unpopularity notwithstanding, he was considered a member of the tribe for all official purposes. Never was he treated as a nonperson at Santee, as he had been while he was enslaved.

It would be a mistake to envision Godfrey as cowering in the corner of his farmhouse during his forty years at Santee. His government jobs and his horse-trading business would have required him to mingle with other reservation residents, and his success as a farmer would have won him some measure of respect from his neighbors. He could not have been a total recluse, for he persuaded two reservation women to marry him. There were undoubtedly Dakotas who turned a cold shoulder to Godfrey, or worse. But it also seems likely that he went about his chores on the farm and interacted with those who did not shun him without suffering serious daily disruptions or hostilities.

During his years at Santee Godfrey's race was reported in three different ways: as half white and half black; as half black and half Dakota; and as fully black (sometimes reduced to the slur that he was a "full-blooded nigger").⁵⁷ Godfrey himself always said that his mother was a black woman and his father a Frenchman. But there are some documents from which it can be inferred that someone (perhaps his children) told the authorities that Godfrey was half Dakota. A 1905 letter from the Santee agent, for example, reported that Joseph Jr. was "3/4 blood Santee the other ¼ being of Negro extraction."⁵⁸ Of course, the only way that Godfrey's son could have had three-quarters Indian blood was for Godfrey to have been half Dakota.⁵⁹ Godfrey and his children might have had multiple incentives to insert some Dakota blood into his veins, including minimizing the hostility they faced from other Indians and assuring their continuing status as enrolled tribal members on the reservation.

Others, almost always critics, claimed that Godfrey had no white blood. After Godfrey had been farming and improving his plot of land on the reservation for more than thirty years, a white resident of nearby Niobrara, F. A. Barns, conceived the idea of stripping him of his title so that Barns could then claim the prime land for himself. In the fall of 1901 Barns wrote an error-filled, punctuation-free letter to the U.S. Indian agent in Washington: "There is a negro full blood here holding land under or as an Indian he was the leader of the Indian masicres in Minesota & has come here in the early day & taken land as an Indian on the santee reservation there is no Indian Blood in him & is a full Blood negro if he has no right to the land I would like to file on it as a homestead I am a old solger[.]"⁶⁰ Though Barns did not name Godfrey initially, he did in a subsequent letter: "His name is Joseph Godfrey and [he] claims to Belong to the Sioux or Santee tribe."⁶¹

This effort to deprive Godfrey of his land came to naught. The commissioner of Indian Affairs informed Barns that Godfrey had received a patent to his farm in 1885 as a homestead under the terms of the 1868 treaty: "[Godfrey] was doubtless a recognized member of the Santee band of Sioux Indians, and the fact that he was not of Indian blood would not under the treaty affect his rights to the land . . . as incorporated members were placed on the same footing as members of blood."⁶² From the bureaucrats' perspective, it made no difference if Godfrey was granted reservation land rights due to his marriage to a Dakota woman or due simply to his acceptance as a member of the Santees. He was an "incorporated member" of the tribe and that was that. Barns apparently abandoned his attempts to obtain the land after 1901, for Godfrey's family inherited his allotment after his death without any problems.⁶³

The 1909 annual Santee census listed Godfrey and the members of his extended family in three separate households. Godfrey's third wife and their children were enumerated as:

Jennie Godfrey	Wife	28	F
John Godfrey	Son	9	M
James Godfrey	Son	1	M

The listing for Godfrey's son's family was:

Joseph Godfrey Jr.	Father	50	M
Louisa Godfrey	Wife	46	F
Edward Godfrey	Son	16	M

Esther, Godfrey's oldest living grandchild, was apparently living apart from her family and was recorded in another entry: "Esther Godfrey, age 22."⁶⁴

An equal number of Godfreys had died before this census, including Joseph's first two wives, a son and a daughter from his marriage to Takanheca, and a daughter from his marriage to Jennie. By 1909 Godfrey had also lost two grandchildren: Cecelia passed away in about 1898 when she was just seven and Anna died about 1901 at the age of seventeen. Significantly, in 1909 every one of Godfrey's descendants and relatives was an enrolled member of the Santee Sioux tribe. They were all, apparently, living on the reservation.

The day after the June 30, 1909 census was taken, Godfrey died. He was most likely working on his farm when he was overcome about noon by what the doctors called "insolation," or sunstroke.⁶⁵ Unless it is promptly treated, sunstroke quickly can lead to an extremely high body temperature (106 degrees or more), convulsions, and a coma.⁶⁶ One report said that Godfrey died "instantly," suggesting that he may already have lapsed into unconsciousness by the time he received medical attention.[67] He expired about 6:00 p.m. on July 1.[68]

Godfrey's Nebraska death certificate states that he was buried on July 2, but little else. Dr. F. A. Bryant, the attending physician, apparently did not furnish the usual cause-of-death information to the county officials, for they noted that inquiries sent to him were "unfortunately not returned." A clerk inserted the reported cause of death. Spaces on the certificate for denoting the deceased's spouse, the names of his father and mother, his birthplace, and other details were left blank. Only three personal facts about Godfrey were officially noted: He was male. He was black. And (incorrectly) he was sixty-eight years old. These bare facts were, the local registrar reported, "all the information available."

Fig. 12. Joseph Godfrey's headstone, Hobu Creek Cemetery, Santee, Nebraska. Photo courtesy of Elroy Ubl.

Godfrey was laid to rest in Hobu Creek Cemetery (also called the Holy Faith Cemetery), located adjacent to the now-unused Episcopal Holy Faith Chapel, about three miles north of the hamlet of Lindy, near the eastern edge of the Santee Reservation.[69] The cemetery sits atop a gentle bulge of Nebraska farm country. A small cluster of fir trees and a seldom-used, cross-topped flagpole offer the only interruptions in the broad expanse of the surrounding prairie. Two rutted lanes serve as the approach to the unfenced, somewhat forlorn graveyard. Godfrey's polished granite gravestone, nestled in unkempt bushes next to the fir trees, is newer and more substantial than many of the other headstones. A willowy floral arrangement is carved on the left side of the smooth face of the stone. The tombstone records the years of Godfrey's life as 1827–1909, though we will probably never know with certainty the year of his birth. Determining the ages of persons born into slavery is often difficult, but the best evidence supports the conclusion that Godfrey was born about 1830.[70]

Eight other Godfreys are also buried at Hobu Creek, all of them related to Joseph by blood or marriage.[71] His three sons who survived to adulthood—Joseph Jr., John Joseph, and James—lie there, as does Sally, his daughter with Jennie, who died in infancy. The two granddaughters who predeceased him, Anna and Cecelia, are also interred there, as is Ivy Saul Godfrey, the wife of Godfrey's son John. Godfrey's third wife is also buried at Hobu under a marker bearing the name she acquired through a second marriage, Jennie Blackowl. The most noteworthy grave at Hobu Creek is that of Chief Wabasha, regally identified on his stone as Wabasha III.

The epitaph on Godfrey's grave is a line from Tennyson: "God's finger touched him, and he slept."[72] That sentiment is fitting for a man who—whether as a slave, fugitive slave, 1862 war participant, murder suspect, prosecution witness, prison inmate, or reservation resident— seldom slept in peace.

NOTES ON CHAPTER 12

1. Meyer, *History of the Santee Sioux,* 175. Meyer titled his chapter covering the years 1870–1900 "The Quiet Decades" (175–97).
2. Isaiah Lightner et al. to E. A. Hay, April 21, 1878, NA, RG 75, BIA, LR, M175, roll 523, frames 614–17.
3. Petition to U.S. President signed by eight Dakota leaders, April 20, 1878, NA, RG 75, BIA, LR, M175, roll 523, frame 619.
4. Ibid.
5. Receipt, September 30, 1867, signed by Joseph Godfrey with an "X," NA, RG 75, St. Peter's Agency, 1868–70, M234, roll 766. See also NA, RG 75, E978, Records of Employees, Rosters of Agency Employees, 1853–1909, vol. 2, entries for Godfrey at pp. 7, 19, and 20. Initially Godfrey was paid only about one-third as much as white employees on the reservation, but his salary later rose to equal those employed in similar jobs.
6. Letters dated August 30 and September 9, 1872, NA, RG 75, BIA, LR, M175, roll 769, frames 611–13. A later report indicates that "Joseph Godfrey, Male, Indian" worked in 1879 for eleven and a half days digging a well, at the rate of seventy-five cents per day. An 1880 record documents the payment of fifty cents to Joseph Godfrey for "making fence to protect crops." NA, RG 75, BIA, LR, M175, roll 528, frames 727–28, and roll 529, frame 74. These records probably refer to Godfrey, though they may refer to his son, Joseph Jr.
7. In his 1912 deposition Joseph Godfrey Jr. said that his father's second marriage occurred not long after the Dakotas were sent to Santee. He also testified that Takanheca died in 1873, apparently in a smallpox epidemic on the reservation. See Godfrey heirship file and Santee Agency Census. In 1870 Takanheca had a son, Edward, whose father was George Wakandaymani. Santee Episcopal Mission Baptismal Register, 1843–1904, pp. 126–27, CWS, recording the birth of Edward in May 1870 at Santee, copy furnished to me by Dr. Valere Beeck. Reputedly Wakandaymani's English surname was Quinn, and thus he was the same Dakota man who later made strident (sometimes false) criticisms of Godfrey.
8. Meyer, *History of the Santee Sioux,* 158–64.
9. Ibid.
10. Ibid.
11. Santee list, NA, RG 75, BIA, LR, M175, roll 768, frames 659–63.
12. Carl Crosley, telephone interviews with author, 2004–5. I gratefully acknowledge the friendly assistance of Carl Crosley, both in describing the Godfrey property and in discussing his recollections of the Godfrey family.
13. Webster's report and letter, June 2–3, 1873, NA, RG 75, BIA, LR, M175, roll 768, frames 855–61.
14. Lightner to Commissioner of Indian Affairs, March 20, 1880, NA, RG 75, BIA, LR, M175, roll 528. See also Meyer, *History of the Santee Sioux,* 183–84.
15. Lightner report, February 2, 1878, NA, RG 75, BIA, LR, M175, roll 523, frames 541–50.
16. Lightner to Commissioner of Indian Affairs, with report, February 11, 1880, NA, RG 75, BIA, LR, M175, roll 528, frames 781–91.

17. The conclusion that Godfrey suffered from racism at Santee is an inference from both earlier and later racist comments about him made by Dakota people.
18. Information generously furnished to me in a 2005 telephone interview of Nebraska resident Charles Mulhair, who interviewed Frazier in about 1986.
19. Story related to me by Jerry Redwing at the Dakota Letters Symposium, Sisseton Wahpeton College, Sisseton, SD, July 26–27, 2005.
20. *Mankato Daily Review,* December 26, 1914, quoting historian Thomas Hughes.
21. Liska, *Ponca Curse,* 134.
22. Meyer, *History of the Santee Sioux,* 180–81. The configuration of Godfrey's final allotment is shown on a 1920 map and atlas of Knox County for Union Township by Anderson Publishing Company, available online at Knox County, Nebraska, GenWeb Project, http://negennet.net/knox/1920atlas/unionmap.htm, accessed May 1, 2012.
23. Carl Crosley, telephone interviews with the author, February 2005.
24. Eli Huggins to Folwell, August 9, 1918, Folwell Papers, MHS, box 47, quoting missionary John Williamson, who also told Huggins that Godfrey, despite his accomplishments as a farmer, was "detested by whites and Indians alike."
25. W. E. Meagley to Commissioner of Indian Affairs, January 27, 1905, , NA, RG 75, BIA, LR, CCF 1907–39, E121, Santee Agency, box 2707. By the early 1900s the duties of agents were assumed by superintendents. Meyer, *History of the Santee Sioux,* 297.
26. Luella Emery, telephone interview with the author, November 20, 2002. Emery, born in 1922, was apparently the only grandchild from Godfrey's third marriage (to Jennie Goodteacher). Her father was John Godfrey, the eldest child of Joseph and Jennie. Emery is now deceased.
27. Santee Episcopal Mission Baptismal Register, book 1, CWS.
28. The records of the Episcopal Church in South Dakota indicate that Joseph Godfrey Jr. was married to Louise "Blackstone" at Santee Agency, Nebraska, on May 28, 1880, by Rev. W. W. Fowler. See letter from the church secretary, Mrs. Kenneth Olson, "to whom it may concern," August 3, 1977, furnished to me by Godfrey descendant Delores Espinoza. In most entries the family surname is given as Stone. The Santee Agency Census records for 1885 show that Joseph Godfrey Jr. was then twenty-six years old, living apart from his father, and married to Louise Stone. Martha Stone (Hapistan), Louise's mother, also lived in their home. . Also see Santee Mission Record Book, book 1, 302.
29. W. E. Meagley to Commissioner of Indian Affairs, January 27, 1905, RG 75, BIA, LR, CCF 1907–39, E121, Santee Agency, box 2707, which deals with the payment of funds to Joseph Godfrey Jr. from the proceeds of the sale of Anna's allotted property after her death.
30. Santee Agency Census.
31. The legal description of the allotment of Joseph Godfrey Jr. is found in a report of the Santee Indian Competency Commission, October 26, 1910, NA, RG 75, BIA, LR, CCF 1907–39, E121, Santee Agency, box 5, file 24448-1911(127). This three-member (white) commission assessed the competence of each farmer to whom an allotment had been assigned, perhaps to determine whether they were suitable to be released from government trust restrictions. A portion of the allotment is shown on a map of Hill Township from a 1920 atlas of Knox County by Anderson Publishing Company, available online at Knox County, Nebraska, GenWeb Project, http://negennet.net/knox/1920atlas/hillmap.htm, accessed May 1, 2012.

32. W. E. Meagley to Commissioner of Indian Affairs, January 27, 1905, RG 75, BIA, LR, CCF 1907–39, E121, Santee Agency, box 2707, file 24448-1911(127); and Santee Indian Competency Commission report, October 26, 1910, NA, RG 75, BIA, LR, CCF 1907–39, E121, Santee Agency, box 5, file 24448-1911(127).
33. The Santee Agency Census taken as of June 30, 1895, shows Emma, age fifty-six, living with Godfrey. Another source gives her date of death as December 18, 1895, though it also lists her age as sixty, not fifty-six. Santee Episcopal Mission Baptismal Register, book 1, pp. 532–33, CWS.
34. The Santee Agency Census for June 30, 1899, shows Jennie G. Godfrey, wife, age eighteen, living with Godfrey, age sixty-three. The text reflects the age for Godfrey that is probably closest to being correct.
35. The Santee Agency Census shows Jennie Goodteacher, age seventeen, as the only child living with her parents on June 30, 1898.
36. C. F. Hauke to Leech, December 17, 1917 (quoting testimony), George Blackowl Estate, NA, RG 75, BIA, LR, CCF 1907–39, E121, file 34941-1915(350).
37. Depositions of Joseph Godfrey Jr. and Henry Trudell, Godfrey heirship file.
38. The June 30, 1900, Santee Agency Census lists an unnamed boy, three months old, in Godfrey's household. He is identified in all later census records as John Godfrey. The same census lists the Godfrey grandchildren.
39. Sally Godfrey's name comes from the Santee Episcopal Mission Baptismal Register, book 2, pp. 82, 96, and 218, CWS, which lists her birth date (February 3, 1905), the date she was baptized (April 9, 1905), her death (May 20, 1905), and her burial in Holy Faith Cemetery (May 23, 1905). She was called Sarah on the 1905 annuity roll, which indicates that she was born on February 13, 1905, and died on May 22, 1905. Santee Sioux annuity rolls, MHS, M405, roll 2, 1905. Joseph Godfrey Jr. testified in 1912 that his father and Jennie had only one daughter, named Margaret. Deposition of Joseph Godfrey Jr., Godfrey heirship file. In the June 30, 1908, Santee Agency Census James is listed as being one year old.
40. These abuse reports arose in the context of disputes over the division of the property of Jennie's second husband. In 1918 Edward Martin, the government-employed farmer at Santee, wrote, "Reports have come to me frequently that she is abused by him [her father] but being an idiot, she makes no complaint." Martin to A. W. Leech, January 9, 1918. For John Godfrey's remarks about his mother's abuse, see John Godfrey to Stephens, January 14, 1918. The reservation superintendent, on the basis of such evidence, concluded that "William Goodteacher sometimes abuses his daughter." A. W. Leech to Commissioner of Indian Affairs, April 8, 1918. All three letters are in George Blackowl Estate, NA, RG 75, BIA, LR, CCF 1907–39, E121, file 34941-1915(350).
41. Meyer, *History of the Santee Sioux*, 169.
42. Lightner to E. A. Hay, NA, RG 75, BIA, LR, M175, roll 523, frames 528–32. See also Meyer, *History of the Santee Sioux*, 169.
43. In 1862 the Sisseton chief Tatankanazin (Standing Buffalo) had sent a letter to Sibley informing him that he and his people were friendly and had no intention of joining in the war. For Sibley's response on September 24, 1862, see *MCIW*, 2:250. But Tatankanazin was a common Dakota name, so no connection with the chief may have been intended.

44. Santee Reservation census records sometimes (but not always) indicate the Dakota names of those enrolled. Godfrey's name, Tatankanajin, first appears on the 1887 census, and it is repeated in many of the entries for later years. Joseph Godfrey Jr.'s name first appears in 1890 with the spelling Wanjinhedan. In later years, starting with 1898, his name is spelled Wanyuhedan. The Indian name of three-year-old John Godfrey, Pejihokxidan, appears in the 1903 census. I gratefully acknowledge the translation of these Dakota names by Louis Garcia.
45. See comments attributed to Dr. George Quinn in McIntyre to Carter, February 14, 1910, Woolworth Papers, MHS. Also see the July 23, 1909, *Morton Enterprise* article, discussed in afterword.
46. Receipt, September 30, 1867, NA, RG 75, St. Peter's Agency, 1868–70, M234, roll 766. The fact that Godfrey never learned to read or write during his time on the Santee Reservation is further documented by his "X" signatures in 1892 and 1894. See Santee Sioux annuity rolls, MHS, M405, roll 2. The annuity rolls show that Joseph Godfrey Jr. sometimes signed with an "X" (see entries for 1892 and 1894) and sometimes signed his name (1902). He spoke English, but he could read and write only "a very little" in English. He could read and write in Dakota. See Santee Indian Competency Commission report, October 26, 1910, NA, RG 75, BIA, LR, CCF 1907–39, E121, Santee Agency, box 5, file 24448-1911(127).
47. See Stevens, "Panorama of the Indian Massacre of 1862," with script, MHS; Bell, "Sioux War Panorama," 279–81; and Heilbron, "Documentary Panorama."
48. Stevens, "Panorama of the Indian Massacre of 1862," MHS.
49. *St. Paul Dispatch*, March 26, 1886.
50. Ibid.
51. Buck, *Indian Outbreaks*, 10, 227–28.
52. Ibid., 238. Buck, a racially insensitive critic, also claimed that Godfrey stayed at Santee only to live "off the rations and annuities issued by the government to his dusky spouse" (238).
53. Transcript of an undated interview of a Dakota man, Archie Redfox, by Louis Garcia, furnished to me by Garcia in 2005. According to the interview notes, Redfox was born in 1901 and died in 1989. He thus would have been six years old when Godfrey died. Garcia noted that Springfield was likely the destination to which Redfox was referring.
54. Account of George Rouillard, in Liska, *Ponca Curse,* 133. Godfrey was transported from Davenport to Santee in 1866 when he was released from prison, so there is no truth to the claim that white soldiers chased him from Mankato to the reservation.
55. Indian agent McIntyre to Theodore Carter, February 14, 1910, Woolworth Papers, MHS. Though most of the information in this letter was received from the unreliable Dr. George Quinn, these comments may have come from the agent himself; they also have a ring of truth since they are partially corroborated by other sources.
56. *Mankato Daily Review*, December 26, 1914 (quoting historian Thomas Hughes).
57. William Goodteacher, the father of Jennie Goodteacher Godfrey, referred to Godfrey as a "full-blooded nigger." See George Blackowl Estate, , NA, RG 75, BIA, LR, CCF 1907–39, E121, file 34941-1915(350). Godfrey's death certificate gives his "color" as "Black." Certified copy of Nebraska Certificate of Death (no. G316), July 1, 1909.
58. W. E. Meagley to Commissioner of Indian Affairs, January 27, 1905, RG 75, BIA, LR, CCF 1907–39, E121, Santee Agency, box 2707.
59. Later records did not perpetuate this mistake, for a 1923 distribution list indicated that Joseph Godfrey Jr. had one-half "degree" of Dakota blood. See Santee Sioux Annuity Records, MHS, M405, roll 2.

60. Barns to U.S. Indian agent, September 9, 1901, NA, RG 75, Office of Indian Affairs, LR, 1881–1907, 1901, box 1976, doc. 50128.
61. Barns to A. C. Tanner, October 13, 1901, NA, RG 75, Office of Indian Affairs, LR, 1881–1907, box 1992, doc. 57485.
62. OIA Commissioner to Barns, November 12, 1901, NA, RG 75, Office of Indian Affairs, LS, doc. 57485-1901.
63. See Godfrey heirship file.
64. Santee Agency Census.
65. Godfrey's death certificate gives "insolation" as the cause of death.
66. Sunstroke's effects are taken from *Dorland's Medical Dictionary*.
67. Deposition of George Goodteacher, 1912, Godfrey heirship file.
68. *Niobrara Tribune*, July 8, 1908. Dr. F. A. Bryant, a visiting physician filling in for the local doctor, treated Godfrey before his death. His unfamiliarity with his patient may have contributed to the dearth of information in Godfrey's death certificate.
69. I am grateful to a dedicated New Ulm historian and author, Elroy Ubl, for the information in this chapter about Godfrey's grave and the Hobu Creek Cemetery. Ubl generously furnished a detailed description of his visit to the cemetery and the gravesite's location—with color photographs of the cemetery and Godfrey's gravestone.
70. Varying accounts indicate other birth years, ranging from 1826 to 1835. In addition to the age Godfrey gave Heard, the annual Santee Agency Census gave an age that was consistent with an 1834–35 birth year. At the other extreme, a Nebraska obituary gave his age as "about 83" at the time of his death, which would indicate a birth year of 1826—close to the age given on his tombstone. See *Niobrara Tribune*, July 8, 1909.
71. A listing of the graves at Hobu Creek Cemetery is available from the Knox County, Nebraska, GenWeb Project, http://negennet.net/knox/cemeteries/hobocreek.htm, accessed May 1, 2012.
72. Alfred, Lord Tennyson, *In Memoriam A. H. H.*, 85, stanza 5.

AFTERWORD

Shortly after Godfrey's death, obituary-type articles appeared in newspapers in Nebraska and Minnesota, but the two states' coverage differed sharply. The *Niobrara (NE) Tribune* offered a basically accurate description of Godfrey's early years, reporting that he and his mother "were said to have been slaves" but that "young Godfrey cast his lot with the Indians." His race was not specifically mentioned, but it could readily be inferred from the mention of slavery. One interpretation of the "cast his lot" phrase would be consistent with the truth: that Godfrey ran away from his master to live with the Dakotas.

The Nebraska paper's version of the events of 1862 was limited to one paragraph: "[Godfrey] was to have been hung in connection with the murder of a teacher and her pupils near Morton, but escaped his fate. Some say it was because he turned state's evidence against the Indians, and others have it that when his name was called he in some manner got an Indian to take his place."[1] The grisly idea that Godfrey killed "a teacher and her pupils" must have reflected local folklore, since it finds no support in trial records or any other account. The suggestion that he might have avoided being hanged by getting "an Indian to take his place" offers a classic example of the means by which recollected history is distorted: almost certainly, the genesis of this falsehood lies in the true accounts of the two Dakota men who were hanged by mistake at Mankato.

The *Tribune* also reported a more positive side of Godfrey's life in Nebraska: "Very seldom was he known to leave his farm. While in Knox county he has always led a quiet life and his neighbors speak well of him. . . . [Godfrey] leaves a wife and three children to mourn him. Another land mark in the History of Knox county has passed away and many incidents of his life will remain unknown."

In contrast, the obituary that appeared in the *Morton (MN) Enterprise* was an unremitting attack on Godfrey ("the name that makes old pioneers shudder"), a man "despised by whites and Indians alike" during the forty-seven years since the 1862 war.[2] Indeed, the *Enterprise* story is the single most damning piece ever written about Godfrey's role in the 1862 conflict. In breathlessly lurid and highly specific terms, it depicts him both as the most bloodthirsty killer among the Dakotas and as their brilliant, Machiavellian leader. According to the *Enterprise*, Godfrey, due to his linguistic wizardry (he could speak English, French, and German "fluently") and encyclopedic familiarity with the local white population ("He knew personally every settler, every child in every family"), acted as the behind-the-scenes mastermind of the 1862 killings ("his influence was strongly felt among the Indians"). The *Enterprise* implicated Godfrey in a dizzying array of "atrocities" culled from only a "partial list." He is blamed for the "killing of the Zimmerman family," looking "with glee" at "the headless body of Dr. Humphrey," the "ambuscade [of settlers] . . . at Beaver Creek," the attacks at Milford and on the Patoille wagon, and "the massacre of Captain Marsh and his men."

Reprinting the Morton newspaper's pejorative account in full, the *St. Paul Dispatch* added its own racially tinged headline: "NEGRO ARCH FIEND OF SIOUX MASSACRE DIES."[3] Another Minnesota newspaper, reprinting the *Enterprise* story, inserted the editor's racial gloss as a subheadline: "WAS A VERY BAD NEGRO."[4]

Neither the *Enterprise* nor any other Minnesota newspaper reported Godfrey's enslavement. He was simply a "full blooded negro" who "lived . . . with an Indian woman" at the time of the 1862 outbreak. (Godfrey's detractors often insisted that he was fully black, while the "lived with" characterization dehumanized him by failing to credit his marriage to Takanheca.) The *Enterprise* article has an aura of verisimilitude because of its specificity. But these very details reveal its fundamental falsity. If one were to stick pins in the locations where Godfrey is supposed to have been on August 18 and 19 alone, for example, it would soon become obvious that one man could not possibly have committed the peripatetic slaughters that the *Enterprise* attributed to him.

But the main problem with the *Enterprise* diatribe lies not in its over-the-top distortion of Godfrey's role in 1862. If that were the case, it would be worth dissecting so as to glean kernels of truth from the hyperbole. Instead, the newspaper's blast should be seen for what it is: a total fabrication by a small-town, white editor who hoped to make money by concocting tall tales of the 1862 Indian war.

O. W. Smith, the editor of the *Enterprise,* has recently been unmasked as the creator of another fictitious story (also published in 1909) related to the 1862 war: the supposed eyewitness account of a Dakota man, George Crooks, who purportedly witnessed the New Ulm assault on the Indian prisoners as an eight-year-old child. In the first four editions of their seminal work, *Through Dakota Eyes,* coauthors Gary Clayton Anderson and Alan R. Woolworth reprinted Crooks's account as originally published by Smith in the *Enterprise*. But in the latest printing of their book Anderson and Woolworth, relying on their discovery of Crooks's own repudiation of the story, informed their readers that the Crooks account was "false" and "invented."[5] Similarly, Smith's 1909 Godfrey obituary should be seen as fictitious, a source to be disbelieved in its entirety unless its claims of "fact" can be found in other reliable accounts.[6]

Though the widely published *Enterprise* obituary left lasting false impressions of Godfrey, Smith's overblown rhetoric spurred an aging former soldier, Theodore Carter, to rally to Godfrey's defense. Within a month of the article's appearance Carter wrote to the U.S. Indian agent at the Santee Reservation: "I do not believe that he was the fiend that he is represented to be in the [*Enterprise*] newspaper article. . . . I like to see fair play, and I believe that his being a mulatto is the cause of most of the prejudice against him."[7] Unfortunately, because Carter did not publish his rebuttal of the Godfrey obituary for more than three years, and then only in one outstate newspaper, the most widely read postscript to Godfrey's life was the sensational invention of O. W. Smith.⁸

On the Santee Reservation, Joseph Godfrey Jr. continued to thrive as a successful farmer after his father's death.⁹ But his half brothers, John and James, had more difficult lives. They were initially left in the care of their developmentally disabled mother. Sometime during the winter after her husband died, Jennie responded to two-year-old James's crying by putting him in the frigid outdoors, an act that apparently left him physically disabled for the rest of his life. James lived with mental impairment, but it is unclear whether that condition was present at birth or was caused by the near-freezing incident. The next summer Jennie eloped with a fifty-five-year-old Dakota man from the Yankton Reservation, George Blackowl. She abandoned her two sons, who were raised for a time in the family of their older stepbrother, Joseph Godfrey Jr.¹⁰

Godfrey left no will. His only property was the 160-acre allotment of land on the reservation. In a probate-type federal heirship proceeding in 1912, the farm was awarded jointly (one fourth each) to his living heirs: Joseph Godfrey Jr., John and James Godfrey, and Jennie Godfrey Blackowl.¹¹

The Godfrey family, it appears, faced ostracism on the reservation due to the color of their skin. At a 1915 hearing following the death of Jennie's second husband the question arose as to whether Jennie had the mental capacity to transfer her inheritance from Blackowl to her father, William Goodteacher (who, it was alleged, had abused her). In this context the "Examiner of Inheritance," relying on concerns expressed by Jennie's uncle, Stephen Blacksmith, said, "Jennie has two sons, but they are part negro, and no one cares to have much to do with them on account of their negro blood. . . . [Blacksmith] thinks that unless you defeat the purpose of William Goodteacher he will have all of the property belonging to Jennie, and her two children will have nothing and on account of their negro blood will have a hard time. Further, James would have to go to the poor house."¹² The testimony of Goodteacher himself seems to support this claim of racial enmity, for he repeatedly referred to his former son-in-law as a "nigger." The court, relying on the evidence of Goodteacher's bias and abuse, refused to allow him to acquire Jennie's assets.

Joseph Godfrey Jr.'s son, Edward, was Godfrey's only grandchild from his first marriage who had children. Edward married Carrie Primeaux, an enrolled member of the Rosebud Sioux tribe in South Dakota. He moved there and the couple had many children. Today Godfrey's living descendants comprise two main branches. Those who trace their ancestry from Godfrey's marriage to Takanheca (and from Joseph Godfrey Jr.) are enrolled in tribes in North Dakota and South Dakota, while those who descend from his marriage to Jennie (and from John Godfrey, since James apparently had no children) are enrolled as members of the Santee tribe in Nebraska.

At least some members of both branches of the family, apparently acting independently, began to deny or conceal their black heritage sometime after Godfrey's death. One of Godfrey's South Dakota descendants recalled that family members "didn't talk about black blood." She grew up not knowing about her African American roots, and when she later asked her grandfather whether she had any black blood, he replied, "By the time you were born, it ran out."[13] Godfrey's Nebraska descendants also reported that the family "hid" their black heritage, though some of them no longer do so.[14]

The Godfrey families' concealment of their black roots was an understandable reaction to racial insensitivity on and around the reservation. As late as 1984 a Santee tribal member described Godfrey as "a full-blooded nigger." Whites living near Santee used the same racial slur. One man, referring to Godfrey's grave on the reservation, said to another white resident, "You wouldn't believe it . . . , but there's a nigger buried in the cemetery."[15]

Virtually all of Godfrey's living descendants identify themselves as Indians. That they do so almost certainly would have pleased their namesake ancestor, who fled from the abuses of a white-dominated society and chose, in good times and bad, to live among the Dakotas.

Writers who have expressed opinions about Godfrey, both before and after his death, have generally fallen into one of two opposing camps. Isaac Heard and Theodore Carter accepted the final appraisal of the military commission and Lincoln. Unconvinced that Godfrey had killed anyone, sympathetic to his claims that he acted under duress, and grateful for his evidence in the trials, they portrayed Godfrey as a decent and honest man who had the misfortune to be swept up in terrible events that were beyond his control. Carter gave a general endorsement of his character: "I became well acquainted with him, and found him a bright man who certainly did not show that he was capable of committing [murders]."[16]

Historian William W. Folwell also adopted a supportive stance toward Godfrey after he relocated and carefully reviewed the missing Dakota trial transcripts in 1909, the year of Godfrey's death.[17] Marion P. Satterlee, whose 1862 victim lists are the most detailed ever compiled, published Folwell's notes on the Dakota trials. In his accompanying commentary, Satterlee credited Godfrey with telling "the only connected story of the Milford murders."[18] Elsewhere, Satterlee wrote that Godfrey "established many facts sustained by other evidence. . . . It is not probable that he ever killed anybody."[19]

Two of the best and most balanced books about the war take a neutral stance on Godfrey. Kenneth Carley, in *The Dakota War of 1862*, notes that the evidence against Godfrey was "more convincing" than that against many of the other trial defendants, but he also describes him as "an intelligent, articulate witness who rebutted in detail" the testimony of Dakotas who were "his late colleagues in the war." Anderson and Woolworth, in *Through Dakota Eyes*, strike an even more positive note about Godfrey by publishing Heard's book version of the story. Following Heard's lead, they give Godfrey undue credit for convicting "most" of the Dakota defendants, but their coverage implies no criticism of his credibility.[20]

On the other hand, some writers have agreed with Sibley, arguing that Godfrey deserved to be hanged despite his state's evidence testimony. Prominent in this group were two men who fought on the white side in 1862 and wrote two of the most chauvinistic pro-white histories of the conflict: Daniel Buck and Jacob Nix. Such critics almost always claimed that Godfrey, no matter what the judges or anyone else said, was guilty of multiple murders. Sometimes they supported their arguments with specific "facts," such as those published in the *Enterprise* obituary; other times they made only vague allegations.

Buck, Nix, and others who shared their views vilified Godfrey by comparing his deeds with those of historical blackguards.[21] Buck called him a "Judas Iscariot criminal" and decried the practice (still common today) of convicting "one murderer by the evidence of another murderer."[22] In the 1960s a writer for *True West* magazine picked up on Buck's characterization and wrote an article about Godfrey (much of it flagrantly false) called "Black Judas."[23]

Nix, Buck, and others who shared their anti-Dakota views argued that Godfrey deserved to die despite his helpful testimony in the trials. Such writers dealt at length with alleged Indian atrocities, exaggerated the number of white deaths, and were largely silent about any mistreatment of the Dakotas before, during, or after the war. Against that biased backdrop Godfrey was viewed as a witness who helped send guilty Dakotas to the gallows, with not a whiff of a suggestion that any warriors—let alone hundreds of them—were unjustly punished. Buck, writing forty-two years after the war, rued the fact that more Dakotas were not executed, arguing that "nearly all" of the 303 men sentenced to death merited that penalty.[24] Nix declared that the thirty-eight Dakotas hanged "received their hundredfold deserved reward."[25] It is hardly surprising that men with such views believed that Godfrey too should have been put to death.

Since the 1970s, however, the pendulum of historical coverage has swung far in the opposite direction, as evidenced by the wildly enthusiastic response to Dee Brown's classic book *Bury My Heart at Wounded Knee,* subtitled "an Indian history of the American West." It is safe to say that more people owe their knowledge of Dakota War history to chapter 3 of *Bury My Heart at Wounded Knee*—more than five million copies of which are in print—than to all other sources combined.

Yet ironically, even as *Bury My Heart at Wounded Knee* reversed the thrust of the Dakota War story from an anti- to a pro-Dakota emphasis, Godfrey continued to be depicted as a villainous character. Brown singled out Godfrey, the "willing informant," as a scapegoat for the miscarriage of justice in the 1862 trials.[26] While Buck contended that the postwar punishment and the hanging of only thirty-eight men was far too lenient, Brown argued that white justice was totally unfair.[27] But these two diametrically opposed historians agreed on one point: that Godfrey should be seen as a blackguard.

If the characterization of Godfrey as either a scapegrace or a scapegoat is unjustified, what is his proper place in history? He is wrongly cast as a consummate villain, but it would be equally wrong to depict him as a hero. Rather, what most distinguishes Godfrey's life is the remarkable series of life-and-death dilemmas he faced.

Godfrey's first life-risking choice was between the abuses of slavery and the perils he faced as a fugitive slave. At the outset of the 1862 conflict his choices were utterly stark: to stay with the Dakotas, who distrusted and threatened him, or to flee (with or without his family) to the whites, who had enslaved him and were suspicious of his association with the Indians. At Milford he was given two blunt options: join the massacre or be killed. Godfrey faced his next dilemma during the trials, when he was forced to choose between testifying against the Dakotas or ascending the gallows in silence. His final decision was whether to reunite with his family at Santee and live among vengeful Dakotas after his release from prison. All of Godfrey's life-or-death choices were related to his race, which was generally a handicap. But sometimes (such as during the trials or when Lincoln considered his fate) his racial uniqueness may actually have saved him.

If Godfrey does not neatly qualify for either glory or ignominy, however, his fascinating story affords us a chance to reappraise the treatment of African Americans in early Minnesota and to look again at the 1862 conflict through the eyes of someone who fits into neither of the two main warring camps. Just as Godfrey does not deserve many of the calumnies heaped upon him, nor does either side in the war merit the strongly biased depictions that have been written from both extremes. Neither whites nor Dakotas held a monopoly on virtue or evil in 1862.

The telling of Godfrey's story tends to make each side look worse than their respective partisans would wish. Perhaps that is rough justice, for neither whites nor Indians, on balance, have been fair to Joseph Godfrey.

NOTES ON AFTERWORD

1. *Niobrara (NE) Tribune*, July 8, 1909.
2. *Morton (MN) Enterprise*, July 23, 1909.
3. *St. Paul Dispatch*, July 24, 1909.
4. *Bird Island (MN) Union*, July 30, 1909.
5. See Anderson and Woolworth, *Through Dakota Eyes*, fifth printing, 261–62. The phony Crooks story purports to be the eyewitness account of an eight-year-old Dakota boy who accompanied the pinioned prisoners through New Ulm. There is ample evidence to support the conclusion that the Dakotas were transported in separate groups by different routes in November 1862: the male Dakotas who had been tried, with a small number of Dakota jail aides, were taken in carts to a camp near Mankato, passing near New Ulm en route; but the much larger group of Dakotas—older men, women, and children, including George Crooks—walked via another route to Fort Snelling, bypassing New Ulm. The now-debunked Crooks account blends the stories of the two groups by placing young Crooks with the prisoners. See Zeman, "Through the Heart of New Ulm: The Persistence of Place in Stories of the 1862 Dakota exile" in Bakeman and Richardson, *Trails of Tears*, 123–47.
6. Other facts supporting the conclusion that O. W. Smith fabricated stories include: (1) Smith was publishing a local paper and trying to sell dime-a-copy tracts about the Dakota War and thus had a financial incentive to invent stories. See his account of Hachin Wakanda (Lightning Blanket), first published in the *Enterprise* on August 28, 1908, and reprinted in a ten-cent tract titled "The Story of the Battle of Fort Ridgely," MHS. (2) Smith refused to modify or withdraw his Crooks account even after another local newspaper published a complete refutation attributed to Crooks himself. See "Geo. Crooks Not the Man," *Redwood (MN) Gazette*, February 24, 1909. The Crooks repudiation of the story outlines very specific falsehoods that could be corroborated independently, such as the fact that Crooks's brother was not killed at New Ulm (as reported by Smith) but died years later of natural causes. Smith failed to publish either a retraction or a response to George Crooks's complaint that Smith's story was invented. (3) Smith also failed to respond and refused to publish corrections when Theodore Carter twice wrote him to point out factual inaccuracies in his Godfrey obituary and to ask Smith for the source of his claims. To facilitate Smith's reply, Carter even enclosed stamped, self-addressed envelopes, but he never heard from Smith. See Carter to Editor, *Morton Enterprise*, November 29 and December 23, 1909, Carter Papers, MHS, box 2. Another local paper also called the Godfrey obituary a "very hazy Indian yarn." *Fairfax (MN) Standard*, July 29, 1909. Smith responded to this criticism in an ad hominem attack on the Fairfax editor and with vague assertions that his statements about Godfrey could be verified by reading uprising histories (which, of course, is also false). *Morton (MN) Enterprise*, August 6, 1909.

7. Carter to Agent, Santee Indians, August 18, 1909, Carter Papers, MHS, box 2. Carter apparently received no response to this letter, but he did later get a letter from Santee Indian agent McIntyre, dated February 14, 1910, Woolworth Papers, MHS. Most of McIntyre's letter is based on information from a Dakota man, Dr. George Quinn. It includes a hearsay report of Quinn's claim that Godfrey had boasted of killing "a whole family" near New Ulm, an account that, Quinn added, a deceased Dakota man named John Henry (an eyewitness) had verified to him. Carter apparently did not credit these second- and third-hand reports, for he did not mention them in his later article about Godfrey. Similarly, Quinn's accounts are not credited in the text of this book, for he was said to have been a highly unreliable person. Historian Return I. Holcombe told Folwell that Quinn was "a bright fellow, but not truthful" and that he "had a way of mixing truth and falsehood." Holcombe, interview by Folwell, January 22, 1908, Folwell Papers, MHS, box 114. More seriously, Quinn was said, in the context of legal proceedings relating to half-breed scrip, to have given false testimony; letters were written by Santee Agency officials alerting judges that Quinn had been paid to give false evidence in litigation. See, for example, Iron Elk heirship case, NA, RG 75, BIA, LR, CCF, 1907–39, E121, file 19641-1910.
8. *St. Peter Herald*, December 20, 1912.
9. "Application for a Patent in Fee," September 15, 1913, Godfrey heirship file, describes Joseph Godfrey Jr. as a "very progressive" and "industrious" farmer.
10. Godfrey heirship file.
11. Ibid.
12. Cassidy to Leech, January 9, 1918 (misdated 1917), George Blackowl Estate, NA, RG 75, BIA, LR, CCF 1907–39, E121, file 34941-1915(350).
13. Delores Espinoza, telephone conversation with the author, March 5, 2006. Espinoza is a great-great-granddaughter of Joseph Godfrey.
14. Jerry Godfrey, telephone conversation with the author, November 20, 2002. He is a great-grandson of Joseph Godfrey.
15. Liska, *Ponca Curse*, 133, quoting tribal member George Rouillard.
16. *St. Peter Herald*, April 20, 1906.
17. Folwell, *History of Minnesota*, 2:199.
18. Satterlee commentary in Folwell, Satterlee, and Brown, *Court Proceedings*, 7–8.
19. Satterlee, "Comments on the Trials of Dakota Indians," Folwell Papers, MHS, box 80, p. 1.
20. Carley, *Dakota War of 1862*, 68; Anderson and Woolworth, *Through Dakota Eyes*, 85.
21. Clarence Paine compared Godfrey with Simon Gerty, a white man raised by the Seneca Indians who joined in a massacre of whites. See also Clarence Paine, Godfrey biography, October 4, 1907, MHS, M582, roll 1; and Barr, "Monster So Brutal." Nix likened Godfrey to a turncoat Greek man who was summarily executed by a Turkish leader despite his helpful spying on his own people. Nix, *Sioux Uprising*, 130. Another writer likened Godfrey to Titus Oates, a Protestant clergyman who was notorious as a serial perjurer and for touching off an anti-Catholic pogrom in seventeenth-century England. Unsigned review of *History of the Sioux War and Massacres of 1862 and 1863*, by Isaac V. D. Heard, *North American Review* 98, no. 202 (January 1864): 266–70.
22. Buck, *Indian Outbreaks*, 228.
23. Shannon, "Black Judas."
24. Buck, *Indian Outbreaks*, 225.
25. Nix, *Sioux Uprising*, 154.
26. Brown, *Bury My Heart*, 59.

27. A respected Dakota scholar, Elden Lawrence, carries this anti-Godfrey argument to its natural conclusion, contending that Godfrey deserved to be hanged "twenty times over" and that his trial testimony should be disregarded as that of "a liar and a murderer." Lawrence, *Peace Seekers*, 134, 138.

APPENDIX

Whiting-Ruggles Report

"Message of the President of the United States in answer to a resolution of the Senate of the 5th instant in relation to the Indian barbarities in Minnesota," 37th Congress, 3rd Session, Executive Doc. 7, Exhibit E, 1862.

SIR: Having, by your directions, examined the records of the convictions of Sioux Indians by the military commission ordered by Brigadier General Sibley, we submit the following list of those who were convicted of rape and murder, viz:

No. 1. O-TA-KLA, *alias* GODFREY, a negro.—Engaged extensively in the massacres, and, though sentenced to be hung, recommended to have his punishment commuted to imprisonment for ten years, because of valuable testimony and information he furnished the commission.

No. 2. TE-HE-HDO-NE-CHA.—Engaged in the massacres; took a white woman prisoner and *ravished* her.

No. 4. TAZOO, *alias* PLAN-DOO-TA.—Convicted of participating in the murder of Mr. Patville, and of ravishing a young girl.

APPENDIX

No. 5. Wy-A-Tah-To-Wah.—Confesses to have participated in the murder of Mr. Francis Patville, and to have been engaged in three battles.

No. 6. Hin-Han-Shoon-Ko-Yag-Ma-Ne.—Convicted of the murder of Alexander Hunter, and of having taken and had Mrs. Hunter a prisoner until she was rescued from him by another Indian.

No. 10. Muz-Za-Bom-A-Du.—Convicted of the murder of an old man and two children.

No. 11. Wah-Pa-Du-Ta.—Confesses that he was engaged in the massacres, and that he shot a white man.

No. 12. Wah-He-Hud.—Convicted of participating in the battles, and of murder.

No. 14. Sua-Ma-Ni.—Convicted of the murder of two persons.

No. 15. Ta-Te-Mi-Ma.—Convicted of murder, and of the capture of women and children.

No. 19. Rda-In-Yan-Kua.—Took a prominent part in all the battles, including the attack on New Ulm, leading and urging the Indians forward, and opposing the giving up of the captives when it was proposed by others.

No. 22. Do-Wan-Sa.—Convicted of the murder of a white woman, and of the design to ravish her daughter, who was wounded by him and killed by another Indian before he had carried his design into execution.

No. 24. Ha-Pan.—Confessed that he was in all the battles and at the murder of Mr. Patville, and that he aided in taking a white woman (Miss Williams) prisoner.

No. 35. Shoon-Ka-Ska, (White Dog.)—Was the leader of the party that attacked Captain Marsh's company, and was the man who detained Captain Marsh in conversation until the Indians crossed the river and surrounded the command, and then gave them the signal to fire.

No. 67. Toon-Kan-Chah-Tay-Mane.—Said in the presence of witness that he shot a man in an ox-wagon, and was in several battles.

No. 68. E-Tay-Hoo-Tay.—Told witness that he killed Divoll and seven white persons across the river; that the second day after crossing the river he killed a man and a woman.

No. 69. Om-Da-Cha.—Took witness, David Faribault, prisoner, who says he shot two persons at his house.

No. 70. Hay-Pee-Don, or Wamne-Omne-Ho-Ta.—Cut Mrs. Thieler with a hatchet after she had been shot by another Indian, and fired many shots at the fort.

No. 96. Mahpe-O-Ke-Na-Ji.—Convicted of the murder of Antoine Young, and of participating in the murder of another man, four women, and eleven children.

No. 115. Henry Milord, a half breed.—Convicted of participating in the murder of a white man and woman.—(See cases 138 & 175.)

No. 121. Chaskay-Don, or Chaskay-Etay.—Convicted of shooting and cutting open a woman who was with child.

No. 138. Baptiste Campbell, a half breed.—Confessed that he was one of the party who murdered a man and woman, and that he shot first.—(See cases 115 and 175.)

APPENDIX

No. 155. Tay-Ta-Ka-Gay.—Convicted of murdering or of participating in the murder of Amos W. Huggins.

No. 170. Ha-Pink-Pa.—Convicted of the murder of Garvie.

No. 175. Hypolite Ange, a half-breed.—Confesses that he was one of the party that murdered a white man, and that he fired at him.—(See cases 115 and 138.)

No. 178. Na-Pa-Shue.—Convicted of participating in a massacre, and boasted he had killed nineteen persons.

No. 210. Wa-Kan-Ta-Ka.—Convicted of the murder of a white man not named.

No. 225. Toon-Kan-Ka-Yag-E-Na-Jin.—Convicted of participating in the murder of a white man at the Big Woods.

No. 254. Ma-Kat-E-Na-Jin.—Convicted of participating in the massacres near New Ulm, and of encouraging the young men to do so.

No. 264. Pa-Ze-Koo-Tay-Ma-Ne.—Convicted of participating in the murder of a party of eight white men.

No. 279. Ta-Tay-Hde-Don.—Convicted of participating in the massacre at Beaver creek, and of taking captive a white woman.

No. 318. Wa-She-Choon, or Toon-Kan-Shkan-Shkan-Mene-Hay.—Convicted of participating in the murder of LaButt's son.

No. 327. A-E-Cha-Ga.—Convicted of participating in the murder of an old man and two girls.

No. 333. HA-TAN-IN-KOO.—Convicted of participating in the murder of a man at Green lake; admits he struck him with an axe after he had been shot by others of the party.

No. 342. CHAY-TON-HOON-KA.—Proved to have been one of a party that committed massacres at Beaver creek.

No. 359. CHAN-KA-HADA.—Is proven to have been of the party, and present when Patville was killed, and to have saved Mary Anderson (who had been wounded) from being killed, and to have taken her prisoner.

No. 373. HDA-HIN-HDAY.—Convicted of the murder of Mrs. Adams's child, and others. Was one of the party that brought Mrs. Adams in.

No. 377. O-YA-TAY-A-KOO.—Convicted of participating in the murder of Patville.

No. 382. MA-HOO-WAY-WA.—Convicted of participating in the massacre at "Travellers' Home," and of murdering a man on the road near there.

No. 383. WA-KIN-YAN-NA.—Convicted of participating in the murder, near the "Travellers' Home," of an old man, two young girls, and two boys.

To facilitate your reference to these particular cases we have withdrawn the papers from the records of the commission and submit them herewith. With great respect, your obedient servants,

GEORGE C. WHITING.
FRANCIS H. RUGGLES.
EXECUTIVE MANSION, December 5, 1862.

ACKNOWLEDGMENTS

In addition to my family, two people provided indispensable support for this book. When I decided, in 1999, to explore the possibility of writing about Joseph Godfrey, I discussed my interest with Alan R. Woolworth, a longtime research fellow at the Minnesota Historical Society. Though officially retired, Alan still maintained an office at the society. He shared with me hundreds of Godfrey-related documents he had collected, a personal treasure trove that would have taken me years to compile. In just one afternoon Alan convinced me that there was a sufficient nucleus of materials to undergird a biography of this relatively obscure black Minnesotan. Without Alan's superb scholarship and generosity, this book would never have been written.

Alan also introduced me to Carrie Reber Zeman, who, I soon found, shares my insistence on using primary sources to document historical truths. Both this book and I have benefited beyond measure from the scores of breakthrough findings that Carrie has passed along from her prodigious research efforts. As one of countless examples I could cite, I would still be ignorant today of the dramatic way in which Godfrey broke loose from slavery had Carrie not wended her meticulous way through more than one hundred boxes at the Minnesota Historical Society containing the research and correspondence files left by historian William Watts Folwell. Thanks to Carrie's findings, Godfrey's story is far more detailed and richer than it would have been without her contributions of original source materials.

My dear wife, Elizabeth, has borne the brunt of my sometimes feverish fixation on this story. Her loving support has been firm and steadfast even when I deserved more exasperation than she evinced. A former journalist and editor, Elizabeth also helped transform my clunky first drafts into more readable prose. Our five wonderful children—Melissa, Rachel, Maria, Howie, and Matthew—and their spouses have listened patiently to my Godfrey tales and avoided saying (even if they thought it) that I might have found a better activity for my retirement years than delving into history's dusty corners. Maria's father-in-law, Admiral Dennis Blair, also showed great patience in helping me understand the military aspects of Godfrey's story.

Many archivists, librarians, historians, and researchers also deserve thanks for contributing to this book. In particular, Darla Gebhard, research librarian at the Brown County Historical Society, spurred my initial interest in Godfrey by producing files that linked him to the scene where my ancestor was killed; she has since assisted in many other ways. Stephen E. Osman and Bruce White each gave me copies of army pay vouchers that led to the all-important paymaster records at the National Archives.

A coterie of diligent Minnesota researchers has provided strong assistance even though I, as a New Yorker, cannot attend their regular meetings. In addition to Carrie Zeman and Stephen Osman, that group includes Mary Bakeman, Curtis Dahlin, Lois Glewwe, John Isch, John LaBatte, Corinne Monjeau-Marz, Thomas G. Shaw, and Jeff Williamson.

Rhoda Gilman, Henry Sibley's biographer, is allegedly retired but still very active in Minnesota history, and she deserves special thanks for her assistance and unwavering encouragement. I also remain very appreciative of the careful and thoughtful editorial skills of Ann Regan at the Minnesota Historical Society Press, which initially contracted to publish an early version of this story.

William D. Green and Christopher P. Lehman each gave me the benefit of their unique knowledge of Minnesota's early African American history. Louis Garcia translated the Dakota-language letter dictated from

ACKNOWLEDGMENTS

prison by Godfrey and helped in many other ways.

Ann Bailly and Bruce Faribault spoke freely with me about Alexis Bailly and the Faribault family, despite the fact that my questions suggested coverage of their ancestors that is not always positive.

I am especially grateful to Dakota people who have assisted me, including descendants of Joseph Godfrey. They include Clarence Campbell, Santee Reservation archivist; Carl Crosley, who now farms the land once owned by Godfrey; Delores Espinoza, Godfrey's great-great-granddaughter (who gave me extraordinary help in developing a Godfrey family tree); Jerry Godfrey, a great-grandson; and Carrie Godfrey.

I am also grateful to the Reverend Clifford Canku, who invited me to attend and make a presentation at the Dakota Letters Symposium, held in July 2005 on the Sisseton-Wahpeton Reservation in South Dakota. The purpose of this symposium was to discuss Dakota-language letters written from the Davenport prison, principally in 1863; I was privileged to be the only non-Dakota presenter. Other speakers or participants in that symposium whose words and kindnesses were greatly appreciated are the Reverend Sydney Byrd, Sara Childers, Dr. Eldon Lawrence, Dr. John Peacock, and the Reverend Michael Simon. I came away from that symposium with a deeper understanding of the cultural and historical-interpretation chasms that continue to separate white Americans from many Dakota people.

Four researchers assisted me in finding and copying invaluable source materials. My thanks go to Candace Clifford, Mary Louise Clifford, Krista Ottino, and Carolyn M. Essig.

My literary agent, John Ware, has been a faithful friend and supporter throughout this project. Michele Hodgson, long a good friend, and Joy Margheim performed magnificently as copy editors of the final drafts of this book.

I am also indebted to a host of other people, including Carolyn Ruth Anderson, Annette Atkins, Dr. Valere Beeck, Scott W. Berg, Kirsten Delegard, Mark Diedrich, Robert and Nancy Goodman, David Grabitske, James Hansen (Wisconsin Historical Society), Rich Hermanek, Bruce Kohn, Barbara Luecke, Charles Mulhair, Lilah Pengra, Kate Roberts, Elwin Rogers, Virginia Driving Hawk Sneve, Kathryn Zabelle Derounian-

Stodola, Terry Strauss, Jimmy Sweet, Brian Szott, Clark Thomas, Elroy E. Ubl, Lea VanderVelde, Richard Williams, and Mary Wingerd.

ABBREVIATIONS

National Archives Records

BIA	Bureau of Indian Affairs
CCF	Central Classified Files
E	Entry
LR	Letters Received
LS	Letters Sent
M	Microfilm
NA	National Archives and Records Administration
RG	Records Group

Other Abbreviations

CCHS	Chippewa County (Minnesota) Historical Society
CWS	Center for Western Studies, Augustana College, Sioux Falls, SD
Godfrey heirship file	Joseph Godfrey heirship file, NA, RG 75, CCF, entry 121, file 110773-1913(312)

MCIW	*Minnesota in the Civil and Indian Wars, 1861–1865, Official Report and Correspondence.* 2 vols. St. Paul, MN: Board of Commissioners, 1892
MHS	Minnesota Historical Society
NMM, MHS	Northwest Missions Manuscripts and Index, Minnesota Historical Society
Pay Vouchers	NA, RG 217, E516, Settled Accounts, Army Paymaster
Santee Agency Census	NA, RG 75, M595, rolls 475 (1885–98), 476 (1898–1910), and 477 (1911–17)
Scrip Rolls	Records Relating to Mixed-Blood Claimants under the Treaty of Prairie du Chien, 1855–56, NA, RG 75, Miscelaneous Reserve Papers; also available as MHS microfilm 550
St. Louis Freedom Suits	Circuit Court Case Files, Office of the Circuit Court–St. Louis, Missouri State Archives, Office of the Secretary of State, http://stlcourtrecords.wustl.edu, accessed March 20, 2012
Dakota Trials Records	1862 Dakota trials records, three microfilm rolls. Original records in NA, Center for Legislative Archives, U.S. Senate Records (for further details, see chapter 4, note 2)
Winnebago trials	Winnebago trial records, House of Representatives, Committee of Indian Affairs, Center for Legislative Archives, 37th Congress, H.R. 37A, E.7.8

WORKS CITED

Archival Collections

Minnesota Historical Society, St. Paul, MN
    Bailly, Alexis. Papers.
    Carter, Theodore G., and Family. Papers.
    Dakota Conflict of 1862 Manuscripts Collection.
    First Presbyterian Church (Minneapolis, MN). Parish Record Books.
    Folwell, William Watts, and Family. Papers.
    Jarvis, Nathan S. Letters.
    Northwest Missions Manuscripts and Index.
    Paine, Clarence S. Biographical data on Joseph Godfrey.
    Pond Family Papers.
    Riggs, Stephen R., and Family. Papers.
    Satterlee, Marion and William W. Papers.
    Schwandt Schmidt, Mary. Papers.
    Sibley, Henry H. Papers.
    Taliaferro, Lawrence. Papers.
    Whipple, Henry B. Papers.
    Williamson, Thomas S. Papers.
    Woolworth, Alan R. Papers.

National Archives and Records Administration, Washington, D.C.
- RG 46, Legislative Center, 37th Congress, Senate 37A-F2, box 43
- RG 46, U.S. Senate Records, 38A-H7, Committee on Indian Affairs
- RG 48, LS, Indian Division, Department of the Interior, M606, roll 4
- RG 48, LR, Indian Division, Department of the Interior, M825, roll 20
- RG 75, BIA, LR, Central Classified Files 1907–39, E121
  - File no. 110773-1913(312) (Godfrey heirship file)
  - File no. 19641-1910 (Iron Elk heirship file)
  - File no. 34941-1915(350) (George Blackowl Estate)
  - File no. 24448-1911(127) (Santee Indian Competency Commission report, Joseph Godfrey Jr.)
- RG 75, BIA, LR, M175
- RG 75, E529, Miscellaneous Sioux Reserve Papers
- RG 75, E978, Records of Employees, Rosters of Agency Employees, 1853–1909
- RG 75, M234, St. Peter's Agency, 1868–70
- RG 75, M595, rolls 475–77, Santee Sioux Agency Census Lists (1885–1917)
- RG 75, Office of Indian Affairs, LR, 1881–1907
- RG 75, Office of Indian Affairs, LS
- RG 94, E173, Indian Prisoners
- RG 94, M617, Returns from U.S. Military Posts, 1800–1916 (also available at http://www.ancestry.com)
- RG 94, M1523, "Courts-Martial and Military Commission Proceedings against Union Soldiers, 1861–1866"
- RG 94, LR, Adjutant General, M619, roll 483
- RG 153, Records of Judge Advocate General, Courts Martial file no. KK 516
- RG 217, E516, Settled Accounts, Paymaster (Pay Vouchers)
- RG 393, E343, pt. 3, Letters and Telegrams Sent, District of Minnesota

RG 393, E346, pt. 3, LR, District of Minnesota, 1862–63
RG 393, E347, pt. 3, Telegrams Received, District of Minnesota, Department of War, 1862–66
RG 393, E3436, pt. 1, Letters Sent and Received, Department of Northwest, Headquarters
RG 393, E3449, pt. 1, Unentered Letters, Department of Northwest, 1862–65, Headquarters Records
RG 393, E3450, pt. 1, Telegrams Received, Department of Northwest
RG 393, E3480, pt. 1, LS, Department of Northwest, 1862 (Sibley's letters from Camp Release)

Other Repositories
Blue Earth County Historical Society, Mankato, MN
Brown County Historical Society, New Ulm, MN
Center for Western Studies, Augustana College, Sioux Falls, SD
Chicago Historical Society, Chicago, IL
Chippewa County Historical Society, Montevideo, MN
Dakotah Prairie Museum, Aberdeen, SD
Hennepin County Historical Society, Minneapolis, MN
Library of Congress, Washington, D.C.
    Abraham Lincoln Papers
Missouri State Archives, Office of the Secretary of State, Jefferson City, MO
    Circuit Court Case Files, Office of the Circuit Court–St. Louis
New-York Historical Society, New York, NY
Saskatchewan Archives Board, Regina, Saskatchewan, Canada
Southern Minnesota Historical Center, Minnesota State University, Mankato, MN
Stearns History Museum, St. Cloud, MN

Books, Articles, and Other Sources

American State Papers: Military Affairs. 7 vols. Washington, D.C.: Gales and Seaton, 1832–61. Available online at Library of Congress, "A Century of Lawmaking for a New Nation: U.S. Congressional Documents and Debates, 1774–1875," http://memory.loc.gov/ammem/amlaw/lawhome.html.

Anderson, Gary Clayton. *Kinsmen of Another Kind: Dakota-White Relations in the Upper Mississippi Valley, 1650–1862*. Lincoln: University of Nebraska Press, 1984.

———. *Little Crow, Spokesman for the Sioux*. St. Paul: Minnesota Historical Society Press, 1986.

Anderson, Gary Clayton, and Alan R. Woolworth, eds. *Through Dakota Eyes: Narrative Accounts of the Minnesota Indian War of 1862*. St. Paul: Minnesota Historical Society Press, 1988.

Appell, Livia. "Slavery in Minnesota." *Minnesota History Bulletin* 5, no. 1 (1923): 40–44.

Bachman, Walt. "*The Death of Ernst Dietrich.*" Unpublished manuscript, 1996. MHS library.

Bakeman, Mary Hawker, and Antona Hawkins Richardson. *Trails of Tears: Minnesota's Dakota Indian Exile Begins*. Roseville, MN: Park Genealogical Books, 2008.

Baker, James H. "Address at Fort Snelling in the Celebration of the Centennial Anniversary of the Treaty of Pike with the Sioux." In *Collections of the Minnesota Historical Society*, 12:291–301. St. Paul: Minnesota Historical Society, 1908.

———. *Lives of the Governors of Minnesota*. Collections of the Minnesota Historical Society, 13. St. Paul: Minnesota Historical Society, 1908.

Barr, Daniel P. "'A Monster So Brutal': Simon Girty and the Degenerative Myth of the American Frontier, 1783–1900." *Essays in History* 40 (1998).

Barton, Winifred W. *John P. Williamson, a Brother to the Sioux*. New York: Fleming H. Revell, 1919.

Basler, Roy P., ed. *The Collected Works of Abraham Lincoln*. Vols. 5–8. New Brunswick, NJ: Rutgers University Press, 1953.

Bauer, K. Jack. *Zachary Taylor: Soldier, Planter, Statesman of the Old Southwest*. Baton Rouge: Louisiana State University Press, 1985.

Bell, John. "The Sioux War Panorama and American Mythic History." *Theatre Journal* 48, no. 3 (1996): 279–99.

Belliveau, Walter. "The Life of Alexis Bailly, Minnesota Pioneer." Typescript, 1928. MHS library.

Berghold, Alexander. *The Indians' Revenge; or, Days of Horror: Some Appalling Events in the History of the Sioux*. Reprint, San Francisco: P. J. Thomas, 1891.

Bliss, John H. "Reminiscences of Fort Snelling." In *Collections of the Minnesota Historical Society*, 6:335–53. St. Paul: Minnesota Historical Society, 1894.

Brown, Dee Alexander. *Bury My Heart at Wounded Knee: An Indian History of the American West*. New York: Holt, Rinehart and Winston, 1971.

Bryant, Charles S. *A History of the Great Massacre by the Sioux Indians, in Minnesota*. Cincinnati: Rickey and Carroll, 1864.

Buck, Daniel. *Indian Outbreaks*. 1904. Reprint, Minneapolis: Ross and Haines, 1965.

Carley, Kenneth. *The Dakota War of 1862*. St. Paul: Minnesota Historical Society Press, 1976.

———. "The Sioux Campaign of 1862; Sibley's Letters to His Wife." *Minnesota History* 38, no. 3 (September 1962): 99–114.

Chomsky, Carol. "The United States–Dakota War Trials: A Study in Military Injustice." *Stanford Law Review* 43, no. 1 (1990): 13–98.

Clodfelter, Micheal. *The Dakota War: The United States Army versus the Sioux, 1862–1865*. Jefferson, NC: McFarland, 1998.

Connolly, A. P. *A Thrilling Narrative of the Minnesota Massacre and the Sioux War of 1862–63*. Chicago: A. P. Connolly, 1896.

Coppée, Henry. *Field Manual of Courts-Martial*. Philadelphia: Lippincott, 1863.

"Crawford County, Wisconsin, Marriages, 1818–1848," *Minnesota Genealogical Journal* 1 (May 1984): 39–58.

Curtiss-Wedge, Franklyn, ed. *The History of Renville County, Minnesota.* 2 vols. Chicago: H. C. Cooper Jr. and Co., 1916.

Davis, Jane Spector. "Two Sioux War Orders: A Mystery Unraveled." *Minnesota History* 41, no. 3 (Fall 1968): 117–25.

De Bow, J. D. B. *Statistical View of the United States, Embracing Its Territory, Population—White, Free Colored, and Slave.* Washington, D.C.: A. O. P. Nicholson, 1854.

Diedrich, Mark. *Famous Dakota Chiefs.* Rev. ed. Rochester, MN: Coyote Books, 1999.

———. *Little Crow and the Dakota War: The Long Historical Cover-Ups Exposed.* Rochester, MN: Coyote Books, 2006.

Dietz, Charlton. "Henry Behnke: New Ulm's Paul Revere." *Minnesota History* 45, no. 3 (Fall 1976): 111–15.

Ehrlich, Walter. *They Have No Rights: Dred Scott's Struggle for Freedom.* Contributions in Legal Studies, vol. 9. Westport, CT: Greenwood Press, 1979.

Fehrenbacher, Don Edward. *The Dred Scott Case: Its Significance in American Law and Politics.* Oxford: Oxford University Press, 1978.

Fisher, Louis. "Military Tribunals: Historical Patterns and Lessons." Congressional Research Service, report RL32458, July 9, 2004.

Flandrau, Charles E. *The History of Minnesota and Tales of the Frontier.* St. Paul, MN: E. W. Porter, 1900.

Folwell, William Watts. *A History of Minnesota.* 4 vols. St. Paul: Minnesota Historical Society, 1921.

Folwell, William Watts, Marion P. Satterlee, and Samuel J. Brown. *The Court Proceedings in the Trial of Dakota Indians Following the Massacre in Minnesota in August 1862.* Minneapolis: Satterlee Print Co., 1927.

Fonda, John H. "Reminiscences of Wisconsin." In *Collections of the State Historical Society of Wisconsin*, ed. Lyman Copeland Draper, 205–84. 1868. Reprint, Madison: Wisconsin Historical Society, 1907.

Frazer, Joseph Jack. *Iron Face: The Adventures of Jack Frazer, Frontier Warrior, Scout, and Hunter. A Narrative Recorded by "Walker-in-the Pines" (Henry Hastings Sibley)*. Edited by Theodore C. Blegen and Sara A. Davidson. Chicago: Caxton Club, 1950.

Fridley, Russell W., Leota M. Kellett, and June D. Holmquist, eds. *Charles E. Flandrau and the Defense of New Ulm*. New Ulm, MN: Brown County Historical Society, 1962.

Fritsche, L. A. *History of Brown County, Minnesota, Its People, Industries and Institutions*. Vol. 1. Indianapolis, IN: B. F. Bowen, 1916.

Gilman, Rhoda R. *Henry Hastings Sibley: Divided Heart*. St. Paul: Minnesota Historical Society Press, 2004.

Goodman, Nancy, and Robert Goodman. *Joseph R. Brown, Adventurer on the Minnesota Frontier, 1820–1849*. Rochester, MN: Lone Oak Press, 1996.

Green, William D. "Eliza Winston and the Politics of Freedom in Minnesota, 1854–60." *Minnesota History* 57, no. 3 (Fall 2000): 106–22.

———. "Minnesota's Long Road to Black Suffrage, 1849–1868." *Minnesota History* 56, no. 3 (Summer 1998): 69–84.

———. *A Peculiar Imbalance: The Fall and Rise of Racial Equality in Early Minnesota*. St. Paul: Minnesota Historical Society Press, 2007.

Hamilton, Holman. *Zachary Taylor*. 2 vols. 1941. Reprint, Norwalk, CT: Easton Press, 1989.

Hans, Fred M. *The Great Sioux Nation. A Complete History of Indian Life and Warfare in America*. Chicago: M. A. Donohue, 1907.

Hart, Joseph. "Rule of the Bone." *City Pages* (Minneapolis–St. Paul), September 24, 1997.

Heard, Isaac V. D. *History of the Sioux War and Massacres of 1862–1863*. New York: Harper and Brothers, 1864.

Heilbron, Bertha L. "Documentary Panorama." *Minnesota History* 30, no. 1 (March 1949): 14–23.

Heitman, Francis B. *Historical Register and Dictionary of the United States Army, from Its Organization, September 29, 1789, to March 2, 1903*. Vol. 1. Baltimore: Genealogical Publishing, 1994.

Holcombe, Return I., and William H. Bingham, eds. *Compendium of History and Biography of Minneapolis and Hennepin County, Minnesota*. Chicago: H. Taylor, 1914.

Hubbard, Lucius F., William Pitt Murray, James H. Baker, Warren Upham, Return I. Holcombe, and Frank R. Holmes. *Minnesota in Three Centuries, 1655–1908*. Semi-centennial ed. 4 vols. New York: Publishing Society of Minnesota, 1908.

Hughes, T. *History of Blue Earth County and Biographies of Its Leading Citizens*. Chicago: Middle West, 1909.

Hyman, Colette A. "Survival at Crow Creek, 1863–1866." *Minnesota History* 61, no. 4 (2008): 148–61.

Kane, Lucile M. "The Sioux Treaties and the Traders." *Minnesota History* 32, no. 2 (June 1951): 65–80.

Kellogg, Deren E. "Lincoln's New Mexico Patronage: Saving the Far Southwest for the Union." *New Mexico Historical Review* 75, no. 4 (October 2000): 511–34.

Kolchin, Peter. *American Slavery, 1619–1877*. New York: Hill and Wang, 1993.

Laviolette, Gontran. *The Dakota Sioux in Canada*. Winnipeg, MB: DLM Publications, 1991. Originally published as *The Sioux Indians in Canada* (Regina, SK: Marian Press, 1944). Page numbers in the notes refer to the 1991 edition.

Lawrence, Elden. *The Peace Seekers: The Indian Christians and the Dakota Conflict*. Sioux Falls, SD: Pine Hill Press, 2005.

Lehman, Christopher P. *Slavery in the Upper Mississippi Valley, 1787–1865: A History of Human Bondage in Illinois, Iowa, Minnesota and Wisconsin*. Jefferson, NC: McFarland, 2011.

Lincoln, Abraham. "Lincoln's Sioux War Order." *Minnesota History* 33, no. 2 (Summer 1952): 77–79.

Liska, Danny. *The Ponca Curse*. Niobrara, NE: Bigfoot Publishing, 1990.

Litwack, Leon F. *North of Slavery: The Negro in the Free States, 1790–1860*. Chicago: University of Chicago Press, 1961.

Luecke, Barbara K., and John Luecke. *Snelling: Minnesota's First First Family*. Eagan, MN: Grenadier Publications, 1993.

WORKS CITED

Mahan, Bruce E. *Old Fort Crawford and the Frontier*. 1926. Reprint, Prairie du Chien, WI: Prairie du Chien Historical Society, 2000.

McConkey, Harriet E. Bishop. *Dakota War Whoop: Indian Massacres and War in Minnesota*. Abridged ed. 1864. Reprint, Chicago: Lakeside Press, 1965.

McManus, Edgar J. *Black Bondage in the North*. Syracuse, NY: Syracuse University Press, 1973.

Meyer, Roy Willard. *History of the Santee Sioux: United States Indian Policy on Trial*. Rev. ed. Lincoln: University of Nebraska Press, 1993.

———. "The Red Wing Indian Village." Typescript, 1975. SMHC Manuscript Collection 1216. Southern Minnesota Historical Center, Minnesota State University, Mankato.

Minnesota in the Civil and Indian Wars, 1861–1865, Official Report and Correspondence. 2 vols. St. Paul, MN: Board of Commissioners, 1892.

Monjeau-Marz, Corrine L. *The Dakota Indian Internment at Fort Snelling, 1862–1864*. St. Paul, MN: Prairie Smoke Press, 2005.

Neill, Edward D. "Occurrences in and around Fort Snelling, from 1819 to 1840." In *Collections of the Minnesota Historical Society*, 2:102–42. St. Paul: Minnesota Historical Society, 1889.

Newson, T. M. *Pen Pictures of St. Paul, Minnesota, and Biographical Sketches of Old Settlers: From the Earliest Settlement of the City, Up to and Including the Year 1857*. St. Paul, MN: T. M. Newson, 1886.

Nichols, David A. *Lincoln and the Indians: Civil War Policy and Politics*. Columbia: University of Missouri Press, 1978.

Nix, Jacob. *The Sioux Uprising in Minnesota, 1862: Jacob Nix's Eyewitness History*. Translated by Gretchen Steinhauser. Edited by Don Heinrich Tolzmann and Eberhard Reichmann. German/English ed. Indianapolis: Max Kade German-American Center, Indiana University-Purdue University at Indianapolis and Indiana German Heritage Society, 1994.

Papers Relating to Talks and Councils Held with the Indians in Dakota and Montana Territories in the Years 1866–1869. Washington, DC: Government Printing Office, 1910.

Parker, Donald Dean. *The Recollections of Philander Prescott: Frontiersman of the Old Northwest, 1819–1862*. Lincoln: University of Nebraska Press, 1966.

Paulson, Robert J. *Franz Massopust, German-Bohemian Pathfinder and Founder of New Ulm, Minnesota: A Tragic Family Saga*. Roseville, MN: Park Genealogical Books, 2004.

Pond, Samuel W. *The Dakota or Sioux in Minnesota as They Were in 1834*. 1908. Reprint, St. Paul: Minnesota Historical Society Press, 1986.

———. *Two Volunteer Missionaries among the Dakotas; or, The Story of the Labors of Samuel W. and Gideon H. Pond*. Boston: Congregational Sunday-School and Publishing Society, 1893.

Porter, C. Fayne. "Little Crow, the Sioux." In *Our Indian Heritage: Profiles of 12 Great Leaders*, 113–28. Philadelphia: Chilton Books, 1964.

Ravoux, A. *Reminiscences, Memoirs, and Lectures of Monsignor A. Ravoux, V.G.* St. Paul: Brown, Treacy, 1890.

Report of the Commissioner of Indian Affairs for the Year 1858. Washington, D.C.: Government Printing Office, 1859.

Report of the Commissioner of Indian Affairs for the Year 1859. Washington, D.C.: Government Printing Office, 1860.

Report of the Commissioner of Indian Affairs for the Year 1862. Washington, D.C.: Government Printing Office, 1863.

Report of the Commissioner of Indian Affairs for the Year 1863. Washington, D.C.: Government Printing Office, 1864.

Report of the Secretary of the Interior for the Year 1864. Washington, D.C.: Government Printing Office, 1865.

Riggs, Maida Leonard. *A Small Bit of Bread and Butter: Letters from the Dakota Territory, 1832–1869*. South Deerfield, MA: Ash Grove Press, 1996.

Riggs, Stephen R. *Mary and I: Forty Years with the Sioux*. 1880. Reprint, Williamstown, MA: Corner House Publishers, 1971.

———. *Tah-koo wah-kan; or, The Gospel among the Dakotas*. 1869. Reprint, New York: Arno Press, 1972.

Roddis, Louis H. *The Indian Wars of Minnesota*. Cedar Rapids, IA: Torch Press, 1956.

Satterlee, Marion P. "The Indian Massacre in Brown County, in August 1862." Typescript, n.d. MHS library.

———. *Outbreak and Massacre by the Dakota Indians in Minnesota in 1862: Marion P. Satterlee's Minute Account of the Outbreak . . .* Edited by Don Heinrich Tolzmann. 1923. Reprint, Bowie, MD: Heritage Books, 2001.

[Schilling, Cecelia Ochs]. "A Nine Year Old Girl's Experiences in 1862 Massacre." *Southern Minnesotan*, 1931, 9–10, 23–24.

Schultz, Duane P. *Over the Earth I Come: The Great Sioux Uprising of 1862.* New York: St. Martin's Press, 1992.

Shannon, Ed. "Black Judas." *True West*, September–October 1960, 22–23, 36.

Shine, Greg. "A Slave Freed at Fort Vancouver: The Manumission of Monimia Travers." National Park Service, Fort Vancouver National Historic Site. http://www.nps.gov/fova/historyculture/a-slave-freed-at-fort-vancouver.htm.

Sibley, Henry Hastings. *The Unfinished Autobiography of Henry Hastings Sibley.* Edited by Theodore Christian Blegen. Minneapolis: Voyageur Press, 1932.

Sibley, James Scarborough. *The Sibley Family in America, 1629–1972: Genealogical Data.* 2nd ed. 2 vols. 1972. Reprint, Midlothian, TX: J. S. Sibley, 1982.

Skelton, William B. *An American Profession of Arms: The Army Officer Corps, 1784–1861.* Lawrence: University Press of Kansas, 1992.

Smith, O. W. Story of the Battle of Ft. Ridgely, Minn., August 20 and 22, 1862 as Told by Hachin-Wakanda (Lightning Blanket). Morton, MN: O. W. Smith, 1908.

Spangler, Earl. *The Negro in Minnesota.* Minneapolis: T. S. Denison, 1961.

Straus, Terry, and Denene DeQuintal, eds. *Race, Roots, and Relations: Native and African Americans.* Chicago: Albatross Press, 2005.

Swanson, Deborah. "Joseph Farr Remembers the Underground Railroad in St. Paul." *Minnesota History* 57, no. 3 (Fall 2000): 123–29.

Sweet, Jannette DeCamp. "Mrs. J. E. DeCamp Sweet's Narrative of Her Captivity in the Sioux Outbreak of 1862." In *Collections of the Minnesota Historical Society*, 6:354–80. St. Paul: Minnesota Historical Society, 1894.

Taliaferro, Lawrence. "Auto-Biography of Major Lawrence Taliaferro: Written in 1864." In *Collections of the Minnesota Historical Society*, 6:189–255. St. Paul: Minnesota Historical Society, 1894.

Temple, Seth J. *Camp McClellan during the Civil War*. Davenport, IA: Contemporary Club, 1928.

Thompson, Jerry D. *Confederate General of the West: Henry Hopkins Sibley*. 1987. Reprint, College Station: Texas A&M University Press, 1996.

Tolzmann, Don Heinrich, Mary Schwandt, and Minnie Buce Carrigan. *German Pioneer Accounts of the Great Sioux Uprising of 1862*. Milford, OH: Little Miami, 2002.

Turner, Lois. "An Analysis of Negro Slavery in Minnesota, 1819–1861." Thesis (Med), Macalester College, 1965.

Upham, Warren and Rose Barteau Dunlap. "Minnesota Biographies, 1655–1912." In *Collections of the Minnesota Historical Society*, 14. St. Paul: Minnesota Historical Society, 1912.

U.S. Department of the Interior and U.S. Sioux Commissioners. *Claims for Depredations by Sioux Indians*. Fairfield, WA: Ye Galleon Press, 1974.

VanderVelde, Lea. *Mrs. Dred Scott: A Life on Slavery's Frontier*. Oxford: Oxford University Press, 2009.

VanderVelde, Lea, and Sandhya Subramanian. "Mrs. Dred Scott." *Yale Law Journal* 106, no. 4 (1997): 1033–122.

Wakefield, Sarah F. *Six Weeks in the Sioux Tepees: A Narrative of Indian Captivity*. Edited by June Namias. 1864. Reprint, Norman: University of Oklahoma Press, 1997.

War of the Rebellion: A Compilation of the Official Records of the Union and Confederate Armies. Ser. 1, vols. 13, 22. Washington, D.C.: Government Printing Office, 1885.

Watson, Samuel J. "Professionalism, Social Attitudes, and Civil-Military Accountability in the United States Officer corps, 1815–1846. PhD diss., Rice University, 1996. Available online at http://scholarship.rice.edu/handle/1911/16973?show=full.

Welsh, William. *Taopi and His Friends; or, The Indians' Wrongs and Rights*. Philadelphia: Claxton, Remsen, and Haffelfinger, 1869.

West, Nathaniel. *The Ancestry, Life, and Times of Hon. Henry Hastings Sibley*. St. Paul, MN: Pioneer Press, 1889.

Whipple, Henry B. *Lights and Shadows of a Long Episcopate; Being Reminiscences and Recollections of the Right Reverend Henry Benjamin Whipple, D.D., LL.D., Bishop of Minnesota*. New York: Macmillan, 1899.

Wiener, Frederick Bernays. "*Courts-Martial and the Bill of Rights: The Original Practice.*" Harvard Law Review 72 (1958): 266–304.

Willand, Jon. *Lac Qui Parle and the Dakota Mission*. Madison, MN: Lac Qui Parle County Historical Society, 1964.

Williamson, John Poage. *An English-Dakota Dictionary*. 1902. Reprint, St. Paul: Minnesota Historical Society Press, 1992.

Wingerd, Mary Lethert, and Kirsten Delegard. *North Country: The Making of Minnesota*. Minneapolis: University of Minnesota Press, 2010.

Zeman, Carrie R. *The Population of Fort Ridgely during the Siege of the Dakota Conflict of 1862*. 3rd ed. Morton, MN: Lower Sioux Agency Historical Site, 2004.

INDEX

Page numbers in italics indicate illustrations.

Abe (slave of Henry Wilson), 37
abolitionism, 41, 43, 78, 133, 235. *See also* slavery
Acton MN, 84, 140
Aechaya (Aechga) (trial 327), 207–8, 225n21, 355
agriculture, 71–72, 73, 78n44, 83; and the Santee Sioux Reservation, 318–19, 320
Ainse, Pelagie, 23n5
Aldrich, Cyrus, 255–56
Alexander, Edmund B., 65, *66*, 67, 76n23
Alexander, Thomas L., 59, 60, 75n6
Allord, Joseph (trial 334), 225n29
Amdaychu (trial 69), 279n23, 354
American Fur Company, 2, 17–18, 19–20, 29, 126. *See also* fur trade
Ampatutokacha (Ampetutokeca), 221
Ampaynechaga, 272
Anderson (slave of Edmund Alexander), 76n23

Anderson, Gary Clayton: *Through Dakota Eyes*, 150, 343, 346
Anderson, Mary, 88, 110n29, 151, 152–53, 272; death of, 89, 157; saving of, by Chankahda, 210, 259
Ange, Hypolite (trial 175), 191, 279n24, 355
annuities, 72–73, 78n47, 92, 101, 183; delays in, 83, 84
Anpetuwaxte, 298
antiblack sentiment, 83–84, 233, 329; among the Dakotas, 70, 77n38, 216, 322–23; and pejorative terms, 70, 77n38, 84, 133, 175, 178, 216, 263, 297, 337n17, 344; in the press, 70, 178–79, 254, 263–64, 297, 342. *See also* racism
anti-Indian sentiment, 101, 201, 232, 252, 255–56; and mob violence, 228–31, 243–45, 246n7, 246n12, 294; in the press, 180, 232, 234–35, 244, 288–89, 297. *See also* racism
antislavery laws. *See* laws

376

INDEX

Armistead, Lewis, 61, 76n22
Astor, John Jacob, 2, 18
Auge, Hypolite (trial 175), 191, 279n24, 355

Bachman, Henry, 97
Bailey, Hiram S., 124, 127
Bailley, Alex. *See* Bailly, Alexis
Bailly, Alexis, 51, 57n60, 58; as American Fur Company representative, 2, 17–18, 19, 29; as Courtney's owner, 1, 13, 14–15, 26n37, 29, 30–31, 32, 49, 55n44; and liquor trafficking, 17, 34, 35, 52n13; race of, 3; and Wabasha trading post, 29, 32–33, 34–35
Bailly, Lucy (Mrs. Alexis Bailly), 2, 23n5, 54n40; and whipping of children, 15–16, 19, 27n44
Baker, Nathan, 303
Balcombe, Maj., 236
Barnes, Lucy Emma, 111n43, 112n47, 120–21
Barnes, Mary Elizabeth, 111n43, 112n47, 120–21
Barnes, Sarah Thompson (Mrs. William Barnes), 36, 92, 111n43, 112n47, 120–21
Barnes, William Henry, 111n43, 112n47, 120–21
Barns, F. A., 332–33
Battle of Wood Lake. *See* Wood Lake battle
Bay, Alexi. *See* Bailly, Alexis
Bee, Barnard, 67, 76n23
Beeson, John, 252
Behnke, Henry, 87
Big Eagle. *See* Wamdetanka (trial 34)
Birch Coulee battle, 95, 97–98, 105, 127, 130; casualty totals, 98; Godfrey's presence at the, 154–55, 160; testimony about the, 154–55, 160, 187, 188, 190, 191, 207, 212, 213, 236–37, 248n47, 290. *See also* Dakota War of 1862
Black Bondage in the North (McManus), 21
Blackowl, George, 344
Blackowl, Jennie (Mrs. George Blackowl). *See* Goodteacher, Jennie (Mrs. Joseph Godfrey)
Blacksmith, Stephen, 344
Bliss, John, 17, 27n47, 33
Bonga, George, 56n55
Bonga, Pierre, 56n55
Boudre, Benjamin, 32, 62
Boudre, Benjamin (son of Courtney), 62
Boudre, Catherine, 62
Boudre, Courtney. *See* Courtney
Boudre, Margaret, 61–62
Boudre, William. *See* William (son of Courtney)
Boutillier, Charles, 276, 284nn81–82
Bradley, George, 185, 292
Brown, Dee: *Bury My Heart at Wounded Knee*, 215, 347
Brown, Joseph R., 120, 127, 132, 273, 295, 296; and agriculture policies, 71, 78n44; and annuity payments, 72, 78n44; and identification of condemned Dakotas, 267, 281n52; as jailer, 132, 273, 295, 296. *See also* Indian agents
Brown, Samuel, 111n45, 230–31, 246n1
Brown, Susan Frenier (Mrs. Joseph Brown), 120
Brunson, Alfred, 36
Brunson, Benjamin, 77n28
Bryant, F. A., 334, 340n68
Buce, Bertha, 118
Buce, Caroline, 118
Buce, Minnie, 118

377

INDEX

Buck, Daniel: *Indian Outbreaks*, 329–30, 339n52, 346–47
Burnside, Ambrose, 251
Bury My Heart at Wounded Knee (Brown), 215, 347

Campbell, Baptiste (trial 138), 191, 198n41, 269, 279n24, 354
Campbell, Joseph, 117
Camp Kearney. *See* Camp McClellan
Camp Lincoln, 243, 247n30; "confessions" of Dakota prisoners at, 271–72, 286; executions at, 232, 264–65, 267–68, 273–76; and gravesite of Dakotas, 276, 294; jail (Leach Building) at, 233, 267, 272–73, 276, 282n55, 284n68, 285–86, 287–88, 291–92, 310n4; location of, 233, 247n25; mob attack on, 244–45; naming of, 232; religious conversions at, 268–70, 287–88, 291–92; transfer of prisoners from, 294–95; Winnebago trials at, 234, 235–39, 248n53. *See also* executions
Camp McClellan, *268*, 300–302; conditions at, 298, 301; deaths of prisoners at, 301, 315n80; and horse races, 305, 316n99; missionaries at, 299–300, 302–3; number of prisoners at, 296; pardons for prisoners at, 303–5, 306–7; and prison list (1866), 307, 317n106; relaxing of prison routine at, 301, 305; transfer of prisoners from, 308–9
Camp Release, 123, 168, 199; arrests made at, 123, 168, 183; and captive handover, 119–22; conditions at, 122, 170–71; Dakota camp outside, 117, 118–19, 122–23, 168, 170–71; and disarming of Dakotas, 122, 168, 182–83, 196n24, 197n28; and execution suspension at, 183–84, 185–86; Godfrey's trial at, 138–62; Indian traders at, 131–32; jail at, 124, 132, 133, 138, 168, 182; military commission appointment at, 124–31, 133; Sibley's arrival at, 117–19, 133; trials (1–29) at, 138–62, 167–77, 179–82, 261, 280n32; trials (30–139) at, 185–94, 201
Camp Sibley. *See* Lower Sioux Agency
captives, 105, 109n12, 111n45, 170, 260, 264, 281n51; and Godfrey's behavior, 91, 123, 124; handover of, at Camp Release, 117–22; lists of, 111n43, 112n47, 119–21, 135n17, 135n18, 191; from the Lower Sioux Agency, 85; mixed-blood, 98, 99, 112n47, 120, 135n18; negotiations for the, 98–99, 103, 105; from the Patoille wagon attack, 88–89, 150–53; and rape, 89, 110nn28–29, 124, 168–69; testimony of, 129–30, 156–60, 165n37, 167, 170, 173–74, 177, 187, 188, 189, 190, 191, 196n16, 225n24, 258, 261, 279n23. *See also* Dakota War of 1862
Cardinal, Margaret, 169, 279n27
Carley, Kenneth: *The Dakota War of 1862*, 226n37, 346
Carter, Theodore G., 91, 181, 233, 245, 284nn81–82, 345–46; on Godfrey's boasting, 91, 181; on Godfrey's obituary, 343–44, 349n6, 350n7
Caska-ite. *See* Chaskaydon (trial 121)
casualty totals, 85, 95, 102–3, 108n11, 109n17, 109n19, 115nn79–80, 243; at Birch Coulee battle, 98; Dakota, 95, 96–97, 98, 102–3, 109n19, 115n78, 174, 209, 301; at Kandiyohi

INDEX

County, 96; at Lake Shetek, 96, 109n19; at Milford, 86–87, 109n19, 174, 209; recruiting party, xvi, 87, 149. *See also* Dakota War of 1862

census, 23n2, 62; Minnesota Territory (1850), 48–51, 55nn51–53, 56n58, 57n60; Minnesota Territory (1860), 111n43; Santee reservation (1909), 333

Chankahda (trial 359), 153, 210, 259, 272, 356

Chankpeyooha, 271

Charles (slave of Samuel Woods), 50, 56n58

Chaska (Chaskaydon). *See* Chaskaydon (trial 121)

Chaska (protector of George Spencer). *See* Wakinyantawa (Chaska)

Chaska (protector of Sarah Wakefield). *See* Wechankwashtodopee (trial 3)

Chaska (Robert Hopkins). *See* Hopkins, Robert (trial 163)

Chaskaydan, 214

Chaskaydon (trial 121), 261, *269*, 282n54, 307, 354

Chaskayetay. *See* Chaskaydon (trial 121)

Chatfield Democrat, 263–64

Chaytanhoonka (trial 342), 279n24, 356

Chippewas. *See* Ojibwes

Chomsky, Carol, 165n31, 195n2

Choonkaka (Winnebago trial 7), 248n51

Civil War, 82, 83–84, 101, 244, 251; end of the, 306; military trials during the, 125, 126, 136n40, 136n44, 167, 195n3, 248n44; recruiting for the, xv–xvi, 83, 84, 86, 147–48

Cloudman (Chief), 16

"colonization," 252, 255, 278n2. *See also* slavery

commission, military. *See* military commission

cookhouse trials (Lower Sioux Agency), 200, 201–14, 215–21, 224n14, 226n32, 241; hanging list from the, 203, 205, 206, 207, 208, 210, 211, 214, 218, 221, 226n33. *See also* trials

Courtney: birth year of, 3, 30; children of, by Benjamin Boudre, 61–62; freedom suit of, 29–31, 32, 46, 52n3; and Maria Fasnacht, 7, 12, 30, 32, 62; marriage of, to Benjamin Boudre, 32, 61–62; marriage of, to Charles Weidimer, 62; ownership of, by Alexis Bailly, 13–15, 16, 19, 22, 26n37, 30–31, 49; ownership of, by John Garland, 3–4, 8–9, 10, 12–13, 30; ownership of, by Samuel S. Rayburn, 29, 30–31; pay vouchers for, 4–6, 13, 23n9, 24n11, 24n13, 26n32, 27n38; physical description of, 13; in Prairie du Chien, 12, 32, 61–62; pregnancies of, 13–14, 27n39, 29. *See also* Godfrey, Joseph; slavery

Crawford, Charles (trial 136), 198n41, 231

Crooks, George, 343, 349nn5–6

Crooks, Ramsay, 18, 126

Crooks, William, 124, 126, 131, 173, 286, 293

Crosley, Carl, 321

Crow Creek, Dakota Territory (reservation), 296–98, 301, 307, 314n59. *See also* reservations

Culbertson, John, 11

Custer, George Armstrong, 318

customs, Dakota, 98, 111n45, 322; and captives, 88, 153, 169; and "civilizing" measures, 71–72, 73, 78n44, 82–83; clothing (breechclouts), 73, 81, 82; governance traditions, 84–85;

379

INDEX

customs, Dakota (*continued*)
hunting, 63–64; and "kill" counting, 90–91, 106–7, 147, 170, 193, 206, 261; marriage, 63, 76n15; scalping, 192–93; and the soldiers' lodge, 72, 81, 84–85, 98, 140, 260, 266, 281n51; of war, 48, 87–88, 89–91, 106–7, 110n22, 123, 153, 169, 192. *See also* language, Dakota

Cut Nose (trial 96). *See* Mahpeokenajin (trial 96)

Dakota War of 1862, xviii, 81–82, 109n14; Acton deaths, 84, 140; and ambush of Marsh's troops, 95, 141, 149, 187, 189, 236, 238, 260, 271, 279n29; and Birch Coulee battle, 97–98, 105, 127, 155, 160, 187, 191; causes of the, 72, 82–85; and child killers, 259–60; Dakota casualties after the, 301; and deception by Dakotas, 86, 87, 95, 96–97, 109n14, 143, 144, 145, 189, 260, 279n29; and federalization of Sibley's troops, 102, 114n71; and Fort Ridgely attacks, 95, 96; Kandiyohi County killings, 96, 113n53; and "killing patterns," 85, 86–87, 88, 92–94, 108n11, 109n12, 112n47, 113n53; Lake Shetek killings, 96–97, 109n19; Lower Sioux Agency deaths, 85, 93, 140, 141, 199; map, *104*; Milford massacre, xvi–xvii, 85–88, 89, 90–91, 109n14, 144–50, 154, 172, 174, 208–9, 247n30; and New Ulm attacks, 96, 97, 113n51, 139, 144, 154, 155, 160, 191; Patoille wagon attack, 88–89, 109n14, 124, 150–51, 153, 155, 157, 169–70, 210; and retribution desire among white troops, 105–6, 117–18, 124, 134n3; and the Slaughter Slough massacre, 96–97; and the soldiers' lodge, 72, 81, 84–85, 98, 140, 260, 266, 281n51; and surrender at Camp Release, 117–19; surrender terms in, from Sibley, 99–100, 102, 103, 105–7, 119, 122, 168, 182; Wood Lake battle, 102, 103, 127, 130, 154–55, 160, 192–93, 237. *See also* captives; casualty totals; trials

The Dakota War of 1862 (Carley), 226n37, 346

Dan (slave of Henry Wilson), 37

Dane, Jerome, 177

Davenport, William, 33, 52n5

Davenport IA, prison at. *See* Camp McClellan

Dawasin, 192

Day, George E. H., 306, 316n104

Day, William, 11, 35–36

death sentences. *See* hanging list

death totals. *See* casualty totals

Detroit MI, 5, 30

Dietrich, Ernst, xv–xvi, 86, 206, 243; death of, xvi, xvii, 87, 147–49

Dietrich, Hedwig, 97

Dietrich, Pauline (Mrs. Ernst Dietrich), 97, 113n55, 312n27

Divoll, George, 85, 173, 287, 293

Dole, William P., 252–53

Dousman, Hercules, 20

Dowansa (trial 22), 176–77, 195n4, 201, 258–59; arrest of, 168, 196n15, 353

Drake, Charles D., 29, 30, 31

Dred (slave). *See* Scott, Dred

Echagoheyayaywin (trial 384), 226n37

Egbert, S. B., 28n65, 54n33, 63–64, 76n21

380

INDEX

Eliza (slave). *See* Johnston, Eliza (slave of Lawrence Taliaferro)

Emancipation Proclamation, 132, 251–52. *See also* slavery

Emerson, John, 11, 33–34, 46, 52n7, 55nn43–44

Emery, Joseph, 163n11

Emery, Luella, 337n26

Espinoza, Delores, 311n11, 337n28, 350n13

Etayechasnamane (trial 240), 213

Etayhoota (trial 68), 279n23, 354

Etheldred (slave of John Emerson). *See* Scott, Dred

Etheldred (slave of William Price), 52n5

executions, 185, 283n67; at Camp Lincoln, 232, 264–65, 267–68, 273–76; and misidentification of condemned prisoners, 265, 267, *268, 269, 270, 271,* 280n44, 280n46, 281n52, 282nn53–54; and public opinion, 231–32, 244, 252–54, 263–64; scaffold for the, 274–75, 284n70; spectators at the, 273, 275; of Union soldiers, 125, 136n40, 136n44, 167, 195n3, 248n44. *See also* hanging list; trials

Eyojanjan (trial 237), 226n32

Fanny (slave of Ebenezer Swift), 76n23

Faribault, Alexander, 2, 23n5, 35, 38, 290

Faribault, David, Jr. (trial 134), 96, 97, 155, 296; pardon of, 166n39, 289–91, 296, 298–99, 311n25; parentage of, 311n25; testimony of, 158–59, 166n39, 196n16; trial of, 191–92, 198n41

Faribault, David, Sr., 2, 23n5, 38, 93, 272–73; as captive, 132; against

Godfrey, 159–60; and liquor trafficking, 35, 52n13; pardon request of, for son, 289–91, 296, 311n25; testimony of, 173–74, 177, 187, 188, 189, 190, 191, 196n16, 258, 261, 279n23

Faribault, Emily, 23n5, 131, 290

Faribault, Jean Baptiste, 2, 3, 23n5, 35, 38, 131; and slave ownership, 14–15

Faribault, Lucy. *See* Bailly, Lucy (Mrs. Alexis Bailly)

Faribault, Oliver, 2, 23n5, 43–44, 51, 57n60, 61, 132; death of, 54n33, 58; and liquor trafficking, 35; trading post of, 38–39

Faribault, Pelagie (Mrs. Jean Baptiste Faribault), 23n5

Faribault Springs (trading post), 38–39

Fasnacht, Jacob, 7, 25n18

Fasnacht, Maria (Mrs. Jacob Fasnacht), 7, 12, 25n18, 30, 32, 62

Fenske, Julius, xvi, xvii, 149

Fifth Infantry Regiment, 5, 6, 9, 10, 33

First Infantry Regiment, 2, 25n24; slaveholding officers in the, 9–10, 11, 33, 52n5

Flandrau, Charles, 87, 105, 113n54, 128, 133; and execution of Dakotas, 200–201, 224n8

Folwell, William Watts, 43, 53n31, 109n12, 197n28, 197n31, 226n37, 302, 346; and victim lists, 108n11, 115n80

Fonda, John H., 44

Forbes, William, 131

Forsnot, Maria. *See* Fasnacht, Maria (Mrs. Jacob Fasnacht)

Fort Crawford (WI), 6, 12, 33, 54n41, 75n9

Fort Howard (WI), 5, 24n11

381

INDEX

Fort Ridgely (MN), 73, 93, 97, 112n47; siege of, 95, 96; slaveholding at, 60–61, 64–65, 66, 67, 94

Fort Snelling (MN), 2, 41, 54n41, 75n9; internment camp at, 285, 286, 291, 294–95, 301; religious conversions at, 292; slaveholding at, 5–13, 17, 20–21, 24n15, 25n28, 27n47, 33–34, 37, 46, 49, 50, 52nn5–7, 59–60, 64, 65–67; transfer of Dakotas from, to Crow Creek, 297–98, 301; transfer of Dakotas to, from Camp Release, 182–84, 196n24, 349n5; transfer of Dakotas to, from Lower Agency, 228, 230–31, 246n1; trials at, 293, 312n42, 313nn43–44

Fowler, Emily (Mrs. Stephen Fowler), 23n5, 131, 290

Fowler, Stephen, 131–32, 290–91, 298, 311n21

Frazier, Cornelia, 323

Frazier, Jack, 187

Frederick (slave of Lawrence Taliaferro), 26n31

freedom suits, 36, 45–46; of Courtney, 29–31, 46, 52n3; of Rachel, 17, 31–32, 34, 37, 46, 52n3. *See also* slavery

Frenier, Antoine, 130, 137n55, 137n57, 139, 202

Freniere, Louis (trial 131), 198n41

Freniere, Narcisse (trial 236), 226n32

fur trade, 1–2, 33, 34, 38–39; and the American Fur Company, 2, 17–18, 19–20, 29, 126; Henry Hastings Sibley's connections to the, 18, 19–20, 22, 29, 68, 126, 131–32; and treaty funds, 58, 82, 94–95

Galbraith, Thomas, 83–84, 171, 183, 278n14, 296–97

Garland, James, 3

Garland, John, 25n28, 43–44, 69, 77n33; and ownership of Courtney, 3–5, 8–9, 10, 12–13, 23n9, 24n11, 24n13, 30, 31; pay vouchers of, 4–6, 13, 23nn8–9, 24n11, 24n13, 26n32, 69, 77n33

General Order No. 23, 273, 284n68

Glascon (slave of Zachary Taylor), 10, 25n26

Godfrey, Anna, 324, 325, 333, 335, 337n29

Godfrey, Carrie Primeaux (Mrs. Edward Godfrey), 345

Godfrey, Cecelia, 324, 333, 335

Godfrey, Chaska. *See* Godfrey, Joseph, Jr.

Godfrey, Edward, 324, 325, 333, 345

Godfrey, Emma (Mrs. Joseph Godfrey). *See* Icazontewin (Mrs. Joseph Godfrey)

Godfrey, Esther, 324, 333

Godfrey, George, 78n49

Godfrey, Gusse. *See* Godfrey, Joseph

Godfrey, Hapan, 73, 78n49, 291, 312n26, 312n28

Godfrey, Ivy Saul (Mrs. John Godfrey), 335

Godfrey, James, 325, 333, 335, 338n39, 344, 345

Godfrey, Jennie (Mrs. Joseph Godfrey). *See* Goodteacher, Jennie (Mrs. Joseph Godfrey)

Godfrey, John Joseph, 325, 333, 335, 337n26, 344, 345

Godfrey, Joseph, xviii, 3, 37, 51, 54n40, 242–43, 348; age of, 27n39, 76n21, 140, 163n6, 335, 338n34, 340n70; arrest of, at Camp Release, 123–24; as Bailly family slave, 1–2, 15–16, 19, 22, 29, 32–33, 34–35; behavior of, during Dakota War, 91–92, 94,

INDEX

96, 100, 102, 111n41, 123, 156–58; and the Birch Coulee battle, 98, 155; birth of, 1, 13–14, 21; birth year of, 14, 27n39, 335, 340n70; and bragging about war exploits, 91–92, 94, 111n41, 123, 124, 155, 159–60, 165n37, 166n40, 179, 181; at Camp Lincoln, 234, 236–38, 239; at Camp Release, 141–44, 145, 146, 147, 148, 150–51, 152, 153–54, 163n10, 164n19, 166n39, 171–72, 175, 176–77, 181, 186–92, 193, 201, 261; and Catholicism, 287–88, 311n11; chaining of, in jail, 139, 163n5, 193; children of, 63, 73, 78n49, 228, 291, 292, 297, 309, 312n26, 312n28, 320, 321–22, 325, 333; as cook, 293, 295; credibility of, 161–62, 188–89, 201–2, 212, 219, 220, 238, 270; and Dakota culture, 48, 63, 90–91, 326; and the Dakota language, 16, 40, 48, 326, 329n46; death of, 333–35, 340n65, 340n68, 341–44; decision of, to flee Dakota War, 81–82, 142; descendants of, 324, 325, 333, 335, 337n26, 338n39, 344–45; description of, by Mary Schwandt, 89, 110n27; as driver (during Dakota War), 87–89, 96, 143, 145, 146, 147, 148, 151, 155, 157, 165n32; escape of, from Oliver Faribault, 42–45, 46–47, 54n33; as Faribault family slave, 38–40, 132; as farmer, 81, 140, 320, 321, 322, 323–24, 331, 332–33, 337n31; at the Fort Ridgely attacks, 96; fugitive slave status of, 45, 46–47, 59, 61, 62–63, 66–67, 73–74, 94, 132; half-siblings of, 61–62; headstone of, *334*, 335; and Henry Hastings Sibley, 19, 22, 132; in his trial, 140–55, 160, 161, 163n10, 164n19, 166nn39–40, 169–70; as horse trader, 165n32, 324, 331; illiteracy of, 326–27, 339n46; as inquisitor, 202, 205–6, 208–9, 211–14, 217–18, 225n28; in jail, at Camp Lincoln, 233–34, 267, 272–73, 276, 282n55, 284n68, 287–88, 292–93; in jail, at Camp McClellan, 296, 300–301, 303, 305; in jail, at Camp Release, 168, 182, 193; and "kills" number, 90–91, 147, 178, 179; laborer and teamster work of, 319–20, 336n5, 336n6; land allotment to, at Santee, 321, 323, 332–33, 344; as "leader" of attacks, xvii, 149, 179, 247n30, 263–64; letter of, to Riggs, 304–5; at Lower Sioux Agency, 201–2, 203–14, 215–19, 220, 224n17, 225n28; marriage of, to Icazontewin, 320, 321, 324, 336n7, 338n33; marriage of, to Jennie Goodteacher, 324–25, 337n26, 338n34; marriage of, to Takanheca, 63, 76n15, 309, 317n116, 320; and the Mdewakanton Dakota band, 34–35, 47–48; and the Milford massacre, xvi–xvii, 86–87, 90–91, 100, 109n14, 144–52, 154, 156–57, 172, 174–75, 205–6, 208–9, 247n30; and mitigation of sentence, 181–82, 184, 197n31, 216, 218–20, 222–23, 226n36, 227n43, 240, 242–43, 249n66, 255, 262, 265–66, 282n53; motivation of, for testifying, 215–17; name variations of, 63, 75n12, 326, 339n44; at the New Ulm attacks, 96, 113n51, 155, 160; obituaries of, 341–44, 349n6; origin stories of, 21–22, 28n63, 28n65; and "otakle" name, 91, 111n37, 139, 155;

INDEX

Godfrey, Joseph (*continued*)
"outsider" status of, xviii–xix, 322–23; and pardon lists, 304; at the Patoille wagon attack, 88–89, 124, 150–51, 153, 155, 157, 210; physical descriptions of, 42, 89, 139–40, 163n6, 233, 272–73; Prairie du Chien visit of, 61–62, 75n9, 75n12; in the press, 177–80, 233, 263–64, 296, 303, 308, 327, 329, 341–44, 349n6; race designation of, 331–32; and religion, 287–88, 311n11, 324; on the Santee Reservation, 319–33; separation of, from Courtney, 29, 31, 32; sketch of, 272–73, *274*; in Stevens's paintings, 327, *328*; testimony of, 233, 258–60, 276–77, 290, 305, 329; and Thomas Williamson, 302–3; threats to, by Dakotas, 81, 82, 86, 91–92, 94, 96, 97, 111n39, 111n41, 141, 142–43, 146, 147, 155, 181, 217, 218; threats to, by white vigilantes, 329, 330–31; treatment of, by historians, 303, 316n92, 345–48, 350n21, 351n27; trial verdict of, 180–81; voice of, 89, 140, 352; with Wakute's band, 34–35, 47, 48, 60, 63–64; and war paint, 82, 143, 156, 159; and watches from Milford victims, 89, 110n27, 243; whipping of, by Lucy Bailly, 16, 19; on the Whiting-Ruggles list, 256–60, 262; and the Wood Lake battle, 102, 155. *See also* Courtney; slavery; trial, Godfrey's
Godfrey, Joseph (father of Joseph Godfrey), 1, 14
Godfrey, Joseph, Jr., 78n49, 309, 317n116, 320, 333, 335, 336n7; and annuity, 72, 78n47; baptism of, 292; birth of, 63; as farmer, 324, 344; marriage of, 324, 337n28; race of, 332, 339n59
Godfrey, Louise (Mrs. Joseph Godfrey). *See* Takanheca (Mrs. Joseph Godfrey)
Godfrey, Sarah ("Sally"), 325, 335, 338n39
Godfrey, Takanheca. *See* Takanheca (Mrs. Joseph Godfrey)
Godfroi, Joseph, 1, 14
Goodteacher, Jennie (Mrs. Joseph Godfrey), 324–25, 333, 335, 337n26, 338n34; abuse of, by father, 325, 338n40, 344–45; mental impairment of, 325, 344
Goodteacher, Maggie, 324
Goodteacher, William, 54n40, 324, 339n57; and abuse of daughter, 325, 338n40, 344–45
Good Thunder, 286–87, 293, 312n41
Grant, Hiram, 124, 127, 130, 133
Gwynne, Thomas P., 52n5

"half-breeds." *See* mixed-bloods
Halleck, Henry, 115n76, 197n37, 310n3
hanging list, 221, 226n37, 227n42, 266, 272, 352–356; from Camp Lincoln trials, 237, 238, 239, 248n50; from Camp Release trials, 169, 170, 172, 175, 177, 184, 187, 188, 190, 194, 196n16; from the cookhouse trials (Lower Sioux Agency), 203, 205, 206, 207, 208, 210, 211, 214, 218, 221, 226n33; and identification of prisoners, 265, 267, *268*, *269*, *270*, *271*, 280n44, 280n46, 281n52, 282nn53–54; Lincoln's review of the, 185–86, 222, 223, 244, 262–63, 264–66, 286; and lying of defendants, 214; Riggs's transcription of the, 221–22, 226n39; and

384

secrecy, 215; Sibley's approval of the, 184, 221; and standards for death sentencing, 187, 188, 193, 214; telegraph submission of the, 185–86, 248n56. *See also* executions; trials; Whiting-Ruggles report
Hannibal (slave of John Bliss), 27n47
Hapan (trial 24), 177, 353
Hapinkpa (trial 170), 355
Harney, Benjamin F., 7, 8, 25n19
Harney, William S., 7, 106
Harris, Nathaniel, 7, 24n14
Hastings MN, 1, 35
Hataninkoo (trial 333), 279n24, 356
Haynook (Winnebago trial 5), 248n51
Haypee (trial 366), 212–13
Haypeedon (trial 70), 354
Hays, Samuel, 77n31
Hayzeka (Winnebago trial 13), 248n52
Hdahinhday (trial 373), 279n26, 356
Heard, Isaac, 1, 199, 202, 216, 249n62, 249n66, 345–46; on Godfrey's trial testimony, 141–44, 145, 146, 147, 148, 150–51, 152, 153–54, 163n10, 164n19, 166n39; letter of, to the *St. Paul Pioneer and Democrat*, 240–43, 249n62, 249nn65–66; as military commission recorder, 127–28, 137n55, 140, 141–42; on pace of trials, 203; physical description of, 128; and publication of *History of the Sioux War and Massacres of 1862–1863*, 128, 306; on testimony against Godfrey, 175, 249n63
Helen (daughter of Henry Hastings Sibley), 53n28, 77n30
Henle, Anton, xv, xvi, xvii, 87, 109n17, 144, 146, 149
Henle, Anton, Jr., 146
Henle, Martin, xvii, 109n17
Henle, Mary, xvii, 146

Hetty (slave of Francis Lee), 60, 65
Heuyers, Carl, 163n11
Hinhanshoonkoyagmane (trial 6), 353
Hinman, S. D., 292
History of the Sioux War and Massacres of 1862–1863 (Heard), 128, 306. *See also* Heard, Isaac
Hobu Creek Cemetery, *334*, 335
Holt, Joseph, 255, 299
Hoonthan (trial 33), 188
Hoopahotakaycha (trial 32), 187–88
Hopkins, Robert (trial 163), 121, 261, 265, 267, 280n30, 298, 303
Horace (slave of Lawrence Taliaferro), 26n31
Hotaninkoo (trial 333), 279n24, 356
Huggins, Alexander, 41–43, 47, 53n31, 121
Huggins, Amos, 121
Huggins, Eli, 41, 42–43, 53n31, 73, 78n50
Huggins, Josephine (Mrs. Amos Huggins), 121, 135n24
Hungkonetah (Winnebago trial 1), 236, 237, 239, 248n47, 248n53
Hunt, Franklin E., 76n23

Icazontewin (Mrs. Joseph Godfrey), 320, 321, 324, 335n7, 338n33
Indian agents, 2, 101, 171, 285, 337n25; and "civilizing" policies, 71–72, 78n44, 82–83; and the fur trade, 17–18; and the Renville Rangers, 83–84; on the Santee reservation, 320, 321, 322, 330–31, 332; and slavery, 6–7, 11–12, 13, 26n31, 33, 37, 46. *See also individual agent names*
Indian Outbreaks (Buck), 329–30, 339n52
Isle Royale, 296

INDEX

Jack (slave of Martin Scott), 8, 33, 52n6

James (slave of Alexander Reynolds), 76n23

James Henry (slave of Thomas Stockton), 17, 32

Jane (slave of Edmund Alexander), 66, 76n23

Jane (slave of John Bliss), 27n47

Jane (slave of Zachary Taylor), 10, 25n26, 56n56

Jenny (slave of Francis Lee), 59–60, 65

Joe (slave of Francis Lee), 59–60, 65

Johnson, Andrew, 307

Johnson, Eliza (slave). *See* Johnston, Eliza (slave of Lawrence Taliaferro)

Johnston, Alexander, 24n14

Johnston, Eliza (slave of Lawrence Taliaferro), 6–7, 24n15, 24n17, 27n40

Johnston, Susan (slave of Lawrence Taliaferro), 24n15, 24n17, 27n40

Jones, Llewellyn, 50, 56n57

Julius (slave of William Davenport), 33, 52n5

Kandiyohi County killings, 96, 113n53. *See also* Dakota War of 1862

Kansas-Nebraska Act of 1854, 64–65, 67, 76n22. *See also* slavery

Kasa. *See* Godfrey, Joseph

Ka-win-gay, 271, 272

Kunchahooka (Winnebago trial 4), 238

Kunckkatrinme, 156

LaBathe, Francois, 111n44, 200

LaBatte, Bernard, 159, 240

Labelle, Louis (trial 139), 192–93, 201

LaCroix Creek. *See* Birch Coulee battle

Lagree, Joseph, 177–78, 179

Lake Shetek killings, 96–97, 109n19. *See also* Dakota War of 1862

The Landing (park), 39, *40*, 53n24

Langham, Elias T., 13

language, Dakota, 16, 35–36, 129, 326, 339n46; and pejorative terms, 70, 77n38. *See also* customs, Dakota

Lassuillier, Baptist, 275

Lawrence, Elden, 111n37, 316n92, 351n27

laws: Fugitive Slave Act (1850), 45; Kansas-Nebraska Act of 1854, 64–65, 67, 76n22; Missouri Compromise, 5, 11, 17, 32, 33, 61, 64, 67; Northwest Ordinance of 1787, 5, 17, 32; and priest/penitent privilege, 130; prohibiting black immigration, 69–70; and protection of slaves, 44

Leach Building. *See* Camp Lincoln

Lee, Francis, 59–60, 65, 76n22

Lehman, Christopher P., 69, 77n31

Lightner, Isaiah, 322

Lincoln, Abraham, 101, 248n44, 297; assassination of, 306, 316n104; and the Emancipation Proclamation, 132, 251–52; execution order of ("Lincoln Order"), 262–63, 264–66, 280n33; and Godfrey's reprieve, 262, 265–66; and hanging list review, 185–86, 222, 223, 244, 262–63, 264–66, 286; and inaction on Dakota death sentences, 299, 314n71, 314n72; pardon petitions to, 289–91, 296, 302, 311n25, 315n85; pardons granted by, 166n39, 289–91, 296, 298–99, 303–4, 311n25; petition to, from Dakota leaders, 266–67, 281n51; politics of, 83–84, 132–33, 254, 255, 306; Pope's resentment of, 101; and public opinion regarding Dakotas, 252–

386

INDEX

54, 255–56, 278n12; and Sibley's promotion, 102; and Sibley's request for more executions, 286; and slavery, 132, 251–52, 254–55; and trial transcript review, 239–40, 251, 255, 256–58, 261–62, 278n12, 279n20
Lincoln Order, 262–63, 264–66, 280n33
Lindholm, A. T., 327
Little Buffalo, John. *See* Chaskaydon (trial 121)
Little Crow, 96, 103, 117, 151–52, 155, 178, 234; at the Birch Coulee battle, 97, 98; and captives, 99, 264; and missionaries, 36; and public opinion, 179; Sibley's expedition against, 298, 305–6; and the soldiers' lodge, 84–85, 140; at the Wood Lake battle, 102
Little Priest. *See* Hungkonetah (Winnebago trial 1)
Littler, B. M., 296
Louisa (slave of Josiah Snelling), 8, 26n29
Lower Reservation, 60, 66, 81. *See also* Fort Ridgely (MN); Lower Sioux Agency
Lower Sioux Agency, 63, 185, 189; deaths at, 81, 85, 93, 95, 140, 141, 173, 199, 237; move of Sibley's camp to the, 199–200; removal of Sibley's camp from the, 228–29, 246n1; trials held at the, 200, 201–14, 215–21, 224n14, 226n32, 241. *See also* Lower Reservation
Lowry, Sylvanus, 69, 77n31
Lucy (slave of Francis Lee), 60, 65
Lucy (slave of Thomas Gwynne), 52n5
lynching schemes. *See* mob violence
Lynd, James, 85, 93

Magasan, 317n109
Magatonka (trial 236), 226n32
Magner, John, 187, 189

Mahoowaywa (trial 382), 144, 163n10, 208–9, 227n42, 259, 356
Mahpeokenajin (trial 96), 276, 279n26, 284nn81–82, 327, 354
Mahpeyakahoton (trial 246), 225n29
Mah-wha. *See* Mahoowaywa (trial 382)
Makamanewashechoon (trial 41), 189–90
Makanahtakay (trial 362), 112nn47–48, 217, 218, 226n33
Makanashota (trial 385), 225n28
Makatanajin (trial 9), 225n24
Makatenajin (trial 254), 206–7, 259, 355
Mankato MN, 97, 232, 233, 247n25; executions at, 273–76; move of Dakota prisoners to, 228–30, 246nn1–2. *See also* Camp Lincoln
Mankato Record, 233, 235–36, 264, 292, 307–8; and antiblack sentiment, 70, 177–79
Margaret (slave of Edmund Alexander), 66, 76n23
Margaret (slave of Franklin Hunt), 76n23
Marpiyawakanhdi, 298
Marsh, John, 95, 141, 149, 187, 189, 236, 238, 260, 271, 279n29
Marshall, William R., 185, 228, 231, 246n1, 273; and antislavery politics, 127, 131; as military commission judge, 124, 126–27, 181, 223
Martin, Edward, 338n40
Mary (slave of Josiah Snelling), 8, 10, 26n29
massacre vs. battle distinction, 105, 185, 193–94, 203, 225n24; and Lincoln's trial transcripts review, 256, 263, 279n20, 299. *See also* trials
Massopust family, 86, 87–88, 109n15; and Godfrey's testimony, 144, 145, 205, 207, 209, 225n21. *See also* Milford (MN) massacre
Mayhpeyahota (trial 286), 227n42

387

Mayo, William W., 276, 284nn81–82
Maypehaypeya (trial 285), 227n42
McClellan, George, 251
McIntyre, Frank E., 330–31
McKenny, J. S., 263–64
McManus, Edgar: *Black Bondage in the North*, 21
Mdewakanton band, 34–35, 85, 134n16
Mendota (St. Peter) MN, 16, 19–20, 23n2, 29, 170, 276, 284n81, 311n12; and the fur trade, 1–3, 18; and lynching schemes, 244
Messmer, Joseph, xvi, 109n17, 149, 164n18
Messmer, Mary Anne, 146
métis, 3, 18–19. *See also* mixed-bloods
Mexican-American War, 37, 59, 125, 136n40
Meyer, Roy W., 318
Mey family, 86, 109n16, 195n11, 209. *See also* Milford (MN) massacre
Milford (MN) massacre, xvi–xvii, 86–87, 90–91, 109n14, 109n19, 174–75; casualty totals, 86, 174; Godfrey's testimony about the, 144–50, 154, 172, 205–6, 208–9; killing pattern at the, 86, 89; lack of witnesses from the, 230, 247n30; and the recruiting party, xv–xvi, xxn3, 85–86, 87, 109n14, 147–49. *See also* Dakota War of 1862
military commission, 26, 136n40, 136n42, 136n44, 196n23; and changing standards for sentencing, 210, 225n24, 232; and "demeanor" of witnesses, 219–20; formation of the, 124–31, 133; members of the, 126–30, 131, 185; and narrative recording of trials, 158; and order of trials, 156; second (Fort Snelling), 293, 312n42, 313n43, 313n44; and secrecy, 179–80, 215; and speed of trials, 167, 185, 195n2, 203, 209, 217, 220–21, 226n32, 240–41; and trial irregularities, 154, 158, 167, 203, 209, 214, 236, 260. *See also* trials
military pay vouchers. *See* pay vouchers, military
Miller, Steven, 243, 264, 276, 280n44; and executions, 265, 267–68, 273, 275; as governor, 306; and mob violence, 244–45; and shortages at Camp Lincoln, 285–86, 310n4
Milord, Henry (trial 115), 193, 198n41, 271–72, 279nn23–24, 354; Godfrey's testimony against, 190–91
Minnesota: antiblack sentiment in, 70, 297; anti-Indian sentiment in, 201, 228–32, 234–35, 243–45, 252, 255–56, 288–89, 297; antislavery sentiment in, 64–65; black population in, 48–49, 70; and the census, 48–51, 55n51, 55n52, 55n53, 56n58, 57n60, 111n43; constitution of, 68, 69–70, 73, 74; demographics of, 2, 3, 18–19, 46, 48–49, 70; as free state, 78–79; map (Minnesota Territory 1849), 45; outlaw status of Dakota Indians in, 305; and public opinion, regarding executions, 231–32, 244, 252–54, 263–64, 288–89; and public opinion, regarding pardons, 307–8; and public opinion, regarding Winnebagoes, 234–35; and refugee fund, 97, 113n55; size of, as territory, 56n59; slavery's decline in, 37–38, 59; slavery's heyday in, 10–12, 20–21, 22, 26n31, 34, 48, 65–66; slavery's illegality in, 5, 8–9, 10–11, 17, 32, 34, 49, 59–61, 64–65, 68–69, 73, 132–33, 329;

slaves born in, 14, 21, 27n40; slave trading in, 6–7, 11–12, 14–15, 24n14, 26n31, 33, 37, 46; territory status of, 46, 68; and voting rights, 68, 69, 77n28

missionaries, 282n54; banning of, from Camp McClellan, 299–300; and "civilizing" policies, 82–83; competition between, for conversions, 268–69, 311n13; and conversions of Dakota prisoners, 268–70, 283n57, 283n63, 287–88, 291–92; and criticism of trials, 252–54, 289, 299–300; and literacy lessons, 291, 292; pardon requests of, 261, 280n30, 302; in Prairieville, 39, 40–41; at the Santee reservation, 318; and slavery, 36, 41–43, 121. *See also* Riggs, Stephen R.; *and individual missionary names*

Missouri, 17, 29–30, 31–32

Missouri Compromise, 5, 11, 17, 32, 33, 61, 64, 67. *See also* slavery

mixed-bloods, 18, 23n5, 83–84, 111n44, 124–25, 126, 155, 177; at Camp Lincoln (jail), 265, 268, 269, 287–88, 302; as captives, 91, 98, 103, 112n47, 120, 135n18, 191; and census forms, 55nn52–53; during the Dakota War, 85, 92–93, 96, 99, 111n44, 137n57, 218; and the Lake Pepin tract, 34; métis, 3, 18–19; religion of, 268, 269, 287–88, 302; testimony of, 129–30, 156, 158–59, 166n39, 177, 186, 187, 196nn16–17; and trial length, 217, 226n32; trials of, at Camp Release, 190–93, 198n41; trials of, at Lower Sioux Agency, 217, 226n32

mob violence, 228–31, 243–45, 246n7, 246n12, 294. *See also* anti-Indian sentiment

Monekasdayhekah (Winnebago trial 2), 237–38, 248n50

Monimia (slave of Llewellyn Jones), 50, 56n57

Monroe, George, 11

Morton (MN) Enterprise, 342–44

Mukatenajin (trial 254), 206–7, 259, 355

Muzzabomadu (trial 10), 146, 147, 163n13, 164n16, 165n31, 195n4, 195n11, 271; arrest of, 168; captive of, 151, 153; trial of, 171–72, 201, 258, 353

Myrick, Andrew, 85, 173, 237

Nancy (slave of William Davenport), 33, 52n5

Napashue (trial 178), 355

Nehanamenah (Spirit of the Moon), 15

New Ulm MN, 60, 84, 246n1; attacks on, 96, 97, 113n51, 139, 144, 154, 155, 160, 191; lack of witnesses from, 230; and the Milford massacre, xvi, xvii, 87; mob violence at, 228–30, 246n7, 246n12; poisoned whiskey left at, 97, 113n54. *See also* Dakota War of 1862

Nicolay, John, 265

Niobrara (NE) Tribune, 341–42

Niobrara (Nebraska Territory), 308, 321, 332, 341. *See also* Santee Sioux Reservation

Nix, Jacob, 346–47

Northwest Ordinance of 1787, 5, 17, 32. *See also* slavery

Ochs, Cecelia, 164n29

Oechagay (trial 186), 210, 225n24

Office of Indian Affairs, 2, 71–72, 78n44, 285, 332; and reservation

Office of Indian Affairs (*continued*)
sites, 296–97, 314n59. *See also* Indian agents
Ojibwes, 2, 46, 296; as enemies of Dakotas, 48, 72, 83, 86, 89–90, 110n22
Olin, Rollin C., 124, 127, 128
Oliver's Grove MN, 1, 35
Omdacha (trial 69), 279n23, 354
Otaheyaya (trial 259), 214
O-ta-kia. *See* Godfrey, Joseph
Otakle (Many Kills). *See* Godfrey, Joseph
Otanka (trial 13), 234, 236, 237, 238–39; credibility of, 238–39, 248n53
Other Day, John, 221
Otineyapa (trial 280), 294, 307, 313n51, 317n110
"outrages against women." *See* rape
Oyatatonka (trial 290), 225n28
Oyatayakoo (trial 377), 164n24, 210–11, 259, 356
Oyataykokejaje (trial 381), 221, 227n42

Pahwashtay (trial 29), 279n29
Paine, Clarence, 21, 28n57, 350n21
"Panorama of the Indian Massacre of 1862" (Stevens), 327, *328*
Pantaninneyay (trial 258), 213–14
Patoille, Francois, 88, 110n29, 150, 157
Patoille wagon attack, 88–89, 124, 157, 169–70, 210; Godfrey's account of the, 150–51, 153, 155. *See also* Dakota War of 1862
pay vouchers, military: of Benjamin F. Harney, 25n19; of Edmund B. Alexander, 66; of Francis Lee, 59–60, 65; of Henry Wilson, 37; of John Bliss, 27n47; of John Emerson, 33–34; of John Garland, 4–6, 13, 23nn8–9, 24n11, 24n13, 26n32, 69, 77n33; of Joseph Plympton, 24n15, 24n17; of Josiah Snelling, 8, 26n29; of Llewellyn Jones, 50, 56n57; of Martin Scott, 33, 52n6; of Thomas Alexander, 60, 75n6; of Thomas Stockton, 12, 26n36; of William Davenport, 52n5; of William Day, 11, 26n30; of Zachary Taylor, 25n26, 56n56. *See also* slavery
Payzhihota (trial 62), 190
Pazekootaymane (trial 264), 355
Pejihokxidan (Medicine Boy). *See* Godfrey, John Joseph
Peter (slave of Benjamin Harney), 7, 25n19
Plympton, Joseph, 6–7, 24n15, 24n17
Pond, Gideon, 40, 291
Pond, Samuel, Jr., 38
Pond, Samuel W., 38, 57n60, 89, 90; at Faribault Springs, 40–41, 42, 51. *See also* missionaries
Pope, John, 169, 289, 294; and additional troops, 101, 114n69; and arrests of Dakotas, 182–84, 197n28; arrival of, in Minnesota, 100–102; and cost of Dakota internment camps, 285–86, 310nn2–3, 310n4; dislike of, for Sibley, 101, 102, 115n76, 182, 196n25; on execution location, 185, 232, 275; on executions, 184, 185, 196n25, 197n30, 200, 201, 232, 275; and extermination of Dakotas, 101; and Lincoln's approval of executions, 185–86, 222, 223, 239–40, 248n56; orders of, to break up Lower Agency camp, 228; orders of, to capture more Dakotas, 184–85; orders of, to disarm Dakotas, 182–83, 196n24, 197n28; and resentment of Lincoln, 101, 114n65; Sibley's dispatches

to, 119, 124, 133, 135n18, 224n5; on Winnebago trials, 232. *See also* Sibley, Henry Hastings

Prairie du Chien WI, 1, 2, 29, 32, 61–62, 75n9; slavery in, 6, 7, 12, 30, 44

Prairieville, 39–41

Prescott, Lucy, 15

Prescott, Mary (Mrs. Philander Prescott), 15

Prescott, Philander, 15–16, 93, 310n8

press: and antiblack sentiment, 70, 177–79, 254, 263–64, 297, 342; and anti-Indian sentiment, 180, 232, 234–35, 244, 288–89, 297; and execution reporting, 275–76; on Godfrey, 177–80, 233, 263–64, 296, 303, 308, 327, 329, 341–44, 349n6; and Heard's letter on trials, 240–43, 249n62, 249nn65–66; on Henry Hastings Sibley, 288–89, 291, 311n14; and Lincoln's executions order, 264, 280n38, 280n40; and pardon of Dakotas (1866), 307–8; on "resurrected" bodies, 294, 301–2; on slavery, 67, 69–70, 297; on Stephen Riggs, 253. *See also* public opinion

Price, Hiram, 306

Price, William H., 52n5

Primeaux, Carrie, 345

Provincalle, Antoine (trial 132), 198n41, 296

Provincalle, Joseph, Jr. (trial 137), 198n41

public opinion: and antiblack sentiment, 133, 233, 297, 329, 344; and anti-Indian sentiment, 201, 228–32, 234–35, 243–45, 252, 255–56, 297; of executions, 231–32, 244, 252–54, 263–64, 288–89; of pardons, 307–8. *See also* press

Putnam, Era, 62

Putnam, Maria (Mrs. Era Putnam). *See* Fasnacht, Maria (Mrs. Jacob Fasnacht)

Quinn, George, 54n40, 312n41, 336n7, 339n55, 350n7

Quinn, Peter, 93, 189

Rachel (slave of Thomas Stockton), 13, 30; freedom suit of, 17, 31–32, 34, 37, 46, 52n3

racism: antiblack sentiment, 83–84, 133, 175, 329; antiblack sentiment among Dakotas, 70, 77n38, 83–84, 216, 233, 322–23, 337n17, 339n57, 344–45; antiblack sentiment in the press, 70, 177–79, 254, 263–64, 297, 342; anti-Indian sentiment, 101, 201, 232, 252, 255–56; anti-Indian sentiment and mob violence, 228–31, 243–45, 246n7, 246n12, 294; anti-Indian sentiment in the press, 180, 232, 234–35, 244, 288–89, 297; of historians, 91, 111n41, 303

Ramsey, Alexander, xvii, 23n2, 315n86; election of, to the U.S. Senate, 306; as governor, 58, 69, 94–95, 223, 239; and treaties with the Dakotas, 58, 82

Randal, Benjamin H., 56n58

rape, 89, 110n28, 110n29, 125, 260; "gang," 169, 255–56, 262–63; investigation of, 124, 129; of Mattie Williams, 89, 110n29, 169, 255–56; prosecution of Union soldiers for, 125, 136n40, 136n44; trials, at Camp Release, 168–69

391

Ravoux, Father, 269, 272, 283n63, 287, 311nn11–12. *See also* missionaries
Ray, Francis (trial 133), 198n41
Rayburn, Samuel S., 29, 30, 32
Rdainyankna (trial 19), 260, 279n23, 353
recruiting party (New Ulm), xv–xvi, 85–86, 87, 109n14, 147–49; monument to the, xxn3. *See also* Dakota War of 1862
Redfox, Archie, 330, 339n53
Red Iron, 157
Red Owl (Chief), 298
Red Wing band (Wakute's band), 63
Redwood. *See* Lower Sioux Agency
Redwood ferry ambush (on Marsh's company), 95, 141, 149, 187, 189, 236, 238, 260, 271, 279n29. *See also* Dakota War of 1862
Renville Rangers, 83, 84, 137n57
Republican Party, 64–65, 126–27, 254, 255
reservations: Crow Creek, 296–98, 301, 307, 314n59; Lower Reservation, 60, *66*, 81; Sisseton and Wahpeton, 85; and the Upper Sioux Agency, 85, 170–71. *See also* Lower Sioux Agency; Santee Sioux Reservation
"resurrected" Dakota bodies, 276, 284n81, 284n82, 294, 301–2
Reynolds, Alexander W., 76n23
Rice, Henry, 23n2, 278n11
Riggs, Mary, 311n13
Riggs, Stephen R., 135n24, 137n55, 182, 186, 189, 200, 300; and captive list, 119–21, 135nn17–18; and "confessions" of Dakotas, 270–72, 283n60, 286; and conflicts of interest, 120, 130, 253, 269, 271–72, 305–6; and conversions, 269–70, 283n63, 291; and the Dakota language, 129, 292; Godfrey's letter to, 304–5; on Godfrey's origins, 28n63; and hanging list preparation, 221–22, 226n39, 226n41, *268*; and identification of condemned Dakotas, 265, 267–68, 281n52, 282n54; military commission appointments of, 127, 293; and military commission duties, 128–30, 159, 171, 186, 192, 203, 217, 221–22, 236, 271–72; missionary work of, 41, 119–20, 134n16; opinion of, of Dakota executions, 253, 278n7, 313n43; opinion of, on punishments for Indians, 196n23; pardon requests of, 226n32; rape inquiries of, 124, 125, 129, 168–69; release requests of, for acquitted prisoners, 294, 298; and trial transcripts delivery, 240, 249n58. *See also* missionaries
Roberts, Benjamin S., 300, 314n73
Robertson, Thomas (trial 135), 99, 187, 188, 190, 279n24; trial of, 191, 192, 198n41
Robinson, Joe (slave of Henry Hastings Sibley), 20, 22
Rocque, Augustin, 18
Roos, Charles, xvi–xvii, 87, 109n16, 209, 247n30; and description of Godfrey, 63, 149, 177, 179, 247n30
Rouillard, George, 323
Ruggles, Francis H., 56, 279n23, 279n29. *See also* Whiting-Ruggles report

Santee Sioux Reservation, 318–19, 336n7; boundaries of the, 320; and form of government, 325–26; and land allotments, 320–22, 323–

24, 332–33, 337n21; map, *319*; missionaries at the, 318
Sarah Ann (slave of Lewis Armistead), 61
Satterlee, Marion, 102–3, 108n11, 115nn78–80, 163n11, 195n11; on Godfrey, 91, 346
scalping, 110n27, 192. *See also* customs, Dakota
Schilling, Adolph, 147, 164n18
Schneider, John, xvi, xvii, 149
Schwandt, Mary, 21, 110n28, 210; as captive, 88–89, 151–52, 153, 172; testimony of, 157–58, 165n37
Schwandt Schmidt, Mary. *See* Schwandt, Mary
Scott, Dred, 29, 33, 34, 37, 47, 52n7; freedom suit of, 45–46; and *Scott v. Sandford*, 67–68, 74, 76n25, 171
Scott, Harriet, 45–46, 47, 55n43, 55n44
Scott, Martin, 8, 33, 52n6
Scott, Winfield, 125, 136n40
Shakopee II (Standing Cloud), 39–40, 53n22
Shakpaydan (Chief), 39–40, 53n22
Sheardown, S. B., 284n82
Shetek Lake massacre, 96–97. *See also* Dakota War of 1862
Shoonkaska (trial 35), 189, 260, 271, 279n29, 354
Sibley, Henry Hastings, 19, 23n2, 249n62, 275, 286, 293, 310n8; appointment of, to fight the Dakotas, 94–95; and approval of Dakota death sentences, 184; and arrests of Dakotas, 123, 182–84, 197n28, 287; and captive negotiations, 98–100; and Charles Flandrau, 133, 200–201; children of, 53n28, 77n30; and "confessions" of condemned Dakotas, 271–72, 286–87; in the Dakota War, 94–95, 97–100, 102, 103, 105–6; and execution planning, 222, 264–65, 275; expedition of, to Dakota Territory, 298, 305–6; and fur trade, 18–20, 22, 29, 58, 68, 126, 131–32; and Godfrey as slave, 19, 22, 132; and Indian traders as advisors, 131–32; and leniency on Godfrey's sentence, 181–82, 184, 197n31, 216, 218–20, 221, 222–23, 226n36, 227n43, 242–43, 249n66, 255, 258, 306, 329; and Lincoln's review of execution list, 185–86, 222, 223, 239–40, 262, 264–65; and military commission formation, 124–31, 133, 185; and mob violence, 229–30, 246n1; and Order No. 55, 124–25, 126, 128; and Order No. 65, 185; orders of, on Camp Lincoln command, 243, 285–86, 310n4; orders of, to disarm Dakotas, 182–83; orders of, to move camp to the Lower Sioux Agency, 199–200; orders of, to move Dakotas from Camp Release to Yellow Medicine, 170–71; orders of, to move Dakotas to Fort Snelling, 228–29, 246nn1–2; orders to, from Pope, 182–83, 184–85, 196n25, 197n28, 200, 232, 294; and pardon of David Faribault Jr., 166n39, 289–91, 298; politics of, 83, 132–33; Pope's dislike of, 101, 102, 115n76, 182, 196n25; and the Presbyterian church, 41, 53n28; and the press, 288–89, 291, 311n14; and promises of protection to surrendering Dakotas, 99, 100, 102, 103, 105, 119, 122, 123, 134n12, 183, 184, 193–94, 263, 266, 301; promotion of, 102, 115n76; and racial terms of conflict, 126; reprieves granted by, 166n39,

INDEX

Sibley, Henry Hastings (*continued*) 221, 226n33, 227n42, 272, 289–91; and sexual relationships with Native women, 18, 53n28, 77n30; and slave ownership, 20, 22, 33, 37, 53n28, 68; and surrender of Dakotas, 99–100, 102, 103, 105–7, 117–19, 122–23, 134n12, 168; and treaties of 1851, 58, 60, 82, 94–95; and verdict ratification, 184, 220, 221; and Winnebago trials, 232, 234, 236, 248n44. *See also* Pope, John; trials
Sibley, Henry Hopkins, 59, 138, 163n2
Sibley, John, 18
Sibley, Solomon, 5
"Sibley tents," 138, 163n2
Simon (Anawangmani), 100
"Sinewy" (Takanheca). *See* Takanheca (Mrs. Joseph Godfrey)
Sisseton band, 83, 103, 134n16
Sixth Infantry Regiment, 59
Skaya, Angelique, 27n44
slavery: and abolitionism, 41, 43, 78, 133, 235; abolition of, 308; and "colonization," 252, 255, 278n2; and corporal punishment of slaves, 15–16, 20, 28n61, 42, 44, 54n42; decline of, in Minnesota, 37–38, 59, 68; and the Emancipation Proclamation, 132, 251–52; at Fort Ridgely (MN), 60–61, 64–65, 66, 67, 94; at Fort Snelling (MN), 5–13, 17, 20–21, 24n15, 25n28, 27n47, 33–34, 37, 46, 49, 50, 52nn5–7, 59–60, 64, 65–67; "heyday" of, in Minnesota, 10–12, 20–21, 22, 26n31, 34, 48, 65–66; illegality of, in Minnesota, 5, 8–9, 10–11, 17, 32, 34, 49, 59–61, 64–65, 68–70, 73, 132–33, 329; and the Kansas-Nebraska Act of 1854, 64–65, 67, 76n22; and marriage between slaves and Indians, 16, 36–37, 53n18; and military officers as slave owners, 4, 6–11, 12–13, 24n11, 24nn13–15, 24n17, 25n28, 26n32, 32, 33, 37, 49, 56n56, 59–61, 65–66, 75n6, 76n23; and the Minnesota constitution, 68, 69–70, 73, 74; and missionaries, 36, 41–43, 121; and the Missouri Compromise, 5, 11, 17, 32, 33, 61, 64, 67; and the Northwest Ordinance of 1787, 5, 17, 32; and partus sequitur ventrem doctrine, 14; and the press, 67, 69–70, 297; and price of slaves, 3–4, 13–14, 15; and risks for fugitive slaves, 42, 44–45, 69, 73–74; and sanctuary for slaves, with Indians, 47–48, 55n47; and *Scott v. Sandford*, 67–68, 74, 76n25, 171; and Sibley as slave owner, 20, 22, 33, 37, 53n28, 68; and slave catchers, 69, 77n32; and slaves born in Minnesota, 14, 21, 24n17, 27n40, 29; and slave trading in Minnesota, 6–7, 11–12, 14–15, 24n14, 26n31, 33, 37, 46; and the Underground Railroad, 47, 73, 112n46. *See also* Courtney; freedom suits; Godfrey, Joseph; pay vouchers, military; *and individual slave names*
Smith, Caleb, 263–64
Smith, John, 320
Smith, O. W., 343–44, 349n6
Snamani (trial 14), 280n32, 283n63, 353
Snana, 89
Snelling, Josiah, 5, 8, 9, 10, 24n14
soldiers' lodge (Dakota), 72, 81, 84–85, 98, 140, 260, 266, 281n51. *See also* Dakota War of 1862
Spencer, George, 111n45, 121, 135n22, 293, 313n46
Spirit Walker, 121

394

Stanton, Edwin, 101, 114n69
Steimle, Adolph, xvi, 149
Stevens, John, 327, *328*
Stocker, Caroline, 164n29
Stocker, Joseph, 164n29
Stockton, Thomas B. W., 12–13, 17, 24n13, 26n36, 55n44
Stone, Louise (Mrs. Joseph Godfrey, Jr.), 324, 333, 337n28
St. Paul MN, 70, 101, 114n67, 280n38; black community in, 48–49, 66, 112n46; epidemics in, 291, 312n27; white refugees in, 97, 113n55, 312n27
St. Paul Pioneer and Democrat, 178, 179–80, 240–41, 280n40, 297
St. Paul Press, 127, 223, 232, 244, 280n40, 308
St. Peter MN. *See* Mendota (St. Peter) MN
Suamani (trial 14), 280n32, 283n63, 353
Sunkaska. *See* Shoonkaska (trial 35)
Susan (slave of Lawrence Taliaferro), 24n15, 24n17, 27n40
Swan, Mary. *See* Schwandt, Mary
Sweeny, Robert O., 163n6, 181, 272–73, *274*
Swift, Ebenezer, 76n23
Swisshelm, Jane, 77n31, 235, 244, 288

Tahohpewakan (trial 238), 226n32
Tahomiinwashtay (trial 28), 279n29
Takanheca (Mrs. Joseph Godfrey), 74, 297, 309, 317n116; annuity given to, 72–73, 78n47; children of, 63, 73, 78n49, 228, 292, 320, 336n7, 345; death of, 320, 336n7; decision of, to flee Dakota War, 81–82, 142; in jail, 286, 291, 312n26; marriage of, to Godfrey, 63, 76n15, 320
Taliaferro, Lawrence, 2, 13, 17–18, 24n15, 27n40, 37; and slave trading, 6–7, 11–12, 24n14, 26n31, 33, 46. *See also* Indian agents
Taopi, 99, 175, 286–87, 305, 310n8
Tatanka Cistina. *See* Chaskaydon (trial 121)
Tatankanajin (Sisseton chief), 103, 338n43
Tatankanajin (Standing Buffalo). *See* Godfrey, Joseph
Tatayebomboo (trial 30), 187
Tatayhdedan, 272
Tataykagay (trial 155), 355
Tatehdedon (trial 279), 355
Tatemima (trial 15), 283n62, 292, 303; reprieve of, 272, 280n32, 282n53, 283n63, 353
Tawapahajata (trial 248), 213
Taxunkamaza, 287
Taylor, William, 47, 92, 93, 94, 112n46
Taylor, Zachary, 9, 10, 12, 25n26, 56n56
Taytakagay (trial 155), 355
Tazoo (trial 4), 89, 151, 153, 177, 260, 352; conviction and sentencing of, 110n29, 169
Teentahotonwa (Indian settlement), 39–41
Tehehdonecha (trial 2), 168–69, 260, 352
telegraph line, 101, 114n67, 185–86, 197n37, 222, 227n42; and cost of hanging list submission, 239, 248n56
Tenth Infantry Regiment, 65, 68–69
Third Regiment, 10
Thompson, George, 37, 92, 93–94, 111n43, 120, 135n17; in Dakota War, 94, 112n47
Thompson, James (slave of William Day), 11, 26n30, 49, 66, 92, 111n43, 112n48; children of, 36, 56n55, 120–21; and the Dakota language, 16, 35–36; and Fort Ridgely sanctuary, 93, 112n47, 121;

Thompson, James (slave of William Day) (*continued*)
freedom of, 28n60, 36–37; marriage of, to Dakota woman, 27n45, 36, 70; testimony of, 217, 218, 226n33

Thompson, Mary (Mrs. James Thompson), 27n45, 36, 70, 92, 94, 112n47, 120; and the census, 55n51, 56n55

Thompson, Sarah. *See* Barnes, Sarah Thompson (Mrs. William Barnes)

Thompson, William (slave of Lawrence Taliaferro), 6, 7, 24n14

Through Dakota Eyes (Anderson and Woolworth), 150, 343, 346

Tom (slave of Alexander Reynolds), 76n23

Toonkanahanmane (trial 31), 187, 188

Toonkanechataymane (trial 67), 279n23, 354

Toonkankoyagenajin (trial 225), 279n23, 355

Toonkanmane (trial 218), 213

Toonwanwakinyachatka (trial 105), 299, 314nn71–72

Travelers' Home (Milford MN), xv, xvii, 87, 109n17, 144, 146, 154, 172, 206. *See also* Milford (MN) massacre

Travers, Monimia (slave of Llewellyn Jones), 50, 56n57

treaties, 34, 71, 101, 320, 321; and diversion of funds to traders, 58–59, 60, 82, 94–95

trial, Godfrey's, 139–40; charges and specifications, 138–39; decision and sentencing in, 180–81; and delay in deciding, 161–62, 166n42, 170, 180, 217; evidence in, 160–62; Godfrey's testimony at, 140–55, 160, 161, 163n10, 164n19, 166nn39–40, 169–70; length of, 167, 195n2; and leniency in sentencing, 181–82, 184, 197n31, 216, 218–20, 222–23, 226n36, 227n43, 240, 242–43, 249n66, 255, 262, 265–66, 282n53; witnesses' testimony, 155–60, 165n37, 169, 170, 174–76, 279n23. *See also* Godfrey, Joseph; trials

trials: at Camp Lincoln, 234, 235–39, 248n50, 248n53; at Camp Release, 138–62, 167–77, 179–82, 185–94, 201, 261, 280n32; cookhouse (Lower Sioux Agency), 200, 201–14, 215–21, 224n14, 226n32, 241; Fort Snelling, 293, 312n42, 313nn43–44; hanging list from, 169, 170, 172, 175, 177, 184, 187, 188, 190, 194, 196n16; hanging list from cookhouse, 203, 205, 206, 207, 208, 210, 211, 214, 218, 221, 226n33; irregularities in, 154, 158, 167, 203, 209, 214, 236, 260; and the massacre vs. battle distinction, 105, 185, 193–94, 203, 225n24, 256, 263, 279n20, 299; speed of, 167, 185, 195n2, 203, 209, 217, 220–21, 226n32, 240–41. *See also* executions; military commission; trial transcripts

trial transcripts, 315n83; loss of the, 302, 307, 315n84, 317n106; narrative format of the, 158; review of, by Lincoln, 239–40, 251, 255, 256–58, 261–62, 278n12, 279n20. *See also* trials; Whiting-Ruggles report

Underground Railroad, 47, 73, 112n46. *See also* slavery

Union soldiers, executions of, 125, 136n40, 136n44, 167, 195n3, 248n44

INDEX

Upper Sioux Agency, 85, 170–71. *See also* Yellow Medicine MN
Urban, Pauline, 118
U.S.-Dakota War of 1862. *See* Dakota War of 1862
Usher, J. P., 314n59

Vanderburgh, Charles E., 73, 74
voting rights, 68, 69, 77n28

Wabasha (Chief), xvii, 33, 34, 47, 48, 60, 63, 170, 201, 293; death of, 325; gravesite of, 335; and guilty warriors, 119, 134n12; as informant, 286–87, 293, 310n8, 312n41, 326; opposition of, to Dakota War, 99, 107, 108n10, 266–67, 281n51; petition of, to Lincoln, 266–67, 281n51, 326; plea of, for Dakotas to remain in Minnesota, 296
Wabasha (first Dakota chief), 18
Wabasha MN, 1, 29, 32–33, 34–35
Wabashaw County MN, 50–51, 56n59
Wahcoota (Chief). *See* Wakute (Chief)
Wahetaymaza (trial 130), 225n22
Wahhehud (trial 12), 196n16, 279n23, 353
Wahinkpe, 287
Wahohna (trial 12), 196n16, 279n23, 353
Wahpadoota. *See* Wahpaduta (trial 11)
Wahpaduta (trial 11), 63, 75n14, 77n38, 168, 309; and "civilizing" measures, 71–73; conviction and sentencing of, 175; and the Dakota War, 81–82, 142, 153–54, 164n29; testimony of, against Godfrey, 77n38, 174–75, 257, 258, 353; trial of, 172–76, 196n16, 279n23

Wahpekute band, 85, 134n16
Wahpeton band, 83, 134n16
Wakandape (trial 299), 225n28
Wakandaymani, George. *See* Quinn, George
Wakantanka (trial 210), 144, 204–5, 225n18, 259, 270, 355
Wakefield, Sarah, 122, 124, 133, 135n34, 167, 250n69; and defense of Chaska (Wechankwashtodopee), 119, 121, 123, 261; on Godfrey, 123, 135n34, 167
Wakinyanhde (trial 300), 227n42
Wakinyanna (trial 383), 144, 163n10, 165n31, 205–6, 227n42, 259, 356
Wakinyantawa (Chaska), 111n45, 121, 135n23, 287; retrial of, 293, 313n46
Wakinyanwashtay (Good Thunder), 286–87, 293, 312n41
Waki-ya-ni. *See* Wakinyanna (trial 383)
Wakkeintawa. *See* Wakinyantawa (Chaska)
Wakute (Chief), 33, 34, 35, 47, 48, 60, 63, 108n10, 201; and captives, 89, 151–52, 157; and "civilizing" measures, 71, 72; and guilty warriors, 119, 134n12; opposition of, to Dakota War, 107, 266–67, 281n51; petition of, to Lincoln, 266–67, 281n51
Wamdetanka (trial 34), 134n12, 187, 298, 303–4, 312n41
Wamneomnehota (trial 70), 354
Wanjuhedan (Little Feather Ornament). *See* Godfrey, Joseph, Jr.
Wapaheduta. *See* Wahpaduta (trial 11)
Wa-She-Choon (Toon-Kan-Shkan-Shkan-Mene-Hay). *See* Washechoon (trial 318)
Washechoon (trial 318), *270*, 279n23, 282n54, 355

INDEX

Washechoonna (trial 332), 267, *270*, *271*, 282n53, 282n54, 294
Washechoonsapa (trial 260), 53n18, 214
Wasicunna. *See* Washechoonna (trial 332)
Wasoohdehayya (trial 358), 225n29
Wazaka (Winnebago trial 6), 248n51
Waze, 272
Wazekootay (trial 213), 88, 215
Wazeyeta, 81, 140
Weanku, 192–93
We-a-ta-tow. *See* Wyatahtowah (trial 5)
Webster, Joseph, 321
Wechankpedoota (trial 367), 237–38, 248n49
Wechankwashtodopee (trial 3), 282n53; misidentification of, 267, *268*, *269*, 282n54, 307; Wakefield's defense of, 119, 121, 123, 261
Weidimer, Charles, 62
Weidimer, Courtney (Mrs. Charles Weidimer). *See* Courtney
Weidimer, Jonas, 62
Weidimer, Joseph, 62
Wesley (slave of Thomas Alexander), 60, 75n6
West, Emily J., 93
Whipple, Henry B., 253–54, 278n11, 278n12, 289
White Dog (trial 35). *See* Shoonkaska (trial 35)
Whiting, George C., 256, 279n23, 279n29. *See also* Whiting-Ruggles report
Whiting-Ruggles report, 352–56; and Godfrey's case, 256–58, 262; on Godfrey's testimony, 258–60; and the massacres/battle distinction, 256, 279n20; omissions on the, 261; publication of the, 280n38. *See also* trial transcripts
Whitney, J. C., 171, 183

Wicahpewastewin (Good Star Woman), 231
Wi-can-hpi-wa-ste-da-pi (Chaska). *See* Wechankwashtodopee (trial 3)
Wilkinson, Morton, 110n29, 255–56, 262–63, 315n86
William (slave of Barnard Bee), 76n23
William (slave of Edmund Alexander), *66*, 76n23
William (slave of Lawrence Taliaferro), 6, 7, 24n14
William (son of Courtney), 27n39, 29, 30–31, 32, 62
Williams, Mattie, 88, 110n27, 151, 153, 157, 172, 177, 210, 279n27; rape of, 89, 110n29, 169, 255–56; testimony of, 158, 225n24
Williams, Thaddeus, 252
Williamson, Jane, 94, 272, 280n30
Williamson, John, 231, 292, 337n24
Williamson, Thomas S., 229, *268*, 282n54, 299–300, 305–6, 315n80, 315n83; and clemency requests, 252–53, 272, 280n30, 283n62, 289, 302–3, 315nn85–86; and conversions, 269, 272, 283n63, 291; on Godfrey, 302–3; on surrender of Dakotas, 106, 116n87. *See also* missionaries
Wilson (slave of William Price), 52n5
Wilson, Henry, 37
Windom, William, 255–56, 315n86
Winnebagoes, 97, 185, 275; move of, to Dakota Territory reservation, 298; and public opinion, 234–35; trials of, 232, 234, 235–39, 248n50, 248n53
Winston, Eliza (slave of Colonel Christmas), 73, 74, 78n52
Wiyakamani, 313n44
Wood, Robert C., 25n28
Woodbury, Mary, 156–57, 165n35

398

INDEX

Wood Lake battle, 102, 103, 127, 130; Godfrey's presence at the, 154–55, 160; scalping at the, 192–93, 237. *See also* Dakota War of 1862

Woods, Samuel, 50, 56n58

Woolworth, Alan: *Through Dakota Eyes*, 150, 343, 346

Wowinapa (son of Little Crow), 306, 316n95

Wyatahtowah (trial 5), 155, 168, 169–70, 195n4, 353

Yellow Medicine MN, 85, 170–71, 182, 185, 201; and disarming of Dakotas, 183, 197n28

Zeller, Max, 109n14

Zettel family, 86

www.ingramcontent.com/pod-product-compliance
Lightning Source LLC
Chambersburg PA
CBHW022036220526
45357CB00059B/198